TAKE IT OFF!

1,414
Tax Deductions
Most People
Overlook

TAKE IT OFF!

1,414 TAX DEDUCTIONS MOST PEOPLE OVERLOOK

*Completely revised and enlarged
1980 edition*

Robert S. Holzman, Ph.D.

Thomas Y. Crowell, Publishers
New York / Established 1834

LIBRARY OF CONGRESS CATALOGING IN PUBLICATION DATA

Holzman, Robert S
  Take it off!

  Includes bibliographical references.
  1. Income tax—United States—Deductions. I. Title.
HJ4653.D4H63 1980   343'.73'052   79-18542
ISBN-0-690-01843-6
ISBN-0-690-01844-4 pbk.

79 80 81 82 83 10 9 8 7 6 5 4 3 2 1

Foreword
to the 1980 edition

THIS SIXTH EDITION of *Take It Off!* contains 180 more deductions than were included in the 1979 version. This is the *net* increase, for several previously described deductions were eliminated by recent legislation, such as the Federal gasoline tax in most circumstances. The additions include changes made by the Revenue Act of 1978, most of which affect for the first time 1979 income that is to be reported in 1980. Other newly included deductions arise from new developments, such as purchases of laetrile. Many 1978 court decisions and Internal Revenue Service rulings and interpretations have been added, as well as previously approved deductions which had not been listed in former editions. For example, the sections on medical expenses, casualty losses, charitable contributions, employees' expenses, and work clothes have been greatly amplified.

In order to make this new edition more useful, 133 additional cross-references have been added.

Court decisions continue to emphasize the need for knowing the *authority* for what you are deducting. If you claim something to which you are not entitled, the result may not only be loss of the deduction but also the imposition of interest plus a penalty. You cannot prove that your disallowed deduction was not the result of negligence if you are unable to show your authority for having claimed it, for taking a deduction without a basis for taking it implies that the required reasonable care had not been taken to report taxable income properly. In addition, declared one court, any unauthorized deductions which are claimed "create doubt as to the accuracy of the total deduction." That places the entire tax return under a cloud of suspicion. In a 1978 decision, one court approved of a negligence penalty where a taxpayer had claimed a deduction which he had no reason for believing was correct.

These decisions emphasize the value of the book's section entitled "Who Says So?" Every deduction mentioned here has an authority listed (court decision, Treasury regulation, Internal Revenue Service explanation, etc.) to show *why* you are claiming it. That disposes of the question of your entitlement to the deduction.

ROBERT S. HOLZMAN

Preface

TAX DEDUCTIONS, the courts have frequently stated, are a matter of legislative grace. You are not entitled to any deduction unless Congress specifically has provided for it. The courts, in interpreting the laws, have approved the deductibility of many other items and subitems. In addition, the Internal Revenue Service, in practical implementation of the tax laws, has authorized the taking of deductions in various forms. So in order to keep one's taxes at their legitimate minimum, it is necessary to know what deductions are *allowed*; none can be presumed. As the United States Supreme Court has said, the legal right of a taxpayer to reduce his taxes or to eliminate them altogether *by means which the law permits* cannot be doubted.

By means which the law permits . . . Your barber, bartender, taxi driver, and other helpful acquaintances are brimful of bright ideas for tax deductions. But when you have that encounter session with a steely-eyed Internal Revenue Agent and he questions your deductions with a suspicious "Who says so?" the moment of truth has arrived. A disallowed deduction means more than payment of what you would have paid in the first place had you not been so venturesome. There is interest (deductible). There are penalties (nondeductible). If you are so distinguished a businessperson or are presumptively so well versed in taxation that you are deemed to have known better, there can be fraud penalties. The entire climate of a tax audit can change. Should a Revenue Agent find improper deductions so readily, not illogically he will believe that there's more gold to be found in your return, and now he will really get to work on it.

This book, as it must be, is thoroughly documented. Each deduction named bears an identifying footnote number, which leads to the answer to that infuriating question of the Revenue Agent, "Who says so?" The so-sayer may be the Internal Revenue Code itself. It may be the Treasury Regulations. It may be an official government release. It may be a court decision. But it won't be your spouse's second cousin. Or, for that matter, your spouse.

Who needs tax deductions? If the zero bracket amount wipes out your entire Federal income tax liability, that's fine (in one limited sense, anyway). But if you still have taxable income, there are almost certain to be some valid deductions awaiting discovery. One cannot accept a defeatist attitude that he really has nothing to deduct. For a modest start, there is the modest cost of this book. Do you have medical expenses (such as a wig), revolving credit accounts with department stores, or sessions with a tutor of some sort to patch up chinks in your executive armor before Higher Authority discovers them? When you take your best customer to that appropriately expensive restaurant after getting a particularly lucrative order, do you know what proportion of the tab you may properly deduct? Were you ever "taken" by a glib-tongued dealer or salesman? If you are summoned to appear as a witness before a Congressional committee (and 1973 showed that this can happen even to the most respectable and unsuspecting of gentlefolk), under what circumstances can you deduct the fees of the lawyer who counsels you there? Do you regularly take work home from your place of business at night? Are you involved in litigation? Are you an investor? Have you any expenditures which involve estate planning, insurance, or taking heavy paraphernalia to your place of work?

An allowable deduction requires more than merely *taking* it. If you find a Supreme Court authority here for a certain deduction, there is still the matter of proving *your* right to it. Can you demonstrate *your* entitlement to that deduction for business entertainment or charitable contributions or child care expense? One clever lawyer proved that his client, an entertainer, was entitled to deduct the cost of expensive dresses as *business expense* rather than personal apparel which could be worn for everyday use; he had her demonstrate in the courtroom the sheer impossibility of sitting down in her exquisite form-fitting finery. But, generally, your right to a deduction is substantiated by such unspectacular routines as keeping pieces of paper. Do you keep letters from your customers on business letterheads which thank you for that lovely evening at the fights where you discussed the new winter line? (A good place to file such correspondence is right next to a purchase order dated a few days later.) Do you remember to take photographs immediately after casualty losses? In order to get a deduction, you may have to plan a transaction in advance to have the proper dates on receipts or in employee manuals. Should your transaction be with stipulated related parties, the Internal Revenue Service can refuse to recognize losses or certain other consequences for tax purposes; so it might be better to make your sales or deals with more distant relatives or with outsiders. Some of the deductions, such as the net operating loss carry-over, may be of sufficient complexity in operation to require the assistance of tax counsel.

If you are entitled to a tax deduction, take it. As Judge Learned Hand once wrote, a person does not owe a patriotic duty to pay one cent more in taxes than he is required to do. But if a deduction is not proper in your situation, don't take it. It has been held that when a taxpayer persistently claimed deductions such as had been disallowed in prior years, he was guilty of fraud, that is, willfully seeking to evade taxes which by now he had learned were due.

Even though courts have stated that taxation is not based upon logic or equity, the rule of reason must not be overlooked in claiming deductions. Ordinary food cannot be deducted as medical expense, even though your health would be affected should you terminate your input. The cost of a business suit is not deductible, although without such garb you would be unable to retain your job in most walks of life. But tax deductions may be allowed even where an expenditure seems to stretch beyond the reasonable concept of a word or phrase, as where clarinet lessons as well as the cost of the clarinet were properly deducted as medical expense. Whether unrepaid advances to your business can be deducted may depend upon your own personality; the nastier it is, the greater is your chance of getting the deduction.

It is strongly advisable to think about your tax deductions before the filing date of your tax return. In order to become legitimately a minimum taxpayer on nonminimum income, you must become accustomed to deductive thinking.

TAKE IT OFF!

1,414
Tax Deductions
Most People
Overlook

Abandonment loss. If business assets are rendered economically useless to a taxpayer, the remaining undepreciated cost may be written off when the property cannot be used or disposed of.[1] Such was the case where a place of business became useless because the state had condemned its parking lot for use as a highway. Without a parking lot for customers, there would be no customers, and the business would have to move to a new location.[2]

A deduction is permitted only where there is a complete elimination of all value, coupled with recognition by the owner that the item no longer has any utility or worth to him.[3]

If a taxpayer has elected to amortize research and development expenses, abandonment of the research projects results in an allowable deduction for any amounts not yet deducted.[4]

Ordinarily, an architect's fees are not currently deductible but must be considered a cost of the building he designed to be depreciated over the period of its useful life. But if a proposed building never leaves the drawing-board stage and the plans are abandoned, the architect's fees are deductible at that time.[5]

When a water well used by a farmer for irrigation and other agricultural purposes dried up, no casualty-loss deduction was allowed on the ground that the loss was the result of long-term deterioration rather than something sudden and hence did not meet the statutory definition of a casualty.[6] But a well can be abandoned by some overt act, such as by filling or sealing the well excavation or casing, which terminates the existence of the well and all economic benefits therefrom. So the abandonment is deductible as a business loss.[7] *See also* **Farmers.**

Abnormal Retirement. *See* **Obsolescence.**

Abortion. A woman who, at her own request, undergoes an abortion operation to terminate her pregnancy can claim the expense as a medical deduction if the operation is performed in a

A

general hospital and the operation is not illegal under state law. This is true because the operation is for the purpose of affecting a structure or function of the body and therefore is a deductible expense.[8] See also **Medical expenses.**

Absconding, losses from. See **Casualties; Reliance upon misrepresentation.**

Accident, as casualty loss. Although the types and variations of deductible casualty loss are virtually beyond count, the triggering event must fall within the general framework of a fire, storm, or the like. Thus, payments for the support of a minor child could not be claimed as a casualty loss resulting from an accident.[9] But a deductible casualty loss can result from an everyday accident as in a case where a diamond disappeared after an automobile door had slammed against an individual's ring.[10] Here the court observed that "the casualty need not be of great or near-tragic proportions in order to qualify."

Sonic-boom damage to a residence caused by jet aircraft qualified in one instance for the casualty-loss deduction.[11] Similarly, vandalism qualified.[12] Loss from damage to the exterior paint of a house, which was caused by sudden and severe smog containing an unusual concentration of chemical fumes, constituted a casualty loss for tax purposes. The painted surface of the house was eaten through in one night by smog, which caused the paint to blister and to peel from the wood. The home had recently been painted, and the damage was the result of an identifiable event, sudden in nature, fixing a point at which loss to the damaged property could be measured; it also was unexpected in the context in which the damage occurred.[13]

Accident and health insurance premiums. See **Medical expenses.**

Accounting, businessperson's guidance in. Amounts paid by a businessperson to an accountant to instruct an employee in keeping the business books were deductible.[14] Similarly, the cost of instruction from an accountant in how to figure costs to bid on government contracts was allowable.[15] See also **Education.**

Accounting expenses. The costs of accounting work performed in applying for a Federal income tax ruling are deductible.[16]

Accounting fees are deductible if they represent an ordinary and necessary business expense, as opposed to expenses of purchasing capital assets.[17]

An investor may deduct fees paid to a certified public accountant and to a bookkeeper in connection with his investment activities.[18]

If a person incurs accounting expenses to produce both taxable and tax-exempt income, but he cannot identify specifically the expenses which produce each type of income, then he must prorate them in order to determine the amount deductible.[19]

Account juggling, losses from. See **Check kiting.**

Acquisition fees. See **Mineral leases, cost of acquiring.**

Actors. The cost of clothing destroyed while performing stunts as an actor was held to be deductible.[20] An actor who lost some teeth during the screening of a fight sequence was allowed a deduction for replacement parts.[21] A prominent actor was allowed to deduct the cost of clothing which was suitable for personal wear and which was in current fashion. This clothing was purchased specifically for television use and was kept at the studio. At the end of the shooting season, this garb was placed in mothballs and was never taken home.[22]

Amounts paid for hairpieces suitable only for professional use were deductible by an actor whose income would have been affected adversely by a mature appearance.[23] A motion picture actor was allowed to deduct expenses incurred in keeping himself in first-class condition to meet the requirements of his calling, including massage treatments, a physical trainer, rent for handball courts and gymnasium facilities, plus sundries.[24]

Acupuncture. Payments for acupuncture treatments are deductible even though the person performing them may be acting in a manner not approved by the appropriate medical association. The determination of what is medical care depends on the nature of the services rendered, not on the experience, qualifications, or title of the person rendering them.[25] See also **Medical expenses.**

Additional first-year depreciation. In the case of property used for business purposes, an individual may elect, for the first taxable year in which a depreciation deduction is allowable, to include as part of the reasonable allowance for depreciation an additional allowance of 20 percent of the cost of the property. This 20 percent may apply to any property he selects. The property must be subject to depreciation (land, for example, is not), must be used in trade or business or for the production of income, and have a useful life of six years or more at the time of acquisition. The maximum amount of the cost on which this election may be taken is $10,000, or $20,000 where a husband and wife file a joint Federal income tax return. These dollar limitations apply to each taxpayer and not to each trade or business in which he has an interest. It must be tangible personal property, either new or used.[26] *See also* **Depreciation.**

Advanced degree, study for. An individual held a temporary appointment as a tutor at a university. It was made clear to him that it was necessary for him to make substantial progress toward attaining his doctorate to keep his position as a tutor. The expenses of tuition, etc., in working for his doctorate were deductible because that doctorate was necessary to earn the income that the Internal Revenue Service would tax.[27]

An assistant professor at a university had no assurance of continued employment unless he was granted tenure, that is, a status of permanency after he had served for a certain length of time. It was university policy to require a doctor's degree before tenure was granted. To influence the university to grant him tenure, he gave written assurance that he would start work on his doctorate at once. He was granted tenure, and the Internal Revenue Service sought to disallow education expenses after the date that tenure was granted. But the deduction was allowed because the assistant professor had made his commitment to get the advanced degree primarily to hold his present status, even though he knew that possession of the degree would also bring promotion and more money. Had he terminated his studies once tenure had been granted, his conduct obviously would have been that of deceit, and the university could have found effective ways of showing its disapproval. Therefore the expense of earning his doctorate was still deductible inasmuch as it was a necessary requirement of maintaining his present status.[28] *See also* **Education; Teachers, expenses of.**

Advances. *See* **Loans and advances; Bad debts.**

Advertising. In the main, the cost of advertising is deductible because it is regarded as a stimulus for getting business.[29] As one court observed, "In the tremendous competition of today [a businessman who did not advertise] would be more like a bashful boy who threw his sweetheart a kiss in the dark. He knew what he was doing, but nobody else did."[30]

Deductible advertising can be in as original and unorthodox

a form as a businessperson's imagination and ingenuity can conceive. The advertising expense is not confined to any stereotyped pattern that might have been set by unimaginative competitors.[31] Some discretion must be left to a taxpayer in deciding what kinds of advertising and promotion are necessary to obtain and to hold business.[32] For example, the principals of a retail dairy company took an African safari, the expenses of which were deductible by the business. The firm maintained a museum, and tickets distributed by milk-truck drivers invited customers to visit it. The business had maintained a museum even before this safari, and the obtaining of more exotic specimens involved such "roughing it" by the principals who made the trip that it scarcely seemed describable as a pleasure jaunt. The court was convinced that it was extremely good advertising at a relatively low cost and that conventional advertising of equal value could not have been obtained for the same amount of money.[33]

A restaurant was allowed to deduct the cost of wolfhounds that never left the premises except to attend dog shows where they were entered in the name of the restaurant. Furthermore, the cost of show horses was deductible when it could be established that they were entered in horse shows in the name of the restaurant and wore the colors which adorned the front of the restaurant.[34]

Advertising expense sometimes takes the form of an expense that is not for advertising. This verbal paradox simply means that in order to advertise, an expenditure is made with advertising as the objective but not the medium. To be deductible for tax purposes, payments in lieu of advertising have to be something that is designed to achieve the same function as advertising, with the same limitations. Thus, expenses of selling associate memberships in a recreation club were deductible by a real estate company. The company had no advertising program; instead, property was sold to persons who became interested when, from the club premises, they could see other picturesque land which was for sale. This was deemed to be a substitute for ordinary advertising.[35]

Deduction is allowed for advertising which emphasizes and promotes government objectives, such as conservation.[36] Expenditures for institutional or goodwill advertising which keeps the taxpayer's name before the public are generally deductible provided the expenditures are related to patronage the taxpayer might reasonably expect in the future. Deduction is allowed for the cost of advertising which keeps the taxpayer's name before the public in connection with encouraging contributions to such organizations as the Red Cross, purchase of United States Savings Bonds, or participation in similar causes. In like fashion, expenditures for advertising which present views on economic, financial, social, or other subjects of a general nature, but which do not involve lobbying or attempts to influence legislation, are deductible.[37]

The advertising need not be of the taxpayer's product or service. A landlord could advertise on behalf of a tenant whose prosperity would help the landlord to collect the rent. Had the tenant failed, the landlord might have had trouble in leasing the aged building and other properties in the neighborhood.[38]

An insurance agent could deduct matured claims against an insurance company that he represented, and which he paid to clients out of his own pocket, to "promote the taxpayer's business," as the court stated.[39] (That, after all, is what advertising is all about.)

Advertising deductions are permitted for companies whose production facilities are devoted entirely to governmental work, so that their names and the qualities of their products will be known to the public when they return to non-governmental production. But in evaluating the amount of the deduction, cognizance must be taken of the taxpayer's prior advertising budgets, public patronage reasonably to be expected in the future, and the unavailability of components used in the advertised products.[40]

Ordinarily, an expenditure is not currently deductible if the benefits to be obtained are expected to last for more than one year. But advertising and promotion for a campaign covering the next five years were deductible at the time of the expenditure.[41]

The general rule is that a deduction is not permitted for advertising in a political convention program. Deduction is permitted for such advertising in connection with a convention for nominating candidates for the offices of President and Vice President of the United States, providing the cost of the advertising is reasonable in light of the business expected to be received (1) directly as the result of the advertising, or (2) as a result of the convention's being held in an area where the taxpayer has a principal place of business.[42]

The cost of tickets for benefit performances, purchased to maintain goodwill in the community, was deductible as a form of advertising.[43] A tavern owner was permitted to deduct as advertising the cost of a Christmas party given for the children of the neighborhood to promote goodwill with their parents.[44] A restaurant could deduct the cost of an automobile given to the patron who drew a winning ticket.[45]

To promote sales and net profits, a business agreed to pay to an approved charitable organization a certain amount for each label from one of its products that the charitable organization mailed to the business enterprise. In return, the charitable organization agreed to permit the use of its name in the business's advertising and to obtain testimonial letters for use in a sales campaign. The amounts turned over to the charity by the business were deductible as ordinary and necessary expense, without the percentage limitations imposed upon charitable contributions.[46] *See also* **Contributions; Employees; Ordinary and necessary business expenses.**

Air-conditioning equipment. Ordinarily, the cost of property with a life of more than one year cannot be deducted for tax purposes; if the property is used for business purposes, the cost can be written off as depreciation over the period of its life. If equipment with a life of more than one year is purchased for medical reasons, the cost is deductible only to the extent that it does not add value to the property of a house in which it may be permanently installed. If air-conditioning equipment is acquired to relieve an allergy or to facilitate breathing for patients with a heart condition, deduction is allowed under the following conditions: The initial cost of the air-conditioning equipment plus the operating expense minus the resale or salvage value is allowed, *provided* that the medical need for the equipment is substantiated by evidence and that the equipment is used primarily for the alleviation of a person's illness, and provided further that the equipment does not become a permanent part of a dwelling. If you can't take it with you, then you can't take it off your taxes.[47] *See also* **Medical expenses.**

Airline pilot, expenses of. A commercial pilot could deduct the cost of uniforms worn only on duty, as well as costs for the maintenance and replacement of navigation instruments, computers, and plotters.[48]

Alcoholics Anonymous. An individual who joined an Alcoholics Anonymous club in his community pursuant to competent medical advice could deduct as medical expenses the transportation costs of attending the meetings of the club. This was true because the medical adviser stated that membership in AA was necessary for the treatment of a disease involving the excessive use of alcohol.[49]

Alcoholism, treatment for. An individual entered a therapeutic center for alcoholism, where he remained as an inpatient for several months. The center was maintained for alcoholics by a private, nonprofit organization, and inpatients were required to pay for their care, which included room, board, and treatment at the center. Amounts thus paid were deductible as medical expense.[50]

Alimony (periodic payments). Periodic payments (alimony) made by a husband to a wife (or vice versa) are deductible by the spouse making the payments, if such payments are made after a legal divorce or separation. Such periodic payments (whether or not they are made at regular intervals) must be made to satisfy a court order or decree divorcing or legally separating the husband and wife, or to satisfy a written form relating to such divorce or legal-separation action.[51]

When, for reasons of economy or otherwise, a couple continues to live in the same house, deduction of alimony depends upon whether they actually were living separately. This is a fact and not a definition, and deduction was allowed in a case where the court was persuaded that they were indeed living separately.[52]

Periodic payments are defined as payments of a fixed amount for an indefinite period (e.g., $10,000 per year until death or until remarriage) or as payments of an indefinite amount for either a fixed period (e.g., 10 percent of a husband's income for ten years) or an indefinite period (e.g., 10 percent until death). The payments need not be made at regular intervals, such as on the fifteenth of each month, to be defined as periodic payments.[53]

If the period for the payments is fixed and it is for more than ten years, the payor may deduct each installment payment, but only to the extent that the sum of the installments does not exceed 10 percent of the total specified in one taxable year. This 10-percent limitation applies to installment payments made in advance of their due date, but not to delinquent installment payments received by the payee during one taxable year. For instance, suppose that under a court order John Smith owes Mary Smith, his ex-wife, $100,000 to be paid over a period of twelve years. If in the first year of his obligation he gives Mary $20,000 he can claim only $10,000 of that money during that taxable year.

In addition to the alimony payments themselves, the husband (or wife) may deduct any other amounts which are a part of the alimony settlement. For instance, a husband under a separation agreement was obligated to pay his ex-wife $20,000 a year as long as she lived and was unmarried and also to pay $5,000 a year to his mother-in-law "for and in behalf of" his ex-wife. He could deduct the payments made to the mother-in-law.[54]

Annual vacation payments to one's former wife, as provided in the divorce decree, were deductible.[55]

A separation agreement between two spouses provided among other things that the husband would pay a specified amount each year to the wife for the payment of her "contemplated life insurance." This agreement was incorporated into the divorce decree. The wife purchased the insurance, the husband having no ownership or any rights under the policy. He could deduct the payments for the insurance as alimony, even though they were not labeled as such in the divorce decree.[56]

Whether mortgage payments made by one spouse on property awarded to the other spouse under a divorce decree are deductible depends upon whether these payments were part of a property settlement or were support payments. The payments were deductible as alimony when they were made in discharge of a general obligation of support.[57]

If, under a divorce decree or alimony settlement, an individual pays his ex-spouse's medical and/or dental expenses, these may be deducted as alimony provided that they qualify as periodic payments and that separate returns (other than a joint return for the two parties involved) are filed.[58]

The spouse receiving the payments must include these payments in his or her gross income, but they may be deducted by that spouse as medical expenses if deductions are itemized.[59]

A deduction is also allowed for periodic payments made in lieu of alimony (but which amount to the same thing), or an allowance for support is correct if the payments provided for that support are made during the year in which the payor's income tax is filed. The amount of payment has to be included in the income of the payee, however, for the deduction to be legal.[60]

The above could cover payments made by a husband (or a wife) periodically under a divorce decree granting legal separation from bed and board.[61]

A separation agreement between two spouses provided that the wife would waive alimony rights. There was a property settlement which, among other things, required the wife to convey her interest in the family house to the husband, who was obliged to sell it and to give her a specified amount out of the proceeds. Until money was received from the sale of the house, he was bound to pay her $170 a month rent for an apartment, unless the actual rent came to a lesser figure. He was permitted to deduct the rental payments he gave to her, even though he gave her the required rents rather belatedly in the form of a lump-sum payment.[62]

Payments made under a divorce decree of questionable validity are deductible because a divorce decree is presumed to be valid for tax purposes until a court having proper jurisdiction either declares the divorce invalid or formally invalidates it by a subsequent divorce decree.[63]

A wife brought suit against her husband for divorce and was awarded $200 a week as alimony. Subsequently he won an annulment on the ground that she had been married to a prior husband at the time of the marriage. Although the court held his marriage to her had been void from the beginning, he gave her $150 a week for support. Inasmuch as his payments were made in recognition of a general legal obligation arising from the marital relationship, which was made specific by the annulment decree, he was allowed to deduct these amounts as alimony, even though under state law that is not what they were.[64]

Where arrears (overdue alimony payments) are paid by one spouse in a lump sum, this sum is treated for tax purposes in the same manner as periodic payments would have been treated if paid when due. See above.[65]

Payments for child support are not deductible by the payor, nor are they included in the income of the payee, such as alimony must be, even if provided for under the same decree or order as the deductible alimony payments.[66]

Regardless of what the parties may have intended, if the decree, and the agreement prepared in accordance with the decree, makes no reference to how much of the payment is for child support, the entire amount is treated for tax purposes as alimony and is therefore deductible by the payor and must be included in the income of the payee.[67]

The payor gets a tax deduction for any portion of the payment he makes which is not specifically earmarked in the agreement for support of the children.[68]

Expenses which are incurred by the alimony-receiving spouse in getting an increase in that alimony are deductible.[69]

Legal fees to collect previously awarded (and delinquent) alimony are deductible.[70]

Under the terms of a property-settlement agreement approved in the divorce decree, a husband had to pay, in addition to alimony and child support, the premiums on two life insurance policies on his own life. Policy A was assigned absolutely to the ex-wife, she being designated, in legal terms, as the irrevocable beneficiary and the children as irrevocable contingent beneficiaries. Policy B designated the children as beneficiaries, and the ex-wife was contingent beneficiary. Policy B was not assigned to the ex-wife and remained in the husband's custody. The premiums paid on Policy A were deductible by the husband, but those on Policy B were not.[71]

An individual was ordered by a divorce decree to pay stipulated annual sums to his former wife. He made some payments in cash, he paid bills from her creditors which she forwarded to him, and he rounded out the required payment in the taxable year by having his broker send her the balance in a margin account he had opened in her name some years previously. Although the divorce decree had provided that his alimony payments to her were to be in cash, the payments to her creditors were deemed equivalent to his having paid these amounts to her, followed by her payments to the creditors. The margin account had been created by his funds, he alone gave the broker instructions to execute transactions, and he paid all the margin calls with his own funds. There was no evidence that he had ever given her the brokerage account as a gift or otherwise, and hence it still was his when he had the account converted into cash for her. Inasmuch as he had paid to or for her the amount mentioned in the divorce decree with his own funds, he was entitled to the alimony deduction even though the payments had not been in the form of cash flowing directly from him to her.[72]

For taxable years beginning after December 31, 1976, alimony is deductible by persons using the zero bracket amount as well as by taxpayers who itemize their deductions.[73] See also **Interest; Legal fees; Medical expenses; Taxes.**

Ambulance hire. See **Medical expenses.**

Amortization. See **Depreciation; Election to deduct or to capitalize; Expenditures for benefits lasting more than one year; Investors.**

Annuities from charitable organizations. The purchaser of an annuity may recover tax-free each year the cost of his annuity divided by the number of years in his life expectancy, that is, he excludes from income each year the *cost* divided by the number of years in his life expectancy.[74] For example, Amos Turner is fifty years old when he purchases an annuity for $3,000. His life expectancy is twenty more years, so he divides the $3,000 by 20, which is $150. The $150 is excluded from his income that year. In response to one of the many advertisements which appear in newspapers and magazines, an individual may buy an annuity from a charitable organization. If he pays more than the going rate for comparable annuities from a commercial company, the annuity cost which may be recovered over the years tax-free is limited to the fair market value of the annuity. The balance of his cost is deductible as a charitable contribution.[75]

Annuity contract, refund. The original purchaser of a single premium *refund* annuity contract who surrendered it for a cash consideration was permitted to deduct the difference between the basis of the contract (the cost less amounts previously recovered under the contract) and the amount received upon surrender.[76]

Answering service. An attorney who had given up his professional office when he became a state employee, but who continued to handle some of his former clients on a "moonlighting basis," could deduct the charges of a telephone answering service which received calls on what had been his business phone.[77]

Antitrust suits. *See* **Legal fees.**

Apartment used for business purposes. When a businessperson regularly travels to another city to take care of his commercial affairs, his hotel expenses there are deductible. But if he maintains an apartment in the city to which he travels from his home, a portion of the rent is deductible, the amount depending upon the business as opposed to the personal use made of it. One individual lived in Cleveland and maintained a three-room apartment in New York which was used by himself and by several employees when in the latter city on business. He was permitted to deduct 75 percent of the full rental.[78]

Apportionment of realty taxes. *See* **Taxes.**

Appraisal fees. *See* **Casualties; Contributions; Farmers; Investors; Taxes.**

Appreciated-value property, contributions of. *See* **Contributions.**

Arbitration. Fees paid to an arbitrator are deductible where the dispute was business-oriented.[79]

Architect's fees. *See* **Abandonment loss.**

Armed Forces. In general, the cost of uniforms, including laundry, cleaning, repair, or alterations, is not deductible because the uniform takes the place of civilian clothing. Where local military regulations require that the fatigue uniform be worn, and then only while on duty or while traveling to and from duty, provided the individual does not leave his car or other means of transportation, the cost of such uniforms and their maintenance is deductible to the extent that it exceeds any uniform gratuity or allowance received.

Here are examples of uniforms which may qualify if these tests are met: Navy dungaree working uniforms and chief petty officer and officer khaki working uniforms (wash khakis); Marine fatigues; Army fatigue (field or utility) uniforms and wash khakis; and Air Force fatigue (utility) uniforms for men and three-piece field suits for women.[80]

In the case of a member of a Reserve component of the Armed Forces who is required to wear his uniform for temporary periods when on active duty for training, when attending Reserve school courses, or when attending training assemblies, and who is prohibited by military regulations from wearing his uniform except on such occasions, the uniform does not merely take the place of articles required in civilian life.[81] Then the cost of uniforms and their maintenance is deductible.

Students of Armed Forces service academies cannot deduct the cost of uniforms to the extent that they replace regular clothing, but deductions may be taken for the cost of their status insignia which are purchased.[82]

All members of the Armed Forces are permitted to deduct the cost of items or equipment specially required of them which do not take the place of civilian clothing. Examples include the cost of all items of insignia of rank and corps, including gold lace and devices on the uniform coat, black braid on the aviation winter working uniform, collar devices, shoulder marks, chin straps, cap devices, and the excess cost of a cap for officers which is attributed to the gold lace on the visor; the cost of campaign bars, wings, full-dress belts, epaulets, and aiguilettes. Deduction likewise is allowed for the expense of altering uniforms and equipment upon change of rank by promotion or demotion.[83] The cost of company bars is deductible.[84] The cost of a sword is an allowable deduction,[85] presumably because it is not something which can be expected to be used in civilian life.

As previously noted, the cost of cleaning fatigues is deductible, but the cost of haircuts is not.[86]

A person in the Armed Forces may deduct the cost of professional magazines which are appropriate to his work.[87]

The cost of a correspondence course is deductible if it meets the regular educational-expense requirements. (See **Education.**) The deductible educational expenses of a veteran of the Armed Forces do not have to be reduced by tax-exempt educational benefits received from the Veterans Administration.[88]

If a member of the Armed Forces is on temporary or temporary additional duty, travel and other expenses (such as those incurred for meals, lodging, taxicabs, laundry, and cleaning) in excess of reimbursements are deductible while he is away overnight from home, be it a ship, base, or station.[89]

Reserve personnel required to work and to drill on the same day at each of two different loctions within the same city or general area may deduct one-way transportation expenses in going from one place of business to another. When they return home before drills, one-way expenses, not to exceed those from place of work to place of work, may be deducted. But roundtrip transportation expenses are deductible only when such duty area is situated beyond the city or general area which constitutes the principal place of business, provided free transportation between such locations is not furnished by the Armed Forces. This applies to all personnel who are employed at two locations on the same day.[90] This rule applies regardless of whether the individual attends such drills in the evening after his regular working hours or on an otherwise nonworking day.[91]

Travel expenses, including meals and lodging, of Reserve personnel who under competent orders, with or without compensation, are required to remain away from their principal place of business overnight in the performance of authorized drills and training duty are deductible.[92]

A member of the Armed Forces who is serving on temporary active duty in the Ready Reserve and who has a principal or regular place of business or employment which he has not given up and to which he will return after his period of service, is considered in a travel status, that is, provided he is stationed away from the general area where his civilian place of employment or other business is located. In such cases, a member who pays for his meals and lodging at his official post of duty is entitled to a deduction for expenses necessarily incurred for that purpose to the extent that such expenses exceed any nontaxable basic subsistence and quarters allowances received for these expenses. In determining the amount deductible, the expenses are limited to those which are directly attributable to the member's own presence at his military post and do not include expenses for members of his family.[93]

A naval officer may deduct as a traveling expense the cost of his meals aboard ship while the ship is away from its home port.[94]

Losses incurred by military and naval disbursing officers in replacing shortages which were not due to negligence are deductible.[95]

Losses sustained as a result of destruction or seizure of personal property in the course of military or naval operations, to the extent not reimbursed by insurance or otherwise, are deductible.[96]

A United States Army retiree could deduct legal fees in connection with a suit instituted by him to contest the rank and rate of retirement pay at which he had been retired. Here the court found that he should have been retired at a higher rank and awarded him back pay which he included in his income.[97] A noncommissioned Army officer could deduct the expenses connected with his successful litigation to obtain an increase in his retirement pay.[98]

An individual who was in the Army Reserve was charged with falsifying his educational accomplishments on two Statements of Personal History and on an Army Reserve Qualification Questionnaire, as well as falsifying time and attendance vouchers while employed as a budget and finance officer. After employing counsel, he defended a court-martial arising out of the charges, was acquitted, and was retained as an officer in the Army Reserve. Inasmuch as conviction could have resulted in loss of his position, his expenses were deductible.[99]

A captain in the Army Reserve could deduct the legal expenses of defending himself in a court-martial which had been appointed to try him on the charge of conduct unbecoming an officer in that he had dishonorably refused to pay his wife the alimony provided for her. It was held that he was engaged in the trade or business of being an officer. This was a business expense, for if he had been convicted, he would have been discharged from the trade or business.[100]

A member of the Armed Forces was allowed to deduct expenses incurred in moving his dependents to his new duty station in a foreign country. They were not eligible for moving at government expense because he was in pay-grade E-4 with less than four years of active military service and hence did not qualify. It did not matter that his dependents had to renew their visas every ninety days, for they were members of his household and he met the requirement of being a full-time employee in the general area of his new principal place of work for twelve months. Nor did it matter that the new duty station had a rule which denied housing to family members who had not been moved at government expense.[101]

The cost of moving to report for active duty by a member of the Armed Forces on permanent change of duty may be deductible even though he used a tax table or the zero bracket amount in computing his Federal income tax. Moving expenses may qualify for deduction even if the new place of employment is at least fifty miles (now thirty-five) from the old residence and if the employment meets the thirty-nine- or seventy-eight-week tests.[102] Such also is the case where he had no old place of employment when he entered the service. See **Moving expenses.**

If an individual had received a reenlistment bonus which he had previously included in gross income on a Federal income tax return, and because his enlistment is terminated, he must refund a portion of the bonus, he is entitled to a deduction for that amount.[103]

Personal money allowances received by certain high-ranking military officers for their discretionary use are includible in gross income but are deductible in determining adjusted gross income, whether or not the officer itemizes his deductions. But if the expenses exceed the personal money allowance, he may claim an itemized deduction for such excess as a business expense provided he itemizes deductions.[104]

Amounts reimbursed to military attachés for entertaining in connection with their official duties are similarly treated, subject to proper substantiation.[105]

The unreimbursed expenses incurred by a veteran as a member of the American Legion in attending a Legion convention as a delegate, as well as unreimbursed expenses directly connected with and solely attributable to the rendition of such voluntary services by him to the Legion, constitute deductible charitable contributions. This applies equally to other organizations which have tax-exempt status.[106]

See also **Education.**

Artificial teeth and limbs. See **Medical expenses.**

Asset Depreciation Range system (A.D.R.). See **Depreciation; Repairs.**

Assets. See **Depreciation; Obsolescence; Purchase of stock to get assets.**

Assistant, lunches for. *See* **Entertainment.**

Athletic club dues. *See* **Entertainment.**

Attorneys' fees. *See* **Legal fees.**

Author. *See* **Research; Travel.**

Automobile use. *See* **Casualties; Commuting; Contributions; Employees; Medical expenses; Mileage allowance.**

"Away from home." *See* **Travel.**

"Who Says So?"

Except in a few areas which most persons never encounter, the burden of proof in a tax matter is on the taxpayer. Unless an individual uses the zero bracket amount with its minimal opportunity for tax savings, he must be prepared to demonstrate an authority for every deduction claimed.

This section of the book lists the authorization or citation for each deduction which has been mentioned alphabetically. The authorities may be the Internal Revenue Code, Treasury Regulations, or various administrative rulings by the Internal Revenue Service. A substantial number of the citations represent court decisions. The monographs, booklets, and brochures listed are all publications of the Internal Revenue Service, except for *Armed Forces Federal Income Tax*, which was issued by the office of the Judge Advocate General of the United States Navy, and *Protecting Older Americans Against Overpayment of Income Taxes*, published by the Special Committee on Aging of the United States Senate.

I.R.S. letter rulings are Internal Revenue Service letters sent in response to specific questions asked by taxpayers. These rulings may not be cited as precedents but they are useful in forming an opinion as to how the Service will apply its thinking to situations of a like kind.

A

1. Regulations Section 1.167(a)-9.
2. *Tanforan Co., Inc., v. United States*, 313 F. Supp. 796 (D.C.,N.D.Cal., 1970).
3. *Commissioner v. McCarthy*, 129 F.2d 84 (7th Cir., 1942).
4. *A.J. Industries, Inc. v. United States*, 503 F.2d 660 (9th Cir., 1974).
5. *Continental Trust Company et al.*, 7 B.T.A. 539 (1927).
6. Revenue Ruling 55-367, 1955-1 CB 25.
7. Revenue Ruling 56-599, 1956-2 CB 122.
8. Revenue Ruling 73-201, 1973-1 CB 141.
9. *William Morse, Jr., et al.*, T.C. Memo. 1968-222, filed September 30, 1968.

10. *John P. White et al.*, 48 T.C. 430 (1967).
11. *Your Federal Income Tax*, 1976 edition, page 149.
12. *Burrell E. Davis*, 34 T.C. 586 (1960).
13. Revenue Ruling 73-201, 1973-1 CB 140.
14. *Clanton Motors, Inc.*, B.T.A. Memo., Docket No. 89957, entered June 29, 1939.
15. *Kamen Soap Products, Inc.*, T.C. Memo. 1956-157, filed June 29, 1956.
16. Revenue Ruling 67-401, 1967-2 CB 123.
17. *Malone & Hyde, Inc., v. United States*, 568 F.2d 474 (6th Cir., 1978).
18. *Albina Bodell*, T.C. Memo., Docket No. 109651, entered January 9, 1943.
19. *Tax Deduction on Investment Income and Expenses*, I.R.S. Publication 550, 1976 edition, page 23.
20. *Charles Hutchison*, 13 B.T.A. 1187 (1928).
21. *Reginald Denny*, 33 B.T.A. 738 (1935).
22. *Oswald "Ozzie" Nelson et al.*, T.C. Memo. 1966-224, filed October 11, 1966.
23. *Reginald Denny*, 33 B.T.A. 738 (1935).
24. *Charles Hutchison*, 13 B.T.A. 1187 (1928).
25. Revenue Ruling 72-593, 1972-2 CB 180.
26. I.R.C. Section 179.
27. *Marlor v. Commissioner*, 251, F.2d 615 (2d Cir., 1958).
28. *Devereaux et al. v. Commissioner*, 292 F.2d 637 (3d Cir., 1961).
29. Regulations Section 1.162-14.
30. *Southwestern Electric Power Company v. United States*, 312 F.2d 437 (Ct. Cl., 1963).
31. *Poletti et al. v. Commissioner*, 330 F.2d 818 (8th Cir., 1969).
32. *Duffey v. Lethert*, D.C., Minn. 1963.
33. *Sanitary Farms Dairy, Inc.*, 25 T.C. 463 (1955).
34. *Rodgers Dairy Company et al.*, 14 T.C. 66 (1950).
35. *Aptos Land and Water Company, Inc.*, 46 B.T.A. 1232 (1942).
36. I.T. 3581, 1942-2 CB 88.
37. Regulations Section 1.162-15.
38. *Hennepin Holding Co.*, 23 B.T.A. 119 (1931).
39. *Edward J. Miller*, 37 B.T.A. 830 (1938).
40. I.T. 3581, 1942-2 CB 88.
41. *Consolidated Apparel Co.*, 17 T.C. 1570 (1952).
42. I.R.C. Section 276(c).
43. *Victor J. McQuade*, 4 B.T.A. 837 (1926).
44. *A. D. Miller*, T.C. Memo., Docket No. 23754, entered January 18, 1951.
45. I.T. 1667, II-I CB 83.
46. Revenue Ruling 63-73, 1963-1 CB 35.
47. Revenue Ruling 55-261, 1955-1 CB 307.
48. *Dean L. Phillips*, T.C. Memo., Docket Nos. 18410-18, entered June 9, 1950.
49. Revenue Ruling 63-273, 1963-2 CB 112.
50. Revenue Ruling 73-325, 1973-2 CB 75.
51. Regulations Section 1.71-1(b).
52. *Sydnes v. Commissioner*, 577 F.2d 60 (8th Cir., 1978).
53. Regulations Section 1.71-1(d).
54. *Robert Lehman*, 17 T.C. 652 (1951).
55. *Illene Isaacson et al.*, 58 T.C. 659 (1972).
56. *Phillips et al. v. Commissioner*, T.C. Memo. 1977-296, filed August 31, 1977.
57. *Mace v. United States*, D.C., S.D. Cal., 1964.
58. Revenue Ruling 62-166, 1962-2 CB 21.
59. *Income Tax Deductions for Alimony Payments*, I.R.S. Publication 504, 1976 edition, page 1.

60. I.R.C. Section 215(a).
61. *Income Tax Deductions for Alimony Payments*, I.R.S. Publication 504, 1976 edition, page 2.
62. *Hinish et al. v. Commissioner*, T.C. Memo. 1978-207, filed June 6, 1978.
63. *Income Tax Deductions for Alimony Payments*, I.R.S. Publication 504, 1976 edition, page 2.
64. *Andrew M. Newburger et al.*, 61 T.C. 437 (1974).
65. Revenue Ruling 55-457, 1955-2 CB 527.
66. I.R.C. Section 71(b).
67. *United States v. Paurowski*, 457 F.2d 1401 (4th Cir., 1973).
68. *Commissioner v. Lester*, 366 U.S. 299 (1961).
69. *Elsie B. Gale*, 13 T.C. 661 (1949), *aff'd on another issue*, 191 F.2d 79 (2d Cir., 1951).
70. *Jane V. Elliott*, 40 T.C. 304 (1963).
71. Revenue Ruling 70-218, 1970-1 CB 19.
72. *Robert W. Drummond et al.*, T.C. Memo. 1976-55, filed February 26, 1976.
73. Tax Reform Act of 1976, Section 502.
74. I.R.C. Section 72.
75. Revenue Ruling 70-15, 1970-1 CB 20.
76. Revenue Ruling 61-201, 1961-2 CB 46.
77. *Leisner et al. v. Commissioner*, T.C. Memo. 1977-205, filed July 5, 1977.
78. *Wallace L. Chesshire*, T.C. Memo., Docket No. 30969, entered February 19, 1952.
79. *James A. Mount*, T.C. Memo., Docket No. 9401, entered November 29, 1946.
80. *Armed Forces Federal Income Tax*, 1976 edition, page 40.
81. Revenue Ruling 55-109, 1955-1 CB 261.
82. *Your Federal Income Tax*, 1976 edition, page 107.
83. *Armed Forces Federal Income Tax*, 1976 edition, page 40.
84. I.T. 1965, III-I CB 201.
85. Regulations Section 1.262-1(b)(8).
86. *Richard W. Drake*, 52 T.C. 842 (1969).
87. *Charles A. Harris et al.*, T.C. Memo., Docket No. 34256, entered January 28, 1953.
88. *Tax Information on Educational Expenses*, I.R.S. Publication 508, 1976 edition, page 1.
89. *Armed Forces Federal Income Tax*, 1976 edition, page 27.
90. *Ibid.*
91. Revenue Ruling 55-109, 1955-1 CB 261.
92. *Armed Forces Federal Income Tax*, 1976 edition, page 27.
93. Revenue Ruling 63-64, 1963-1 CB 30.
94. Revenue Ruling 55-571, 1955-2 CB 44.
95. *Armed Forces Federal Income Tax*, 1976 edition, page 39.
96. *Ibid.*
97. Revenue Ruling 72-169, 1972-1 CB 43.
98. I.T. 3325, 1939-2 CB 151.
99. Revenue Ruling 64-277, 1964-2 CB 55.
100. *Howard v. Commissioner*, 202 F.2d 28 (9th Cir., 1953).
101. Revenue Ruling 70-520, 1970-2 CB 66.
102. *Armed Forces Federal Income Tax*, 1976 edition, page 26.
103. *Ibid.*, page 40.
104. Revenue Ruling 77-350, 1977-2 CB 21.
105. Revenue Ruling 77-351, 1977-2 CB 23.
106. Revenue Ruling 58-240, 1958-1 CB 141.

B

Bad debts. Business bad debts are deductible in full. Nonbusiness bad debts are deductible as short-term capital losses.[1] A business bad debt must be connected with the taxpayer's trade or business. A business bad debt can arise even out of an isolated transaction if it is related to a person's trade or business.[2]

Ordinarily, where an officer or other employee lends money to the business which employs him, any resulting loss is a nonbusiness bad debt, for an employee is not likely to be in the business of lending money and therefore the loss is not the result of a business transaction. Similarly, loss on his purchase of his employer's stock is a capital loss. But where the loan or purchase was for the purpose of obtaining or retaining one's position, a resultant loss is business-related. An individual as a result of major surgery was virtually unable to use his voice and one arm. He was offered employment only if he lent money to a certain corporation, in the stock of which he was also obligated to make an investment; the justification was that the corporation could not expand sufficiently to offer him employment unless the funds were made available. His subsequent losses were fully deductible as expenses in connection with his business of being an employee. He could not have been employed here or, presumably, anywhere else without his making the advance and the investment.[3]

An individual was informed when he was hired as vice-president and business manager of a corporation that he would be expected to make loans to the company until its cash position improved. He made such loans from time to time. There came a time when he was told that if he did not make further advances, the company would not be able to pay his salary and he would be fired. He declined and was fired. His prior unpaid advances were fully deductible business bad debts. The advances had been made in connection with his trade or business of rendering services for pay.[4]

A father and son created their own corporation in the

used-metal business. They could deduct their losses when their advances to the corporation were not repaid. The father had made loans because, being over seventy, he had reason to feel he never would be able to get another job, and such proved to be the case after the corporation failed. The son was of employable age but was characterized by the court as unemployable for all practical purposes because of his personality, which did not lend itself to serving as an employee for a company other than his own. Both father and son were motivated by the desire to protect their trade or business as employees, and the advances were business bad debts.[5]

The president and sole stockholder of a textile corporation could deduct his advances to a corporation when they became uncollectible. The loans had been made to protect his job. His psychiatrist testified that his patient had very serious personality problems and was unable to work with persons in superior or equal positions. He had to retain his position as executive by owning his company; he could protect his employment only by helping the corporation to survive. The psychiatrist had advised him to form his own company so that he could carry on his trade or business of being a stylist.[6]

The manager of a division of an insurance company received compensation based upon a percentage of the premium income produced by the unit under his control. To develop and to maintain loyalty and dedication which paid off in employee productivity, he made thirty-two loans to his staff members in an eight-year period. When one borrower went into bankruptcy, the loan to him could be deducted fully as a business bad debt. The manager's action in making loans to his employees was appropriate and useful in furtherance of his business as an insurance producer.[7]

If a taxpayer can establish that a debt appears to be recoverable only in part, he has the election of waiting until the debt is fully bad or of charging off that part of the debt which seems to have been worthless at the time of this charge-off. In order to get a deduction for a partially bad debt, it must be a business bad debt and it must actually be charged off on the books to the extent claimed on the tax return.[8] The write-off must be of specific debts; it is not proper to take a flat percentage of total receivables or any other generalized figure.[9]

In the past, worthless debts of political parties could not be written off by frustrated creditors, except in the case of banks. For taxable years beginning after December 31, 1975, deduction is allowed for worthless debts owed by political parties or campaign committees if the debts arose from good-faith sales of goods or services and if substantial efforts were made to collect the debts.[10] Thus, suppliers of campaign office furniture, printers, landlords, and the like, who had been stuck with unpaid bills can now regard campaigns with less bitterness, regardless of which horse comes in.

Spending money in an effort to collect a debt that a person previously had deducted as bad can endanger this deduction, for it suggests that the creditor wasn't fully convinced that the debt *was* uncollectible. Deduction was permitted, however, where suit had been brought against a company, the unpaid account of which had been written off as worthless, when it could be established that the taxpayer still believed the company was unable to pay its debt but there was some possibility of personally involving an officer of the delinquent company.[11]

Bad debts are deductible when they are charged off. Alternatively, amounts added to a reserve for bad debts to bring this reserve up to what experience has shown to be a proper percentage of receivables or sales are deductible.[12]

One of the two standard methods of accounting for bad debts for Federal income tax purposes is the *reserve method*. Based upon past experience, a taxpayer can deduct whatever amount is necessary to bring the year-end balance in the reserve up to an acceptable measuring rod, such as 2 percent of closing receivables. This assumes that in the past, 2 percent of receivables become worthless. But inflation can ruin the validity of this approach. With soaring prices for goods, a single default could exceed the amount in the seller's previous reserve, which had been based upon *last year's* receivables balances. Changed circumstances must be taken into account in determining the reasonableness of a taxpayer's addition to the reserve.[13]

Bankruptcy. A trustee in bankruptcy can deduct costs in connection with a corporate liquidation, except costs connected with the sale of assets, which must be charged against the proceeds of the sale.[14] *See also* **Creditors, payments to; Fiduciaries.**

Bargain sales. *See* **Contributions.**

Baseball player, expenses of. A professional player is permitted to deduct the cost of his own uniforms if he has to supply them.[15]

Beneficiaries. If, on the termination of an estate or a trust, there is a net operating loss carryover or a capital loss carryover, or for the last taxable year of the estate or trust there is an excess of deductions over gross income for that year, the carryover may be used by the beneficiary succeeding to the property of the estate or trust.[16] *See also* **Depreciation; Legal fees; Capital losses.**

Benefit performances, tickets for. Here are the ground rules if one purchases tickets for a benefit performance by an approved charitable organization:
1. If the charity sells one ticket for about the established price for a concert, etc., no part of the "contribution" is deductible.
2. If the charity charges an amount in excess of the established price of the ticket, only this excess is deductible as a contribution.
3. If the buyer of a ticket sold by the charity at the established price has no intention of using the ticket and in fact does not use it, he still gets no deduction. However, he would get the deduction if he refuses to accept the ticket and merely makes his contribution of the same amount to the charity.
4. If a charity solicits contributions on a form where the "contributor" designates his check mark as being for a ticket to an event produced by the tax-exempt organization or as being a straight contribution, the person checking the first option gets no tax deduction.
5. If friends of the charity pay the entire cost of staging an event for which tickets are sent to contributors to the charity, no part of the cost of the tickets is deductible.[17]

If there is no established charge for an event for which tickets are "distributed" by a charitable organization to "contributors," an individual claiming a tax deduction must establish that the amount paid is not the purchase price of the privileges or benefits and that part of the payment, in fact, does qualify as a gift.

The amount indicated on a ticket or other evidence of payment to be a "contribution" does not necessarily have a bearing on the amount deductible. Such a statement, however, may be meaningful if it shows not only the value of the admission or other privilege but also the amount of the gift. If an individual pays $10 to see a special showing of a movie, the net proceeds of which go to a qualified organization, he cannot take too seriously the words "Contribution—$10." If the regular price for the movie is $2, he has made a contribution of $8.[18]

Birth control measures. The purchase of birth control pills by a woman for her personal use was a deductible medical expense because she obtained the pills under a prescription provided by her physician.[19]

A woman who, at her own request, undergoes an abortion operation to terminate her pregnancy can claim the expense as a medical deduction if the operation is performed in a general hospital and if the operation is not illegal under state law. This is true because the operation is for the purpose of affecting a structure or function of the body and therefore is a deductible expense.[20]

A vasectomy performed in a doctor's office under local anesthetic and for the purpose of preventing conception is a deductible medical expense, even if the operation is performed at the man's own request.[21]

Blackout losses. Losses from casualties or thefts sustained during an electricity blackout are deductible. The loss is fully deductible if business property is involved. In the case of nonbusiness property, the deduction is limited to the amount which exceeds $100.[22]

Blind person, expenses of. The expenses paid by a blind person or for him in connection with maintaining a Seeing Eye dog are deductible as medical expenses.[23]

Amounts expended to have someone accompany the payor's blind child solely for the purpose of guiding the youngster in walking throughout the school day constituted medical care.[24]

Corporate executives or professional persons who are blind may have to engage readers in order to perform their business duties satisfactorily. The cost generally is paid by the handicapped persons themselves and not by their employers. The payments are deductible as ordinary and necessary expenses for labor directly connected with or pertaining to the taxpayer's trade or business. But being medical expenses, they are limited in deductibility to the extent that total medical expenses exceed 3 percent of the taxpayer's adjusted gross income. In a case where it is questionable whether an expense is deductible as a business or medical expense, business expense deductibility applies if all three of the following elements are present: (1) the nature of the taxpayer's work clearly requires that he incur a particular expense to perform his work satisfactorily, (2) the goods or services purchased by the expense are clearly not required or used, other than incidentally, in the conduct of the individual's personal activities, and (3) the tax law and its explanatory regulations are otherwise silent as to the treatment of such expenses.[25]

Where an item is purchased in a special form primarily for the alleviation of a physical defect (such as a braille edition of a book or magazine purchased for the blind) and where it is one that ordinarily is used for personal, living, and family purposes, the excess of the cost of the special form over the normal cost of the item is an expense for medical care. Therefore, where a parent has a child attending a school for the blind, amounts paid to purchase braille books and magazines in excess of the cost of their regular printed editions are expenses for medical care.[26]

An individual's child was afflicted with an eye condition that was diagnosed as a disease which eventually would cause the child to become totally blind. At the time the child was enrolled in a state university, and competent physicians recommended that certain special aids be obtained to facilitate the child's further education. The costs of a tape recorder, special typewriter, projection lamp for enlarging written material, and special lenses were considered mitigating the condition of losing the sense of sight and were deductible as medical expenses.[27]

See *also* **Medical expenses.**

Bodyguard. Hiring a bodyguard was a deductible expense in the case of a professional person who was the recipient of a kidnap threat.[28]

Bond, furnishing of. An employee who is required to furnish bond to his employers at his own expense can deduct the cost.[29]

Bondholders' protective committee, payments to. See **Investors.**

Bond premiums. See **Investors.**

Bonds, tax-exempt. See **Tax-exempt bonds.**

Breach of contract, payments for. Damages paid for breach of contract entered into in the ordinary course of a taxpayer's business and directly related thereto normally are considered to represent deductible business expense.[30] See *also* **Settlements.**

Breakage by employee. A research scientist could deduct expenses for breakage he incurred and paid for.[31]

Bribes and kickbacks. Bribes and kickbacks, whether direct or indirect, are not deductible if made to an official of any government (United States, state, or foreign) or to any agency or instrumentality in violation of Federal or state law. They are allowed in the case of other payees unless the taxpayer-payor is convicted of an illegal bribe or kickback in a criminal proceeding or if he enters a plea of guilty or *nolo contendere.* (*Nolo contendere* means that the defendant does not contest the accusation against him.)[32]

If a bribe or kickback, other than to a governmental employee, does not constitute a criminal act in the jurisdiction where it took place, or if the taxpayer is not successfully prosecuted, the deduction is not disallowed.[33]

Some states, such as New York, make it a misdemeanor to give any gratuity to another party's employees without the knowledge and consent of the employer, "with intent to influence such employee's . . . action in relation to his . . . employer's . . . business." The tax deduction is available if the payor gets the consent of the employer of the buyer, inspector, etc.[34] Actually this may not be impossible. The employer may have complete confidence in the integrity of his employees, who have been told that they would be fired if they overpaid for merchandise or approved shoddy performance. And he may believe that if the customer gives the employee a sizable bonus, he will not have to do so.

Even if a type of payment is barred by state law, deduction is permitted when the payment is business-oriented if this law is not enforced by the state. An unenforced law is scarcely a law for this purpose. In one example of this, a wholesale beer distributor gave away free samples in violation of state law and the regulations of the state alcoholic beverage control board. Deduction was permitted in this case because the state officials consciously chose not to enforce these rules and had advised the appropriate enforcement personnel to that effect.[35]

The cost of liquor used to entertain customers was deductible where the state knew of the custom and did nothing about it, although state law banned the practice. The state's nonaction negated the idea of a sharply defined public policy against the practice.[36]

A manufacturer entered into an agreement with other companies to fix prices at a high level. On occasion, the manufacturer granted price rebates on merchandise purchased by certain customers who otherwise would have bought their requirements from companies which were not part of the arrangement. In time, the manufacturer was convicted under a Federal law against deals to maintain higher prices. But the price rebates were not illegal payments; they were paid so the manufacturer could remain competitive with companies not part of the price-rigging scheme. So the rebates were deductible.[37]

Tips to employees of other employers are deductible if such employers are not governmental and there is no local law prohibiting the practice. Tips to employees of a railroad company to expedite the movement of the payor's shipments were deductible where this was essential to the success of the business and where the practice was common.[38] Tips to truck drivers to assure prompt deliveries were allowable.[39]

However, tips to railroad ticket offices to obtain extra services such as were not offered to "ordinary" customers of these offices were disallowed on the ground that they merely gratified the desire of the payor for unusual and extraordinary personal comfort or convenience and therefore were not business expenses but personal expenditures.[40]

Brokers' fees. *See* **Investors.**

Burglary, losses from. *See* **Casualties.**

Business associates, lunches for. *See* **Entertainment.**

Business bad debts. *See* **Bad debts.**

Business expenses. *See* **Ordinary and necessary business expenses.**

Business gifts. Although ordinarily no deduction is allowed for the cost of gifts made directly or indirectly to an individual to the extent that the total expense of all or any gifts made in the same taxable year exceeds $25, deduction is allowed in the following situations:
1.   An item having a cost to the taxpayer of not more than $4, on which the taxpayer's name is clearly and permanently imprinted and which is one of a number of similar items generally distributed.
2.   A sign, a display rack, or other promotional material to be used on the recipient's business premises.
3.   An item of tangible property having a cost to the taxpayer not in excess of $100, which is awarded to an employee by reason of length of service or for safety achievement.[41]

A businessperson could deduct the cost of liquor purchased in reasonable amounts for people who regularly supplied merchandise.[42]

Gifts to subordinates by a sales supervisor were deductible because greater cooperation from these persons was likely to increase his own performance.[43]

Business losses. *See* **Bad debts; Business-related losses; Cancellation and forfeiture; Carry-overs; Family transactions; Partner-**

ships; **Property used in the trade or business and involuntary conversions.**

B

Business overhead insurance. *See* **Insurance.**

Business-related losses. Amounts paid in satisfaction of a claim arising from an individual's trade or business are deductible.[44] Amounts paid in settlement of such a claim, in the exercise of good-faith business judgment, are likewise deductible.[45]

A teller, cashier, or similar party may be required by the conditions of his employment to pay his employer the amount of any shortages before he is permitted to continue on the payroll. This is deductible as an expense in earning one's compensation if he itemizes his deductions. But if he uses the zero bracket amount instead of itemizing deductions, this is not a deduction in determining adjusted gross income.[46]

The cost of rectification of errors made in advising customers of the cost of policies was deductible.[47] A salesman sold securities to a customer with the agreement that he would be entitled to 50 percent of the customer's profits but would absorb 50 percent of his losses. When the transaction ended with a loss, the salesman could deduct the amount he paid in discharge of his obligation under the guaranty agreement, for the guaranty was given in the course of his business activities.[48]

An individual, while driving in connection with his business activities, injured a child. He lost a negligence suit. The judgment was deductible as a business expense; the expenditure was proximately connected with a business activity, not a personal one.[49]

A taxpayer's warehouse was totally destroyed by fire, and properties belonging to its customers were lost. Although some customers were insured under personal policies, and others were covered by the taxpayer's general insurance policy, still other customers had no insurance protection at all. They were unhappy about their losses and complained that they had been insufficiently informed about their insurance options. To preserve customer goodwill and to protect its business reputation, the taxpayer made at least partial monetary restitution to uninsured customers. Although in most instances payments for goodwill are regarded as nondeductible capital expenditures, these payments were allowed to be deducted as ordinary and necessary business expenses to protect the taxpayer's business reputation.[50]

An employee who sells on commission is dependent for his income upon the amount of its wares the employer is willing to make available to him for marketing. When a brokerage firm "suggested" to an employee that he buy stock in the company to provide it with survival funds, he bought shares. True, his arm wasn't actually twisted nor were there threats of discharge if he refused to buy company stock. But it was obvious to him that his employer could control his level of income by restricting new stock which in the past had been a good source of income to him. When the brokerage firm failed, his stock loss was fully deductible as a business transaction—protecting his job and earning power—rather than as a capital loss, such as customarily would accompany a sour investment.[51]

The publisher and editor of a newspaper stated in an interview with a magazine writer that one of his (the publisher's) executive committee members evidently was selling or telling secrets of the publication to competitors. A recently discharged executive sued the publisher for libel and won. Deduction was allowed for the court's award. The libelous statement was made during the course of his trade or business, and allowance of the deduction was not contrary to public policy because it was a private wrongdoing rather than a public one.[52] See **Executives.**

Business reputation, defense of. See **Business-related losses; Executives; Legal fees.**

B

1. I.R.C. Section 166.
2. *Robert Cluett 3d et al.,* 8 T.C. 1178 (1947).
3. *Wallace L. Hirsch et al.,* T.C. Memo. 1971-235, filed September 14, 1971.
4. *Trent et al. v. Commissioner,* 291 F.2d 679 (2d Cir., 1961).
5. *Isidor Jaffee et al.,* T.C. Memo. 1967-215, filed October 30, 1967.
6. *Kent Average Estate,* T.C. Memo. 1969-64, filed April 3, 1969.
7. *Harlan v. United States,* D.C., N.D. Texas, 1974.
8. I.R.C. Section 166(a)(2).
9. Regulations Section 1.166-3(a).
10. Tax Reform Act of 1976, Section 2104.
11. *Bruce V. Green et al.,* T.C. Memo. 1976-127, filed April 22, 1976.
12. I.R.C. Section 166(c).
13. *Gurentz et al. v. Commissioner,* T.C. Memo. 1978-238, filed June 26, 1978.
14. Revenue Ruling 77-204, 1977-1 CB 40.
15. Revenue Ruling 70-476, 1970-2 CB 25.
16. I.R.C. Section 642(h).
17. Revenue Ruling 67-246, 1967-2 CB 104.
18. *The Tax Deduction for Contributions,* I.R.S. Publication 526, 1976 edition, page 3.
19. Revenue Ruling 73-200, 1973-1 CB 140.

20. Revenue Ruling 73-201, 1973-1 CB 140.
21. *Ibid.*
22. Revenue Ruling 55-261, 1955-1 CB 307.
23. I.R.S. News Release, November 12, 1965.
24. Revenue Ruling 64-173, 1964-1 CB (Part 1) 12.
25. Revenue Ruling 75-316, 1975-2 CB 54.
26. Revenue Ruling 75-313, I.R.B. 1975-31, 8.
27. Revenue Ruling 58-223, 1958-1 CB 156.
28. *Frederick Cecil Bartholomew Estate,* 4 T.C. 349 (1944).
29. T.D. 2090, CB December 14, 1914.
30. *Great Island Holding Corporation,* 5 T.C. 150 (1945).
31. *Mathilda M. Brooks,* 30 T.C. 1087 (1958), *rev'd on other grounds,* 274 F.2d 96 (9th cir., 1960).
32. I.R.C. Section 162(c)(3).
33. Senate Finance Committee Report on the Revenue Bill of 1971, Section 162(c)(3).
34. New York Penal Laws, Section 439.
35. *Sterling Distributors, Inc., v. Patterson,* 236 F. Supp. 479 (D.C., N.D. Ala., 1964).
36. *Stacy et al. v. United States,* 231 F. Supp. 304 (D.C., S.D. Miss., 1963).
37. Revenue Ruling 77-243, 1977-2 CB 57.
38. *F. L. Bateman,* 34 B.T.A. 351 (1936).
39. *August F. Nielsen Co., Inc., et al.,* T.C. Memo. 1968-11, filed January 18, 1968.
40. *Julius (Jay) C. Henricks,* T.C. Memo., Docket No. 16192, entered November 8, 1949.
41. I.R.C. Section 274(b).
42. *Rodgers Dairy Co.,* 14 T.C. 66 (1950).
43. *Harold A. Christensen,* 17 T.C. 1456 (1952).
44. *Helvering v. Hampton,* 79 F.2d 358 (9th Cir., 1935).
45. *Levitt & Sons v. Nunan,* 142 F.2d 795 (2d Cir., 1944).
46. *Butchko et al. v. Commissioner,* T.C. Memo. 1978-209, filed June 7, 1978.
47. *Boyle, Flagg & Seaman, Inc.,* 25 T.C. 43 (1955).
48. *Irving L. Schein,* T.C. Memo., Docket No. 32717, entered February 29, 1952.
49. *Plante et al. v. United States,* 226 F. Supp. 314 (D.C., N.H., 1963).
50. Revenue Ruling 76-23, 1976-1 CB 45.
51. *Elmer Carsello et al.,* T.C. Memo. 1976-193, filed June 15, 1976.
52. *Cornelius Vanderbilt, Jr.,* T.C. Memo. 1957-235, filed December 23, 1957.

C

Cancellation and forfeiture. A payment by a lessee for cancellation of a business lease was held to be deductible.[1]

A tenant failed to go through with its commitment on a business lease and its deposits thereupon were forfeited. The amounts were deductible in the year of the forfeiture.[2]

Where a portion of the purchase price of a plantation was forfeited upon failure of the would-be buyer to make the additional payments called for, the forfeited down payments were deductible.[3]

Deduction was allowed when a deposit to guarantee observation of the rules of a service bureau was forfeited.[4]

Capital improvements. Capital expenditures are not currently deductible, but in the case of business assets with a measurable life, annual write-offs are permitted in the form of depreciation and amortization.

In general, all construction costs of a business must be capitalized and written off over the estimated useful life of the facility. But when the purpose of temporary partitions, heating, and the like was to allow existing buildings to operate during major construction operations, the cost was deductible.[5] Deduction was also allowed for the cost of enlarging and improving an office where the work was not in the nature of permanent improvements but was to facilitate the transaction of increasing business.[6]

Expenses related to the installation of capital equipment with a useful life of more than one year customarily must be capitalized. But labor and transportation costs in connection with moving certain of a taxpayer's capitalized assets to another location were deductible, for the relocation did not add to the value nor appreciably prolong the useful lives of these assets.[7]

For capital improvements to one's home for medical reasons, *see* **Expenditures for benefits lasting more than one year; Medical expenses.**

Capital losses. In the case of sales of capital assets after October 31, 1978, an individual may deduct from income 60 percent of the net long-term capital losses which are in excess of the net short-term capital gains.[8]

Long-term capital losses are deductible from long-term capital gains, but $2 of the former are needed to offset $1 of the latter.[9]

If capital losses exceed capital gains, a deduction against taxable income is allowed up to $3,000.[10] The deduction of capital losses against ordinary income for married persons filing separate returns is limited to $500 for each spouse.[11]

To the extent that an individual cannot use a capital loss in the year sustained, he may carry it forward for an unlimited period of time. The unused capital-loss carry-over, after being used to reduce net capital gains of the year to which it is carried, is available to offset ordinary income in the manner just mentioned.[12]

An unused capital-loss carry-over at the time that an estate or trust terminates is allowed as a deduction to the beneficiaries succeeding to the property.[13]

As to capital loss transactions involving certain related parties, *see* **Family transactions.**

Career counseling. Expenses for career counseling are deductible where they assist a person to obtain other employment in the same trade or business. This includes (1) a job evaluation which is an appraisal of a party's capabilities and personal characteristics, (2) establishment of attainable goals consistent with a person's abilities, (3) interview preparations, and (4) evaluation of salary and fringe benefits, including job acceptance protection procedure.[14]

Carrying charges on unproductive realty. *See* **Election to deduct or to capitalize.**

Carry-overs. If an individual has sustained a loss in the operation of his trade or business during a taxable year, or a casualty or theft loss in excess of the year's income, there is a net operating loss. A net operating loss is the excess of allowable deductions over gross income after prescribed adjustments have been made. An individual with a net operating loss may carry the loss as a deduction to certain other taxable years in a stipulated time sequence to reduce tax liability for such years or to obtain a refund of taxes previously paid.[15]

An individual's net operating loss is computed in the same way as his taxable income, with these adjustments:

1.   Taxable income is determined without regard to the particular net operating loss being carried back or over, or to any later net operating loss. But account is taken of any earlier net operating losses being carried back or over from the previous years.

2.   Capital losses may not exceed capital gains. Nonbusiness capital losses may not exceed nonbusiness capital gains, even though there may be an excess of business capital gains over business capital losses.

3.   Deduction of 50 percent of the excess of a net long-term capital gain over a net short-term capital loss cannot be taken.

4.   Personal exemptions and exemptions for dependents cannot be taken into account.

5.   Nonbusinesses deductions cannot exceed nonbusiness income.[16]

If a husband and wife file separate returns for a taxable year but file a joint Federal income tax return for any or all of the years involved in computing the carry-over or carry-back to the taxable year, the separate carry-overs or carry-backs to the taxable year are to be computed as if on separate returns with certain modifications. A husband was engaged in the coal business. His wife served as billing clerk and bookkeeper and she handled sales, all without compensation. In addition, she cosigned company notes, pledged her own property as security for business loans, and paid off some of the business notes with her own funds. The business lost money for the three years ending with her husband's death. Then she took a salaried position in another business. A net operating loss that is incurred in a joint-return year and carried forward to a separate tax return must be allocated to ensure that it is used to offset only the income of the spouse who incurred the loss. But under the facts here, it was held that the losses of the coal business had been incurred equally by each spouse. So when she filed a separate income tax return for the year after the death of her husband, she could carry forward one-half of the losses of the coal business for the preceding three years to offset her business income, which consisted of her salary.[17]

Except for charitable contributions, any deductions claimed by an individual which are based on or limited to a percentage of adjusted gross income (such as medical expenses) must be recomputed on the basis of the adjusted gross or taxable income after the application of these adjustments. The deduction of charitable contributions is determined using the same adjustments except that account is not taken of any net operating losses being carried back.[18]

Except in the case of any foreign expropriation losses (which

are discussed under **Foreign expropriation losses**), a net operating loss must first be carried back to the third year preceding
the year in which it was sustained. Any amount of the loss that
is not used to offset taxable income (adjusted, as mentioned
previously) for the third preceding year is carried back to the
second preceding year.[19] Any amount of the loss that is not
used to offset taxable income for the third and second preceding years must be carried to the first preceding year. If the loss
is not entirely used to offset taxable income as adjusted in the
three preceding years, the balance may be carried over to
specified future years in the order of their occurrence. For net
operating losses incurred in taxable years after December 31,
1975, losses may be carried forward for seven years (previously
the figure had been five). In addition, taxpayers entitled to
carry-back periods for their net operating losses may elect to
forgo the entire carry-back period for a net operating loss in
any taxable year.[20]

Married persons may carry back or forward a loss sustained
by one spouse and reported on a separate tax return to offset
joint income.[21] If the parties consistently file joint returns, they
may carry a net operating loss jointly to the other years irre-
spective of which one incurred the loss.[22] An individual may
deduct a net operating loss from the income of his or her
spouse reported on a joint return only where a joint return can
also be filed at the time the loss is sustained.[23] So a net operating loss sustained by a wife after her husband's death cannot
be carried back and applied against income reported on joint
returns in past years where all the income had been earned by
the husband.[24]

Where, in a community property state such as California,
there is a change in the marital status by divorce, and subsequently one of the parties to the marriage sustains a net
operating loss, the loss may be carried back only to that portion
of the taxable income reported on a previously filed joint return of the community income which is vested in the party
who sustained the loss.[25] (John and Mary, for example, had
until the time of their divorce in 1972 filed joint income tax
returns. All the community income had been produced by
John's businesses. The terms of the divorce gave John title to
those businesses. In 1973 John sustained a net operating loss.
He could carry the loss back in a manner which is ordinarily
applicable in computing business losses, whereas if Mary had
sustained the loss, she could not have done so.)

Such also is the case in a noncommunity property state
where one of the parties dies and the survivor sustains a net
operating loss in a subsequent year.[26]

A husband and wife filed a joint return for one year and separate returns for the following year. The husband had a business loss for the earlier year, while the wife had nontaxable income. The husband's loss for the first year which could be carried forward and claimed as a deduction in the second year had to be reduced by the nontaxable income of the wife for the same year.[27]

A partnership agreement will determine the proportionate loss deductions of the several partners, but if any provision has as its principal purpose tax avoidance, the Internal Revenue Service can disregard it.[28] A partner may deduct his proportionate share of partnership losses for each year, but only to the extent of his adjusted basis in the partnership at the close of each year.[29] He can increase the amount of his loss which is deductible by increasing his basis in any of these manners: (1) by contributing additional capital to the partnership, (2) by lending money to the partnership, or (3) by any increases in the liabilities of the partnership. A partner's basis for his interest is increased by his share of partnership liabilities.[30]

A limited partner's share of partnership liabilities does not exceed the difference between his actual contribution credited to him by the partnership and the total contribution which he is obligated to make under the limited-partnership agreement. But where none of the partners has any personal liability with respect to a partnership liability (as in the case of a mortgage on real estate acquired by the partnership without the assumption by the partnership or by any of the partners of any liability on the mortgage), then all partners, including limited partners, are considered as sharing such liability in the same proportion as they share profits.[31]

A limited partner cannot deduct losses in excess of his investment. But unused losses can be carried forward to offset future income of the partnership.[32]

If an estate or trust, when it is terminated, has a net operating loss carry-over, the carry-over is allowed as a deduction to the beneficiaries succeeding to the property. The same rule applies if the estate or trust, in its last taxable year, has deductions in excess of gross income, not taking the personal exemption into consideration.[33]

The total of the unused loss carry-overs or the excess deductions on termination which may be deducted by the successor beneficiaries is allocated proportionately according to the share of each in the burden of the loss or deduction.[34]

Carry-overs, unused charitable contributions. *See* **Contributions.**

Car telephone. *See* **Medical expenses.**

Cash discounts on purchases. Cash discounts on purchases may be deductible by businesspersons as discounts, or the amounts may be reflected in inventory. The taxpayer has this election on the first tax return where there are such purchases. Once made, this election is irrevocable and permanent.[35]

Cash shortages. A salesman properly deducted the amounts of cash shortages he was obligated to make up to his employer because of mistakes in making change, loss of inventory in his custody, and reimbursements to his customers for which he in turn was not reimbursed.[36] Collections from customers which were lost by a salesman were deductible by him as a business expense.[37] *See* **Armed forces.**

Casualties. A deduction is allowed for any loss sustained during the taxable year which has not been compensated for by insurance or in any other manner.[38]

The amount of the loss to be taken into account for tax purposes is the lesser of (1) the fair market value of the property immediately before the casualty, or (2) the amount of the adjusted basis for determining loss.

In the case of business property, if the fair market value of the property immediately before the casualty is less than the adjusted basis, the amount of the adjusted basis is deemed to be the amount of the loss.[39]

In the case of nonbusiness (or personal) property, the deduction is the amount by which the casualty loss exceeds $100. Or the deduction may be the cost of repairing the damage.[40]

In other words, to determine your deductible loss on personal property, take the following three steps:

1. Determine the difference between the market value of the property immediately before the loss and the market value of the property immediately after the loss. The result is the loss in fair market value.

2. Then determine the adjusted basis for the property. This is, in most cases, the original cost of the property plus the cost of improvement minus previously taken deductions for casualty loss.

3. Take the lower amount of step 1 or step 2 and subtract the salvage value, insurance proceeds (or other compensation for the loss), and $100. The resulting amount is your deductible casualty loss for personal property.

If the property is business property, these steps should be taken:

1. Same as step 1 above.

2. Determine the adjusted basis for the business property. This is usually the original cost of the property plus the cost of improvements minus previously taken deductions and depreciation.

3. Take the lower amount of step 1 or step 2, with the following exception: If the business property has been totally destroyed and the market value of the property before the casualty was less than the adjusted basis for the property, then the deduction taken is the adjusted basis less the compensation received for the loss.

An individual's deductible losses are limited to (1) losses incurred in a trade or business, (2) losses incurred in any transaction entered into for profit, although not connected with a trade or business, and (3) losses of property not connected with a trade or business, where the losses arise from a fire, storm, shipwreck, or other casualty, or from theft.[41] Examples are: subterranean disturbances,[42] ice storm,[43] flood.[44] "Other casualty" means an event or happening which was destructive of the property and was sudden in its occurrence.[45] An "other casualty" must also be unexpected, violent, and not due to the deliberate or willful actions of the taxpayer.[46] An individual's *ordinary* negligence is not a bar to a casualty loss, although *gross* negligence is.[47]

The cost of repairing damage to a person's car was deductible where he carried no insurance and the accident had not been occasioned by his willful act of negligence.[48] The value of a personal car was deductible when the vehicle unexpectedly fell through the ice on a frozen lake on which it was parked.[49] Deduction was allowed when a car was destroyed by overturning on an icy road while the car was in the unauthorized possession of a chauffeur. The driver may have been negligent, but "casualty" for income tax purposes expresses rather the result than the cause of the damage.[50]

An individual owned some *Asparagus plumosus* ferns which he had intended to sell. He was allowed to deduct their cost when they were destroyed by a severe freeze, even though a commercial fern grower might have made proper provisions for heating the plants on cold nights.[51]

Ordinarily, a casualty loss must have the element of suddenness. But a loss sustained in the case of residential property as a result of subsoil shrinkage during a period of drought was deemed to be a casualty loss.[52] Damage to a house because of an "earth movement" following a heavy rain was deductible as a casualty loss. Actually, a clogged drain was the immediate precipitating event. That it might have been prevented by the exercise of due care by the taxpayer did not require that the characterization of the loss as a casualty deduction be denied.[53]

Losses arising from highway mishaps may be deducted even though caused by the ordinary negligence of the taxpayer.[54] Thus, it is necessary in such cases to establish that even though the person was careless, he was not *grossly* negligent. When a physician asked a salesman in a seed store for something which would kill "quack grass" and was given a bottle which allegedly bore a label warning that the product should not be used on desirable vegetation, the resulting loss of the lawn was a casualty. While the taxpayer may not have exercised due care by omitting to read the label, he did rely upon the salesman's recommendation. This was not a case of gross negligence on the part of the taxpayer, which would bar a casualty-loss deduction.[55]

When a water heater in a private home burst, no deduction was allowed for the loss of the boiler, for there was no evidence that the casualty was sudden; quite likely the boiler had been deteriorating gradually for a long period of time. But damage to the taxpayer's rugs and draperies could be deducted, for the injury to them was sudden.[56] A casualty loss may have been indirect. A taxpayer's home was destroyed by fire. As a result, underground water pipes froze and burst. The pipes would not have been uncovered so that freezing occurred, save for the fire, and the damage therefore was part of the casualty-loss deduction.[57]

Loss because of termites rarely qualifies as a casualty-loss deduction because of the absence of suddenness. The rotting away of building foundations, trees, and the like has been some time in coming. Loss was allowed for destruction of trees by southern pine beetles, for this particular form of infestation killed the trees in a matter of days, which was fast enough to constitute the required suddenness.[58]

A taxpayer's truck was damaged severely in an accident, and there was no possibility of recovery. He carried no collision insurance, and the driver of the vehicle which caused the accident could not be found. The amount of the deductible loss was the difference between the trade-in allowed him on a new truck and the amount which would have been allowed had damage not been sustained in the collision.[59]

When there is no proof of the value of an asset damaged, both before and after the event, the cost of restoration to prior condition is deductible.[60]

The cost of repairs to the damaged property is acceptable as evidence of the loss of value if (1) the repairs are necessary to restore the property to its condition immediately before the casualty, (2) the amount spent for such repairs is not excessive, (3) the repairs do not account for more than the damage suffered, and (4) the value of the property after the repairs does not as a result of the repairs exceed its value immediately before the casualty.[61]

The amount of casualty loss to a building which was fully depreciated could not be deducted, but the cost of replacing the damage was ordinary and necessary expense and was deductible as such.[62]

One of the measures of a deductible casualty loss is fair market value of the property immediately before the casualty reduced by fair market value immediately afterwards.[63] Often fair market value of realty immediately after the casualty drops sharply because of buyer resistance. For example, if there is a landslide, hurricane, or the like, potential buyers do not want to purchase property in that area. Ordinarily, the courts do not allow a casualty loss deduction based upon such psychological or economic losses, because the property has not been sold and hence there is no closed transaction by which to measure the amount of loss sustained. But in one case, when Internal Revenue Service appraisers said that loss in value was only temporary, inasmuch as buyers would forget all about a hurricane in nine months, the court came up with a brand-new approach. Fair market value of the property immediately after the casualty could be reduced by a buyer resistance factor: a fair interest rate for a nine-month period on the proceeds likely to be realized on the sale of the property at the end of this nine-month period.[64]

In the case of a tenancy by the entirety, two legally married persons own property, which will pass to the survivor upon the death of one spouse. Neither one can sell without the consent of the other. Where there is a casualty loss to a home owned by husband and wife as tenants by the entirety, if the husband pays for the cost of restoring the house to its original condition, each spouse may claim one-half of the cost on his or her Federal income tax return, assuming the parties itemize their deductions. Neither spouse is permitted to deduct the entire cost if separate returns are filed.[65] Formerly it had been held that if the husband paid the full amount, he could deduct the full amount. The revised rule applies on and after August 18, 1975.

Theft losses are deductible as casualties. The problem here, frequently, is that of establishing the loss as having been caused by a theft rather than by carelessness or by causes unknown. That the victim promptly reports the loss to the police is a factor which tends to corroborate that a theft indeed has taken place. But loss on the theft of a diamond ring was allowed for tax purposes in a case where a new cleaning person failed to come back to work directly after the ring had disappeared. And the victim did not accuse this cleaning person of the theft and did not report the incident to the police, lest she be charged with false arrest as had happened in the case of a personal friend.[66]

If a theft loss is not reported promptly to the police, the victim must offer as a substitute the testimony of anyone who had witnessed the event or its aftermath. If records were burglarized, steps must be taken to reconstruct the records by gathering substitutes, such as copies of checks for travel.[67]

Proof of the amount of a theft loss is difficult in the case of cash, where there is little likelihood that there is any documentation of how much a taxpayer had on his person or in his home. Deduction was allowed in full, however, where the victim had evidence of why he had such a large amount of money with him. Here, the record showed that he was on his way to complete the closing on the acquisition of a house.[68]

In allowing a deduction for theft losses, Congress did not distinguish between losses sustained by the naive or greedy from those suffered by others. "Indeed," commented one court, "gullibility or cupidity of the victim is often the crucial factor that enables the swindler to succeed in his fraud."[69]

An individual paid a contractor who was building a swimming pool for her on the strength of false representations made by the contractor that he had already paid subcontractors and material suppliers. The individual was allowed a deduction, as a theft loss had taken place.[70]

A taxpayer engaged a lawyer to recover property which had been stolen from her. When without authorization the lawyer kept part of the property which he had recovered as his fee, the taxpayer could deduct as a theft loss that portion which the attorney kept.[71]

Losses which are sustained by reason of criminally false pretenses are deductible as casualty losses. Such was the finding in the case where an individual was induced to buy certain annuity contracts by a pension consultant in order to obtain reputed tax savings. Later the consultant told him that a pending change in the law would prevent the alleged tax advantages and offered to buy back the contracts for $500. The offer was accepted. When the trusting client discovered that the contracts were actually worth $104,000, the difference was deductible as a theft loss, having been taken from the taxpayer by the consultant with the intent to defraud. It was no less a theft by reason of the fact that had the victim read the printed words of his contracts he would have been aware of the substantial value they had. He had relied upon the statement of a person in a position to know the circumstances.[72]

An individual loaned money to a corporation in exchange for a short-term note. His decision to make the loan was based on financial statements issued by the corporation. The corporation failed, after which the president was convicted by a court of violating the state securities law through the issuance of false and misleading financial statements. The unfortunate lender could deduct a theft loss, inasmuch as the corporation president knowingly had obtained money by false representation, with intent to defraud.[73]

An individual bought 100 shares of stock in G Corporation. Six years later, the company's directors approved a merger into X Corporation, subject to the approval of two-thirds of the stockholders of each corporation. X Corporation provided G with detailed information about its financial condition, which was included in proxy statements sent to the G stockholders when they voted on the merger plan, which was passed. Each G shareholder got X shares for his stock. Within two years X went into bankruptcy, and an unfortunate investor claimed a theft loss. Deductibility depended upon whether he had lost his money as the result of what the law characterized as theft in the state where all of this took place. It did. Theft was defined by the state's law as the obtaining of money by the false representation of a material fact with intent to defraud and with knowledge of the falsity of the statement, as a result of which the perpetrator obtains money or something else of value from someone who has relied upon the false representation to his own detriment.[74]

A taxpayer paid out sums of money to enter into certain tax-avoidance schemes by reason of misrepresentations. He would not otherwise have paid out these sums. It was determined that he was swindled and had sustained a theft loss. It mattered not that the person sponsoring the scheme thought his machinations would succeed and therefore lacked any intent to commit a fraud.[75]

Whether money paid out as a result of fraud, trickery, and deceit is deductible may depend upon whether the *modus operandi* was treated as theft under the laws of the state where the incident took place. A loss such as that incurred on the sale of forged notes is treated differently in different states.[76]

A hatcheck girl in a nightclub became friendly with a wealthy older man, who provided her with a nice home and valuable gifts, including a block of Xerox stock. The nightclub owner learned of her considerable net worth and began dating her, sometimes taking along his brother and their attorney. Collectively, they convinced the well-endowed but financially unsophisticated woman that she should turn over $300,000 to them for investment purposes. That was the last she saw of the money. But at least it qualified for a casualty-loss deduction, for under the law of that state, "theft" includes obtaining money by false pretenses.[77]

Money lost in a confidence game known in the profession as a "Spanish swindle" was deductible, for the transaction had occurred in Mexico, where local law defined the activity as theft.[78]

Sums withdrawn by a husband from a joint checking account with his wife may be deductible as theft losses if this action takes place in a state where intraspousal thefts are recognized as "legitimate" thefts.[79]

A child was kidnapped. Under threats of injury to the child, the kidnappers extorted ransom payments from the taxpayer. Theft loss is defined by state law. But to be permitted a theft loss in this circumstance, the Internal Revenue Service has ruled that a taxpayer needs only to prove that his loss resulted from a taking of property which is illegal under the law of the state where it occurred and that the taking was done with criminal intent. So even though the ransom demand and payment did not amount to the statutory crime of "theft" under local law, the taking of the taxpayer's money had been illegal under the laws of the state where the incident took place, and the taking could be presumed to have been done with criminal intent. Hence, the theft-loss deduction was allowed.[80] But inasmuch as the first $100 of a nonbusiness casualty loss is nondeductible, a $500,000 payment to a kidnapper would be deductible only to the extent of $499,900.

Ordinarily, expenses to prevent a casualty are not deductible, for the expenditures are likely to involve acquisition of property with an estimated useful life of more than one year. But deduction is allowed where the preventive measures do not add to the value of property. In one example, a plant had sustained cave-ins under flooring, and further trouble of the same sort was anticipated. Drilling and grouting to forestall this was a deductible expense.[81]

An individual used temporary dikes to protect his personal residence (property that was not held for investment or used in his trade or business) as well as his business property from flooding. The dikes were constructed of earth and sandbags and were removed immediately after the floodwater receded. The cost of constructing and removing the temporary dikes was not allowed as a casualty loss with respect either to the business or the nonbusiness properties. But the cost of constructing and removing the temporary dikes to protect business property was deductible as an ordinary and necessary business expense.[82]

One type of expense which was incurred for the purpose of preventing an accident and which was held to be deductible was the cost of vasectomy.[83]

Ordinarily, a casualty loss, as by storm, is deductible in the year the event took place. But if the casualty is sustained in what the President of the United States subsequently proclaims to be a disaster area, the loss may be deducted in the taxable year immediately preceding the year in which the casualty occurred.[84] This is optional.

Appraisal fees paid in order to establish the amount of a casualty loss sustained to residential property by reason of a prolonged drought are deductible.[85]

A fee was paid to an insurance adjuster to develop data to be used in connection with proving the amount of a tax-loss deduction to be claimed. This was deductible. Because settlement with the insurance company had already been made, this was not an expenditure dealing with the appraisal of property but was an expense in connection with the determination of one's income tax.[86] The cost of hiring adjusters to collect insurance claimed on business property was deductible. The claim was for money damages, not to protect title or to improve or to increase the value of any capital asset.[87]

A major problem in the claiming of a casualty-loss deduction is *proof*. Unless one thinks to take action immediately after a casualty has occurred, it may not be possible to prove the amount and extent of the loss. The day after her home was wrecked by a storm, an individual went through the house and wrote down a list of the articles she saw, adding items she remembered having been there, though many had been blown or washed away. She inserted her recollection of where each item had been purchased and what it had cost. There were almost 1,900 items on the list. The Internal Revenue Service allowed $1,500.19 for loss of household and personal effects; the Tax Court allowed $12,000, or the difference between the lower amount of fair market value or adjusted basis immediately before the casualty and the value immediately afterward.[88]

Loss deduction could be established by photographs which were taken immediately after a storm and which depicted valuable trees destroyed by a hurricane.[89]

Another individual documented the tornado damage sustained by his residential property by exhibiting contemporary photographs of destroyed trees, damage to the supporting piers of the foundation of his house, and the like.[90] Along the same line, at the time of Hurricane Agnes in 1969, the Internal Revenue Service announced that photographs of damage done by the storm would be helpful in establishing the amount of loss.[91]

After Hurricane Camille, a taxpayer's photographs were accepted as establishing the amount of the damage sustained.[92]

Vandalism qualifies as a casualty loss, as where a house was broken into and a stove, washing machine, dryer, and deep freeze were taken.[93] Looting also qualifies as a casualty.[94]

Mine cave-in damage to one's property is regarded as a casualty for tax purposes.[95]

It is almost mandatory in the case of loss by theft or vandalism to prove that the casualty was reported immediately to the police. But deduction may still be alllowed if an individual can show why the police were not notified. A teacher discovered that persons unknown had broken into his house and that various items of property were missing. The Internal Revenue Service sought to disallow the loss deduction because the incident had not been reported to the law-enforcement authorities. But a pushed-in window indicated unlawful entry. And there were special reasons why he had not reported his loss. Juveniles were known to be stealing from unoccupied homes in the vicinity, and the youths he suspected were his own students, whom he could scarcely accuse of the crime without some proof. In addition, the nearest policeman was a sheriff some thirty miles away.[96]

A loss for tax purposes due to the nationalization of property by a foreign government takes place at that time when the taxpayer no longer has a reasonable prospect of recovery.[97]

Losses due to flooding of buildings and basements as a result of a storm are deductible casualty losses.[98]

An individual purchased real estate for long-term investment. Oil was discovered under the ground, so the fair market value of the property shot up. Then salt water filtered into the oil deposit and ruined it. Down went the value of the property, and a casualty-loss deduction was claimed. The Internal Revenue Service sought to disallow this on the theory that there was no loss affecting cash flow. The Service insisted that there was a loss of only unexpected and unrealized appreciation of the original investment in land. The court disagreed. There is no tax distinction between casualty losses to property which has appreciated in value and to property which has not. The only thing that counts is that as a result of a casualty involving the taxpayer's property, there was a permanent loss of value in the marketplace.[99]

Casualty or theft losses and casualty gains with respect to (1) depreciable property and real estate used in a trade or business, and (2) capital assets held for more than twelve months are consolidated. If the casualty losses exceed the casualty gains, the net loss is treated as an ordinary loss, fully deductible, without regard to whether there may be noncasualty gains of business depreciable and real property. If, however, the casualty gains exceed the casualty losses, the net gain on business depreciable and real property must be consolidated for tax purposes with other gains and losses on such properties.[100]

Included in a loss, such as a fire, are cleanup expenses after the fire.[101]

Cleanup expenses after a hurricane include such items as labor and stump removal.[102]

In determining the measure of a deductible casualty loss, sales tax is included in the value of property.[103]

A casualty loss, to the extent not reimbursable by insurance or otherwise, is deductible even if the property owner actually benefits. Such was the situation where a business lost a valuable merchandising right. Subsequently, an even more valuable merchandising right was obtained from a different source, a right which could not have been obtained had the original one still had been held. Declared the court: "A deduction cannot be denied simply because the loss may not be wholly disadvantageous to the taxpayer."[104]

See also **Check kiting; Drought losses; Farmers; Reliance upon misrepresentation.**

Ceilings to charitable contributions. See **Contributions.**

Cemetery company, contributions to. See **Contributions.**

Charge accounts, interest on. See **Interest.**

Charitable contributions. See **Contributions.**

Check kiting. Two persons worked out a scheme for kiting checks: that is, checks drawn on one bank were deposited in a second bank, from which moneys were taken out before the original check cleared. A time came when one of the banks discovered it had paid out dollars from an account which was bare. The money was not recovered. The overdraft was not regarded as a claim against the bank's reserve for bad debts but was a fully deductible loss, as state law characterized check kiting or account juggling as theft.[105]

C

Child care and disabled dependent care. This book is concerned solely with tax *deductions*. But an exception is made in the case of this item, for prior to 1976 it had been a deduction. Now it is a *credit*, that is, it can be used to reduce the tax you have computed on Form 1040 itself. You may claim up to 20% of your qualifying employment-related expenses, which, however, are limited to $2,000 for one qualifying individual or $4,000 for two or more qualifying individuals. In addition, the employment-related expenses may not exceed your earned income if you are not married at the end of your taxable year, or if you are married at that time, the lesser of the earned income of you or your spouse. Employment-related expenses must have been incurred for the primary purpose of assuring the well-being and protection of a qualifying individual and are considered employment-related if they were incurred to enable you (and your spouse, if married) to be gainfully employed. Employment-related expenses include: household expenses, child care expenses, disabled dependent care expenses, and disabled spouse care expenses.

To qualify, you (together with your spouse, if married) must furnish more than half the cost of maintaining a home that is your principal residence as well as that of a qualified individual, which means: (1) your dependent under age 15 for whom you are entitled to a personal exemption, (2) your dependent (or a person you could claim as a dependent if it were not for the gross-income test used in determining dependent status) who is physically or mentally incapable of self-care, or (3) your spouse who is physically or mentally incapable of self-care.

Child care expenses are not confined to services performed within your household. Disabled dependent or disabled spouse care expenses are includable only if they are for services performed in your home to enable you to be gainfully employed.[106]

Payments for child care services by a taxpayer to certain relatives formerly qualified for the child care credit only if the services constituted "employment" as defined for Social Security purposes. Under the Social Security definition, child care services rendered by a grandparent generally do not constitute employment. But for taxable years beginning after December 31, 1978, payments to grandparents for the care of their grandchildren may qualify for the child care credit.[107]

Child care center for employees' children. See **Ordinary and necessary business expenses.**

Child support. *See* **Alimony.**

Chiropodists, payments to. *See* **Medical expenses.**

Chiropractors, payments to. *See* **Medical expenses.**

Christian Science practitioners, payments to. *See* **Medical expenses.**

Christmas cards. *See* **Ordinary and necessary business expenses.**

Christmas gifts to employees. *See* **Compensation.**

Cigars. Ordinarily, it is impossible to justify the cost of cigars as a tax deduction. But the full cost was deductible by a businessperson who could establish that he (or she) was a nonsmoker of the items.[108]

Claim of right. If income is received in any taxable year under circumstances where it appears from all the facts available at the time that an individual has an unrestricted right to this income (known as a "claim of right"), but subsequent to that year it is established that he really was not entitled to the income in the first place, his repayment in a later year ordinarily does not affect his tax in the year of the original receipt; his deduction for the repayment is in the year when it is made. But if the deduction is more than $3,000, he may elect to take the deduction either in the year of original receipt or in the year of repayment.[109]

This election as to the year of deduction is not available in the case of the return of embezzled funds of more than $3,000, inasmuch as they had not been received under a claim of right. Repayment of amounts embezzled in prior years is deductible in the year in which the repayment is made. The election does not apply to the repayment by corporate officers or employees of compensation they must repay to their corporation, as where they had agreed to reimburse the corporation for any portion of their compensation which has been disallowed to the corporation as a deduction as a result of a tax audit by the Internal Revenue Service.[110]

Claims, satisfaction of. *See* **Business-related losses.**

Claim settlements. *See* **Settlement payments.**

Cleanup expenses. *See* **Casualties.**

Client reimbursement. *See* **Ordinary and necessary business expenses.**

C

48

Clothing. *See* **Actors; Uniforms; Work clothes.**

Clothing, cleaning of. Where uniforms or work clothes not adaptable to general use must be worn on the job, cleaning expenses are deductible as well as the cost of the garb.[111] *See* **Uniforms; Work clothes.**

Club dues. *See* **Entertainment.**

Coaching. *See* **Education.**

"*Cohan* rule." *See* **Entertainment.**

Collection of income, expenses for. *See* **Legal fees.**

Commercial bribes. *See* **Bribes and kickbacks.**

Commissions. *See* **Referral fees.**

Commitment fees. Where a loan is for an extended period, commitment fees must be amortized over the period of loan or mortgage.[112] Where the amortization of the fees paid for a construction loan falls within the construction period, the amount amortized must be capitalized as a part of the cost of construction.[113]

    See also **Interest.**

Commodity futures contract, purchase of. *See* **Farmers.**

Commuting. The expenses of getting from one's home to his place of business, and vice versa, are deemed to be personal and not tax-deductible. If an individual has several regular places of business, he may drive to one or more places of work on any given day. On days when he drives to any one place of work and then returns home, there is no deductible transportation expense. On days that involve stops at more than one place of work, no deduction is allowed for the cost of his transportation from his home to the first work location and from the last work location back home. But transportation costs incurred between work locations are deductible business expenses.[114]

    A physician who performed services at his office, a hospital, nursing homes, and patients' residences was permitted to deduct automobile expenses incurred in traveling 150,000 miles in one year, except for 920 miles which the court deemed to represent actual commuting expenses. Declared the court: "The nature of a medical doctor's business, when he is engaged in the private general practice of medicine, making house calls and visiting the various medical institutions, precludes an arbitrary application of the commuter expense rule holding that every time a physician leaves his home on business he is 'commuting.' ..."[115]

An individual can deduct expenses in excess of ordinary commuting expenses which can be shown to have been incurred in transporting job-related tools and materials to and from a work site.[116] A person who can establish that transportation costs were incurred in addition to ordinary commuting expenses and that such additional costs are attributable solely to the necessity of transporting work implements to and from work is entitled to deduct such additional costs. A reasonable and feasible method of allocation of transportation costs is to compute the portion of the cost of transporting the work implements by the mode of transportation used in excess of the cost of commuting by the same mode of transportation without the work implements.[117]

An individual has the opportunity of showing (if he can) that he would not have used his automobile to drive to and from his work except for the necessity of transporting his tools. One court found that a taxpayer would have used the car to get to and from work even though there was no necessity for him to lug his equipment, and 50 percent of the total costs could be deducted as pertaining to business rather than to personal considerations.[118]

A musician may deduct the expenses of using his car to carry instruments between his residence and his place of work if such transportation is necessary because the instruments are too bulky to be carried otherwise and he would not use his automobile except for that reason.[119]

But "incidentals of his profession" are not given the same favorable treatment as tools. A commercial airline pilot transported his flight bag and his overnight bag in his car which he regularly drove from his home to his place of employment. Inasmuch as he would have used his car even if he went to the airport empty-handed (a nondeductible commuting cost), the United States Supreme Court refused to allow any deduction or allocation, in the justices' language, "because by happenstances the taxpayer must carry incidentals of his occupation with him."[120]

An individual worked about forty miles from his home. He showed that there was a public bus within one hundred yards of his home, with scheduled trips every thirty minutes. The court believed that that was the way he would have traveled were it not for the tools he had to carry. Inasmuch as the car was deemed to be for carrying the tools and not for his personal commuting, deduction was proper in this instance.[121]

Expenses of driving between jobs were held to be deductible, as well as the cost of extra trips to pick up tools and the like which had been left at a prior place of employment because the equipment was not needed at the next assignment.[122]

For examples of deductions where physicians had advised incapacitated persons to go to work as a therapy measure, *see* **Medical expenses.**

Companion. See **Blind persons, expenses of; Medical expenses.**

Compensable injuries. In the case of losses resulting from a patent infringement, a breach of fiduciary duty, or antitrust injury for which there is a recovery under the Clayton Act, a special deduction is allowed which has the effect of reducing the amounts required to be included in income to the extent that the losses to which they relate did not give rise to a tax benefit. This is accomplished by a provision that when a "compensable amount" is received or accrued during a taxable year for a "compensable injury," a deduction is allowed for the compensable amount or, if smaller, the unrecovered losses sustained as a result of the compensable injury. Compensable injuries are those sustained as a result of patent infringement, a breach of contract, or a breach of fiduciary duty, or an antitrust injury for which there is a recovery under Section 4 of the Clayton Act.[123]

Compensating use tax. See **Taxes.**

Compensation. Compensation paid for business services is deductible. But even if no services are performed, compensation may be deductible, as in the case of payments to employees who are on vacation. Similarly, payments of a guaranteed annual wage and of dismissal pay are deductible although they are not paid for services.[124] Payments to onetime employees who are now in the Armed Services are deductible when they are made as an inducement to return after separation from military duty.[125] Payments to an employee absent from work as a result of being summoned to serve the Federal government in any capacity at nominal consideration are deductible if he plans to return to the employer at the end of his service.[126]

Persons who work in civilian businesses sometimes are invited to accept governmental positions for a period which is not intended to be permanent. For example, a successful corporation executive may be called to Washington to serve as a member of the Cabinet at a salary which is far less than he had been earning in civilian life. Where such a person intends to return to his private employer at the conclusion of his government service, continuance of salary payments (or portions of them) by his civilian employer are deductible as ordinary and necessary expenses.[127]

An employer may deduct the cost of turkey, hams, or other items of merchandise of nominal value given to employees at Christmastime. There is an annual limitation of $25 for such gifts.[128]

A businessperson who absorbs the employee portion of Social Security taxes can deduct them as compensation, providing the rule of reasonableness is followed.[129] The cost of flowers sent to an employee in a hospital is deductible.[130] Improvements to a recreation lodge conveyed to a foremen's association for use by its employees for recreation purposes were deductible.[131]

Loans and advances to an employee which the employer does not expect him to repay are deductible as compensation if they are for personal services actually rendered and the total is reasonable when added to other compensations.[132]

Group term life insurance premiums paid or incurred by the employer on policies covering the lives of employees who designate their own beneficiaries are deductible by the employer if he does not retain any incidents of ownership and he is not directly or indirectly the beneficiary under the contract. This is true for both permanent group life and nonpermanent group life insurance.[133] Group hospitalization and medical-care premiums which the employer pays for the benefit of his employees are deductible.[134] Medicare premiums for both active and retired employees are deductible.[135]

Amounts paid by an employer to employees because of injuries, including lump-sum amounts paid or accrued as compensation for injuries, are allowable deductions, which, however, are limited to amounts not compensated for by insurance or otherwise.[136]

Compensation, repayment where excessive. *See* **Executives.**

Competition, payments to eliminate. *See* **Expenditures for benefits lasting more than one year.**

Compromise of taxes, fees in connection with. *See* **Legal fees.**

Compromise payments. *See* **Settlement payments.**

Condemnation awards, expenses related to. Where awards upon the condemnation of property by governmental authority were held to be taxable to the person whose property was seized, deduction was allowed for legal, engineering, and appraisal fees he incurred in getting this award.[137]

Condominiums and cooperative housing corporations. An individual who qualifies as a tenant-stockholder of a cooperative housing corporation may deduct from his gross income amounts paid or accrued within his taxable year to the cooperative housing corporation which represents his proportionate share of (1) the land and building, and (2) the interest allowable to the corporation on its indebtedness contracted in the acquisition, construction, alteration, rehabilitation, or maintenance of the building. The deduction cannot exceed the amount of the tenant-shareholder's proportionate share of the taxes and interest. His proportionate share of the stock of the corporation is that proportion owned by him of the total outstanding stock of the corporation. For taxable years beginning after December 21, 1969, if the corporation has issued stock to a governmental unit, then in determining the total outstanding stock, the governmental unit is deemed to hold the number of shares it would have held if it had been a tenant-stockholder.[138]

When a tenant-stockholder uses the proprietary lease or right of tenancy, which he has solely by reason of stock ownership in a trade or business or for the production of income, rather than for personal use, the stock is subject to depreciation or (in the case of a lease) amortization.[139]

An individual qualifies as a tenant-stockholder even though he is entitled to occupy more than one dwelling unit in the cooperative housing corporation. He need not actually live in any of the units himself and may rent them to other parties.[140]

In a condominium arrangement, a purchaser owns outright a dwelling unit in a multidwelling structure, and he also owns a proportionate undivided interest in the common elements of the structure, such as land, lobbies, elevators, and service areas. Real estate taxes on the individual owner's interest in the land and on the common parts of the structure are deductible on a proportionate basis.[141] If he is liable to the local taxing authority for the tax assessment on his interest in the condominium, he may deduct taxes which he pays with respect to the apartment.[142] He may deduct interest on an overall mortgage if the amount he pays is specified in his purchase deed. He also may deduct interest on an individual mortgage on his particular property. He may deduct for his share of casualty losses, such as uninsured boiler explosion, in the same manner as other homeowners.[143]

Ordinarily, a condominium is purchased for its tax advantages, notably the deduction by the purchaser of interest and property taxes not available to a person who rents his home or apartment, despite the fact that a major portion of his rent actually represents interest and taxes on the property. But a condominium also can represent a transaction entered upon for profit, all the expenses of which are deductible. Upon the advice of an investment counselor, an individual bought a condominium. The purchaser's facilities were made available for rental by outsiders, and use by the owner was negligible. Accordingly, depreciation and other costs incurred in owning and operating the property were deductible by the owner as business expenses.[144] *See also* **Interest; Taxes.**

Similarly, such expenses were deductible where he notified the manager that he wanted to rent his unit, hired a real estate agency to manage rentals for a year, and placed advertisements in the *Wall Street Journal* and elsewhere. Although he was not too successful in finding tenants at first, over a period of four years he had been able to convert from a totally unrented apartment to a continuously rented one. He almost never went to the apartment, spending less than four weeks there in his five years of ownership.[145]

Con games. *See* **Casualties.**

Conservation expenditures. *See* **Farmers.**

Construction costs. *See* **Capital improvements; Expenditures for benefits lasting more than one year.**

Contact lens insurance. *See* **Medical expenses.**

Contested inheritance, expenses of. Expenses paid or incurred for the production or collection of income are deductible. Legal fees incurred in settling a claim for an inheritance are not deductible insofar as what is received is characterized as inherited property, for such property is excludible from gross income and hence the legal fees allocated to obtaining the property are not related to the production or collection of income. But legal fees for any part of what is received which represents improperly withheld income is deductible, legal fees being prorated according to the type of payment involved for this purpose.[146] *See* **Legal expenses.**

Contraceptives. *See* **Medical expenses.**

Contract, breach of. *See* **Settlement payments.**

Contracts, expenses. A business was obligated to deposit United States Government bonds as security for the performance of a contract. Such bonds were purchased, and after the completion of the contract, the bonds were promptly sold. The resultant loss was deductible as an ordinary and necessary business expense, not as a capital loss of limited availability. The cost of procuring security for the performance of the contract was not distinguishable from the ordinary premium expense of a surety company, a usual part of a contractor's cost.[147] Penalties for nonperformance of a contract are deductible. If a taxpayer makes a contract to construct a building by a certain date and is obligated to pay a certain amount for each day the building is not finished after the date set for completion, the amounts paid or incurred by him are deductible.[148] *See also* **Family transactions.**

Contributions. Within certain limits (to be defined later in this section), an individual may deduct contributions for exclusively public purposes to:

1.   The United States or any of its political subdivisions.

2.   A domestic corporation, trust, or community chest, fund, or foundation organized and operated exclusively for religious, charitable, scientific, literary, or educational purposes or for the prevention of cruelty to children or animals.

This applies provided that no part of the earnings goes for the benefit of any individual and no substantial part of the activity is lobbying. Under certain circumstances, the recipient of the contribution may be a veterans' organization or cemetery company.[149]

The Internal Revenue Service publishes a list of organizations, contributions to which are deductible within specific limits. If an organization's name is deleted from this list by the I.R.S. because it no longer is entitled to recognition as charitable, etc., deduction ordinarily is allowed where the contribution had been made *before* removal of the name. But deduction is not allowed if the contributor knew the exempt status was going to be revoked or if he was himself in any way responsible for activities leading to the revocation of charitable status.[150] Deduction was permitted where exempt status subsequently was revoked, for here the donor, although he enjoyed a close personal relationship with the charitable organization's president, had no reason to know about any questionable activities.[151]

Deduction is allowed for contributions made after October 4, 1976, to organizations "to foster national or international sports competition, but only if no part of its activities involve the provision of athletic facilities or equipment ... "[152]

A charitable contribution is allowable even if it is made without the slightest charitable impulse. In the words of one court:

Community good will, the desire to avoid community bad will, public pressures of other kinds, tax avoidance, prestige, conscience-salving, a vindictive desire to prevent relatives from inheriting family wealth—these are a few of the motives which may lie close to the heart, or so-called heart, of one who gives to charity. If the policy of the income tax laws favoring charitable contributions is to be effectively carried out, there is good reason to avoid unnecessary intrusions of subjective judgments as to what prompts the financial support of the organized but non-governmental good works of society.[153]

An attorney owned a number of low-income houses which had no indoor plumbing and provided little more than shelter. A storm of criticism about substandard housing in the city arose, as a result of which he donated the use of these houses to a tax-exempt organization, for the use of the existing tenants without rent for a three-year period, after which they were scheduled for demolition under an urban renewal program. He could deduct the value of this gift, measured by the income flow he was giving up, even though the purpose of the contribution was to avoid further controversy attaching to his name and destroying his effectiveness as a lawyer.[154]

For Federal income tax deduction purposes, the mere delivery of a check to an approved charitable organization is considered a payment and is sufficient to permit a deduction.[155]

In general, contributions in the form of appreciated-value property are deductible only to the extent of the donor's costs, and the appreciation element is not included in the amount of the deduction. But there are some important exceptions to this general rule:

1. In the case of gifts of appreciated-value property which, if sold, would have produced ordinary income or short-term capital gain, the appreciation is not part of the tax deduction. Let's say that Fred Jones gives some stock held for less than one year to charity. The stock cost Fred $500 initially but now is worth $700. He can use as a basis for his charitable deduction only the $500 which he originally paid for the stock and must forget the appreciated $200 value of the stock as far as his tax deduction goes. In other words, the amount of the appreciation in value results in a reduction of the contribution deduction to

the extent of the appreciation. Inventory is an example of this type of appreciated-value property.

The charitable deduction for gifts of property which would to some extent, at least, produce ordinary income if sold, as a result of various depreciation recapture rules, also is reduced by the amount subject to recapture as ordinary income.[156]

2. Gifts of property which would produce long-term capital gain if sold are deductible at fair market value when they are made to organizations which can use the property for the purpose for which the donee's tax-exempt status has been granted, e.g., sculpture donated to an art museum.

In the case where tangible property is given to an exempt organization whose use of the property is unrelated to the purpose constituting the donee's basis for tax exemption (e.g., that same piece of sculpture donated to a haven for dogs and cats), the amount of the deduction is reduced by 40 percent of the appreciation which would have been a long-term capital gain if the property had been sold at fair market value.

Consider a piece of sculpture originally purchased by Erma Black for $400. Its market value is now judged to be $4,000. If Erma donates the sculpture to her favorite art museum, her deduction for charity is $4,000. If she decides to donate the same sculpture to a dog and cat haven, she can now deduct only $1,840, or the original purchase price ($400) plus half of the appreciated value (40 percent of $3,600, or $1,440).[157]

3. Similarly, appreciation is taken into account in determining the amount of deduction in the case of gifts of appreciated-value property to certain private foundations.

4. In the case of so-called "bargain sales" to charitable organizations, where the taxpayer sells property to such an organization for less than its fair market value (often at his cost), the cost or other basis of the property must be allocated between the portion of the property "given" to the charity and the portion "sold" on the basis of the fair market value of each portion.[158]

Thus, if an individual sold land with a fair market value of $20,000 to a charitable organization (not a private foundation) at his cost of $12,000, he would be required to go through the following steps: He must find the percentage that the actual sale price of the property is to the property fair market value. In this case it is 60 percent. He must then apply this percentage to the adjusted basis of the land (in this case $12,000) and he finds that he has a recognized taxable gain of $4,800 on which he must pay taxes. (Sixty percent of $12,000 is $7,200, which when subtracted from $12,000 equals the gain of $4,800.) This is his allocation for that part of the property "sold" to charity.

His deduction of that part "given" to charity is allocated as 40 percent of the potential $20,000 realization, or $8,000. He would be required to include the $4,800 as gain from the sale of a capital asset in his tax return and would be allowed a charitable deduction of $8,000.

As previously mentioned, contributions to valid charitable organizations are deductible at fair market value in most situations. Fair market value, in turn, is defined as what a willing buyer pays a willing seller where each has knowledge of all of the facts. So if a charitable organization promptly sells the gifted property to a third party, the price customarily measures the amount of the donor's deduction. But he has the opportunity to show that the actual sales price was not realistic under the circumstances. In one case, it was shown that the charitable organization had no need for this property, a yacht (it might just as well have been a work of art or a home), and the property was sold as rapidly as possible to avoid maintenance and insurance charges. This haste to sell may very well have resulted in a lower price than more leisurely and careful selling efforts would have brought. If the donor can show that such indeed was the case, his deduction is not limited to the price at which the actual sale has taken place.[159]

The contribution may be in the form of any kind of property which the donor possesses. He may deduct the value of a form of assignment he makes to a charitable organization. For example, a man signs a dance-lesson contract and pays for a specified number of hours at a stated price per lesson. He may contribute to a charitable organization his right to receive dancing lessons which he purchased from the dancing school.[160]

If a person has any interest in property, the value of his interest can be the basis of a deductible contribution when he gives or assigns it to an approved charity. For example, where an individual owns a policy of insurance upon his own life and he gives this policy to a charity, he is entitled to a deduction on his tax return. The amount of the deductible contribution is what insurance people call the interpolated terminal reserve, which is rather similar to the cash surrender value.[161]

A "restrictive easement" in favor of the Federal government to enable the government to preserve the scenic view which at the time was open to certain public properties was found to be deductible for a taxpayer complying with this restrictive easement. In one case, a taxpayer generously donated the "restriction" of his parcel of land, which presented a scenic view to a nearby Federal highway. The restrictions he imposed pertained to the type and height of buildings, type of activities for which they could be used, size of parcels to be sold, etc. His "restrictive easement" enabled him to claim a charitable deduction.[162]

Other restrictive easements which a taxpayer may grant provide that the donor agrees to restrictions on the use of his property, such as limitations on the type and height of buildings that may be erected, the removal of trees, the erection of utility lines, the dumping of trash, and the use of signs.[163] Although contribution deductions are no longer permitted for interests in property which consist of less than a taxpayer's entire interest in the property, deduction is allowed in the case of an undivided portion of his entire interest. So deduction is permitted for a charitable contribution of an open-space easement in gross forever. An easement in gross is a mere personal interest in, or right to use, the land of another party. In order to value the easement, the difference between the fair market value of the total property after the grant is the fair market value of the easement given up.[164] Here is an illustration. A governmental body, in order to preserve open space in a particular location and to prevent its development with a structure of any kind, secured from the owner of farm land a contribution of an easement for all time to prohibit development, but to permit continued use as farm land.

A taxpayer transmitted an open-space easement in gross for all time to an approved operating foundation, which qualified as a tax-exempt organization. The deed of easement provided for a thirty-foot-wide right-of-way along the edge of the taxpayer's property to be used by the foundation for the creation and maintenance of a recreation trail that was to be used year-round by the general public for hiking and skiing purposes. The donor agreed not to interfere with use of this property by the public. The fair market value of the easement, as determined by a realtor or other expert in values, was allowable as a charitable deduction.[165]

In the event that a taxpayer who is the recipient of a reversionary interest from the principal of a trust declines the interest in favor of a charitable organization, he is allowed the deduction of that amount as a charitable deduction.[166]

Ordinarily, no charitable deduction is allowed for a donation of less than the donor's entire interest in property to a charitable organization. Deduction is allowed, however, if the interest is a *remainder* interest in a personal residence or farm. Similarly, a partial interest can be deductible if transferred to a trust. A donor may take a charitable contribution deduction for an outright transfer of property to a qualified organization even though he transfers less than his entire interest in the property. In such a case, he is entitled to a contribution deduction in the amount which would have been allowed had he transferred the same property in trust for the charitable organization.[167]

A donor may deduct the value of an undivided portion of his entire interest which he contributes. If he owns 100 acres of land and donates an undivided 50 acres to a qualified charity, a deduction is allowed for that portion which he gives away.[168]

For a contribution to a charitable organization to produce a tax deduction, the donor must rid himself of all dominion and control over the property given. The owners of manuscripts and similar materials related to the theater, radio, and television donated this property to the New York Public Library for use by the public at large. The contributors stipulated, however, that none of the materials could be copied without the donors' permission. The Internal Revenue Service claimed that full control of the property had not been relinquished by the donors because of this restriction. The court concluded, however, that the donation had a genuine charitable intent and amounted to a completed gift despite certain very minor restrictions imposed upon its use.[169]

Charitable contributions of individuals generally are limited to 50 percent of adjusted gross income. The limitation is 30 percent for gifts of appreciated-value property unless in computing the amount of the contribution the appreciation element is reduced by one-half.

The limitation of 20 percent of adjusted gross income is imposed on contributions to private foundations which are not operating foundations unless within two and one-half months after the year of receipt they distribute the contributions to an operating foundation or to a public charity, college, etc., in which event the higher contribution limitation is available.[170]

One of the major problems in the case of contributions to charities is whether the donor receives anything in return. In the words of one court, "If a payment proceeds primarily from the incentive of anticipated benefit to the payor beyond a satisfaction which flows from a generous act, it is not a gift."[171]

But it is not always true that there is automatically something wrong with a contribution which also benefits the donor. Two businessmen gave some modest acreage in their real estate enterprise to the local school board. The Internal Revenue Service claimed this was not a charitable contribution because at the time the enterprise was trying to get the planning board to approve its subdivision plan. Also, the presence of a school right in the middle of the subdivision would attract family buyers to the area, and the properties would be enhanced in value. But the court saw nothing objectionable about that. It was a transfer without consideration to an organization which qualified under the tax law as a charity. The fact that the donors may have derived financial benefits was quite irrelevant.[172]

A business firm contributed land to a state highway department. This land ran through the firm's property. The highway department improved and beautified the lands given by the taxpayer and by other parties at the same time. A contributions deduction was permitted. The contributions section of the law, observed the court, is not to be construed as applicable only in the event the donor receives no benefit. Nor are the motives of the donor in making his contributions relevant if compliance with the tax law is otherwise realized.[173]

Voluntary payments by merchants and property owners to a municipality to provide public parking facilities in the general area of the businesses and properties of the contributors were deductible as contributions *only* in cases where the parking was not limited to use by contributors and their customers and where the amount of the contributions was not based on the proximity or probable use of the facilities by contributors, their tenants, or customers.[174]

A hopelessly ill individual paid a substantial sum of money into the building fund of a nursing home one day prior to her acceptance as a patient in the home's infirmary. This was allowed as a contributions deduction, as there was no showing that such payment was required to procure her admission there or that the home thereafter charged and collected less for her regular care than it otherwise would have charged her.[175]

Contributions to nonprofit volunteer fire companies are deductible as contributions.[176] It does not matter that the contributor may be getting something very substantial in return, such as his life.

Contributions to charitable organizations are limited to a specified percentage of the taxpayer's adjusted gross income, as mentioned previously. Ordinary and necessary business expenses, however, are fully deductible, subject only to the requirement that they be reasonable (see **Ordinary and necessary business expenses**), but no deduction is permitted as ordinary and necessary if it would be allowable as a charitable contribution except for the fact that it exceeds that portion of the donor's income which qualifies as a charitable contribution. In other words, you can't sneak extra money into the charitable deduction disguised as a business expense if the only reason for doing so is that you have already used up your allowable 50 percent of adjusted gross income deduction.[177]

The problem is to show that the payment, even to a charitable or similar organization, was really for business rather than charitable purposes.

A business firm was engaged in retailing in a resort city and derived a significant part of its income from the tourist industry. An oil well blowout caused crude oil to pollute the beaches, and tourists stayed away in droves. The local city council solicited voluntary funds to protect local business through an oil pollution control fund, which was to be used to seek ways of preventing pollution problems other than through lobbying. The firm made a contribution to this fund. It was deductible as ordinary and necessary expense; it was not a contribution inasmuch as the donor expected a financial return commensurate with the amount of money he had given. The payment was calculated to improve the donor's future business.[178]

A cement manufacturer's contribution to a Y.M.C.A. building fund was deductible as a business expense. The "Y" would have to buy cement for its building. The manufacturer's contribution was made for the purpose of directly acquiring more business; thus it was a business expense.[179]

A woman who operated her own travel agency dealt primarily with charitable organizations. She made sizable contributions to some of them, which she regarded as sales promotion, for she did not advertise or use promotion techniques as her competitors did. She considered the value of each account when making the contributions and reflected them in a business account. The Internal Revenue Service claimed they were not deductible to the extent they exceeded the contributions limitation. She won. These were payments in the expectation of getting business.[180]

A business firm agreed to pay a certain charitable organization a specified amount for each label of the payor's product which was mailed back to the payor by its customers. In return, the charity agreed to permit its name to be used in connection with the firm's advertising and to secure testimonial letters from prominent individuals extolling the firm's product. It was held that the amounts paid by the firm to the charitable organization were not charitable deductions, subject to limitation as such, but were ordinary and necessary business expenses for the purpose of stepping up the sales of its product.[181]

In order to promote business in the neighborhood of his office, a stockbroker, as an inducement to customers, paid an amount equal to 6 percent of all brokerage commissions to an authorized charitable organization. The purpose of this tax-exempt organization was to reduce neighborhood tensions and to combat community deterioration in the neighborhood in which the broker's office was located. The broker advised the charitable organization of the procedure used in soliciting business, and the latter was agreeable to the technique. Inasmuch as the broker's payment of 6 percent of its commissions to the charity was related to the payor's business and could reasonably be expected to further his business commensurately, the payments were deductible as ordinary and necessary business expenses.[182]

An employer made payments to a nonprofit organization organized and operated for the purpose of eliminating prejudice and discrimination in the securing of housing by minority groups. As part of its activities the exempt organization entered into agreements with various business concerns in the community in which it acted as general adviser and consultant to employees. These payments were deductible without limitation as business expenses.[183]

If a donor to a charitable organization receives (or reasonably expects to receive) a financial benefit that is commensurate with the "gift" he makes, no deduction is allowed. If he receives a financial benefit that is substantial but is less than the value he gives, then the transaction may involve both (1) a gift and (2) a contribution. Then deduction is allowed only for the excess of the value of what he gives over (1). A tax-exempt organization conducted weekend seminars for the purpose of bringing harmony into marriages. A husband and wife attended one such seminar. Participants were not obligated to pay any fee but were invited to make a donation to the actual pro rata participant costs of the seminar. The couple was permitted to deduct any part of its contribution to the extent it could be shown that the contribution exceeded the monetary value of all benefits and privileges received.[184]

An employer could deduct as ordinary and necessary expenses its payments to an association for the purpose of setting up a school for company employees and their families. The payments were a direct business benefit to the employer because they encouraged family persons not to move away to locations where schools were available.[185] A manufacturer could deduct payments made to a local hospital as business expenses. Two-thirds of the population of this community were employees or their dependents.[186]

A contribution to charitable organizations in the form of property is deductible, even though the donor buys it back in a later year, if the contribution has been valid when it was made and if there was no requirement or condition that it be sold back, the charitable organization having all rights to keep the property or to sell it elsewhere.[187]

When a contribution is made to an approved organization in the form of property which the donee can use in connection with its tax-exempt function, the donor is allowed a deduction for the fair market value of the property for its highest and best use. In the case of property on which stands a structure which the donee cannot use, removal costs must be subtracted from the value of the property, unless the donee can make some interim use of it until plans can be put into effect utilizing the land for its highest and best use.[188]

Amounts paid for stock of the Ohio Valley Industrial Corporation, a nonprofit organization, were deductible by a clothier as ordinary and necessary business expenses. The nonprofit organization had been organized to promote business in the area where the clothier operated.[189]

Sometimes an individual is interested in making a contribution to a charitable organization, but he has nothing of value to give, all his wealth being tied up in the family business corporation. A tax-free reorganization may be the solution to this problem. If the corporation is capitalized solely with one-class voting stock, a recapitalization would allow the replacement of such shares by common (voting) stock and preferred stock on a tax-free basis.[190] The individual could then contribute as few or as many of the preferred shares as he chose each year to charitable organizations, thereby obtaining charitable deductions without in any way diluting his control of the voting stock of the corporation and without using his cash or other forms of wealth.

No deduction is allowed for services rendered to a charitable organization. But an individual who gratuitously gives his services to a charity may deduct his unreimbursed travel expenses (including meals and lodging) while away from home in connection with the affairs of the charity.[191] Also the cost and upkeep of uniforms which have no general utility and are required to be worn while performing donated services are deductible.[192] This includes the cost and upkeep of uniforms used in charitable or educational activities, as by a scoutmaster.[193]

A contributions deduction is not allowed for the contribution of one's own services. But an individual's car, however deeply he is attached to it, is not a part of him for tax purposes. When Hurricane Agnes struck the area in which an individual lived, he worked as a volunteer and used his automobile to distribute food to evacuated flood victims. His car expenses, on a mileage basis, were deductible.[194]

A ski buff who volunteered to assist a tax-exempt organization in safeguarding ski areas could deduct the cost of the distinctive parka and trousers the patrol wore as uniforms.[195]

Frequently mayors, councilmen, and other elected or appointed governmental officials serve without compensation in the performance of their official functions. If such a person can show that he had expenses directly connected with these duties and solely connected with these duties (that is, they were not personal expenses), then he can deduct as contributions the amount of such expenses to the extent that he has not been reimbursed for his out-of-pocket expenditures.[196]

Out-of-pocket expenses incurred by an individual for transportation to and from a local hospital or church for the purposes of rendering voluntary services to the Red Cross or a church are deductible, but not meals unless the taxpayer is away from home overnight.[197]

Similarly deductible are out-of-pocket expenses incurred by a civil defense volunteer in the performance of his duties, such as travel expenses to watch simulated emergencies and to attend state meetings of civil defense volunteers.[198]

An approved charitable organization conducted a program of assisting needy unmarried pregnant women. As part of this program these women were placed during the middle of their pregnancies in the homes of families which volunteered their help to the organization. Participating families took these women into their homes and paid for their food and clothing as well as a small weekly allowance, for which they were not reimbursed. Inasmuch as the out-of-pocket expenses incurred by the participating families were directly connected with and solely attributable to the rendition of uncompensated services to the charitable organization, they were deductible as contributions.[199]

Foster parents may deduct unreimbursed out-of-pocket expenses they pay out to provide gratuitous foster home care for children placed in their home by a charitable organization.[200]

If an individual uses his car in connection with rendering gratuitous services, the standard mileage deduction is 7 cents a mile. To take the deduction in this manner is optional with the taxpayer. If the actual cost of operating his car exceeds the 7-cent-per-mile allowance, the taxpayer may deduct his actual expense.[201]

Unreimbursed, reasonable, out-of-pocket expenses incurred by a volunteer who treats selected groups of children to such activities as swimming, going out to dinner, fishing, and the like are deductible in the same manner and to the same extent as other contributions. But the portion of the expense attributable to the admission tickets or similar expenses of the volunteer is not deductible because he is receiving a benefit or privilege for this portion of the expenditure.[202]

Unreimbursed out-of-pocket expenses incurred in sponsoring cocktail and dinner parties to promote a ball held by a charitable organization are deductible.[203]

An individual donated land to a community for a park and properly claimed a charitable deduction. Many years later, a highway project sought to open a roadway through this park. The original donor of the land was permitted to deduct as a contribution the legal fees spent in resisting efforts thus to encroach upon property now owned by a tax-exempt organization.[204]

An individual permitted two charitable organizations to use office space in his premises. Deduction was allowed for the value of the space used by one of the organizations; the other organization was not on the official list of organizations contributions to which are deductible for tax purposes.[205]

Should an individual pay more than fair market value to a qualified charitable organization for merchandise or goods, the amount paid in excess for the value of the item may be a charitable contribution. Assume he pays $20 for a box lunch at a church picnic. If the lunch, plus any entertainment or other services provided, has a fair market value of $1.50, the excess of $18.50 is a contribution to the church, assuming that the net proceeds of the picnic go exclusively to the church.[206]

An appraisal fee paid by a contributor of property to a tax-exempt organization for the purpose of ascertaining the proper amount to claim as a deduction on his income tax return is deductible. It is an expense in connection with the determination of income tax liability.[207]

An individual may deduct the amount he paid to maintain in his home a full-time student in the twelfth or any lower grade at an educational institution located in the United States. The student cannot be a dependent or relative. He can be a foreign student or an American student, but he must be a member of the taxpayer's household under a written agreement between the taxpayer and a qualified organization. The purpose of the agreement must be to provide educational opportunities for the student. If the taxpayer receives any compensation or reimbursement for the student's maintenance, no deduction is allowed. Only money actually spent by the taxpayer is taken into account (the fair market value of the student's lodging or any other similar item is not considered money spent by the taxpayer).

The amount which may be deducted cannot exceed $50

times the number of full calendar months in the taxable year during which the student was a member of the taxpayer's household. Any month in which the student resides there for fifteen or more days is considered a full calendar month for this purpose.[208]

Ordinarily, contributions made directly to individuals, however deserving the recipients may be, are not deductible. Occasionally they are. The officials of a state which had suffered a hurricane disaster appealed to householders to open their homes to the thousands of persons made homeless by the storm. The persons displaced by this disaster were advised to check at centers set up by the Red Cross, Salvation Army, Civil Defense, and the United States Office of Emergency Planning, which tried to find temporary shelters for the displaced people. The charitable organizations assumed the responsibility of caring for the hurricane evacuees. So actual unreimbursed expenses incurred by an assisting individual, which were directly connected with and solely attributable to providing necessities, such as lodging, food, and clothing to the storm victims, were regarded as contributions for the use of the charitable organizations. Deduction was permitted as contributions.[209]

Contributions to individuals, however needy, are not deductible. Under proper circumstances, however, this is possible. Contributions are deductible when made "to or for the use" of an approved organization. One individual set up a fund to provide scholarships for high school students, recipients to be selected by school principals on the basis of need and scholastic merit. The donor actually wrote out all of the checks, each one payable jointly to a selected student and to the college he would attend. The Internal Revenue Service vainly sought to disallow a contributions deduction on the ground that the donees' names were known to the donor and he was making payments to them as individuals. But the court concluded that deduction was proper, for neither the contributor nor anyone acting under his direction had any control over which deserving student would receive a scholarship.[210]

A charitable contribution is a gift "to or for the use of" a corporation, fund, or foundation organized and operated exclusively for charitable, religious, educational, etc., purposes. A donor tends to believe that this means the contribution must be directly to the fund or corporation. But the recipient may be more broadly construed. An individual directed his bank to send a check to a missionary who was serving in South America under the auspices of a church. As instructed, the bank notified the missionary that the money was to be used "for the Presbyterian mission work" in Brazil. So the funds were not for the missionary's personal use but were to be employed in carrying out the church's activities. In substance, the donor contributed the funds to the church, and the missionary received the money as its agent or representative. Result: deductibility.[211]

Although contributions made directly to a foreign organization are not deductible, an individual may deduct contributions to a United States organization that transfers funds to a foreign charitable organization, provided the United States organization controls the foreign organization's use of the funds or if the foreign operation is merely an administrative arm of the United States organization.[212]

If an individual's charitable contributions are of the type that qualify for the 50-percent ceiling discussed earlier, any contributions which he makes in excess of 50 percent of his adjusted gross income may be carried over for use in the next five years to the extent that contributions in those years do not exceed the 50-percent figure at such time. No carry-over is provided in the case of contributions geared to 20 percent of adjusted gross income where such contributions exceed 20 percent in any year.[213]

If husband and wife file a joint Federal income tax return in a taxable year in which they made valid charitable contributions in excess of the percentage of their adjusted gross income allowed by the tax law, this *excess charitable contribution* can be carried forward to each of the next five taxable years, starting with the earliest. But if separate tax returns are filed in a succeeding year, the carry-over must be allocated according to the amount of any excess contribution that each spouse would have computed had separate returns rather than a joint return been filed for the year in which the excess contribution was made. Any agreement made by the spouses as to how they will divide the excess contribution should they subsequently file separate returns will be disregarded by the Internal Revenue Service.[214]

For taxable years beginning after December 31, 1978, the former deduction for political or newsletter fund contributions has been discontinued. There now is a *credit* against the contributor's Federal income tax for political contributions of $50 ($100 on a joint return). Contributions eligible for this credit may be made to (1) candidates for nomination or election to a Federal, state, or local office in general, primary, or special elections; (2) committees sponsoring such candidates; (3) national, state, or local committees of a national political party; and (4) newsletter funds of an official or candidate.[215]

A so-called checkoff system took effect on January 1, 1973. An individual can designate that $1 of his tax liability be set aside in a special fund in the Presidential Election Campaign Fund for the candidates of a political party he specifies. Alternatively, he can direct that the $1 be set aside in a nonpartisan general account in the fund. In the case of a joint return having a tax liability of $2 or more, each spouse may designate that $1 be paid into an account.[216]

See also **Annuities from charitable organizations; Credit card, charges to; Ordinary and necessary business expenses; Retirement homes.**

Conventions. Expenses related to one's trade or business are deductible. Thus deduction was allowed for the cost of attending a professional seminar[217] and a professional convention.[218]

Expenses incurred in attending conventions are deductible if an individual by attending is benefiting or advancing the interests of his trade or business. This test is met if the agenda of the convention or other meetings is so related to the individual's position as to show that attendance was for business purposes. The agenda need not deal specifically with the official duties and responsibilities of the person's position in order for his expenses of attendance to be business-oriented and deductible for tax purposes as business expenses.[219]

A bank required its employees who went to annual conventions of the industry to take their wives as registered participants. At these conventions, executives fraternized with key personnel of other banks with whom they regularly discussed such mutual problems as loans, investments, and leverage lease transactions. Wives entertained and socialized with other bankers and their spouses. The Internal Revenue Service sought to disallow wives' expenses as business deductions on the ground that what the wives did was not *necessary* to the employer's business activities. But it was ruled that the conventions were working sessions and not vacations for the executives or their spouses. The employer found the presence of spouses was so useful in fostering good working relations with other companies that executives *had* to bring their wives. An expenditure qualifies for a necessary expense when it is appropriate and helpful to the taxpayer's business.[220]

Deductions are allowable for expenses incurred in attending not more than two conventions, education seminars, and similar meetings outside the United States, its possessions, and the Trust Territory of the Pacific which take place after December 31, 1976. The amount of the deduction for transportation expenses to and from these foreign conventions cannot exceed the cost of airfare based on coach or economy-class charges. (This limitation, however, does not apply to that portion of travel which is within the United States.) Transportation expenses will be deductible in full only if more than one-half of the total days of the trip (excluding the days of transportation to and from the site of the convention) are devoted to business-related activities. If less than one-half of the total days of the trip are devoted to business-related activities, a deduction will be allowed for transportation expenses only in the ratio of the business time to total time. Deductions for subsistence expenses, paid or incurred while attending the convention, will be limited to the fixed amount of *per diem* allowed to government employees at the location where the convention is held. In order to deduct subsistence expenses up to this limitation for a day, however, there generally must be at least six hours of business-related activities scheduled daily (or three hours for a deduction for one-half day) and the taxpayer must have attended two-thirds of these activities. New substantiation requirements have been imposed in order to justify this deduction.[221]

Previously, transportation costs to foreign conventions were deductible in full only where more than one-half of the total days were devoted to business-related activities. This has been changed to "at least one-half" for conventions beginning after December 31, 1976. The limitations on the deductibility of expenses of attending foreign conventions do not apply to an employer or other person paying the expenses of an individual's attending the foreign convention (either directly or through reimbursement) where that individual is required to include the expenses in his gross income. But this exception does not apply to a payor where the amounts paid are required to be furnished by the payor to the payee on information returns or statements (*i.e.*, Form W-2 or Form 1099) but are not furnished by the payor.[222]

Cooperative housing, deductions of tenant-shareholder in. *See* **Condominiums and cooperative housing corporations.**

Co-owners, transfer of property between. *See* **Family transactions.**

Corporate officers' expenses. *See* **Entertainment; Executives; Legal fees; Travel.**

Corporations. *See* **Contributions; Legal fees; Small business corporation stock; Tax-option corporations.**

Cost depletion. *See* **Depletion.**

Cost of eliminating competition. *See* **Expenditures for benefits lasting more than one year.**

Country club dues. Dues or fees paid to a country club are deductible only if the taxpayer establishes that the facility was used primarily for the furtherance of his trade or business and that the expense was directly related to the conduct of his trade or business.[223] *See* **Entertainment.**

Covenant not to compete, payments for. *See* **Expenditures for benefits lasting more than one year.**

Credit card, charges to. Contributions to approved charitable organizations by use of a credit card are validly made and deductible in the year made; deduction does not await the formal billing day, and payment to the bank or other issuer of the credit card.[224] A similar rule exists in the case of use of a credit card for the payment of medical expenses, such as to a hospital.[225]

Credit cards, interest on. *See* **Interest.**

Credit insurance. *See* **Insurance.**

Creditor insurance policy, premiums on. A seller of real property on the installment plan can deduct premiums covering the lives of purchasers.[226] Premiums on life insurance policies held as security for debts were deductible.[227]

Creditors, payments to. Payments to creditors after a discharge of debts in bankruptcy proceedings were held to be deductible, being expenses to reestablish the bankrupt's credit in the commercial world. An insurance broker wrote insurance in several companies. When one of these failed he paid off claims which had matured against that company and reinsured his customers in another company at additional cost to himself. His payments for such purposes were deductible. Although he was under no obligation to make these payments, he did so in order to retain customers and to promote his business.[228]

Crutches, deduction of cost of. *See* **Medical expenses.**

Cuban expropriation losses. *See* **Foreign expropriation losses.**

Custodian Services. *See* **Investors.**

Customer, medical expenses of. The owner of a bakery could deduct the cost of a physician's treatment of a thumb injury sustained by a customer [Tom Thumb?] in the shop.[229]

C

1. Revenue Ruling 69-511, 1969-2 CB 23.
2. *R. E. L. Holding Corporation* B.T.A. Memo., Docket No. 34961, entered March 23, 1931.
3. *Mrs. E. B. Lawler,* 17 B.T.A. 1083 (1929).
4. *Chicago Lumber Company of Omaha et al.,* 18 B.T.A. 916 (1930).
5. *Robert Buedingen,* 6 B.T.A. 335 (1927).
6. *Connecticut Mutual Insurance Company v. Eaton,* 218 F. 206 (D.C., Conn., 1914).
7. Revenue Ruling 70-392, 1970-2 CB 33.
8. Revenue Act of 1978, Section 402(a).
9. I.R.C. Section 1211(b)(1).
10. Tax Reform Act of 1976, Section 1401.
11. I.R.C. Section 1211(b)(2).
12. I.R.C. Section 1202.
13. I.R.C. Section 642(h).
14. Revenue Ruling 78-93, I.R.B. 1978-11, 7.
15. I.R.C. Section 172(c).
16. Regulations Section 1.172-3(a).
17. *Vivian W. Rose.* T.C. Memo, 1973-207, filed September 17, 1973.
18. *Losses from Operating a Business,* I.R.S. Publication 536, 1976 edition, page 2.
19. I.R.C. Section 172(b)(1).
20. Tax Reform Act of 1976, Section 806(a).
21. Regulations Section 1.172-7(b).
22. Regulations Section 1.172-7(c).
23. Revenue Ruling 65-140, 1965-1 CB 127.
24. *Security First National Bank v. United States,* D.C., S.D. Cal., 1966.
25. Revenue Ruling 60-216, 1960-1 CB 126.
26. Revenue Ruling 65-140, 1965-1 CB 127.
27. *Samuel G. Adams et al.,* 14 B.T.A. 781 (1930).
28. Regulations Section 1.704-1(b)(2).
29. I.R.C. Section 704(d).
30. I.R.C. Section 752.
31. Regulations Section 1.752-1(e).
32. I.R.C. Section 704(d).
33. I.R.C. Section 642(h).
34. *Federal Tax Guide for Survivors, Executors, and Administrators.* I.R.S. Publication 559, 1978 edition, page 15.
35. *Warfell-Pratt-Howell Company,* 13 B.T.A. 506 (1928).
36. *Marshall J. Hammons et al.,* T.C. Memo., Docket No. 31518, entered November 24, 1953.
37. *Marion S. Perkins et al.,* T.C. Memo., Docket No. 31053, entered May 29, 1952.
38. I.R.C. Section 165(a).

39. Regulations Section 1.164-7(b).

40. Regulations Section 1.165-7(a)(2).

41. I.R.C. Section 165(c)(3).

42. *Harry Johnson Grant*, 30 B.T.A. 1028 (1934).

43. *Frederick H. Nash*, 22 B.T.A. 482 (1931).

44. *Ferguson v. Commissioner*, 59 F.2d 893 (10th Cir., 1932).

45. *Louis Broido*, 35 T.C. 786 (1961).

46. *John P. White et al.*, 48 T.C. 430 (1967).

47. *Jack R. Farber et al.*, 57 T.C. 714 (1972).

48. *Elwood J. Clark et al.*, T.C. Memo., Docket Nos. 9059, 9135, and 9167, entered April 1, 1956, *aff'd*, 158 F.2d 851 (6th Cir., 1947).

49. Revenue Ruling 69-88, 1969-1 CB 58.

50. *Shearer v. Anderson*, 16 F.2d 995 (2d Cir., 1927).

51. *Stanley Kupiszewski et al.*, T.C. Memo. 1964-258, filed September 30, 1964.

52. Revenue Ruling 54-85, 1954-1 CB 58.

53. *Sid J. Klawitter et al.*, T.C. Memo. 1971-289, filed November 9, 1971.

54. *Anderson v. Commissioner*, 81 F.2d 457 (10th Cir., 1936).

55. *Jack R. Farber et al.*, 57 T.C. 714 (1972).

56. Revenue Ruling 70-91, 1970-1 CB 37.

57. *Betty L. Young*, T.C. Memo. 1977-38, filed February 16, 1977.

58. *Black et al. v. Commissioner*, T.C. Memo. 1977-337, filed September 27, 1977.

59. *Luther Wickline*, T.C. Memo, 1971-205, filed August 18, 1971.

60. *Dominick Calderazzo et al.*, T.C. Memo. 1967-25, filed February 13, 1967.

61. *Lamphere et al. v. Commissioner*, 70 T.C. 391 (1978).

62. *Ralph S. Clark et al.*, T.C. Memo. 1966-22, filed January 27, 1966.

63. Regulations Section 1.165-7(b)(1)(i).

64. *Cantrell et al. v. Commissioner*, T.C. Memo. 1978-237, filed June 26, 1978.

65. Revenue Ruling 75-36, 1975-1 CB 143.

66. *Frederick C. Moser et al.*, T.C. Memo. 1959-25, filed February 11, 1959.

67. *Blackshear v. Commissioner*, T.C. Memo. 1977-231, filed July 25, 1977.

68. *Harris v. Commissioner*, T.C. Memo. 1978-332, filed August 23, 1978.

69. *Perry A. Nichols et al.*, 43 T.C. 842 (1965).

70. *Evelyn Nell Norton*, 40 T.C. 500 (1963), *aff'd*, 333 F.2d 1005 (9th Cir., 1964).

71. *Vesta Peak Maxwell*, B.T.A. Memo., Docket Nos. 86186-7, entered February 7, 1940.

72. *Robert S. Gerstell et al.*, 46 T.C. 161 (1966).

73. Revenue Ruling 71-381, 1971-2 CB 126.

74. Revenue Ruling 77-18, 1977-1 CB 46.

75. *Perry A. Nichols et al.*, 43 T.C. 842 (1965).

76. *The Morris Plan Company of St. Joseph*, 42 B.T.A. 1190 (1940).

77. *Russell v. United States*, D.C., Ore., 1976.

78. *Curtis H. Muncie*, 18 T.C. 849 (1952).

79. *Vesta Peak Maxwell*, B.T.A. Memo., Docket Nos. 86186-7, entered February 7, 1940.

80. Revenue Ruling 72-112, 1972-1 CB 60.

81. *American Bemberg Corporation*, 10 T.C. 361 (1948), *aff'd*, 177 F.2d 200 (6th Cir., 1949).

82. Revenue Ruling 70-90, 1970-1 CB 37.

83. Revenue Ruling 73-201, 1973-1 CB 140.

84. I.R.C. Section 165(h).

85. Revenue Ruling 58-180, 1958-1 CB 153.

86. *Ben R. Stein et al.*, T.C. Memo. 1972-140, filed June 29, 1972.

87. *Ticket Office Equipment Co., Inc.*, 20 T.C. 272 (1953), *aff'd on another issue*, 213 F.2d 318 (2d Cir., 1954).

88. *Gilbert J. Kraus*, T.C. Memo., Docket No. 22594, entered October 31, 1951.

89. *Carl A. Hasslacher*, T.C. Memo., Docket No. 21662, entered April 7, 1950.

90. *C. E. R. Howard et al.*, T.C. Memo. 1969-277, filed December 18, 1969.

91. I.R.S. News Release 1237, July 16, 1972.

92. *Cantrell et al. v. Commissioner*. T.C. Memo. 1978-237, filed June 26, 1978.

93. *Burrell E. Davis et al.*, 34 T.C. 586 (1960).

94. *Charles Gutwirth et al.*, 40 T.C. 666 (1963).

95. *Tax Guide for Small Business*, 1978 edition. I.R.S. Publication 334, page 111.

96. *Robert W. Jorg*, 52 T.C. 288 (1969).

97. *Frank Fuchs Estate et al. v. Commissioner*, 413 F.2d 503 (2d Cir., 1969).

98. Revenue Ruling 76-134, 1976-1 CB 54.

99. *Cox et al. v. United States*, 537 F.2d 1066 (9th Cir., 1976).

100. I.R.C. Section 1231.

101. *Louis V. Coughlin et al.*, T.C. Memo. 1973-243, filed October 29, 1973.

102. *Cantrell et al. v. Commissioner*, T.C. Memo. 1978-237, filed June 26, 1978.

103. *Daniel B. Kenerly et al.*, T.C. Memo. 1975-139, filed May 12, 1975.

104. *George Freitas Dairy, Inc. et al. v. United States*, . . . F.2d . . . (9th Cir., 1978).

105. Revenue Ruling 77-215, 1977-1 CB 51.

106. *Child Care and Disabled Dependent Care*, I.R.S. Publication 503, 1977 edition.

107. Revenue Act of 1978, Section 121.

108. *Abe Brenner et al.*, T.C. Memo. 1967-239, filed November 28, 1967.

109. I.R.C. Section 1341.

110. Revenue Ruling 65-254, 1965-2 CB 50.

111. *Jerome Mortrud et al.*, 44 T.C. 208 (1965).

112. *Andover Realty Corporation*, 33 T.C. 671 (1960).

113. *H. K. Francis et al. v. Commissioner*, T.C. Memo. 1977-170, filed June 2, 1977.

114. Revenue Ruling 76-453, 1976-2 CB 86.

115. *Bovington et al. v. United States*, D.C., Mont., 1977.

116. Revenue Ruling 63-100, 1963-1 CB 34.

117. Revenue Ruling 75-380, 1975-2 CB 59.

118. *Tyne v. Commissioner*, 385 F.2d 50 (7th Cir., 1972).

119. Revenue Ruling 63-100, 1963-1 CB 34.

120. *Fausner et al. v. Commissioner*, 413 U.S. 838 (1973).

121. *Grayson et al. v. Commissioner*, T.C. Memo, 1977-304, filed September 7, 1977.

122. *Howard A. Pool*, T.C. Memo. 1977-20, filed January 31, 1977.

123. I.R.C. Section 186.

124. Regulations Section 1.162-10(a).

125. *Berkshire Oil Co.*, 9 T.C. 903 (1947).

126. Revenue Ruling 71-260, 1971-1 CB 57.

127. *Ibid.*

128. *Tax Information on Business Expenses*, I.R.S. Publication 535, 1976 edition, page 5.

129. *R. J. Nicholl Co.*, 59 T.C. 37 (1972).

130. *Marvin T. Blackwell et al.*, T.C. Memo. 1956-184, filed August 9, 1956.

131. *Slaymaker Lock Company*, 18 T.C. 1001 (1952).

132. *Tax Information on Business Expenses*, I.R.S. Publication 535, 1976 edition, page 5.

133. *Tax Guide for Small Business,* 1976 edition, page 85.

134. *Ibid.,* page 79.

135. *Ibid.*

136. *Tax Information on Business Expenses,* I.R.S. Publication 535, 1976 edition, page 7.

137. Revenue Ruling 71-476, 1971-2 CB 308.

138. I.R.C. Section 216.

139. Regulations Section 1.216-2(a).

140. Revenue Ruling 66-341, 1966-2 CB 101.

141. *Tax Information for Homeowners,* I.R.S. Publication 530, 1976 edition, page 8.

142. Revenue Ruling 64-31, 1964-1 CB (part 1) 300.

143. *Tax Information for Homeowners,* I.R.S. Publication 530, 1976 edition, page 8.

144. *Wachter et al. v. United States,* D.C., W.D. Wash., 1974.

145. *Nelson et al. v. Commissioner,* T.C. Memo. 1978-287, filed July 26, 1978.

146. *Parker et al. v. United States, . . . F.2d . . . (Ct. Cl., 1978).*

147. *Commissioner v. Bagley & Sewell Co.,* 221 F.2d 944 (2d Cir., 1955).

148. *Tax Information on Business Expenses,* I.R.S. Publication 535, 1976 edition, page 3.

149. I.R.C. Section 170(c).

150. Revenue Procedure 64-25, 1964-1 CB (Part 1) 694.

151. *Cooper et al. v. Commissioner,* T.C. Memo. 1978-178, filed May 15, 1978.

152. I.R.C. Section 170(c)(2)(B).

153. *Crosby Valve & Gage Company v. Commissioner,* 380 F.2d 146 (1st Cir., 1967).

154. *Pearsall et al. v. Commissioner,* T.C. Memo. 1977-230, filed July 25, 1977.

155. I.R.S. Letter Ruling 7816001, August 19, 1977.

156. I.R.C. Section 170(e)(1)(A).

157. I.R.C. Section 170(e)(1)(B).

158. I.R.C. Section 1011(b).

159. *United States v. Wolfson,* 573 F.2d 216 (5th Cir., 1978).

160. Revenue Ruling 68-113, 1968-1 CB 80.

161. Revenue Ruling 69-79, 1969-1 CB 63.

162. Revenue Ruling 64-205, 1964-2 CB 62.

163. I.R.C. Section 170.

164. Revenue Ruling 73-339, 1973-2 CB 68.

165. Revenue Ruling 74-583, 1974-2 CB 80.

166. Revenue Ruling 67-363, 1967-2 CB 118.

167. I.R.C. Section 170(f)(3).

168. *Income Tax Deduction for Contributions,* I.R.S. Publication 526, 1976 edition, page 7.

169. *Lawrence et al. v. United States,* D.C., C.D. Cal., 1974.

170. I.R.C. Section 170(b).

171. *Harold DeJong,* 36 T.C. 896 (1961), *aff'd,* 309 F.2d 373 (9th Cir., 1962).

172. *Ben I. Seldin et al.,* T.C. Memo. 1969-233, filed November 3, 1969.

173. *The Citizens & Southern National Bank of South Carolina v. United States,* 243 F. Supp. 900 (D.C., W.D. S.C., 1965).

174. Revenue Ruling 69-90, 1969-1 CB 63.

175. *O. J. Wardwell Estate v. Commissioner,* 301 F.2d 632 (8th Cir., 1962).

176. *Income Tax Deduction for Contributions,* I.R.S. Publication 526, 1976 edition, page 1.

177. I.R.C. Section 162(b).

178. Revenue Ruling 73-113, 1973-1 CB 65.

179. *Old Mission Portland Cement Company v. Commissioner*, 69 F.2d 676 (9th Cir., 1934).
180. *Sarah Marquis*, 49 T.C. 695 (1968).
181. Revenue Ruling 63-73, 1963-1 CB 35.
182. Revenue Ruling 73-312, 1972-1 CB 44.
183. Revenue Ruling 68-2, 1968-1 CB 61.
184. Revenue Ruling 76-232, 1976-1 CB 62.
185. *Sugarland Industries*, 15 B.T.A. 1265 (1929).
186. *Corning Glass Works v. Commissioner*, 37 F.2d 798 (App. D.C., 1929).
187. *DeWitt et al. v. United States*, 503 F.2d 1406 (1974).
188. *Rainier Companies, Inc., et al. v. Commissioner*, T.C. Memo. 1977-351, filed October 3, 1977.
189. *Commissioner v. The Hub, Incorporated*, 68 F.2d 349 (4th Cir., 1934).
190. I.R.C. Section 368(a)(1)(E).
191. Revenue Ruling 55-4, 1955-1 CB 291.
192. *Income Tax Deduction for Contributions*, I.R.S. Publication 526, 1976 edition, page 2.
193. *Protecting Older Americans Against Overpayment of Income Taxes*, Special Committee on Aging, United States Senate, 1976, page 3.
194. *Wilhelm et al. v. Commissioner*, T.C. Memo. 1978-327, filed August 17, 1978.
195. *McCollum et al. v. Commissioner*, T.C. Memo. 1978-435, filed November 1, 1978.
196. Revenue Ruling 59-160, 1959-1 CB 59.
197. Revenue Ruling 56-508, 1956-2 CB 126.
198. Revenue Ruling 56-509, 1956-2 CB 129.
199. Revenue Ruling 69-473, 1969-2 CB 37.
200. Revenue Ruling 77-280, 1977-2 CB 14.
201. Revenue Procedure 70-26, 1970-2 CB 507.
202. Revenue Ruling 70-519, 1970-2 CB 62.
203. IRS Letter Ruling 7726018, May 29, 1977.
204. *Archbold v. United States*, 449 F.2d 1120 (Ct. Cl., 1971).
205. *Hubert Rutland et al.*, T.C. Memo. 1977-8, filed January 17, 1977.
206. *Income Tax Deduction for Contributions*, I.R.S. Publication 526, 1976 edition, page 4.
207. Revenue Ruling 67-461, 1967-2 CB 125.
208. I.R.C. Section 170(h).
209. Revenue Ruling 66-10, 1966-1 CB 47.
210. *Bauer et al. v. United States*, 449 F. Supp. 755 (D.C., W.D. La., 1978).
211. *Thomas E. Lesslie et al.*, T.C. Memo. 1977-111, filed April 14, 1977.
212. *Miscellaneous Deductions and Credits*, I.R.S. Publication 529, 1976 edition, page 4.
213. I.R.C. Section 170(d).
214. Revenue Ruling 76-267, 1976-2 CB 71.
215. Revenue Act of 1978, Section 113.
216. I.R.C. Section 6096.
217. *Musser v. United States*, D.C., N.D. Cal., 1957.
218. *Robert C. Coffey*, 21 B.T.A. 1242 (1930).
219. Revenue Ruling 63-266, 1963-2 CB 88.
220. *Bank of Stockton*, T.C. Memo. 1977-24, filed January 31, 1977.
221. Tax Reform Act of 1976, Section 602.
222. Revenue Act of 1978, Section 701(g).
223. I.R.C. Section 274(a)(2), as amended by Revenue Act of 1978, Section 361.
224. Revenue Ruling 78-38, I.R.B. 1978-5, 7.

225. Revenue Ruling 78-39, I.R.B. 1978-5, 8.
226. Revenue Ruling 70-254, 1970-1 CB 31.
227. *Charleston National Bank*, 20 T.C. 253 (1953), *aff'd*, 213 F.2d 45 (4th Cir., 1954).
228. Revenue Ruling 56-359, 1956-2 CB 115.
229. *Fred W. Staudt*, T.C. Memo., Docket No. 32244, entered December 17, 1953.

C

D

Day care center. *See* **Ordinary and necessary business expenses.**

Deaf persons, expenses of. Less well known than the Seeing Eye
dog is the Hearing Ear dog. Amounts paid for the acquisition,
training, and maintenance of a Hearing Ear dog for the purpose
of assisting a taxpayer or his dependent who is deaf are deductible. A taxpayer's daughter had a severe congenital hearing
loss. In order to alleviate, in part, the effect of his daughter's
defect in hearing, he purchased a dog and paid to have it
trained by a professional trainer to alert her to dangerous conditions.[1]

Medical care can include such expenses as payments to a
notetaker for a deaf student. The taxpayer for whom the deaf
student is a dependent is allowed the deduction.[2]

Specialized equipment which, when used in conjunction
with a regular telephone, enables a deaf person to communi-
cate with anyone who has identical equipment is deductible as
a medical expense.[3]

When such specialized equipment is used primarily to help
a taxpayer's condition or that of his spouse or dependents, any
amounts spent by him to repair the equipment may also be
deducted as medical expenses.[4]

The cost of instruction in lip reading is deductible.[5] Deduction was allowed for expenses of a school for the teaching of lip
reading.[6] Deduction also is allowed for expenses to qualify an
individual for future normal education or for normal living.[7]

Medical insurance includes health and accident insurance.
A father had a deaf child who had learned lip reading. But if
anything were now to happen to his sight. . . . The father took
out an insurance policy covering the total permanent loss of
sight in the child's right eye. Premiums were deductible as
medical expense.[8]

See also **Medical expenses.** For a study of this problem, see
Alan Ander, "Tax Law Benefits and Problems for the Deaf," a

thesis presented to the Graduate School of Business Administration, New York University, 1977.

Dealers in securities, stock transfer taxes of. See **Taxes.**

Debtor insurance premiums. See **Creditor insurance policy, premiums on; Insurance.**

Debts. See **Bad debts.**

Decedent, medical care of. See **Medical expenses.**

Deceit, loss because of. See **Casualties.**

Defense of title. See **Legal fees.**

Demolition. If land and buildings are acquired for business purposes, and subsequently the building is torn down, tax treatment depends upon the buyer's intention when he acquired the property. If he intended to use the building, and the decision to demolish is made *subsequent* to the acquisition, the cost of the building as well as the demolition expense may be deducted.[9] Such was the case in which the buyer had every intention of using the building it had acquired, but at a later date it was determined that necessary reconstruction work to allow the building to be used was economically unfeasible.[10] Demolition deduction was permitted where it was decided after the acquisition that the building could not be used because of the hidden defects which had been discovered, specifically, rotten beams.[11]

In another case, a demolition loss was deductible when a year after land and building had been purchased, the building had to be torn down as a result of unexpected action by the city in widening a street.[12]

If a lessee has the right to tear down buildings which are on the property in order to erect his own, the landlord is entitled to a demolition-loss deduction.[13]

An automobile distributor erected a building to the specifications of Ford Motor Company. About fifteen years later, Ford insisted that the distributor would have to move to a new location with greatly enlarged facilities in order to retain the franchise. This was done. As the old building was of such a specialized nature that no one wanted it, it was torn down by the distributor at his own expense, for a new tenant required that the land be made available free of any structures. Demolition loss was deductible, as the old building had been constructed for a specific purpose that had to be abandoned by the owner because of an economic event not of his own making. The building became as worthless as if it had been destroyed by fire or other casualty.[14]

Dental expenses. *See* **Medical expenses.**

Dependent care expenses. *See* **Child care and disabled dependent care.**

Dependents. *See* **Family transactions; Medical expenses.**

Depletion. The owner of an economic interest in mines, oil and gas wells, other natural deposits, and timber is allowed a deduction for a reasonable amount of depletion.

Cost depletion is computed by dividing the total number of recoverable units (tons, barrels, etc., determined in accordance with prevailing industry methods) in the deposit into the adjusted basis of the mineral deposit and multiplying the resulting rate per unit (1) by the number of units for which payment is received during the taxable year of the taxpayer if the cash method is used, or (2) by the number of units sold if he uses the accrual method.[15] (The adjusted basis of the mineral deposit is the original cost less depletion allowed. The adjusted basis cannot be less than zero.)

A taxpayer may deduct under the percentage-depletion method a stipulated percentage of his gross income from the property during the taxable year. But the deduction for depletion under this method cannot exceed 50 percent of his taxable income from the property, computed without the deduction for depletion.[16] The stipulated percentage for oil and gas wells, for example, was set at 22 percent by the Tax Reform Act of 1969.[17]

Effective January 1, 1975, the 22-percent depletion allowance for oil and gas wells was terminated, except in the case of (1) regulated natural gas, (2) natural gas sold under a fixed contract, (3) certain geothermal deposits, and (4) independent producers and royalty owners. In the case of (4), the rate drops each year until it reaches 15 percent in 1984 and depends upon a production schedule contained in the Tax Reduction Act of 1975.[18]

Deposit, forfeiture of. *See* **Cancellation and forfeiture.**

Depreciation. The cost of business assets with an estimated useful life of more than one year cannot be deducted as an expense.

But if the useful life can be estimated with reasonable accuracy, these costs in many instances can be amortized with a tax deduction in each year of estimated useful life. That is, gradual using up of the asset used for business purposes is written off. The most common form of this is depreciation.

Depreciation is deductible only in the case of property used in the trade or business or held for the production of income.[19] Where property had been held for the production of income during a taxable year, depreciation was allowed even though, in fact, the property produced no income.[20] Depreciation can be taken on the Federal income tax return for such items as a radio, a cocktail table, a grandfather clock, and a painting if the items are used in the taxpayer's trade or business.[21]

Depreciation may be taken on a professional library, as by a physician.[22] A veterinarian was allowed to take depreciation on names and addresses of pet owners and medical histories of the animals.[23]

Only a taxpayer who has a depreciable interest in property may take the deduction.[24] But the depreciable property may be upon another party's land. A manufacturer of military aircraft erected barricades on each end of a runway on land owned by a municipality. This was done in view of safety requirements in landing aircraft, in order to catch aircraft using the maximum roll-out afforded by the runway. The manufacturer was permitted to take depreciation on the barricades.[25]

Where depreciable business property is held by an estate or a trust, a life tenant is entitled to a depreciation deduction. Income beneficiaries of property held in trust, or heirs, legatees, or devisees of an estate may deduct allowable depreciation not deductible by the estate or trust.[26]

A deduction for a portion of the depreciation is allowable where property is used partially for business and partially for personal purposes.[27] The amount of the allocation is the taxpayer's to prove.

Any reasonable and consistently applied method of computing depreciation may be used, but deductions cannot exceed the amounts necessary to recover the cost or other basis during the remaining useful life of the property.[28] But so-called accelerated depreciation, such as the double-declining-balance method or the sum-of-the-years'-digits method, may be used only in the case of (1) tangible property having a useful life of three years or more where (2) the original use of the property commenced with the taxpayer.[29] (If either of these methods of depreciation is unfamiliar to you, ask your accountant for an explanation.)

The annual depreciation deduction must be in accordance

with a reasonably consistent plan, but it is not necessarily at a uniform rate.[30] Even straight-line depreciation, which customarily is thought of as being a consistent figure year after year regardless of actual usage of the asset, may vary markedly. Depreciation of this type may be taken at a faster rate than previously if it can be proved that during a taxable year the assets were subjected to faster wear and tear than had been contemplated when the rates were set. In the case of road-building equipment, for example, accelerated straight-line depreciation was recognized where the contractor worked the equipment for an excessive number of hours a day, where the equipment was subjected to abnormal weather conditions such as salt water or flooding, and where untrained operators worked with the equipment and subjected it to grueling stresses.[31] Abuse of equipment justified more rapid depreciation even under the straight-line method.[32]

In addition to the depreciation methods mentioned previously, any other method may be used, provided depreciation allowances computed in accordance with such method do not result in accumulated allowances at the end of any taxable year greater than the total of the accumulated allowances which would have resulted from the use of the double-declining method. This limitation applies only during the first two-thirds of the useful life of the property.[33]

For example, there is the operating-day method. Life of an asset, such as a rotary oil-drilling rig, is estimated in terms of the total number of days it can be operated, and the depreciable basis is prorated according to the actual number of days the asset is used.[34]

One of the major depreciation deduction problems is estimating the useful life of an asset, so that annual deductions can be computed. The most recent technique for coping with this is the Asset Depreciation Range (A.D.R.) system.[35]

For taxable years beginning after December 31, 1970, taxpayers have been allowed to elect to use A.D.R. to compute the reasonable depreciation allowance for all eligible property placed in service during a taxable year. Eligible property is tangible personal and real property placed in service by the taxpayer after 1970 for which there is in effect an asset guideline class and an asset guideline period. An election can be made for each year on Form 4832 for assets acquired during that year which, at the taxpayer's choice, may be anywhere in the range of 20 percent above or below the guideline figures. If a taxpayer adopts the *modified half-year convention*, all property placed in service during the first half of a taxable year is considered as placed in service on the first day of that year; all property placed in service during the second half of the taxable year is considered as placed in service on the first day of the second half of the taxable year. If he adopts the *half-year convention*, all property placed in service during the taxable year is treated as if it had been placed in service on the first day of the second half of the taxable year. Special provisons are made for allowances for salvage and for repairs.[36]

Depreciation deductions may be taken without reference to the physical life of the property. Deductions may be taken over the remaining economic life of the property if that is shorter than the physical life.[37]

Special depreciation rules have been provided for expenditures to rehabilitate low-income rental housing under specified conditions. Here, the expenditures may be computed under a straight-line method over a period of 60 months, if the additions or improvements have a useful life of five years or more. The Revenue Act of 1978 provided a three-year extension of this rule in the case of expenditures paid or incurred with respect to low- and moderate-income rental housing after December 31, 1978, and before January 1, 1982 (including expenditures made pursuant to a binding contract entered into before January 1, 1982).[38]

Depreciation may be taken on intangible property with a limited useful life.[39] Patents and sales franchises for a specified number of years are examples.

Normal obsolescence is included in the depreciation allowance, that is, there is a general assumption that in time depreciable property is likely to be supplanted by something better even though there is a remaining useful life. *Abnormal* obsolescence, a write-off necessitated by some specific fact or action, can be a separate deduction. *See also* **Additional first-year depreciation; Obsolescence.**

Development. *See* **Research and experimental expenses.**

Development expenses of farmers. *See* **Farmers.**

Directors. *See* **Executives; Legal fees; Reputation, maintenance of.**

Disability insurance payments. *See* **State disability insurance.**

Disabled dependent care. *See* **Child care and disabled dependent care.**

Disallowance of deductions in transaction with related parties. *See* **Family transactions.**

Disaster area. *See* **Casualties.**

Disaster losses. If a casualty is sustained in what the President of the United States subsequently proclaims to be a disaster area, the loss may be deducted in the taxable year immediately preceding the year in which the casualty is sustained rather than in the year of the happening. This choice is optional. The election is available whenever a deductible disaster loss is incurred, whether or not that loss technically is a "casualty loss" as narrowly defined in the tax law. This choice as to year of tax deduction now is available for *any* kind of loss, even if not casualty related. Now included are such items as obsolescence, worthless stock or securities, losses from sale or exchange of capital assets, loss on stock of affiliated companies, provided the property is used in a trade or business or in a profit-seeking transaction. Individuals, however, may deduct losses to personal property only if the loss arises from a fire, storm, shipwreck, or other such casualty, or from theft.[40] The election to deduct for the preceding year must be made on or before the later of (1) the original due date of the taxpayer's income tax return for the year in which the disaster occurred or (2) the due date of the preceding year's tax return (taking into account any extensions of time for filing which had been granted.)[41]

Dismissal pay. A businessperson can deduct severance pay which he gives, whether in the form of cash or property.[42] *See also* **Compensation.**

Dissenting stockholder, expenses of. *See* **Legal fees.**

Divorce settlements. *See* **Alimony.**

Doctors, professional expenses of. *See* **Commuting; Depreciation; Education; Expenditures for periods lasting more than one year; Insurance; Legal fees; Malpractice insurance; Office at home; Ordinary and necessary business expenses; Subscriptions to periodicals; Travel.**

Doctors' fees. *See* **Medical expenses.**

Dogs. *See* **Advertising; Blind persons, expenses of; Deaf persons, expenses of; Entertainment.**

Donee, expenses of. *See* **Legal fees.**

Down payments, forfeiture of. *See* **Cancellation and forfeiture.**

Dredging expenses. *See* **Repairs.**

Dress clothes. *See* **Uniforms.**

Drought losses. In most instances drought-related losses, to be deductible, must be incurred in a trade or business or in a transaction entered upon for profit. But in 1977, the Internal Revenue Service announced it had changed its mind and now will not go so far as to say that a drought loss may never qualify as a casualty loss.[43]

Drug addicts, treatment of. *See* **Medical expenses.**

Drunkenness. *See* **Alcoholism, treatment for.**

Dues, club. *See* **Entertainment.**

D

1. Revenue Ruling 68-295, 1968-1 CB 92.
2. *Reuben A. Baer Estate*, T.C. Memo, 1967-34, filed February 27, 1967.
3. Revenue Ruling 71-48, 1971-1 CB 156.
4. Revenue Ruling 73-53, 1973-1 CB 139.
5. *Donovan et al. v. Campbell, Jr.*, D.C., N.D. Texas, 1961.
6. *Lawrence D. Greisdorf et al.*, 54 T.C. 1684 (1970).
7. Regulations Section 1.213-1(e)(1)(v)(a).
8. *Donovan et al. v. Campbell, Jr.*, D.C., N.D. Texas, 1961.
9. Regulations Section 1.165-3(b)(1).
10. *Panhandle State Bank*, 39 T.C. 813 (1963).
11. *Parma Company*, 18 B.T.A. 429 (1929).
12. *Hartford Courant Company v. Smith*, D.C., Conn., 1942.
13. *Feldman v. Wood*, 335 F.2d 264 (9th Cir., 1964).
14. *Yates Motor Company, Inc. v. Commissioner*, 561 F.2d 490 (6th Cir., 1977).
15. Regulations Section 1.611-2.
16. Regulations Section 1.613-2.
17. I.R.C. Section 613(b)(1).
18. Tax Reduction Act of 1975, Section 501.
19. I.R.C. Section 167(a)(1),(2).
20. *Riis & Company, Inc., et al.*, T.C. Memo. 1964-190, filed July 14, 1964.
21. *Beaudry v. Commissioner*, 150 F.2d 20 (2d Cir., 1945).
22. *Wolfson et al. v. Commissioner*, T.C. Memo. 1978-445, filed November 7, 1978.
23. *Central Animal Hospital, Inc.*, 68 T.C. 269 (1977).
24. *Reisinger v. Commissioner*, 144 F.2d 475 (2d Cir., 1944).
25. Revenue Ruling 54-579, 1954-2 CB 91.
26. I.R.C. Section 167(b).
27. *Glynn N. C. Jones*, T.C. Memo. 1959-98, filed May 19, 1959.

28. Regulations Section 1.167(b)-o.
29. I.R.C. Section 167(c).
30. Regulations Section 1.167(a)-1(a).
31. *United States v. Livengood et al.*, D.C., E.D. Pa., 1969.
32. *Pilot Freight Carriers, Inc.*, T.C. Memo. 1956-195, filed August 27, 1956.
33. Regulations Section 1.167(b)-4(a).
34. Revenue Ruling 65-652, 1956-2 CB 125.
35. I.R.C. Section 167(m).
36. Regulations Section 1.167(a)-11.
37. *Adda, Inc.*, 9 T.C. 199 (1947), *rev'd on another issue*, 171 F.2d 367 (2d Cir., 1948).
38. Revenue Act of 1978, Section 367.
39. Regulations Section 1.167(a)-3.
40. Treasury Decision 7522, December 15, 1977.
41. Regulations Section 1.165-11.
42. *Albin J. Strandquist et al.*, T.C. Memo. 1970-84, filed April 13, 1970.
43. Revenue Ruling 77-490, 1977-2 CB 64.

D

E

Earning power, payments to protect. An attorney performed some legal chores for an elderly widow, although he did not prepare her will. He was named executor and was bequeathed a very substantial sum when she died. Then her relatives swarmed in, challenging the probate of the will on the ground that he had exerted undue influence upon her before she had prepared the will. To prevent litigation in connection with the will contest and to avoid unfavorable publicity, he agreed to pay a large sum to the deceased widow's relatives, who thereupon dropped the suit which had so savagely attacked him. He could deduct the payment as an expense in connection with his trade or business of being a lawyer, as he legitimately feared the possible damage to his reputation that a hotly contested vengeful lawsuit might cause. His payment was solely to protect his business reputation and his future earnings' flow.[1] See also **Business-related losses; Reputation, maintenance of.**

Easement, contribution in form of. See **Contributions.**

Economic analysis. Expenditures which will produce benefits expected to last for more than one year must be capitalized and not deducted at the time. Economic analysis of projects which never were undertaken, however, could be written off when the projects were abandoned.[2]

Economic value, loss of. See **Casualties.**

Education. Ordinarily, an individual cannot deduct expenses for his education. This is because such expense is regarded as a personal expense or as the expenditure for the acquisition of capital asset (learning), the advantages of which last for more than one year. But certain educational expenses which occur in connection with one's trade or business are deductible. An individual may deduct educational expenses which were necessary under the following conditions:

1. To meet the express requirements of his current employer.

2. To keep his current salary, status, or employment.

3. To maintain or to improve skills required in performing his current duties.[3]

Educational expenses are also deductible when:

1. The courses which an individual takes are *not* required to meet the minimum educational requirements for his employment. In other words, if the minimum educational requirements of the individual's employer is a high-school education, and the employee (already possessing a high-school education) takes a course at a college or business school, then the expenses of the courses he takes to improve his skills are deductible.

2. The education was *not* undertaken to qualify him for a new trade or profession.

Education expenses are related to the retention of one's existing job. Deduction is not allowed for the cost of education required of an individual to meet the minimum educational requirements for qualification in his employment or other trade or business. Once a person has met the minimum educational requirements for qualification in his employment, he is treated as continuing to meet those requirements even though they are changed.[4] A woman who was already certified to teach in Toronto, Canada, thus could deduct the cost of taking courses required to obtain her certification in New Jersey. Having acquired certification to teach in Toronto, she had met the minimum educational requirements for qualification in her employment, and the cost of additional courses required by New Jersey was deductible because they maintained and improved her skills as a teacher.[5]

A business administrator could deduct the expenses of working for a Master of Business Administration degree even when he was not currently employed and used his sharpened skills to get a different job. He wished to participate in a university's M.B.A. program on a full-time basis but could not get a leave of absence from his employer. He resigned and worked full time for two years to get his degree. Then he went to work as an administrator for another business. He was allowed to deduct his expenses in getting this advanced degree because (1) he had worked long enough in the past to show that he was in the business of being a salaried employee; (2) a period of absence does not affect one's status of carrying on a trade or business while attending graduate school; (3) the M.B.A. training would not equip him for a different type of career; (4) the education was expected to equip him to be a better administrator than he was before; and (5) he continued in the same business of being an administrator, although it happened to be for another company.[6]

If one is not diligently seeking a job, he cannot deduct the cost of studying for it. An elementary school principal resigned to work full time for his doctorate. But then he could not find another administrative position. Deduction for his costs was disallowed by the Internal Revenue Service on the ground that he was not actually in the trade or business of teacher or educational administrator while his expenses were incurred. The court allowed the deduction. A person still can be engaged in a trade or business, although currently unemployed, if he previously had been engaged in it and intends to return to the same trade or business. The court stressed the fact that he "was more than an inactive member of his profession."[7] In an earlier case, deduction was disallowed where a teacher lacked diligence in seeking employment after the completion of her graduate courses.[8]

It does not matter that an individual chooses to acquire the additional education to improve his skills by attending a university in a foreign country rather than one in the United States.[9]

Educational costs are deductible, even though the education may lead to a degree and possibly a new trade or profession, if the expense is incurred to meet the express requirements of the individual's employer.[10]

An individual was hired by International Business Machines as a patent trainee with a stipulation that he acquire a law degree in a prescribed four-year course of study. He could deduct the cost of this educational expense, for this was a condition of the retention of his present employment.[11]

When a commercial airline switched from propeller to jet planes, flight engineers on the old type of aircraft could retain their status only if they held commercial pilot's licenses. The cost of the education necessary to acquire such licenses was deductible because the purpose was to meet a specific requirement of the employer for the retention of their status as flight crew members. That the training might also qualify a person for a higher position as copilot was irrelevant if the primary purpose was to retain the existing status.[12]

A high-school teacher had tenure, that is, he had taught for a sufficiently long time that under the school's employment policy he could not be discharged. However, to be eligible to participate in any salary increase made available by the school, he had to obtain additional training. One acceptable method was to take a summer course at a foreign university. The cost of this training was deductible as a business expense. True, because of the tenure he didn't *have* to study further in order to keep his job, but this additional training was undertaken to preserve rights to annual advancements that would be lost if he did not comply with the additional training requirements.[13]

If a person has met the minimum educational requirements for qualification in his employment, but his employer requires him to obtain further education in order to retain his present salary status or employment, that person may deduct the expenses for the education he must get to meet the employer's minimum requirements. If one college course is all that is needed to meet those minimum requirements and the person takes two courses, he may deduct only the cost of the one course.[14]

Educational expenses incurred for the purpose of improving one's skills in his existing position or field of specialization are deductible. An Internal Revenue Service reviewer in the Estate and Gift Tax Division was entitled to deduct law school tuition. It was custom, if not the rule, that all examiners in this division be attorneys, and the custom, observed the court, "should be even more true of a reviewer who is their superior." Inasmuch as in his position a law degree was the custom, the expenditure was primarily for the purpose of maintaining or improving the skills required by his business. The "summit of knowledge," the court concluded, "like the fruit of Tantalus, is never reached."[15]

A practicing physician specializing in internal medicine voluntarily undertook training in the techniques of psychiatry primarily for the purpose of maintaining or improving his skills in the practice of internal medicine. He continued to practice as an internist following the completion of his psychiatric training. The claimed deductions were allowed as education expenses incurred for the purpose of enabling him better to carry on his own practice, notwithstanding the fact that incidental to such education he acquired a new specialty.[16]

A physician, while engaged in the private practice of psychiatry, undertook a program of study and training at an accredited psychoanalytic institute which would lead to his qualification to practice psychoanalysis. His expenditures for such study and training were deductible because the study and training maintained or improved skills required by him in his trade or business and did not qualify him for a new trade or business. A general practitioner of medicine took a two-week course reviewing new developments in several specialized fields of medicine. His expenses for the course were deductible because the course maintained or improved skills required by him in his trade or business and did not qualify him for a new trade or business.[17]

A dentist took postgraduate courses in orthodontics, that division of dentistry dealing with irregularities of the teeth. He had engaged in a general dental practice, but he now attended dental school on a full-time basis, continuing his professional practice on a part-time basis. Upon completion of his post-graduate training he became an orthodontist and limited his practice to patients in need of this field of specialization. He was permitted to deduct the cost of his postgraduate studies, for these expenses were not incurred in connection with qual-ifying him for a new trade or business but were for the purpose of improving his skills as a dentist.[18]

Deductible expenses which are voluntarily incurred for edu-cation to maintain or to improve skills needed for one's occu-pation include refresher courses or courses dealing with cur-rent developments, as well as the academic or vocational courses.[19]

An attorney was permitted to deduct his expenses in attend-ing a tax institute. The institute had as an objective the presen-tation of current developments in the field of taxation. The court noted that the attorney was morally bound to keep cur-rently informed as to the law of Federal taxation. Attendance at the institute, declared the court, "was a way well adopted to keep sharp the tools he actually used in his going trade or business."[20]

Education may include the improving of the managerial skills needed in one's employment, and therefore the expenses incurred in obtaining such improvement are deductible.[21]

A United States Navy captain whose assignments involved primarily command and administration of personnel could deduct the cost of graduate courses which he took on his own initiative as part of a program that led to the degree of Master of Arts in Personnel Administration. The education he under-took was not pursuant to a specific requirement of his em-ployer imposed as a condition to the retention of his salary, status, or employment. But the courses undertaken by him were so closely related to his employment duties that they served to maintain or to improve the skills required of him in his employment. Inasmuch as the courses taken by him were not part of a program of study which would qualify him for a new trade or business and were not required of him in order to meet the minimum educational requirements for qualification in his employment, the expenditures he incurred in taking the courses were deductible.[22]

An individual who was born and educated in Korea was employed by a major corporation as a workmen's compensation supervisor. He was allowed to deduct the cost of courses he took to study methods of comprehension, logic, accounting, and government. These courses helped him to think, to express himself, and to write in the English language, to analyze the reports received, and to comprehend the methods by which laws are enacted and interpreted in the United States. The education improved his skills in his employment in a direct way.[23]

An ordained minister could deduct educational expenses incurred while taking certain undergraduate courses at a college. He chose his courses according to their helpfulness to his ministry: psychology, public speaking, teaching methods, business-related subjects, and drama. Such courses enhanced skills which were appropriate and helpful to him in solving the problems of his congregation. His degree did not qualify him for a new trade or business; he neither sought nor obtained the teaching certificate customarily awarded to those being graduated from his college.[24]

An industrial psychologist employed by a national life insurance firm as an assistant research analyst in industrial psychology could deduct the cost of courses which he undertook in that field in order to improve his skills. The courses were leading to a Doctor of Philosophy degree, but his employer did not insist upon the higher degree as a basis for promotion.[25]

An individual employed as an engineering aide by a major corporation was informed by his superior that he should take a leave of absence and take courses to complete his work for a college degree so that he would have a more secure future with the company, especially during slack periods when lesser-trained employees would be laid off. He did so. Deduction of the cost of taking these courses was permitted, for although he was not required to take the courses, he did so to maintain or improve skills required by his employer.[26]

Voluntarily strengthening one's business weaknesses can be equated with sharpening one's skills. An individual was an executive with a construction company. When the president was killed in an automobile accident, this individual was promoted to the position of vice-president and general superintendent. He felt that although he was generally knowledgeable about the construction business, he was deficient in certain key aspects of corporation management, such as financing, bonding, accounting, and personnel problems. So he went to an experienced management consultant who was then training and advising a number of corporate executives on an individual basis in his own home. The new vice-president deducted his payments as "Business Management Training Consultant Fees." Deduction was allowed despite the Internal Revenue Service claim that a self-educated private tutor, who never had attended an institution of higher learning, cannot qualify as a management consultant. The tax deduction is not limited to formal or institutional education. What the vice-president learned from his tutor served to improve the managerial skills needed in his present employment. In order to *maintain* his employment, which he probably could not have done had his superiors discovered the chinks in his executive armor, he had to learn to cope with problems with which he was unfamiliar.[27]

A professional singer could deduct payments which she made to a voice coach. The payments were to maintain her present employment by profiting from the voice coach's instructions.[28]

A staff photographer for a major New York newspaper also served as a free-lancer. He learned to fly solely to get to the locale of news events quickly and to take aerial views of spot news. This enabled him to improve his skills as to timeliness, range, and graphic portrayal. The time gained might well make the difference between a valuable and a worthless picture, and many events which would have been mundane or even unphotographable from ground level became spectacular from the air. The photographer exhibited to the court "enlightening examples" of how he was maintaining his status as a photographer. His deduction for the flying lessons was allowed.[29]

Expenses for education are not deductible when that education is part of a program of study being pursued by the taxpayer that will lead him to qualifying for a new trade or business. In the case of an employee, however, *a mere change of duties is not the same as a new trade or business* if the change of duties involves the same general type of work as is involved in his present employment.[30]

The most frequent example of nondeductible educational expenses involves law school tuition and related expenses. Or at least, it is the most often brought to court. To a very large proportion of all persons engaged in a trade or business, the advantages of an education in the law would be helpful. But that is not enough to justify a tax deduction, for by getting a law degree a person has at least *qualified* himself for a new trade or business. In the words of one decision, "Law is a field so pervasive as to be 'helpful' to some extent in virtually every type of employment. But that does not mean that everyone who is gainfully employed is entitled to deduct the expenses of acquiring a legal education."[31]

To be entitled to deduct law school expenses, an individual must show that his primary purpose in attending the school is to enable him to do his *present* job better. An insurance claims adjuster could deduct his expenses in attending night law school, for the knowledge he acquired improved the skills required of him as an adjuster. His duties, said the court, involved "frequent contact with legally oriented problems."[32]

Law school expenses were properly deductible by a civilian employee with the Air Force because his employment required him to write technical regulations in the area of procurement and he constantly worked with contracts. His skill as a lawyer would certainly enhance his ability in his present occupation.[33]

A physician served the coroner's office in a major city. His expenses in attending law school were deductible, for his employment dealt with investigations of sudden, violent, and suspicious deaths. His work brought him into constant contact with law-enforcement agencies, lawyers, and the law itself. Certainly an improved knowledge of the law would be an asset to the physician in his present position.[34]

A certified public accountant served as a partner in his father's accounting firm. At the suggestion of his father, the son attended law school. His legal education enabled him to do his accounting work better. He could analyze legal documents to determine their effect upon financial statements and he was better able to understand the laws affecting tax returns which he prepared. But his work for his firm did not change after he obtained his law degree; he never presented himself to the public as a lawyer; and he was satisfied with his earnings as a certified public accountant. There was no indication that he intended to use his law school education or degree to obtain changed or better employment. Therefore the expenses for attending law school were an allowable deduction.[35]

An individual could deduct the costs of attending law school while he was an Internal Revenue Service Special Agent, that is, while he was engaged in the investigation of suspected criminal violations of the tax law. Although he accepted a position with a law firm shortly after obtaining his degree, he had taken the courses to improve and to maintain his skills as a Special Agent. He was an Armed Services veteran on whom the war had left an unerasable mark and for whom government service offered the security his doctor had prescribed. The court felt that he wouldn't have chosen to burden himself with evening law school so that he might leave the security of government service in order to enter the legal profession. Whatever else the legal profession offers, concluded the judge, is difficult to catalog, but its principal attraction has never been security. This indicated to the court that the taxpayer really had gone to law school to improve his skills as a Special Agent, which made the tuition deductible despite his later change of intention.[36]

Very frequently an individual will lose his deduction for law school expenses for either or both of two reasons. First, law school application forms customarily ask why the applicant wishes to attend the school, and applicants fear to say anything except the desire to practice law, lest the admissions committee reject a person whose objective really is something other than being an attorney. But the Internal Revenue Service frequently uses the application form to prove that the individual really was seeking to qualify for a new profession.

Second, even if the individual has not left his old business, he frequently tries his own tax case involving disallowance of the education deduction. That pretty well establishes that he is qualified for a new profession. Persons who do not try their own cases in this situation fare better.[37]

A child was afflicted with dyslexia, a neurological condition which results in great difficulty in learning to read. Education rather than medicine or therapy is the means to offset the effect of dyslexia. The parents were permitted to deduct as medical expenses the fees paid to a teacher for training and study skills which enabled the child to overcome the results of his handicap.[38]

Expenditures for travel as a form of education are deductible only to the extent that the period of travel covered is directly related to the duties of the individual in his employment or other trade or business. There is such a direct relationship only if the major portion of the activities during the period is of a nature which directly maintains or improves skills required by the individual in his employment, trade, or business.[39]

The following examples should give a better idea of how expenditures for travel as a form of education can be deductible.

A concert harpist could deduct train fare to take lessons from the premier harp instructor in the land. In this case the purpose of the travel was to improve the concert harpist's techniques and then to obtain coaching in the best methods of performing particular numbers.[40]

A physician who specialized in the problems of alcoholism

could deduct the expenses of a trip to Europe. While he was there, he visited hospitals and clinics to study their methods and procedures. The expenses contributed substantially to his knowledge and technique of treating the disease of alcoholism.[41]

A high-school teacher of Latin and French could deduct as an expense of maintaining and improving her skills in her employment the money she paid in traveling to various places in the Mediterranean area that had a relationship to the courses she taught.[42] Travel expenses are allowed as educational expenses even where the teacher's activities consisted largely of visiting French schools and families, attending motion pictures, plays, and lectures in the French language, and similar activities.[43]

A school librarian could deduct the costs of a trip abroad. Her principal duty was to lend various forms of assistance to other teachers in their classroom teaching. She acted as "educational resource person," utilizing or making available to teachers and students various relevant audio-visual and other educational media, such as slides, film strips, recordings, and books. Her trip abroad, which took several hundred hours to plan, was centered around subjects the faculty wished to teach. She purchased or took hundreds of slides which were maintained in the school; she collected other materials such as posters and pamphlets for use in the school. Her travel itinerary and travel goals bore close relationship to the emphasis placed on foreign cultures by the social studies department. The trip, in the court's words, "directly maintained and improved important job skills. She is therefore entitled to her deduction."[44]

Travel expenses on sabbatical leave are deductible by a teacher when the places and activities encompassed by the trip are related directly to his teaching position.[45]

An individual may deduct transportation expenses for qualified educational activities which he incurs in going between (1) his place of employment and a school within the same general area, or (2) his place of employment and a school located beyond the general area. But if he returns home before going to school, he may deduct the expense in going from home to school only to the extent it does not exceed the transportation expense which he would have incurred had he gone from work to school.

One individual lives and works in Jersey City and goes to New York City three times a week to attend night classes at a university there. If his educational expenses are deductible under the allowable deduction guidelines, he may also deduct his round-trip transportation expenses, including toll and parking fees.[46]

If an individual travels away from home primarily to obtain education, the expenses of which are deductible, his expenditures for travel, meals, and lodging while away from home are also deductible. But if he, as an incident of the trip, engages in some personal activity such as sightseeing, social visiting, or entertaining or other recreation, that portion of the expenses attributable to the personal activity constitutes nondeductible personal or living expenses. If his travel away from home is primarily personal, his expenditures for travel, meals, and lodging (other than meals and lodging during the time spent in participating in the deductible educational pursuits) are not deductible.

Whether a particular trip is primarily personal or primarily to obtain education depends upon all the facts and circumstances of each case. An important factor to be taken into account is the relative amount of time devoted to personal activity as compared to the time devoted to educational pursuits.[47]

Expenses of a trip involving both educational and personal pursuits may be allocated into deductible and nondeductible expenses. A physician took a cruise on a ship where lectures on developments in medicine were given. He could deduct that portion of the cost which he could establish was appropriate to the time he spent on educational endeavors.[48] See also **Armed forces; Deaf persons, expenses of; Ordinary and necessary business expenses.**

Educational materials. A teacher was allowed to deduct the cost of games and other items he bought to use in his classes for trainable mentally retarded students, or as a student in courses for the handicapped in which he was enrolled.[49]

Efficiency engineer, payment to. See **Expenditures for benefits lasting more than one year.**

Election to deduct or to capitalize. Certain expenditures may be treated as deductible expenses or as capital expenditures at the taxpayer's election.
1.   In the case of unimproved and unproductive real property: annual taxes, interest on a mortgage, and other carrying charges.
2.   In the case of real property, whether improved or unimproved and whether productive or unproductive:

a. Interest on a loan (but not theoretical interest of a tax-payer using his own funds).

b. Taxes of the owner of such real property measured by compensation paid to his employees.

c. Taxes of such an owner which are imposed on the purchase of materials or on the storage, use, or other consumption of materials.

d. Other necessary expenditures paid or incurred for the development of the real property or for the construction of an improvement to the property up to the time the development or construction work has been completed.

3. In the case of personal property:

a. Taxes of an employer measured by compensation for services rendered in transporting machinery or other fixed assets to the plant or installing them there.

b. Interest on a loan to purchase such property or to pay for transporting or installing it.

c. Taxes of the owner thereof imposed on the purchase of such property or on the storage, use, or other consumption of such property, paid or incurred up to the date when such property is first put to use by the taxpayer, whichever date is later.

4. Any otherwise deductible taxes and carrying charges with respect to property which in the opinion of the Commissioner of Internal Revenue are under sound accounting principles chargeable to capital accounts.[50]

Intangible drilling and development costs are deductible expenses or are chargeable to capital, as the taxpayer elects.[51] Development expenses are subject to a similar election.[52] A like election is available in the case of certain mining exploration expenditures.[53]

Research and experimental expenses may be deducted in the year paid or incurred, or the amount may be deferred and amortized ratably over a period of not less than sixty months, as selected by the taxpayer, beginning with the month in which the taxpayer first realizes benefits from these expenditures.[54] Thus, if it takes some time before the research expenses produce income, he is not wasting a deduction by claiming it in a year when there is no income. But if the research pays off more rapidly, the expenses may be deducted should that method have been the taxpayer's election. Research and experimental expenditures for new products or processes which are not related to the current product lines or manufacturing processes of his trade or business are still regarded as research and experimental expenditures which, at the taxpayer's election, may be deducted if paid or incurred in connection with his trade or business.[55]

Ordinarily, a taxpayer likes to take a deduction as soon as possible. But research and development expenditures sometimes require several years to produce financial success. Thus, a taxpayer might prefer to amortize research and development over a period of years, so that expenditures are not claimed until there is income to offset them. An election either to deduct or to amortize is permissible. Previously, a taxpayer merely made this election by taking the deduction at once or on a prorated basis. For taxable years ending after August 29, 1976, the election can be made only by attaching a written statement to this effect to the Federal income tax return for the first taxable year in which the election is applicable. For details of what is to be stated in this election, consult Treasury Regulations Section 1.174-4(b)(1).[56]

See also **Farmers; Removal of impediments to the physically handicapped.**

Elevator in home. See **Medical expenses.**

Eligible charitable contributions. See **Contributions.**

Embezzled funds, return of. Embezzled funds are taxed to the embezzler in the year of their acquisition and are deductible in the year of their return.[57]

Embezzlement. See **Casualties; Claim of right.**

Employee awards. Business gifts are not deductible to the extent that the cost exceeds $25. But an item of tangible personal property having a cost to the taxpayer of not in excess of $100 is deductible, where it is awarded to an employee by reason of length of service or for safety achievement.[58]

Employee benefit-plan losses. Somehow the computations of the advantages of qualified employee benefit plans always assume that an employee will get back more than he puts into the plan. It doesn't always work that way. An employer's pension plan called for employees to contribute part of the cost of the plan. When one employee retired some years later, his retirement contribution from the fund, as a result of investment losses sustained by the fund, amounted to less money than he had contributed over the years. This differential was deductible by him as an ordinary loss in the year of the lump-sum distribution to him.[59]

Another employee was a participant in his employer's contributory stock-bonus plan. The employer went bankrupt, and the employee, his services being ended, received his portion of the stock, which was worthless. In the year he received the stock he was entitled to an ordinary loss deduction in the amount of the contributions he had made over the years.[60]

Employee benefits. See **Compensation; Employee benefit-plan losses.**

Employee loans, unrepaid. See **Bad Debts.**

Employees. Expenses related to one's trade or business are deductible. But these expenses are not confined to that of a business enterprise. The performance of services as an employee constitutes the carrying on of a trade or business. Therefore, the ordinary and necessary business expenses of an employee in connection with his employment are deductible.[61]

Expenses to prevent discharge are deductible because related to the continuance of one's present employment.[62]

Legal expenses paid by an employee who needs help in matters relating to his employment, whether in performing his duties or keeping his job, are deductible.[63]

An employee can deduct the cost of a personal physical examination when the employer requires it.[64]

An employee could deduct club membership costs when he could show that his membership was designed to make his services more valuable to his employer in expectation of an increased salary.[65] A sales manager was allowed to deduct payments for business journals and magazines.[66] A securities salesman properly deducted expenses for a marketing-service publication used by him in pursuance of his selling activities.[67]

Deduction is allowed for living expenses while an individual is away from home on business. This is to lessen the burden of a person who, because of the requirements of his trade or business, must maintain two places of abode and thus incur additional and duplicate living expenses.[68] In furtherance of this purpose, when a person with a principal place of employment goes *elsewhere* to take work which is merely temporary, he may deduct the living expenses incurred at the temporary post of duty, because it would not be reasonable to expect him to move his residence under such circumstances.[69] For this purpose, temporary employment is the type which can be expected to last for only a short period of time.[70]

Outside salesmen, who do their selling away from their employer's place of business, are permitted to deduct all ordinary and necessary expenses paid or incurred in connection with their sales activities. Except for meals, an outside salesman can deduct all such expenses even if he is not away from home overnight. He may deduct the cost of his meals only if he is traveling away from home overnight or if his meals qualify as entertainment expenses.[71] In determining adjusted gross income, an employee can deduct these types of traveling expenses incurred while he is away from home on business if he is not reimbursed by his employer: travel, lodging, baggage, samples, display materials, cost of sample rooms, telephone and telegraph, stenographic services, and expenses (including depreciation) of maintaining and operating an automobile for business purposes. Loss on the sale of a car used for business purposes is deductible by an employee in computing adjusted gross income.[72] Automobile expenses for this purpose specifically include the cost of lubrication, repairs, tires, supplies, parking fees, and tolls. Also included are interest on a car loan, taxes in connection with maintaing the car, and insurance.[73]

An outside salesman who kept valuable samples in his room could deduct as a business expense the cost of a security lock to protect these samples. He could also deduct the cost of a post-office box for business use, and a home telephone used for business purposes before and after his day's visits.[74]

A life insurance company opened a new building, where appropriately new furniture was supplied by the company for all individual offices except that of a district sales manager, who thereupon purchased his own desk, sofa, draperies, etc. The company had not supplied him with new equipment because of a personality conflict between him and the employee designated to furnish the new building. The district sales manager felt that he could not maintain his status with clients, agents, and other persons that he saw in his dilapidated surroundings, but he wanted to avoid interoffice conflicts and hence did not complain. He sought no reimbursement from the company, and none was offered even when the matter became public knowledge. He could deduct depreciation on this equipment, which had been acquired for business reasons, to maintain status in connection with doing his job as an employee.[75]

A legal stenographer was permitted to deduct the cost of advertisements for employment which she inserted in the *New York Law Journal*.[76]

A nurse could deduct amounts she paid to a nurses' registry.[77] A hospital attendant was permitted to deduct the cost of repairs to a watch which he was *required* to wear by his employer.[78] In other cases, where possession of a watch was not required, deduction of repairs was not permitted.

An insurance broker could deduct premium differences absorbed by him when he improperly advised his clients of the costs of policies.[79]

A physician who worked for an employer could deduct premiums he paid for malpractice insurance.[80]

A university research associate was expected by his employer to publish articles on his scientific pursuits. One article of particular value was not accepted by any scholarly publication, possibly because of professional dissension about the research technique used. He finally decided to finance the printing of this piece himself. The cost was deductible on the ground that his employer expected (although did not require) its research staff to publish the results of the research.[81]

The cost to an employee of a routine physical examination to establish his physical fitness in order to retain his position was deductible as a business expense, but any additional expense for medical or physical correction would only be deductible if it met the medical-expense requirements.[82]

Defense of one's professional acts is also deductible.[83]

Liquidated damages paid to one's former employer because of breach of an employment contract are deductible as a business loss if they are attributable to compensation received for services rendered.[84] For example, Jesse Hunt, a mason, worked for the Miller Industrial Corporation under the terms of a contract which called for Hunt to construct a brick wall around the entire perimeter of the Miller complex in one year's time. The entire cost of the project was $20,000, one-half of which was to be paid in advance. The amount of liquidation damages established by the contract was $7,000. After working for three months, Hunt found that he could not complete the project under the terms of the contract for less than twice the original cost agreed upon. In order to save himself from such a big loss, Hunt defaulted on the employment contract, thereby having to pay the $7,000 liquidation damages out of his $10,000 advance. He could properly deduct the $7,000 as a business loss.

An airline flight officer was allowed to deduct the cost of his navigation kits and maps.[85] A college professor may deduct his research, lecturing, and writing expenses.[86]

The initiation fee required to be paid by an individual to a labor union in order to obtain employment is deductible.[87]

A sales representative for a graphics company was obliged to install, maintain, and service equipment sold to his customers. In order to perform this work, it was necessary for him to have a full complement of hand tools. These were not supplied by his employer, and the cost was not reimbursable. He could deduct the cost.[88]

Monthly dues and assessments paid by members of a labor

union are deductible business expenses except for any portion of the assessments used to provide death benefits.[89]

An unemployed electrician was allowed to deduct the costs of going to his union's hall twice daily for extended periods so that he could learn of any jobs that were posted. Although unemployed, he still was engaged in the electrical construction trade, even though not working for any particular employer at these times.[90]

Assessments for benefit payments to unemployed union members are deductible to the extent that they are applied to out-of-work benefit payments to unemployed members capable of working.[91] Payments for union assessments which members are required to make for the support of an old-age pension fund are deductible where a member must pay his assessment in order to remain in the union and to retain his job.[92] An employee who was obligated to pay a fine imposed against him by his union could deduct the amount of the payment when the fine had to be paid in order to remain in the union.[93]

Persons who are not members of a union may deduct check-off fees payable to the union which must be withheld from the compensation of *all* employees under a union contract.[94]

Employee contributions to the New Jersey Nonoccupational Disability Benefit and its New York equivalent are deductible by employees as state income taxes.[95]

An employee may deduct business transportation expenses in computing adjusted gross income even though they are neither reimbursable by his employer nor incurred while traveling away from home.[96] Among the expenses included in traveling expenses are charges for transportation of persons or baggage, expenditures for meals and lodging, and payments for the use of sample rooms for the display of goods.[97] But an employee must be away from home overnight in order to deduct the cost of his meals on business trips.[98]

An employee away from home on business could deduct the cost of his meals and nonalcoholic beverages in excess of the amount of reimbursement he received from his employer.[99]

Despite the rule that an individual cannot deduct the cost of his own meals unless he is away from home overnight on business, employer requirements can create employee deductions. An employee was permitted to take a deduction for the cost of his meals when he was required by his employer to have his meals on the work premises at his own expense. Here, to prevent racial discrimination, all employees were ordered to eat at the same time and place which, because of the requirements of the job, had to be on the employer's premises. Each employee was billed, and could deduct, the proportionate share of actual expenses.[100]

A salaried person ordinarily may not deduct entertainment expenses. But if he can show that his employer required or expected him to incur entertainment expenses in connection with his work, he may deduct the expenses, assuming that he can satisfy the record-keeping requirements.[101] A field manager of a pharmaceutical manufacturer supervised fifteen salesmen. He spent some of his own money on salesmen or their families for bowling, theater, candy, toys, and the like in order to bring about good relations so that the business of his employer could prosper and his own earnings would increase. Deduction was allowed.[102]

An employer's business expenses are deductible by the employer. If an employee pays for company expenses, he is entitled to receive reimbursement, and hence the expenses are not his to deduct, even if, for some reason, he fails to seek reimbursement. But if he is not entitled to reimbursement, the expenses of the employer which he pays are deductible by him provided the expenditures also are in furtherance of his own business career.

An individual was an advertising solicitor for *Time* magazine. He was able to deduct entertainment expense because of evidence that he was expected to entertain company clients and would not be reimbursed. A memorandum from his business manager stated:

Mr. Luce and other Management officers have often emphasized that TIME salesmen are paid high salaries because selling is not a routine job and makes demands on a man's time and money that cannot be accounted for minute-by-minute or penny-by-penny. There are many expenses incidental to selling which a salesman is not expected to recover from the Company on top of his salary. In a very true sense, a salesman's job never ceases. And almost without exception his business life is closely interwoven with his personal social life. I make this point again because there are new men on the TIME staff who may never have heard of it. And because it explains why the Management does not expect an expense account to contain every phone call, every taxi ride, every luncheon and every drink bought by a salesman in the course of his business and social existence.

He was allowed to deduct his expenses.[103]

Deduction by the employee requires that he show that he was expected to pay company entertainment expenses or specified company expenses from his own pocket according to an agreement with his superior.[104] The general manager of a corporation could deduct his expenses of entertaining company customers when a jury was satisfied that he could not have obtained reimbursement from his employer.[105]

A bakery-route salesman working on a strictly commission basis could deduct his expenses in occasionally taking grocers to lunch and in buying soft drinks and coffee for certain customers in order to promote goodwill and to increase his sales and commissions. The court agreed with his labeling of these transactions on his income tax return, "Entertainment expense (to secure and/or retain patronage)."[106] An employee of a management-consulting firm spent much of his time on the road, where he was allowed reasonable traveling and living expenses. He could deduct payments for public stenographers, typewriter rentals, calculator rentals, blueprints, drafting materials, and technical books for which he could not get reimbursement from his employer.[107]

See also **Commuting; Education; Employee benefit-plan losses; Employment, expenses in seeking; Employment agency fees; Interviews; Office at home; Uniforms.**

Employer, expenses of. See **Compensation; Contributions; Conventions; Ordinary and necessary business expenses; Violation of rights, payments to settle.**

Employment, expenses in seeking. In 1975, the Internal Revenue Service reconsidered the position which it had previously taken. The Service now takes the position that expenses incurred in seeking new employment *in the same trade or business* are deductible if the expenses are directly connected with that trade or business as determined by all the facts and circumstances. But such expenses are not deductible if an individual is seeking employment *in a new trade or business* even if employment is secured. If the individual is unemployed at the time of the expenditure, his trade or business would consist of the services previously performed for his past employer where no substantial lack of continuity occurred between the time of the past employment and the seeking of the new employment. Such expenses are not deductible by an individual where there is a substantial lack of continuity between the time of the past employment and the seeking of the new employment, or by an individual who is seeking employment for the first time.[108]

An individual became disenchanted with his employer's future prospects and decided to seek a comparable position elsewhere. Expenses in attending scheduled interviews with interested would-be employers were allowable as deductions from gross income in computing his adjusted gross income.

Expenses for typing, printing, and postage related to the sending out of resumes could be deducted by a person who itemized his deductions.[109]

An attorney worked for a state agency. He was worried lest this agency's activities be curtailed. His transportation expenses in going to another city to take an examination for a position as court administrator were deductible, being expenses in seeking new employment in the same trade or business, that is, being a lawyer.[110]

Employment agency fees. Fees paid to an employment agency for *securing* employment are deductible.[111] But for executives seeking top positions and the compensation packages which go with them, much individualized effort may be necessary to find the ideal place, which no employment agency will undertake without an assured fee (usually substantial, in view of the work necessary), regardless of whether suitable employment ultimately is found. Payments made to an executive-search agency (not an employment agency) were deductible at the time when paid where employment was not found until long after the close of the taxable year when the payment was made.[112] Payments to an executive-search agency were deductible even though the executive never accepted a new position that was offered, his old employer having agreed to match the offered terms.[113]

Such payments were held to be deductible even though, because of economic conditions or otherwise, the payor did not succeed in obtaining a better position.[114] And fees of this nature were deemed to be deductible even though the payor had become disenchanted with the executive-search agency and terminated the relationship before anything was done for him.[115]

The executive vice-president of a corporation was fired by his longtime employer. The ex-officer paid a substantial fee to an executive-search agency, but he was not able to deduct the payment. Expenses incurred in connection with one's trade or business are deductible. But an employee who is out of work cannot be said to be in the trade or business of being an executive. One is not considered to be performing his trade or business when he is out of a job. "It stretches the imagination to say that one is carrying on his trade or business as a corporate executive when he has no corporation for which to be an executive," observed the court.[116] To get the deduction one should be sure to make the payment to an executive-search agency before he loses his position.

Entertainment. No deduction is allowed for entertainment unless an individual establishes (1) that the expenditure was directly related to the active conduct of his trade or business, or (2) in the case of an expenditure directly preceding or following a substantial and *bona fide* business discussion (including business meetings at conventions or otherwise), that the expenditure was associated with the active conduct of the individual's trade or business.[117]

An expenditure is deemed to be directly related to an individual's trade or business if it meets all four of the following tests:

1. At the time of the expenditure, the individual must have more than a general expectation of deriving income or a business benefit other than goodwill at some indefinite future time.

2. During the entertainment period, the individual is actually engaged in a business meeting, negotiation, discussion, or other *bona fide* transaction, other than entertainment, for the purpose of obtaining a business benefit.

3. The principal character of the expenditure must be the active conduct of the individual's trade or business. It is not necessary that more time be devoted to business than to entertainment to meet this requirement.

4. The expenditure is allocable to the individual and a person or persons with whom he engages in the active conduct of trade or business during the entertainment or with whom he would be so engaged if it were not for circumstances beyond the individual's control.

In all the above instances, the expenditure must be in a "clear business setting."

The following expenditures generally are considered not directly related to an individual's business and would not be allowed as deductions:

1. The individual is not present.

2. The distractions are substantial, e.g., meetings or discussions are held at nightclubs, theaters, sporting events, or cocktail parties.

Expenditures for food and drink will be allowed without reference to the above limitations where the circumstances are conducive to business discussions, even if business is not actually discussed. But the surroundings must provide an atmosphere where there are no substantial distractions.[118]

There are nine exceptions to these rules. They are business meals, food and beverages for employees, expenses treated as compensation, reimbursed expenses of employees and independent contractors, recreational expenses for employees, employee or stockholder business meetings, meetings of business leagues, items available to the public, and entertainment sold to customers. Expenses covered by these exceptions are not subject to the regular restrictions for entertainment expenses; they are deductible if they qualify as ordinary and necessary business expenses.[119]

It is not necessary that income or business benefits actually result from every entertainment expenditure for which a deduction is claimed.[120]

"Goodwill" entertainment involves entertainment where business is not discussed. The cost or expense is deductible if the entertainment takes the form of a "quiet" business setting, which directly precedes or follows a substantial business discussion. "The surroundings should be such," declared the Internal Revenue Service, "that there are no substantial distractions to dinner."[121] For example, the parties may completely avoid any business discussions at dinner if these discussions take place right before or after the meal.

If an individual entertains a business customer under circumstances where the cost of entertaining a customer is deductible, and the customer's wife joins the individual and the customer because it is impracticable to entertain the customer without her (e.g., the customer is from out of town and has his wife traveling with him), the cost of entertaining the customer's wife also is deductible as an ordinary and necessary business expense. And if the taxpayer's wife joins them during the entertainment because the customer's wife is present, the cost of entertainment allocable to the taxpayer's wife also is deductible.[122]

If a person takes a customer to lunch for business goodwill purposes, and the customer's wife comes along, the expense will be allowed, even if they do not discuss business, where the surroundings are of the type generally considered conducive to discussing business. Should the host's wife accompany him in entertaining a customer in such surroundings, her part of the bill also is deductible whether or not the customer's wife also is present. The fact that the business-meal entertaining takes place at the taxpayer's home does not disqualify the deduction, as long as the food or beverages are served under circumstances conducive to business discussion. But in the case of business-meal entertaining, the taxpayer must clearly show that the expenditure is commercially rather than socially motivated.[123]

An individual, then, may deduct the cost of entertaining a customer, the customer's wife, and even his own wife under appropriate circumstances. But the deductibility of his own meal when he is not away from home overnight is a big question mark. Widely unnoticed is the fact that a number of decisions have held that unless the taxpayer demonstrates that the cost of a business meal exceeded that amount which he would have been required to spend in any event for his sustenance, no deduction will be allowed, for one's own meals represent a personal, nondeductible cost, and the individual would have had to feed himself even if a customer were not present. The fact that the taxpayer would not have spent nearly so much on his own meal had he not been entertaining a *bona fide* customer is something for him to prove, if he can.[124] Bar bills where a customer was present were not the basis for *any* deduction where there was no indication of purchases for the taxpayer's own consumption.[125]

One court has noted that "if taxpayer can show . . . the maximum cost of his own lunches, a deduction for the remaining amount should be allowed."[126] It is an unusual situation when a taxpayer can do this. In one case, however, the taxpayer was a diabetic who was on a strict diet and did not use intoxicating liquors. He ate most of his meals, except lunches, at home. His lunches cost between 75 cents and $1, except when he entertained customers at lunch or dinner. Then he ordered mostly vegetables and coffee. Sometimes he ate nothing when he was with customers. Here the Internal Revenue Service was not able to assume that the portion of each lunch or dinner check chargeable to the host's food was equal to that chargeable to each guest, for the host had evidence to the contrary.[127] The I.R.S. has announced that this rule as to nondeductibility of an individual's own portion of entertainment expenses will be applied only in "abuse" cases.[128] Where this approach is táken, it is up to the taxpayer to demonstrate that there was no abuse in *his* particular situation.

Deduction of entertainment facility items has been curtailed sharply in the case of items paid or incurred after December 31, 1978, in taxable years ending after that date. Deduction no longer is allowed for expenses of an entertainment, amusement, or recreation facility. "Facility" for this purpose means any real or personal property which is owned, rented, or used by a taxpayer in connection with an entertainment activity, including yachts, hunting lodges, fishing camps, swimming pools, tennis courts, and bowling alleys. Facilities also include airplanes, cars, hotel suites, apartments, and houses (such as beach cottages and ski lodges) located in recreational areas. But business expense deduction is proper provided that a facility is not used in connection with *entertainment*. Thus, expenses of a car used primarily for business purposes other than entertainment still are deductible if properly substantiated.

"Facility" includes dues or fees paid to any social, athletic, or sporting club or organization. But otherwise deductible business meals are not disallowable merely because the expense was incurred in the dining room of a club or organization where dues or fees are not deductible under this rule. Dues or fees paid to a country club are deductible only if the taxpayer establishes that the facility was used primarily for the furtherance of his trade or business and that the expenses were directly related to the conduct of his trade or business.[129]

This illustration was furnished by the Congressional committee which wrote the legislation:

For example, if a salesman took a customer hunting for a day at a commercial shooting preserve, the expenses of the hunt (such as hunting rights, dogs, a guide, etc.) would be deductible provided that the current law requirements of substantiation, adequate records, ordinary and necessary, directly related, etc., are met. However, if the hunters stayed overnight at a hunting lodge on the shooting preserve, the cost attributable to the lodging would be non-deductible but expenses for any meals would be deductible if they satisfied the requirements of current law. The shooting preserve should provide the taxpayer with an allocation of charges attributable to the overnight lodging for the taxpayer and guests.[130]

Proof that an entertainment expense was business-related can come from showing why a particular person was entertained. An individual who was seeking investment advice could deduct the cost of meals furnished to persons in a position to give him such advice.[131] An anesthesiologist was allowed to deduct entertainment costs for physicians who referred patients to him.[132] Deduction was approved for the purchase of tickets from customers to promote goodwill.[133]

A business was unsuccessful in attracting customers during the normal daytime working hours. Dinners were therefore given for important clients. Expenses for these were allowed after the taxpayer produced charts which showed that business growth had paralleled increased promotional activities.[134]

A business could deduct its entertainment expenses where customers of its made-to-order machine parts were invited to partake of the host company's hospitality. Here the customers were urged to bring their own personal manufacturing problems for discussion with the host's staff and with other guests who had had to cope with the same or similar situations. The personal pleasure of persons invited may have been a factor in their attendance, but undeniably they hoped to derive business benefits from being there, and so did the host, who therefore could deduct business entertainment expenses.[135]

Deduction was allowed for the cost of taking partners and

business associates to lunch where there was evidence that business was discussed.[136] A person could deduct the cost of lunches for assistants with whom he discussed business.[137]

Proof is the essential ingredient in the allowance of travel and entertainment expenses. Unlike most deductions, reasonable estimates cannot be used; the so-called "*Cohan* rule," which permits a court to make its own estimate of undocumented expenses where it can be established that there were such expenditures, does not apply to travel and entertainment expenses.[138] In addition to the regular rules which control tax deductions with reference to being ordinary, necessary, reasonable, and the like, a special section of the Internal Revenue Code disallows travel and entertainment expenses which do not meet stringent additional requirements as to documentation.[139] There must be contemporary records for each such expenditure, showing cost, date, place, business purpose, nature of the business benefit expected, and business relationship to the taxpayer of the person or persons entertained.[140]

The strict rules for business entertainment deduction require a contemporary listing of who was entertained, where, etc., as detailed earlier in this section. A liquor salesman bought drinks at bars where he solicited orders, picking up the tab for owners, managers, bartenders, and their friends who happened to be on the spot. He recorded each day where he had spent the money, naming each bar and the proprietor, plus other persons unspecified. The Internal Revenue Service sought to disallow expenses where names were not named. But the court allowed full deduction. The requirement is that persons entertained be identified by name, title, or *other designation.* "Friends" or "customers" was sufficient identification of the business relationship of the expenditures to the salesman's business. The purpose of the substantiation requirement is only to encourage the taxpayer to maintain proper records, not to penalize him unduly for compliance peculiar to his trade or business.[141]

One court has repudiated the Internal Revenue Service regulation that such data be in writing. Even without meeting the Service requirements, declared this decision, a taxpayer can deduct travel and entertainment expenses if he backs up the expenses with adequate records or with sufficient evidence corroborating his own statement. There may be alternative methods of substantiation other than written records. "Thus," ruled this court, "oral testimony of the taxpayer, together with circumstantial evidence available, may be considered 'sufficient evidence' for the purpose of establishing the business purpose required under the new provision.[142] This means that properly substantiated oral testimony may be sufficient to back up travel and entertainment expenses.

If a taxpayer maintains a diary showing each person entertained, no receipts or other corroborating documentary evidence are required in the case of expenditures up to $25, except for lodging, and where receipts are readily available,for transportation.[143]

The tough substantiation requirements can be bypassed if entertainment expenses can be properly categorized under another classification. A business awarded trips to deserving dealer-customers; such trips covered an individual and his spouse. The wives of two of the business's principals acted as hostesses, performing personal services on weeklong trips in the interest of building customer goodwill. The court accepted the denomination of the $1,000 payments to each of the wives as compensation rather than entertainment expense; and hence the lack of detailed substantiation data was not fatal to the deduction.[144]

Deduction is allowed for entertainment of public officials where it is of a type prevalent in the industry and there is no administrative action in the state prohibiting the providing of such entertainment.[145]

Out-of-pocket expenditures spent on entertainment to promote a charitable ball by means of giving cocktail parties and dinners were deductible. It was noted in this ruling that the sponsor of these affairs had no control over the invitation list.[146]

If a taxpayer's substantiation data for entertainment expenses cannot be produced because of loss of such records through circumstances beyond his control, he has the right to substantiate a deduction by reasonable reconstruction of his expenditures.[147]

A persistent question in the case of a closely held corporation is whether the I.R.S. will recognize entertainment expenses incurred by an officer-shareholder as a corporate deduction. This is especially a problem where, as so often is the case with a closely held corporation, substantiation of the *business* nature of the entertainment is sketchy. To safeguard the corporation's interest, some companies in their bylaws provide that if the firm's entertainment expense deduction is disallowed by the Service because the expenditure appeared to be for the officer's personal benefit, he must repay the corporation for its lost deduction. He can then deduct the amount of this reimbursement as an expense in carrying on his trade or business.[148] *See also* **Executives; Ordinary and necessary business expenses.**

Errors, rectification of. See **Business-related losses; Shortages.**

Errors and omissions, policy premiums. *See* **Fiduciaries.**

Estate planning. Estate planning involves many items in connection with the disposition of a person's property, including in most instances Federal income, estate, and gift taxes. A fee related to the preparation of a tax return or the establishment of the tax is one of the relatively few personal expenditures which an individual can deduct for tax purposes. So payments for estate planning are deductible to the extent that it can be shown that the fees paid for the estate planning relate to taxes. An individual therefore should make certain that bills for estate-planning services clearly identify the portion of the charge which relates to taxes rather than the drawing up of a will, setting up of a trust, transfer of insurance policies, and the like.[149]

Excess charitable deductions. *See* **Contributions.**

Excessive compensation, repayment of. *See* **Executives; Repayment of excessive compensations.**

Executives. The president of a gigantic, prestigious, publicly held corporation is after all an employee, and he has the type of deduction available to employees in general. But because of the nature and scope of his duties, an executive may be entitled to various other additional deductions.

Serving as president of a corporation constitutes the carrying on of a trade or business.[150] Thus, expenses in connection with his trade or business are deductible by an officer.

An executive could deduct the cost of entertaining salesmen under his supervision, for this tended to build up business, which in turn affected his compensation.[151] A corporation president was allowed to deduct his membership fees in a Chamber of Commerce whether or not the corporation required him to take out the membership. He used this affiliation as a means of carrying out the essential duties of his employment; it enabled him to keep more readily abreast of business plans and of business and economic conditions in the community.[152]

In order to encourage directors and officers to make the "right" decision regardless of possible personal consequences, some corporations take out liability insurance to indemnify these persons if they are sued or otherwise held financially accountable for business acts. Lower-level executives customarily are not covered by such insurance, perhaps because they are less likely to be sued, perhaps because top management is not willing to have the corporation absorb costs involving the second team. When a corporation took out such liability insurance to indemnify nonofficer executives for the financial consequences of their business acts, and the executives were back-charged their proportionate shares of the premiums, the executives individually could deduct the costs as ordinary and necessary business expenses.[153]

Two individuals who were major but not the sole stockholders of a corporation transferred some of their stock back to the company in order to improve its financial condition. They could deduct their cost of this stock as an expense in connection with being employees, as their solution to the company's financial problem was intended to help the company pay their salaries.[154]

A corporate officer could deduct attorney's fees when defending himself against an effort to remove him from control and management.[155] Legal expenses in resisting attempts to dislodge him as an officer were deductible by an executive.[156] A corporation president properly deducted his expenses in connection with a lawsuit against the corporation for his ouster.[157]

Legal fees in connection with one's business or the production of income generally are deductible. Fees for personal, nonbusiness services are not. But the president of a corporation was permitted to deduct attorneys' fees in connection with changing the trustees of trusts she had created for her children. Some of the stockholders wanted to oust her from her high-salaried position, and the company shares which she had transferred to these trusts (5 percent of the total stock outstanding) might be voted by the trustees against her. So replacement of these trustees with persons willing to vote the stock in her favor constituted a deductible business expense: to continue on the payroll.[158]

An individual was a corporation executive and also a trustee and life-income beneficiary of a trust which owned all of the corporation's stock. Charges against him for mismanagement were filed by the trust's remaindermen. In settlement of this dispute he relinquished his life income in the trust. The value of the transferred interest was an ordinary and necessary business expense as an officer and director of the corporation. His malfeasance in the conduct of his paid corporate duties was a major part of the action against him.[159]

A corporate officer was permitted to deduct amounts he paid to settle a claim that he had violated a position of trust in permitting his wife to profit from transactions in the corporation's securities.[160]

The board chairman of a major steel-manufacturing company swore to all of its tax returns as chief executive officer. He was charged with conspiracy to defraud the government of taxes but was acquitted. The necessity of paying legal fees was occasioned by acts done in connection with his trade or business, and deduction was allowed.[161] Similarly, a corporate officer whose responsibilities included the filing of his company's Federal income tax returns was indicted for having caused the filing of a false corporate return where company funds were diverted to his own use. His legal fees in defending himself were deductible because they arose in connection with acts committed by him in his trade or business as an executive.[162]

Amounts expended in defending a suit against charges of breach of duty as a corporate officer are deductible.[163] Expenditures by an officer and director of a corporation in the successful defense of a stockholder's derivative suit were held to be deductible business expenses. While acting as an officer and director, he was engaged in carrying on a trade or business.[164]

A director of a corporation could deduct amounts paid to settle a stockholders' suit alleging incompetency in his duties.[165]

Stockholders sued the directors of a corporation for recovery of damages based upon alleged wrongful acts and omissions, and a court awarded judgment for a certain sum against one of the directors. He was not permitted to deduct his costs as being incurred in a trade or business, or in a transaction entered for profit. He did not, and did not expect to, receive any compensation or other monetary benefit for his services, having become a director solely out of friendship for the chief stockholder. He rarely attended a board meeting and was totally uninformed about the corporation's financial affairs. He could not be regarded as in the business of being a director. This decision illustrates what *should* be established in order to be allowed the deduction.[166]

An individual was president and a stockholder of a corporation which became insolvent. An employee threatened to sue him personally because the corporation had violated state law by not protecting its employees with Workmen's Compensation Insurance. The president's lawyer advised him that he might be personally liable to the claimant because the corporation could not provide any funds for employee demands. So the official compromised the claim for $2,000, which he paid. Even though his lawyer's advice might have been erroneous, he was justified in relying upon it, and he properly deducted the payment as an expense in connection with being an officer of the corporation.[167]

Stockholders of a corporation brought suit against the officers and directors of a corporation for alleged improper conduct. A settlement was reached under which each defendant would transfer a certain number of his shares or the cash equivalent to an agent for the stockholders. A director who transferred stock to this agent in order to satisfy his obligation was deemed to have made a disposition of his stock. So the difference between what he had paid for the shares and its value at the time of disposition was gain or loss. But inasmuch as his settlement obligation arose from his trade or business of being a director, loss was not capital but was a fully deductible business expense.[168]

A director of a corporation undergoing a reorganization was permitted to deduct his share of a settlement payment (including his attorney's fees) which arose from suits against him and the other directors in their respective capacities as directors.[169]

An executive could deduct the amount of a judgment obtained against him by his corporation for losses resulting from his unauthorized use of corporate funds for speculating in commodities, which he carried on solely for the benefit of the corporation.[170]

A financial consultant acted as an officer and consultant of public utility companies. He served as an officer and director of a corporation undergoing Section 77B Bankruptcy Act reorganization. He paid a sum in settlement of a claim which arose from an alleged breach of fiduciary duty because of certain profits made by his wife with respect to sales and purchases of the corporation's bonds. His payment was deductible, having been made in connection with his trade or business.[171]

Section 16(b) of the Securities Exchange Act of 1934 provides, in part, that for the purpose of preventing the unfair use of information which may have been obtained by an officer, director, or beneficial owner of more than 10 percent of the stock of a corporation, any profit realized by him from any purchase or sale, or any sale and purchase, of any equity security of the corporation within any period of less than six months shall inure to and be recoverable by the corporation. A deduction by reason of an insider's payment to a corporation pursuant to or as a result of this provision in the amount of profits derived in dealings in stock will not be denied on the ground that it frustrates sharply defined public policy.[172]

A corporate executive held various directorships, including a major listed motion-picture producing company. He had purchased enough of that stock to ensure his becoming a director. His purpose was to make a profit by improving the company's performance. When the Securities and Exchange Commission brought the matter to the company's attention, reminding the company that insider profits belong to the corporation, he was so advised. He believed that he was not covered because the violation, if such it was, resulted from inadvertence. But to avoid any adverse impact on his business reputation which a disclosure would occasion, he turned his profits over to the company. That amount was deductible by him as a business expense, to protect his reputation, which he considered to be his most important asset.[173] Although several other decisions have held that such payments are not deductible, those cases involved payment which the insider legally was obligated to make. Here the individual never consulted a lawyer but immediately repaid the amount, not because he felt it was a legal obligation but to safeguard his reputation for integrity. The payment was not made purely because he was required by law to make it; he had a business reason for making the payment.

The president and chief stockholder of a corporation was approached by a potential acquirer of the company, and all financial data were requested. The president became an officer of the acquirer after negotiations were completed. Subsequently the acquirer filed suit against him, alleging that he had fraudulently misrepresented his old company's liabilities, as a result of which substantial losses were incurred by the acquirer. Deeming this suit to be an attack upon his integrity and business reputation, he vigorously defended the suit, incurring substantial legal and accounting fees which he deducted as ordinary and necessary expenses. The court permitted these as expenses in connection with his trade or business of being a corporate officer. Counsel for his new employer had advised him that if the charges were substantiated, he would have to resign as an officer and director because the new employer was a listed company which might be harmed by the publicity.[174]

Expenses to protect one's business reputation are deductible, such as in the case of the president of a personal service corporation which bore his name. The company was unable to pay trade creditors. He feared that if the company with his name went bankrupt, that would damage his own reputation. He could deduct the amount of the company bills which he paid with his own funds.[175]

The chief executive officer of a manufacturing company was responsible for operations. When the shareholders sold their stock to another company, the latter subsequently demanded a reduction in price because of shortages and errors, which was granted. The equivalent of this amount was deducted from moneys payable to the chief executive on account of his allegedly poor performance. He in turn could deduct this amount as an expense in connection with his business of being an executive.[176]

Ordinarily, a shareholder may not take a tax deduction for a payment made on behalf of the corporation. But the payment may be deducted as an ordinary and necessary expense of a trade or business of the shareholder. An individual was an officer and purchasing agent of an industrial-plumbing corporation, I. He also owned all the stock of a corporation, G, which was engaged in residential heating. G was in severe financial trouble, and the directors of his employer company, I, were worried about the impact of the insolvency of a firm with which he was known in the trade to be closely identified. In fact, the I directors felt it would be impossible for him to continue as purchasing agent, where he would have to make terms with creditors who were familiar with the impending bankruptcy of his own company, G. It was remembered that some years before he had also been associated with a bankrupt firm, and suppliers might be reluctant to sell on credit to a company, I, whose purchasing agent had consistently been associated with losers. Feeling that his job was in danger, he attempted to protect his position by personally making settlement with G's creditors. The payments were made by him, not to put new life into G nor to protect his investment in it, but to protect his job with I. Accordingly, he could deduct the payments he made to G's creditors as expenses related to his business of being an employee of Corporation I.[177]

When an executive bought stock in his corporation to prevent a buy-out that would have cost him his job, subsequent loss upon disposition of the stock was fully deductible as a business expense, for the business was transacted in order to maintain his employment.[178]

An executive may deduct as education expense his costs for improving the managerial skills needed in his employment.[179]

An executive could deduct expenses of a telephone in his home during a period when he was confined there by illness.[180]

The executive head of a corporation worked on a commission basis. He employed other persons, whom he personally paid, to help him increase his sales and commissions. The salaries he paid were deductible as expenses in connection with his business of being the head of the company.[181] A corporate officer claiming a deduction for travel and entertainment expenses will get the deduction if he can show that such expenses relate directly to his own business activities.[182]

In general, expenses of corporate entertaining are deductible only by the corporation; the expenses are corporate and not those of the officers, however much they may identify themselves with the company. But if payment of entertainment expenses helps an officer to do his job better, the fact that the corporation also benefits does not bar the officer's deduction. The vice-president of a New York City bank could deduct his substantiated expenses for entertaining persons whose favor the bank wanted, for the entertainment enabled the officer to discharge his implied duty. As the bank had given him to understand that he was to extend hospitality to certain clients, and nothing was said about reimbursement, the expenses were necessary for his office.[183]

A bank officer received "suggestions" from his superiors that he join certain clubs for the better performance of his duties, and after his salary was increased, they made it clear to him that he was personally expected to bear the expense of his club dues. "To be sure," observed the court, "they did not threaten to discharge him if he failed to comply with their suggestions; but the purport of such suggestions was obvious."[184]

A vice-president in charge of production for a major listed tobacco company had responsibilities which included extensive entertaining. It was held that his bills were properly deductible by him because they were incurred in connection with earning his income.[185]

The president of a corporation was not on a guaranteed salary. A significant part of his compensation represented commissions on sales he made for the corporation. He was on an incentive basis, and in order to earn these commissions, it was necessary to entertain prospective customers to get their business. He was entitled to the deduction for this entertainment cost, not being able to get reimbursement from the corporation for his expenses.[186]

In another case, a vice-president and regional manager of a leading paper company had as his principal responsibility the maintenance of "first-name" contacts and relationships with top-echelon officers of major business enterprises throughout his region. To keep such high-level contacts, he joined a number of clubs. His arrangement with the company president was that entertainment expenses for large parties were subject to reimbursement, while usual and ordinary expenses were to be paid from his own funds. To maintain his status position and appropriate image with the company's board of directors and president, he believed that it was necessary that he pay for ordinary expenses. These expenditures were deductible.[187]

A corporate officer who claims deductions for travel and entertainment expenses incurred on behalf of a corporation must bear the burden of proof that *he* is entitled to the deduction. A directors' resolution requiring the assumption of such expenses by him tends to indicate that they are a necessary expense of his office.[188]

An executive may be required by corporate bylaw or otherwise to reimburse the corporation to the extent of any entertainment expense the company paid on his behalf, if the Internal Revenue Service disallows it as unsubstantiated from the point of view of the corporation's business. Then he is permitted to deduct the amount which he pays the corporation to make good its lost deduction.[189]

In an interoffice memorandum a company advised its executives that although entertainment expenses for existing customers would be reimbursed, expenses for potential new business would not be reimbursed by the company and would have to be borne by the individual incurring them unless the president and the treasurer specifically authorized them. An executive's entertainment expenses for potential customers were deemed to be deductible to a considerable extent and perhaps would have been allowed in full had his records been better kept.[190]

Where the officers of a corporation were required to incur travel and other expenses of the corporation without expectation of reimbursement, these expenses were deductible as ordinary and necessary expenses of being an executive of the corporation.[191]

If an executive personally pays the salary of someone to handle his duties when he is not available, the cost of the substitute is a deduction for the executive.[192]

An individual paid a fee to a psychological-study organization for a basic psychological examination and for counseling services to the degree of success he might obtain as a business executive. Through these efforts he actually obtained a position. He could deduct the fees as expenses in securing employment.[193]

If a corporation loses part of a compensation deduction because it is deemed to be unreasonable, the payee (usually an officer or executive) may be called upon, directly or indirectly, to restore to the company the amount of its lost tax deduction. All sorts of pressures may be placed upon him to do so. But if he does repay the amount of disallowed compensation for the prior year, he will not get a tax deduction; business expenses must be ordinary and necessary, and this is neither. It is not ordinary for an executive to pay back money his employer could not justify to the Internal Revenue Service as reasonable. It is not necessary to make the payment in the absence of a legal obligation to do so. But his deduction in case of repayment can be assured in either of these ways:

1. Notation in the directors' minutes. *Actual example:* Salary payments made to an officer of the corporation that shall be disallowed in whole or in part as a deductible expense for Federal income tax purposes shall be reimbursed to the full extent of the disallowance. It shall be the duty of the Board of Directors to enforce payment of such amount disallowed.[194]

2. Corporate bylaws. *Actual example:* Any payments made to an officer of the corporation such as salary, commission, bonus, or rent or entertainment expense incurred by him, which shall be disallowed in whole or in part as a deductible expense by the Internal Revenue Service, shall be reimbursable to the full extent of the disallowance. It shall be the duty of the Directors, as a Board, to enforce payment of each such amount disallowed. In lieu of a payment by the officer, subject to the determination of the Directors, proportionate amounts may be withheld from his future compensation until the amount owed to the corporation has been recovered.[195] *See also* **Education; Employment agency fees; Entertainment; Guarantors; Reputation, maintenance of; Travel.**

Executive-search agency fees. *See* **Employment agency fees.**

Executor's fees. As a general rule, expenses of a casual executor, administrator, or trustee are not deductible. But where an individual undertook the duties of executrix with intent to secure compensation therefor, and she was in fact allowed a substantial fee by the probate court, her services could not be deemed to be so insignificant as to deny them the characterization of business activities.[196] Similarly, a trustee could deduct legal expenses resulting from a suit by a beneficiary which demanded an accounting, sought restoration by the trustee of losses from improper investments, and attempted to have a new trustee appointed. On a do-it-yourself basis, she also could deduct the cost of law texts for her own use.[197]

An individual had been named by the decedent, his father, to be one of his three coexecutors. The son had limited business and financial experience. But the administration of the estate required financial and business skill ordinarily associated with the conduct of large enterprises and available only to persons who had years of intimate knowledge of the details of the business. The other two coexecutors had such experience, and the son felt that his own heavy responsibilities should be delegated to them. He arranged to pay them for relieving him of unfamiliar chores in the form of a percentage of the executors' fees he would receive. The fees he thus paid them were deductible by him as nontrade or nonbusiness expenses incurred for the production of income.[198]

Ex-employee, inducement to return after military duty. *See* **Ordinary and necessary business expenses.**

Expenditures for benefits lasting more than one year. Ordinarily, expenditures for business benefits which will be enjoyed over a period of years must be capitalized rather than expensed currently. Following are areas where the full expense could be taken in the year of payment or incurrence:

1. Survey of future financing requirements.[199]
2. Fees paid to an accountant to investigate the advisability of a change in the taxpayer's accounting system.[200]
3. Management survey.[201]
4. Fees of efficiency engineers to increase the taxpayer's production at reduced cost.[202]
5. In many states, employers subject to the state unemployment insurance law are permitted to make voluntary payments in excess of the regular rate. Inasmuch as the state unemployment insurance tax rate in such places is based upon a ratio of employer contributions to claims filed by ex-employees now out of work, a favorable ratio will entitle the employer to a lower tax rate in the future. Such voluntary payments are deductible as ordinary and necessary expenses when made, although the objective is to reduce the rate of *future* tax payments to the state.[203]

Expenses for obtaining a long-term lease (e.g., a broker's commission or lawyer's fee) are amortizable over the life of the lease, regardless of the taxpayer's accounting method.[204] Any renewal period is to be considered in determining the period over which amortization of cost is allowed, but *only* if less than 75 percent of the cost is attributable to the portion of the lease (excluding the renewal period) remaining on the acquisition date. This rule will apply unless it is established at the close of the taxable year that the lease probably will not be renewed.[205]

Where loan commitment fees are for a short period, they are deductible. They must be amortized over the period of a loan or mortgage for a period of more than a year.[206]

Individuals must capitalize the costs of producing motion pictures, records, and similar properties, including the cost of making prints of a film for distribution. These capitalized costs may be deducted over the life of the income stream generated from the production activity. This provision applies to amounts paid or incurred after December 31, 1975, with respect to property the principal production of which began after that date.[207]

The cost of a license or franchise is amortizable over its life.[208] Where a franchise is indefinitely renewable so that there is no reasonably determinable life over which to spread the cost, there is no amortization deduction.[209] But where the holder of an automobile distributorship franchise which was indefinitely renewable could show that General Motors Corporation had the authority to terminate a franchise upon the holder's death, and in fact frequently did so, he could amortize the cost over his own life expectancy.[210]

A physician paid a onetime hospital-staff-privilege fee. He was permitted to deduct his cost ratably over the number of years in his life expectancy.[211]

Ordinarily, payments to eliminate competition are not deductible. But where the elimination of competition is for a fixed and limited term, the cost could be spread and deducted over that period.[212] Similarly, the cost of a covenant from the former owner of a business not to compete with the new owner is not deductible unless the covenant is for a stipulated number of years, in which event the cost can be amortized.[213]

In general, the cost of construction of property with estimated business usefulness of more than one year must be capitalized over the period of contemplated benefits; in the case of a road, where that period may be unmeasurable, no deductions at all may be available. Payment of the cost of construction of a new highway was deductible by a food processor whose property otherwise would have been substantially destroyed by a new state highway running through it. The cost of a new alternative road to be paid for by the food processor was acceptable to the state for its purposes, and the company could deduct this amount because the expenditure did not add to the value of the property but was for the purpose of reducing or minimizing loss or injury to existing property.[214]

Expenses of a trip to Washington in connection with an additional tax assessed on the taxpayer's trade or business are deductible.[215]

Amounts paid to an appraiser to determine the proper amount of a casualty or theft loss may be deducted.[216]

Amounts paid to a title insurance company to determine whether local tax assessments were properly made against property held by the taxpayer are similarly deductible.[217] See *also* **Removal of impediments to the physically handicapped; Repairs.**

Experimental expenses. In the case of research and experimental expenditures, a taxpayer may elect either to deduct them as expenses or to capitalize them for amortization and deduction over a period of not less than 60 months.[218]

Expenses relating to the acquisition of inventory are not currently deductible but are added to the cost of inventory. That is what you must do with research and experimental costs incurred in the fabrication of your products, the I.R.S. told a manufacturer of office equipment. To the contrary, ruled the court, for research and experimental costs may be deducted, if the taxpayer wants to handle them in that way, even though they relate to inventory or production equipment.[219] Nearly eight years later, the Internal Revenue Service announced that it will be guided by the court's decision.[220] *See also* **Depreciation; Election to deduct or to capitalize; Legal expenses; Mortgage loan fees and commissions; Refinancing fees; Repairs.**

Expropriation losses. *See* **Foreign expropriation losses.**

Extortion payments. *See* **Casualties.**

Eyeglasses. *See* **Medical expenses.**

E

E

1. *McDonald, Sr., et al. v. Commissioner*, T.C. Memo. 1977-202, filed June 29, 1977.
2. *Ranchers Exploration and Development Corporation v. United States*, . . . F. Supp. . . . (D.C., N.M., 1978).
3. *Tax Information on Educational Expenses*, I.R.S. Publication 508, 1976 edition, page 1.
4. Regulations Section 1.162-5(b)(2)(i)(2).
5. *Laurano et al. v. Commissioner*, 69 T.C., No. 60 (1978).
6. *Sherman v. Commissioner*, T.C. Memo. 1977-301, filed September 7, 1977.
7. *Picknally v. Commissioner*, T.C. Memo. 1977-321, filed September 20, 1977.
8. *Peter G. Corbett et al.*, 55 T.C. 884 (1971).
9. *John C. Ford*, 56 T.C. 1300 (1971).
10. Regulations Section 1.162-5(a)(2).
11. *William et al. v. United States*, 238 F. Supp. 351 (D.C., S.D. N.Y., 1965).
12. *Marvin Leroy Lund et al.*, 46 T.C. 321 (1966).
13. *Ruth Domigan Truxall*, T.C. Memo. 1962-137, filed June 5, 1962.
14. *Tax Information on Educational Expenses*, I.R.S. Publication 508, 1976 edition, page 1.
15. *William J. Brennan et al.*, T.C. Memo. 1963-243, filed September 10, 1963.
16. *John S. Watson*, 31 T.C. 1014 (1959).
17. Regulations Section 1.162-5(b).
18. Revenue Ruling 74-78, 1974-1 CB 44.
19. Regulations Section 1.162-5(c)(1).

E

124

20. *Coughlin v. Commissioner*, 203 F.2d 307 (2d Cir., 1953).
21. *Cosimo A. Carlucci*, 37 T.C. 695 (1962).
22. Revenue Ruling 69-199, 1969-1 CB 51.
23. *Ben (Bong) H. Kim et al.*, T.C. Memo. 1969-126, filed June 23, 1969.
24. *John D. Glascow et al.*, T.C. Memo. 1972-77, filed March 28, 1972.
25. *Cosimo A. Carlucci*, 37 T.C. 695 (1962).
26. *Ralph A. Fattore*, T.C. Memo. 1963-219, filed August 20, 1963.
27. *Walter C. Lage et al.*, 52 T.C. 130 (1969).
28. *Frieda Hempel*, T.C. Memo., Docket No. 7993, entered June 23, 1947.
29. *Alan Aaronson*, T.C. Memo. 1970-178, filed June 25, 1970.
30. Regulations Section 1.162-5(b)(3).
31. *Marshall L. Helms, Jr., et al.*, T.C. Memo. 1968-207, filed September 19, 1968.
32. *Richard M. Baum et al.*, T.C. Memo. 1964-37, filed February 18, 1964.
33. *Donald P. Frazee et al.*, T.C. Memo. 1963-217, filed August 19, 1963.
34. *Campbell et al. v. United States*, 250 F. Supp. 941 (D.C., E.D. Pa., 1966).
35. *Walter T. Charlton et al.*, T.C. Memo. 1964-59, filed March 10, 1964.
36. *Welsh et al. v. United States*, 210 F. Supp. 597 (D.C., N.D. Ohio, 1962), *aff'd*, 329 F.2d 145 (6th Cir., 1964).
37. *Ibid.*
38. Revenue Ruling 69-607, 1969-2 CB 40.
39. Regulations Section 1.162-5(d).
40. *Elliott v. United States*, 250 F. Supp. 322 (D.C., W.D. N.Y., 1965).
41. *Duncan v. Bookwalter*, 216 F. Supp. 301 (D.C., W.D. Mo., 1963).
42. *Gladys M. Smith*, T.C. Memo. 1967-246, filed December 8, 1967.
43. *Tax Information on Educational Expenses*, I.R.S. Publication 508, 1976 edition, page 3.
44. *Gibbons, Jr., et al. v. Commissioner*, T.C. Memo. 1978-75, filed February 27, 1978.
45. Revenue Ruling 64-176, 1964-1 CB (Part 1) 87.
46. *Tax Information on Educational Expenses*, I.R.S. Publication 508, 1976 edition, page 3.
47. Regulations Section 1.162-5(e).
48. *Reuben B. Hoover*, 35 T.C. 566 (1961).
49. *Gudmundsson et al. v. Commissioner*, T.C. Memo. 1978-299, filed August 1, 1978.
50. Regulations Section 1.266-1(b).
51. Regulations Section 1.612-4.
52. I.R.C. Section 616.
53. I.R.C. Section 617.
54. I.R.C. Section 174.
55. Revenue Ruling 71-162, 1971-1 CB 97.
56. Revenue Ruling 76-324, 1976-2 CB 77.
57. *James v. United States*, 366 U.S. 213 (1961).
58. Regulations Section 1.274-3(b)(2)(iii).
59. Revenue Ruling 72-305, 1972-1 CB 116.
60. Revenue Ruling 72-328, 1972-2 CB 224.
61. Revenue Ruling 62-180, 1962-2 CB 52.
62. *Nidetch v. Commissioner*, T.C. Memo. 1978-313, filed August 11, 1978.
63. *Other Miscellaneous Deductions*, I.R.S. Publication 529, 1976 edition, page 3.
64. *Protecting Older Americans Against Overpayment of Taxes*, Special Committee on Aging, United States Senate, 1976, page 5.
65. *Albert L. Sanderson*, T.C. Memo., Docket No. 56830, entered January 31, 1957.

66. *Arthur Brookfield*, T.C. Memo., Docket No. 51372, entered March 12, 1956.
67. *Irving L. Schein*, T.C. Memo., Docket No. 32717, entered February 29, 1952.
68. *Ronald D. Kroll*, 49 T.C. 557 (1968).
69. *Emil J. Michaels*, 53 T.C. 269 (1969).
70. *Beatrice H. Albert*, 13 T.C. 129 (1949).
71. *Your Federal Income Tax*, 1976 edition, page 70.
72. I.T. 3728, 1945 CB 78.
73. Form 2106, "Employee Business Expense."
74. *Richard Keith Johnson*, T.C. Memo. 1972-192, filed September 6, 1972.
75. *LeRoy W. Gillis et al.*, T.C. Memo. 1973-96, filed April 24, 1973.
76. *Virginia C. Avery*, T.C. Memo. 1970-269, filed September 23, 1970.
77. *Albert R. McGovern et al.*, 42 T.C. 1148 (1964), *aff'd on another issue*, 6th Cir., 1966.
78. *Oliver W. Bryant*, T.C. Memo., Docket No. 27114, entered May 2, 1952.
79. *Boyle, Flagg & Seaman, Inc.*, 25 T.C. 43 (1955).
80. Revenue Ruling 60-365, 1960-2 CB 49.
81. *Drury v. Commissioner*, T.C. Memo. 1977-199, filed June 2, 1977.
82. Revenue Ruling 58-382, 1958-2 CB 59.
83. S.M. 4078, V-1 CB 226.
84. *Other Miscellaneous Deductions*, I.R.S. Publication 529, 1976 edition, page 3.
85. *Dean L. Phillips*, T.C. Memo., Docket Nos. 18410-2, entered June 9, 1950.
86. *Miscellaneous Deductions and Credits*, I.R.S. Publication 529, 1976 edition, page 1.
87. I.T. 3634, 1944 CB 90.
88. *McCollum et al. v. Commissioner*, T.C. Memo. 1978-435, filed November 1, 1978.
89. Revenue Ruling 72-463, 1972-2 CB 93.
90. *McKinley et al. v. Commissioner*, T.C. Memo. 1978-428, filed October 30, 1978.
91. *Miscellaneous Deductions and Credits*, I.R.S. Publication 529, 1976 edition, page 2.
92. Revenue Ruling 54-190, 1954-1 CB 46.
93. Revenue Ruling 69-214, 1969-1 CB 52.
94. I.R.S. Letter Ruling 7828050, April 13, 1978.
95. Internal Revenue News Release IR-1967, March 10, 1978.
96. I.R.C. Section 62(2)(c).
97. Regulations Section 1.62-1(e).
98. *United States v. Correll*, 389 U.S. 299 (1967).
99. *Floyd DeRieux*, T.C. Memo. 1958-146, filed July 29, 1958.
100. *Robert E. Cooper*, 67 T.C. 870 (1977).
101. *Your Federal Income Tax*, 1976 edition, page 70.
102. *Harold A. Christensen*, 17 T.C. 46 (1952).
103. *Julius (Jay) C. Henricks*, T.C. Memo., Docket No. 16192, entered November 8, 1949.
104. *Holland et al. v. United States*, 311 F. Supp. 422 (D.C., C.D. Cal., 1970).
105. *Fallon et al. v. United States*, D.C., N.D. Texas, 1957.
106. *Marshall J. Hammons et al.*, T.C. Memo., Docket No. 31518, entered November 24, 1953.
107. *Thomas M. B. Hicks, Jr., et al.*, T.C. Memo. 1960-48, filed March 24, 1960.
108. Revenue Ruling 75-120, 1975-1 CB 55.
109. Revenue Ruling 77-16, 1977-1 CB 37.
110. *Leisner et al. v. Commissioner*, T.C. Memo. 1977-205, filed July 5, 1977.
111. Revenue Ruling 60-223, 1960-1 CB 57.
112. *David J. Primuth*, 54 T.C. 374 (1970).

113. *Kenneth R. Kenfield*, 54 T.C. 1197 (1970).
114. *Leonard J. Cremona et al.*, T.C. Memo. 1972-66, filed March 14, 1972.
115. *R. E. Blewitt, Jr., et al.*, T.C. Memo. 1972-247, filed December 12, 1972.
116. *Miller et al. v. United States*, 362 F. Supp. 1242 (D.C., E.D. Tenn., 1973).
117. I.R.C. Section 274.
118. Regulations Section 1.274-2.
119. Revenue Ruling 63-144, 1963-2 CB 129.
120. *Ibid.*
121. *Ibid.*
122. Revenue Ruling 68-144, 1963-2 CB 129.
123. *Ibid.*
124. *Richard A. Sutter*, 21 T.C. 170 (1953).
125. *Hughes v. Commissioner*, 451 F.2d 975 (2d Cir., 1971).
126. *LaForge et al. v. Commissioner*, 434 F.2d 370 (2d Cir., 1970).
127. *Max Plishner et al.*, T.C. Memo. 1962-208, filed August 30, 1962.
128. Revenue Ruling 63-144, 1963-2 CB 129.
129. Revenue Act of 1978, Section 361.
130. *Conference Committee Report on Revenue Bill of 1978.*
131. *Samuel Abrams et al.*, T.C. Memo. 1964-256, filed September 29, 1964.
132. *Wolf v. United States*, D.C., W.D. Mo., 1964.
133. *Victor J. McQuade*, 4 B.T.A. 837 (1926).
134. *First National Bank of Omaha v. United States*, 276 F. Supp. 905 (D.C., Neb., 1967).
135. *Berkley Machine Works & Foundry Company, Inc. v. Commissioner*, T.C. Memo. 1977-177, filed June 13, 1977.
136. *Lennon et al. v. Commissioner*, T.C. Memo. 1978-176, filed May 11, 1978.
137. *LaForge v. Commissioner*, 434 F.2d 370 (2d Cir., 1970).
138. Regulations Section 1.274-5(a)(3).
139. I.R.C. Section 274.
140. Regulations Section 1.274-5(b)(3).
141. *Diller et al. v. Commissioner*, T.C. Memo. 1978-321, filed August 16, 1978.
142. *LaForge et al. v. Commissioner*, 434 F.2d 370 (2d Cir., 1970).
143. Regulations Section 1.274-5(c)(2)(i),(iii).
144. *Andrews Distributing Co., Inc.*, T.C. Memo. 1972-146, filed July 3, 1972.
145. *Dukehart-Hughes Tractor & Equipment Company, Inc., v. United States*, 341 F.2d 613 (Ct. Cl., 1965).
146. I.R.S. Letter Ruling 7726018, March 29, 1977.
147. Regulations Section 1.274-5(c)(5).
148. I.R.S. Letter Ruling 7811004, November 29; 1977.
149. *Sidney Merians et al.*, 60 T.C. 187 (1973).
150. *Ditmars et al. v. Commissioner*, 302 F.2d 481 (2d Cir., 1962).
151. *Harold A. Christensen*, 17 T.C. 1456 (1952).
152. Revenue Ruling 72-192, 1972-1 CB 48.
153. Revenue Ruling 76-77, 1976-1 CB 107.
154. *David N. Smith et al.*, 66 T.C. 622 (1976).
155. *Ingalls v. Patterson*, 158 F. Supp. 627 (D.C., N.D. Ala., 1958).
156. *Stanley V. Waldheim et al.*, T.C. 839 (1956), *aff'd on other issues*, 244 F.2d 1 (7th Cir., 1957).
157. *E. L. Potter*, 20 B.T.A. 252 (1930).
158. *Nidetch v. Commissioner*, T.C. Memo. 1978-313, filed August 11, 1978.
159. *J. Leroy Nickel, Jr., Estate*, T.C. Memo. 1962-55, filed March 15, 1962.
160. *William L. Butler*, 17 T.C. 675 (1951).
161. *Peoples-Pittsburgh Trust Company et al.*, 21 B.T.A. 588 (1930), *aff'd*, 60 F.2d 187 (3d Cir., 1932).

162. Revenue Ruling 68-662, 1968-2 CB 69.
163. *Ditmars et al. v. Commissioner,* 302 F.2d 481 (2d Cir., 1962).
164. *Hochschild v. Commissioner,* 161 F.2d 817 (2d Cir., 1947).
165. *Graham et al. v. Commissioner,* 326 F.2d 878 (4th Cir., 1964).
166. *DePinto et al. v. United States,* ... F.2d ... (9th Cir., 1978).
167. *Frank W. Byrne,* T.C. Memo., Docket No. 4090, entered September 7, 1945.
168. I.R.S. Letter Ruling 7802005, September 29, 1977.
169. I.R.S. Letter Ruling 7728004, April 6, 1977.
170. *Dixon Fagerberg,* B.T.A. Memo., Docket No. 103449, entered February 6, 1942.
171. *William L. Butler,* 17 T.C. 675 (1951).
172. Revenue Ruling 61-115, 1961-1 CB 46.
173. *Nathan Cummings et al.,* 60 T.C. 91 (1973).
174. *Mitchell et al. v. United States,* 405 F.2d 435 (Ct. Cl., 1969).
175. *Conley et al. v. Commissioner,* T.C. Memo. 1977-406, filed November 23, 1977.
176. *Murray R. Denemark et al.,* T.C. Memo. 1976-267, filed August 23, 1976.
177. *James O. Gould et al.,* 64 T.C. 132 (1975).
178. *Steadman et al. v. Commissioner,* 424 F.2d 1 (6th Cir., 1970).
179. *Cosimo A. Carlucci,* 37 T.C. 695 (1962).
180. *Dan R. Hanna, Jr., et al.,* T.C. Memo., Docket Nos. 25706 and 25707, entered June 6, 1951.
181. *John S. Thompson,* T.C. Memo., Docket No. 23817, entered August 14, 1950.
182. *Kornhauser v. United States,* 276 U.S. 145 (1928).
183. *Schmidlapp v. Commissioner,* 96 F.2d 680 (2d Cir., 1938).
184. *Albert L. Sanderson et al.,* T.C. Memo. 1957-23, filed January 31, 1957.
185. *Penn et al. v. Robertson,* 29 F. Supp. 386 (D.C., M.D. N.C., 1939), *aff'd on other issues,* 115 F.2d 167 (4th cir., 1940).
186. *Robert J. Harder et al.,* T.C. Memo. 1958-97, filed May 27, 1958.
187. *Holland et al. v. United States,* 311 F. Supp. 422 (D.C., C.D. Cal., 1970).
188. Revenue Ruling 57-502, 1957-2 CB 118.
189. I.R.S. Letter Ruling 7811004, November 29, 1977.
190. *Herman E. Bischoff et al.,* T.C. Memo. 1966-102, filed May 19, 1966.
191. *John Lockwood et al.,* T.C. Memo. 1970-141, filed June 8, 1970.
192. *Lillian M. Goldsmith,* 7 B.T.A. 151 (1927).
193. Revenue Ruling 71-308, 1971-2 CB 167.
194. Revenue Ruling 69-115, 1969-1 CB 50.
195. *Vincent E. Oswald et al.,* 49 T.C. 645 (1968).
196. *Mildred W. Wallace Estate v. Commissioner,* 101 F.2d 604 (4th Cir., 1939).
197. *A. M. Barnhart Estate,* T.C. Memo. 1959-42, filed February 27, 1959.
198. Revenue Ruling 55-447, 1955-2 CB 533.
199. *Herbert Shainberg et al.,* 33 T.C. 241 (1959).
200. *Meldrum & Fewsmith, Inc.,* 20 T.C. 780 (1953).
201. *Goodwyn Crockery Company,* 37 T.C. 355 (1961), *aff'd on another issue,* 315 F.2d 110 (6th Cir., 1963).
202. *Evans & Howard Fire Brick Company,* 8 B.T.A. 867 (1927).
203. Revenue Ruling 71-246, 1971-1 CB 54.
204. Revenue Ruling 70-408, 1970-2 CB 68.
205. *Tax Information on Business Expenses,* I.R.S. Publication 535, 1966 edition, page 12.
206. *Longview Hilton Hotel Company,* 9 T.C. 180 (1947).
207. Tax Reform Act of 1976, Section 209.
208. *Riis & Company, Inc., et al.,* T.C. Memo. 1964-190, filed July 14, 1964.

209. *Richmond Television Corporation v. United States*, 354 F.2d 410 (4th Cir., 1965).
210. *Hampton Pontiac, Inc., v. United States*, 294 F. Supp. 1073 (D.C., S.C., 1969).
211. Revenue Ruling 70-171, 1970-1 CB 56.
212. *Farmers Feed Co.*, 17 B.T.A. 507 (1938).
213. *Carboloy Company, Inc.*, T.C. Memo., Docket Nos. 101345 and 101920, entered July 2, 1943.
214. *Seufert Bros. Co. v. Lucas*, 44 F.2d 526 (9th Cir., 1930).
215. O.D. 849, CB 123.
216. *Tax Information on Disasters, Casualty Losses, and Thefts*, I.R.S. Publication 547, 1976 edition, page 2.
217. *Byron H. Farwell et al.*, 35 T.C. 454 (1960).
218. I.R.C. Section 174(b).
219. *All-State Equipment, Inc.*, 54 T.C. 1749 (1970).
220. I.R.B. 1978-23, 7.

F

Facelifting. *See* **Medical expenses.**

Faithful performance bonds. *See* **Insurance.**

False pretenses, losses arising from. *See* **Reliance upon misrepresentation.**

False teeth. *See* **Medical expenses.**

Family transactions. In general, tax deductions arising from transactions between members of the same family are allowed in the same manner as any other deductions. The only practical distinction is that the Internal Revenue Service (I.R.S.) is going to be more suspicious about the legitimacy of the deduction and might feel that the taxpayer is trying to beat them out of some tax dollars. This means that the taxpayer has a great burden of proof in establishing his entitlement to deductions resulting from intrafamily transactions.

In one case, a celebrated actress made payments in a contractual arrangement with her stepfather for business assistance. The payments made proved to be far greater than either of them had anticipated due to a "contingency arrangement" in the contract. The I.R.S. claimed that the payment was really a disguised form of support and not a *bona fide* business arrangement. But it was proved that the stepfather performed his role of business adviser under the terms of the contract as well as any unrelated party would have done, and therefore the payments, which were made at the prevailing percentage rate of the theatrical industry, were allowed.[1]

Payments by a famous theatrical producer to his wife for obtaining for him the rights to produce *A Tree Grows in Brooklyn* were deductible as a finder's fee. She also was a theater personage who had been associated closely with the stage for years, and the amount of his payment to her was reasonable in terms of what he received.[2]

Similarly, a salary paid by an individual to his wife as the manager of his ladies' garment factory was fully deductible and considered reasonable because prior to marrying the boss, the woman had worked as a machine operator in the garment factory, and she was thoroughly familiar with all phases of the operation. Her salary became a business deduction for the husband just as if it had been paid to an unrelated person.[3]

A parent may be entitled to the services of his child by having parental rights and duties in respect of the child. But the father is entitled to deduct *reasonable wages* for personal services *actually rendered* by the child as a *bona fide* employee in the conduct of a trade or business or in the production of income.[4] Note the words italicized.

A rookie baseball player entered into a contract with his father, a former semi-professional player and coach, to share equally any bonus the youngster got for signing a contract that his father would procure for him. The son was entitled to deduct the amount which he paid to his father as an expense related to his business.[5]

Other payments made to a relative, if made in good faith for a legitimate business purpose, are deductible in the same manner as payments made to nonfamily members. One individual was permitted to deduct interest payments which he made to his wife for the use of her securities. He had used the securities to provide capital for his business.[6]

A husband could deduct interest on money his wife had advanced him from her own funds to pay off an existing indebtedness. He gave her a note bearing the same interest rate he had been paying a bank, which had thought him a good enough risk to make the loan in the first place. The court felt that she was entitled to a return on the moneys advanced.[7]

Parents may legitimately deduct interest on loans from minor children.[8]

To get a rent deduction on a lease involving one's minor children is difficult but possible. Two physicians owned the building which they leased to their medical partnership. They then transferred the building to a bank as trustee for their minor children, and their medical partnership leased the property back from the trust. The partners could deduct the rent paid to the trust which they had created for the young children. The bank served as an independent intermediary between parents and minor children.[9]

A physician transferred his medical equipment and furnishings to a trust for the benefit of his children, the trust to last for ten years and a month. The assets then were leased back to the professional corporation which the doctor used to conduct his practice. His attorney was the trustee, and the rent income was distributed annually to the children. Here, the rent payments unquestionably were fair in amount. And the trustee was not the father's stooge who meekly followed his wishes. This trustee on several occasions refused the doctor's request to use trust funds for the purchase of equipment which would be leased to the physician's corporation, on the ground that the items were too expensive. So the rent payments were held to be deductible.[10]

A world-famed concert singer could deduct the travel expenses of his wife when he went on a professional engagement to Europe because she was professionally competent to be his theatrical consultant in studying for his roles, choosing costumes, and other necessary chores related to his engagements.[11] In connection with a business matter, legal fees paid to an attorney who happened to be the payor's brother were deductible.[12]

An individual owned a tenement house containing eight apartments. He paid his teen-age sons for janitor and repair services, which were performed after school or on weekends or school-vacation days. The court was satisfied that the sons indeed had rendered some services, but there was nothing to substantiate the $900 business deduction claimed by the father. Because of the absence of substantiating records, the court allowed a deduction of $500 for the work performed by the young sons.[13]

In special cases, a husband can deduct the travel expenses of his wife (or other related person) who accompanies him on a business trip. One man, who was a diabetic, could travel only if accompanied by someone who had been specially trained to deal with the demands of his ailment, which his wife had been. Since the expenses certainly would have been deductible if paid to a similarly trained nonrelative, the family relationship in this case was irrelevant.[14]

A corporation was permitted to deduct the expenses of its president's wife when she accompanied him on business trips. He had a serious heart condition and was permitted by his physician to travel only in the company of a knowledgeable person who knew precisely what to do in a crisis situation. She had been instructed specifically on how to minister to him by her father, a prominent physician. Helpful in rebutting the Internal Revenue Service allegation that the trips amounted to vacations to the wife was evidence that she was not enthusiastic about having to accompany her husband on his trips.[15]

Losses on sales or exchanges of stock or other property are *automatically disallowed* if the transactions took place between an individual and certain designated family members. The designated family members are a spouse, brothers, sisters, ancestors, and lineal descendants (sons, daughters, grandchildren, etc.). This applies in any case, no matter if the price or terms are identical to those offered by unrelated persons.[16]

Losses on the exchanges or sales of stock or other property with family members other than those designated above are not automatically disallowed and will be recognized if legitimate. These include losses that occur in transactions between an individual and his mother-in-law. This can be true no matter how emotionally close the two are.[17]

Losses which occur in transactions with *both* eligible and ineligible relatives can be partially allowed but must be prorated. For example, one individual sold property to his daughter and her husband, receiving their joint promissory note in payment. When they defaulted on the payment, the father claimed a loss on the transaction. In this case, the sale had been to "tenants in common" (the husband and wife shared equally in the possession of the property) and there had been no legally authorized inheritor (for example, the property was not deeded to a blood relative of the father if the two died) nor were there any other legal complications in the ownership of the property. Therefore the half of the loss which was sold to the daughter's husband could be recognized by the father for a tax deduction.[18]

For a real family-style transaction, one that could hardly be more complex, take this example: An individual sold assets to his nieces' husbands at a price previously set as fair by an independent expert. The father of the nieces (the individual's brother) had lent his daughters the money to purchase the assets. The husbands then used the borrowed money (which had been deposited in a joint husband-wife account) for purchasing the assets.

The loss occurring in the transaction was allowed as a deduction, even though this circuitous method was used for the purpose of saving taxes in the first place. The motive behind the sale was immaterial as long as the sale was *bona fide* and there was no evidence that the assets were being held for the benefit of the individual's brother, who had, after all, put up the money for the purchase.[19]

If one spouse decamps with property belonging to another (*decamp* literally means to pack up equipment and leave a camping ground, but in this case it would mean a wife packing up her husband's valuable stamp collection and running away with the gasoline serviceman), the victim can deduct this as a theft loss in the same manner as if a stranger had taken the property, *provided the laws of the state where this took place recognize that the theft of property by one spouse from another is a legal theft.* There is a question arising over what the victim can call the loss of his property in states which do not recognize intraspousal theft, but in any case, where it is recognized (in Iowa and states with similar laws), the loss is deductible.[20]

An individual can include in deductible medical expenses not only those for himself but also those for his spouse and for persons defined as dependents in the Internal Revenue Code.[21]

An individual can deduct expenses proper for his wife to take *only* if a joint return is filed. And a joint return can be filed by a man and woman who are unmarried if they live where common-law marriages (those marriages where a man and woman live together as man and wife but have never gone through an official ceremony) are recognized as lawful (e.g., the District of Columbia).[22]

Not all dispositions of capital assets are taxable (for instance, because the disposition might be more in the nature of an exchange than a sale), but a taxable disposition of capital assets will produce a gain or loss which is not changed by the fact that the parties involved in the transaction are married to each other. Thus, if a husband transfers securities to his wife under a court-approved settlement, and his cost is more than the fair market value at the time of the transfer, that deduction which is proper for a *capital loss* can be taken.

In the case of the husband giving the wife the securities, it is not considered a division of property. It is considered a sale or exchange of the securities for something of value, namely, the husband's freedom.[23]

When a husband gives property to his spouse in a divorce settlement, and this property has appreciated in value since he acquired it, he has disposed of property in a taxable exchange and thus has gain to report. It is not a sale but a taxable exchange, for property was transferred in return for something else. The same rule applies to losses. Where a husband transferred to his wife, in a divorce settlement, certain stock which had gone down in value since he acquired it, he had a loss, deductible to the same extent as other capital losses borne by individuals.[24]

The satisfaction of a legal obligation (the payment of a debt, for example) by the transfer of co-owned property from one co-owner to the other is considered a legal taxable transaction and can be a deduction if a loss is realized by the co-owner transferring the property. For instance, if John Smith by reason of a divorce settlement owes Shirley Smith money which he pays by transferring ownership of a jointly held parcel of land to her, John can claim a loss (and therefore a tax deduction) if the cost of the transfer is costlier to him than if he had paid the money in cash to satisfy the debt. The amount of the deduction is the sum of money above the amount of the debt which John Smith had originally owed.[25]

An individual may deduct a net operating loss from the income of his (or her) spouse on a joint income tax return, but *only if* a joint return can be filed at the time the loss is suffered.[26] *See also* **Alimony; Business-related losses; Carryovers; Casualties; Child care and disabled dependent care; Interest; Medical expenses; Travel.**

Farmers. A farmer is entitled to a certain particularized tax treatment in a manner which is different from that applicable to other taxpayers. The most frequently litigated issue of farmer versus nonfarmer involves deduction of farm expenses and losses. Inasmuch as farming so frequently is engaged in for reasons of pleasure or other not-for-profit purposes, the issue is whether this really is a transaction entered upon for profit. Says the Internal Revenue Service:

A taxpayer is engaged in the business of farming if he cultivates, operates, or manages a farm for gain or profit, either as an owner or tenant. . . . [A] taxpayer who receives a rental (either in cash or kind) which is based upon farm production is engaged in the business of farming. However, a taxpayer who receives a fixed rental (without reference to production) is engaged in the business of farming only if he participates to a material extent in the operation or management of the farm. . . . A taxpayer is engaged in "the business of farming" if he is a member of a partnership engaged in the business of farming.[27]

A farm which had shown losses over a continued period was held to be a business operation which could beget deductible expenses and losses. It was stated by the court that a taxpayer is entitled to embark on his own business enterprises no matter how impractical and that it is not "for the [Tax] Collector to criticize the particulars of the management of the business by the taxpayer."[28] Another court added:

Certainly a taxpayer is entitled to embark on a business enterprise and if in fact that enterprise is a business enterprise is entitled to deduct his losses. The impracticality of the enterprise and the unlikelihood of making a profit are merely factors to be considered along with all other evidence in determining whether the intent of the taxpayer is to make a profit.[29]

A taxpayer has the burden of proving that the transaction was entered upon with the expectation of making a profit. Expenses were adjudged to be deductible where an individual had a panel of experts to advise him on his farming enterprise and where he had an elaborate accounting system so that he could operate the venture in a businesslike way, regardless of what the profit-and-loss statement actually showed.[30]

Whether a farming operation represents a transaction entered upon for profit must be determined from all the facts and circumstances in each case. The Internal Revenue Service will not consider that an individual has operated a farm for profit if he raises crops or livestock mainly for the use of his family, although he derives some income from incidental sales.[31]

A person is presumed to be operating his farm for profit by the Internal Revenue Service if in two or more years out of five consecutive taxable years ending with the current taxable year (seven years in the case of an activity which consists in major part of the breeding, training, showing, or racing of horses), his gross income from the activity exceeds the deductions attributable to it. He may elect to suspend the application of this presumption until there are five consecutive taxable years (seven in the case of horses) in existence from the time he first engaged in farming. If a person makes this election, the presumption will apply to each taxable year in the five- or seven-year period.[32]

The cost of ordinary tools of short life or small cost, such as hand tools including shovels, rakes, etc., may be deducted.[33]

If a farmer does not compute income upon the crop method, the cost of seeds and young plants which are purchased for further development and cultivation prior to sale in later years may be deducted as an expense for the year of purchase, provided the farmer follows a consistent practice of deducting such costs as an expense from year to year.[34]

The purchase of feed and other costs connected with raising livestock may be treated as expense deductions insofar as costs represent actual outlay, but this does not include the value of farm produce grown upon the farm or the labor of the farmer.[35]

The cost of feed, labor, and similar items utilized in raising turkeys could be deducted; these items were valid business expenses and did not have to be considered part of the cost of the turkeys.[36]

A farmer was permitted to deduct as expense a payment for feed to be delivered in the *following* taxable year when a drought situation, which could cause a feed shortage, indicated that the farmer was not merely seeking a tax deduction by claiming an expense and later changing his mind about making the purchase.[37]

A farmer using the cash basis (that is, income was reported for tax purposes when actually received, and expenses were deducted as paid) could deduct a check for feed which he gave to a dealer on the last day of the taxable year, even though deliveries were not to be made until the following year. This was not a mere deposit for future orders. There was a business purpose for the expenditure prior to the time the feed was needed, namely, to protect the farmer against a price rise in the event the market price went up. Also, because he held a valid contract to acquire feed, he was in a preferred position to get delivery of the items purchased in case of a feed shortage.[38]

Deduction was allowed for the cost of seed purchased in advance where the purchaser believed prices would go up, even though there was no evidence that his fears were correct.[39]

Other deductible farm expenses may include farm organization dues, farm magazines, stamps and stationery, advertising, livestock fees, account books, litter and bedding, ginning, typing materials and containers, insect sprays and dusts, trucking, farm business travel, and accounting fees.[40] Veterinary medicine is also deductible.[41]

Management and service fees paid to an agent were deductible.[42]

Repairs to an earthen dam to prevent further leaks were deductible, even though the original dirt in one area was replaced with clay. Declared the court: "Fixing leaks on a dam on a farm . . . can hardly be considered an extraordinary or unsuspected expense. Nor can such expense be considered other than necessary in the conduct of the business of farming."[43]

Removal expenses for dead and blown-down trees were properly deductible.[44]

For taxable years beginning after July 12, 1972, where a farmer is engaged in producing crops and the process of gathering and disposal of such crops is not completed within the taxable year in which the crops were planted, expenses may, with the consent of the Commissioner of Internal Revenue, be determined under the crop method, and these deductions may be taken in the taxable year in which the gross income from the crop has been realized.[45]

A farmer may elect to treat as deductible expenses those expenditures otherwise chargeable to capital account which are paid or incurred by him during the taxable year for the purchase or acquisition of fertilizer, lime, or other materials to enrich, to neutralize, or to condition land used in farming. And those expenditures which otherwise would be chargeable to capital account but which were paid or incurred for the application of such listed items and materials to the land may likewise be treated as deductible expenses.[46] If a farmer chooses to capitalize these expenditures over a period of years, the portion of the cost deducted each year need not be the same if the benefits are clearly greater in the early years.[47]

Amounts expended in the development of farms, orchards, and ranches prior to the time when the productive state is reached may at the election of the taxpayer be regarded as investments of capital to be recovered over the period of expected useful life.[48]

Expenses attributable to the planting, cultivation, maintenance, or development of any citrus or almond grove (or part of one) which are incurred before the close of the fourth taxable year beginning with the year in which the trees are planted must be capitalized. But current deduction is allowed where such a grove is replanted after having been lost while in the taxpayer's hands by reason of freeze, disease, drought, pests, or casualty.[49]

A farmer may deduct his soil and water conservation expenditures which do not give rise to a deduction for depreciation and which are otherwise not deductible. The amount of the deduction is limited each year to 25 percent of the taxpayer's gross income from farming. Any excess may be carried forward and deducted in succeeding taxable years. As a general rule, once a farmer has adopted this method of treating soil and water conservation expenditures, he must deduct all these expenditures, subject to the 25-percent limitation, for the current and subsequent taxable years. If a farmer does not adopt this method, such expenditures increase the basis of the property to which they relate.[50]

A taxpayer engaged in the business of farming may elect to deduct certain expenditures paid or incurred by him in any taxable year in the clearing of land to make the "land suitable for use in farming," but only if such expenditures are made in furtherance of his business of farming. The amount deductible for any taxable year is limited to the lesser of $5,000 or 25 percent of the taxable income derived from farming. Expenditures in excess of the amount thus deductible are treated as capital expenditures and constitute an adjustment to the basis of the land.[51]

Clearing of land includes (but is not limited to) (1) the removal of rocks, stones, trees, brush, or other natural impediments to the use of the land in farming, (2) the treatment or moving of earth, including the construction, repair, or removal of nondepreciable earthern structures such as dikes or levees, if the purpose of such treatment or moving of earth is to protect, level, contour, terrace, or condition the land to permit its use as farming land, and (3) the diversion of streams and watercourses, including the construction of nondepreciable drainage facilities, provided that the purpose is to remove or to divert water from the land to make it available for use in farming.[52]

Also included with land-clearing expenses are stump blasting, grass planting, and river protection.[53]

As a general rule, penalties are not deductible for tax purposes. But if a farmer participates in an acreage-reserve program, and he markets an amount in excess of his quota, the marketing-quota penalty imposed on him is deductible as business expense.[54]

Qualified notices of allocation issued by farming cooperatives to their members are written notices of rights of redemption given by the cooperative separately to each patron. They are taxable, to the extent of their stated dollar value, when received and are redeemable in cash within a period of at least ninety days after issuance unless the taxpayer has consented with the cooperative to include the notices to the extent of their stated dollar value in income when received. A loss incurred on the redemption of a qualified written notice of allocation, received in the ordinary course of one's farming business, is deductible as an ordinary loss. The loss is measured by the difference between the stated dollar amount included in income upon receipt and the amount received upon redemption.[55]

The cost of a commodity futures contract purchased solely for protection against commodity price fluctuation is a form of business insurance and is deductible as an ordinary and necessary business expense.[56] But the cost of a futures contract purchased for speculative purposes is not deductible.[57]

The Federal use tax on highway motor vehicles paid on a truck or truck-trailer used in a farming business is a deductible expense.[58]

To the extent that there was no prospect of recovery by insurance or otherwise, deduction was allowed for flood damage to land planted with cranberries.[59] Deduction was allowed for frost destruction of grass on land purchased for purposes of harvesting.[60] Where a windstorm damaged the topsoil of a farm, a casualty-loss deduction was allowed to the extent of the difference in the fair market value of the farm immediately before and immediately after the happening. The court regarded the precipitating event as sufficiently unexpected and unusual to constitute a casualty, although the Internal Revenue Service had argued that this type of windstorm occurred every year, usually in February or March (this one hit in March).[61] Casualty-loss deduction was allowed in the case of damage from drought and early freeze in the case of plants and shrubs.[62]

Appraisal fees for the purpose of establishing a casualty loss by reason of subsoil shrinkage resulting from prolonged drought were deductible.[63]

Property used in the business of farming, or for the production of income from rent and royalties (if subject to an involuntary conversion after having been held for more than one year), is included in the definition of "Section 1231 property." Gain on the *net* of all transactions involving Section 1231 property held for more than one year is treated as long-term capital gain. If the netted result of transactions in Section 1231 property of the taxable year results in a loss, the loss is fully deductible.[64]

The following transactions represent areas where losses involving Section 1231 property are fully deductible:

1. Livestock acquired before 1970 (not including poultry) held for draft, breeding, or dairy purposes and held for twelve months or more.

2. Cattle and horses acquired after 1969 for draft, breeding, dairy, or sporting purposes and held for twenty-four months or more.

3. Livestock (except cattle, horses, and poultry) acquired after 1969 for draft, breeding, dairy, or sporting purposes and held for twelve months or more.

If diseased livestock held for the above purposes are destroyed or disposed of by or on account of the disease, any recognized gain or loss must be included.

Section 1231 property also includes:

1. Depreciable property used in the business, such as farm machinery, trucks, barns, sheds, livestock, etc., except for gain attributable to depreciation.

2. Real estate used in the business, such as a farm or ranch land, except for gain attributable to depreciation or for soil and water conservation and land-clearing expenses.

3. Unharvested crops on land used in farming if the crop and land are sold, exchanged, or involuntarily converted at the same time and to the same person. Growing crops sold with a lease on the land, even though to the same person in a single transaction, are not included. Also not included is a sale, exchange, or involuntary conversion of an unharvested crop with land, where the taxpayer retains any right or option to reacquire the land, directly or indirectly (other than a right customarily incident to a mortgage or other security transaction).

4. Timber, the cutting of which the taxpayer has elected to treat as a sale, and timber disposed of under a contract by which he retains an economic interest in the timber.

5. Coal or iron ore disposed of under a contract by which the taxpayer retains an economic interest in the coal or iron ore.

6. Property held for the production of rents or royalties.

7. The taxpayer's distributive share of partnership gains and losses from the sale, exchange, and involuntary conversion of the above items held for more than one year (or the period specified for livestock under specified circumstances), except for gain attributable to depreciation.

8. Involuntary conversions of business property and capital assets held for more than one year (or the holding periods specified for livestock) resulting from casualties and thefts (whether insured or uninsured) or from condemnations for public use.[65]

A deduction is denied in the case of a contribution to an approved charitable organization (except in transfer in trust) of a partial value of a charitable contribution (not in trust) of an irrevocable remainder interest in a farm which is not the donor's entire interest. For example, if an individual contributes (not in trust) to an approved charitable organization a remainder interest in a farm and retains an estate in the farm for life or for a specified number of years, a deduction is allowed for the value of the remainder interest not transferred in trust.[66]

Legal expenses incurred in defending an action for damages by a tenant injured while at work on the taxpayer's farm were deductible as business expense.[67] See *also* **Casualties; Hobby losses.**

Feasibility studies. A taxpayer can deduct most forms of expense related to his business. But this refers to the business in which he is then engaged. Legitimate expenses for feasibility studies as to the desirability of going into fields in which a taxpayer is not yet engaged are not deductible, being *pre-business* expenses. One taxpayer had a division to study locations for future expansion and to see how customers' requirements could be satisfied. Operating expenses of this division were deductible even though they related to locations which did not then exist and perhaps never would. The studies involved a way of adjusting the scope of the business' operations to changing conditions and to changing consumer demands in order to maintain its competitive position as the geographical area which it served grew beyond the convenient range of existing facilities.[68] See **Investors; Ordinary and necessary business expenses; Research and experimental expenses.**

Fidelity bond premium. See **Insurance.**

Fiduciaries. The business which begets business deductions may be any form of activity entered upon with a reasonable expectation of profit. One who regularly engages in the business of serving *for pay* as a trustee, who is required to pay a sum as a liability growing out of the conduct of fiduciary affairs, such as a lawyer who devoted about half of his time to acting as an attorney and as a trustee, may deduct amounts claimed against him.[69] Such deduction was not allowed in the case of a trustee who was not in the *business* of being a trustee.[70] A casual executor, administrator, or trustee cannot deduct business expenses, not being engaged in a trade or business as fiduciary. But it is possible that a person's activities in handling a single estate may be of sufficient scope and duration to constitute his being engaged in a trade or business as fiduciary.[71] (A fiduciary is one who holds something in trust for another party.)

An individual accepted the trusteeship of a trust containing assets with a definite dollar value. He was not regularly engaged in the business of performing services as a trustee. Pursuant to the laws of the state where the trust was created, he was entitled, without court allowance, to annual commissions of 6 percent of all the income from the trust which was handled by him. In order to protect his personal estate from claims or lawsuits which could arise from his activities as trustee, he purchased a one-year trustees' errors and omissions policy with his own funds. Inasmuch as the premium was reasonable in amount compared to the commissions he expected to receive during the policy term, the premium was deductible as an ordinary and necessary expense paid or incurred for the collection of income.[72]

When an individual engages a fiduciary in connection with the production of *taxable* income or for the management, conservation, or maintenance of property held for the production of taxable income, the fee is deductible. Thus, to the extent that tax-free municipal bonds in a trust produce taxable income or are held for that purpose, the fee of the fiduciary, whether measured by the income or by the value of the municipals in the trust, is deductible. A reasonable basis for determining the extent to which the fiduciary's fee was related to taxable income and thus was deductible is the ratio of taxable income to nontaxable income over the life of the trust.[73] *See also* **Legal fees; Termination of trust or estate; Unused carry-over of fiduciary.**

Finance charges. *See* **Interest.**

Finder's fee. Reasonable amounts paid as a commission to a person for obtaining something of business value (not a capital asset), or referring parties to the payor, are deductible as ordinary and necessary business expenses.[74] See **Family transactions.**

Fines and penalties. See **Settlement payments; Union fines.**

Fire damage. See **Casualties.**

Firemen. See **Uniforms.**

Fishermen. See **Work clothes.**

Fixed mileage allowance. See **Mileage allowance.**

Floods. See **Casualties.**

Food additives. See **Medical expenses.**

Foreign conventions. Under the Tax Reform Act of 1976, deductions for the cost of attending foreign conventions may be subject to severe limitations.[75] See **Conventions.** But these rules do not apply to deductions incurred by individuals in attending conventions in the Commonwealth of Puerto Rico.[76]

Foreign expropriation losses. If an individual has net operating losses as a result of expropriation by a foreign government, they may not be carried back but may be carried forward ten years. In the case of Cuban expropriation losses, the carry-over period is twenty years (under the Tax Reform Act of 1976, Section 2126). To qualify, the individual must have been a citizen or resident of the United States on December 31, 1958. This rule applies also to investment property.[77] See *also* **Casualties.**

Foreign income taxes. See **Taxes.**

Foreign organizations, contributions to. See **Contributions.**

Foreign study. See **Education.**

Forest management expenses. Forest management expenses of the owner of timber land were deductible despite the fact that sales of timber were treated as capital gain, even though a small part of those expenses was attributable to the negotiation and supervision of timber-cutting contracts. Here the court declared that selling expenses related to the disposal of timber are treated in a manner somewhat inconsistent with that accorded selling expenses related to most other kinds of capital assets.[78]

Forfeited interest, premature withdrawal. *See* **Premature withdrawal of interest.**

Forfeitures. *See* **Cancellation and forfeiture.**

Forgiveness of rent. *See* **Rent, forgiveness of.**

Forwarding fees. *See* **Referral fees.**

Foster parents. Foster parents may deduct as charitable contributions unreimbursed out-of-pocket expenses which they pay to provide gratuitous foster home care for children placed in their home by a charitable organization.[79]

Founder's fee. *See* **Retirement homes.**

Fraud, loss resulting from. *See* **Casualties; Reliance upon misrepresentation.**

Fringe benefits. *See* **Compensation; Ordinary and necessary business expenses.**

Futures contract in commodities. *See* **Farmers.**

F

1. *Olivia de Havilland Goodrich et al.,* 20 T.C. 323 (1953).
2. *Mary Sinclair et al.,* B.T.A. Memo., Docket No. 91164, entered March 14, 1939.
3. *Blanche Rosenzweig,* T.C. Memo, 1955-57, filed March 22, 1955.
4. Revenue Ruling 72-23, 1972-2 CB 43.
5. *Cecil Randolph Hundley, Jr.,* 48 T.C. 339 (1967).
6. *M. A. Long,* 8 B.T.A. 737 (1927).
7. *Dorzbeck v. Collison,* 195 F.2d 69 (3d Cir., 1952).
8. *Cook et ux. v. United States,* D.C., W.D. La., 1977.
9. *Serbousek et al. v. Commissioner,* T.C. Memo. 1977-105, filed April 11, 1977.
10. *Lerner et al. v. Commissioner,* 71 T.C., No. 24 (1978).
11. *John Charles Thomas,* B.T.A. Memo., Docket No. 91164, entered March 14, 1939.
12. *George S. Groves,* 38 B.T.A. 727 (1938).
13. *Charles Tschupp et al.,* T.C. Memo. 1963-98, filed April 4, 1963.
14. *Allenberg Cotton Co., Inc., et al. v. United States,* D.C., W.D. Tenn., 1960.
15. *Quinn et al. v. United States,* D.C., Md., 1977.

16. I.R.C. Section 267.
17. Revenue Ruling 71-50, 1971-1 CB 106.
18. *Walter Simister, Jr., et al.,* 4 T.C. 470 (1944).
19. *Maurice B. Saul et al.,* T.C. Memo., Docket No. 7679, entered June 26, 1947.
20. *Vesta Peak Maxwell,* B.T.A. Memo., Docket Nos. 86186-7, entered February 7, 1940.
21. I.R.C. Section 213.
22. *James M. Ross,* T.C. Memo. 1972-112, filed May 25, 1972.
23. *Wallace et al. v. United States,* 439 F.2d 757 (8th Cir., 1971).
24. *Worthy W. McKinney,* 64 T.C. 263 (1975).
25. *United States v. Davis,* 370 U.S. 65 (1962).
26. *Zeeman v. United States,* 275 F. Supp. 235 (D.C., S.D. N.Y., 1967), *aff'd on this issue,* 395 F.2d 861 (2d Cir., 1968).
27. Regulations Section 1.182-2.
28. *Wright v. United States,* D.C., Nev., 1965.
29. *Leonard F. Barcus et al.,* T.C. Memo. 1973-138, filed June 25, 1973.
30. *Plant v. Walsh,* 280 F.2d 722 (D.C., Conn., 1922).
31. *Farmer's Tax Guide,* 1976 edition, page 24.
32. I.R.C. Section 183.
33. Regulations Section 1.162-12(a).
34. *Ibid.*
35. *Ibid.*
36. *McCulley v. Kelm,* 112 F. Supp. 832 (D.C., Minn., 1953).
37. *Cravens v. Commissioner,* 272 F.2d 895 (10th Cir., 1959).
38. *Mann et al. v. Commissioner,* 483 F.2d 673 (8th Cir., 1973).
39. *De La Cruz et al. v. Commissioner,* T.C. Memo. 1978-8, filed January 9, 1978.
40. *Farmer's Tax Guide,* 1976 edition, page 27.
41. Schedule F listing for Form 1040.
42. *De La Cruz et al. v. Commissioner,* T.C. Memo. 1978-8, filed January 9, 1978.
43. *Evans et al. v. Commissioner,* 557 F.2d 1095 (5th Cir., 1977).
44. *Thomas O. Campbell et al.,* T.C. Memo. 1973-101, filed April 25, 1973.
45. Regulations Section 1.162-12(a).
46. Regulations Section 1.180-1.
47. *Farmer's Tax Guide,* 1976 edition, page 25.
48. Regulations Section 1.162-12(a).
49. I.R.C. Section 278(b)(1).
50. I.R.C. Section 175.
51. I.R.C. Section 182.
52. Regulations Section 1.182-3(a).
53. *Arthur William Peterson et al.,* T.C. Memo. 1970-181, filed June 29, 1970.
54. Regulations Section 1.61-4(a)(4) and 1.61-1(b)(4).
55. *Farmer's Tax Guide,* 1976 edition, page 23.
56. *Corn Products Refining Company v. Commissioner,* 350 U.S. 46 (1955).
57. *Henry I. Seroussi,* T.C. Memo. 1962-233, filed August 29, 1963.
58. *Farmer's Tax Guide,* 1976 edition, page 26.
59. *F. H. Wilson,* 12 B.T.A. 403 (1928).
60. *Flona Corporation v. United States,* 218 F. Supp. 354 (D.C., S.D. Fla., 1963).
61. *Barry et al. v. United States,* 175 F. Supp. 308 (D.C., W.D. Okla., 1958).
62. *Alfred M. Cox et al.,* T.C. Memo. 1965-5, filed January 14, 1965, *aff'd on another issue,* 354 F.2d 659 (3d Cir., 1966).
63. Revenue Ruling 58-180, 1958-1 CB 153.
64. I.R.C. Section 1231.
65. *Farmer's Tax Guide,* 1976 edition, page 40.
66. Regulations Section 1.170A-7(b)(4).

67. O.D. 1117, CB No. 5 (1921).
68. *North Carolina National Bank et al. v. United States*, ... F. Supp. ... (D.C., W.D.N.C., 1978).
69. *John Abbott*, 38 B.T.A. 1290 (1938).
70. *Commissioner v. Heide*, 165 F.2d 699 (2d Cir., 1948).
71. *A. M. Barnhart Estate*, T.C. Memo. 1959-42, filed February 27, 1959.
72. Revenue Ruling 72-314, 1972-1 CB 44.
73. *Whittemore, Jr., et al. v. United States*, 383 F.2d 824 (8th Cir., 1967).
74. *Mary Sinclair et al.*, T.C. Memo. 1960-113, filed May 31, 1960.
75. I.R.C. Section 274(h).
76. Revenue Ruling 78-23, I.R.B. 1978-3, 7.
77. I.R.C. Section 165(i).
78. *McMullan et al. v. United States*, ... F.2d ... (Ct. Cl., 1978).
79. Revenue Ruling 77-280, 1977-2 CB 14.

F

G

Gambling losses. Income from gambling is taxable, but it may be offset or even canceled completely by gambling losses.[1] The difficulty is that significant gambling "wins" are reported to the Internal Revenue Service by the racetrack or other payor, at least in theory. The taxpayer has to prove the losses himself. When a taxi driver who went to the track several times a week finally won a $21,854 twin double on April 5, this payout was reported by the track. Forewarned, he showed a Revenue Agent $23,680 in losing tickets he allegedly had purchased between April 6 and May 21. The only trouble was that many of the losing tickets unmistakably bore heel marks, such as often appear on tickets that disgusted bettors throw away after their horses have lost. Instead of $23,680 the court allowed him $2,000 as a deduction against gambling gains.[2] Damon Runyon could have written a dandy story on this one, but the bettor did not do too badly, considering the nature of his "evidence."

A factory worker was a racetrack addict. To offset wagering gains one year, he showed "losing" tickets of almost as large an amount. But unlike other taxpayers who had displayed randomly numbered tickets which often bore heel marks or other evidence that they had been picked off the turf by persons whose horses had not come in, his tickets were clean and untorn, most bearing sequential serial numbers which indicated that they had been issued to the same purchaser at the same time. A racetrack companion testified that he never had seen the taxpayer pick up ticket stubs from the ground to which they had been flung by unsuccessful bettors. The court allowed two-thirds of the amount claimed as offsets against gambling wins.[3]

To prove gambling losses, the Internal Revenue Service recommends that an accurate diary or similar record regularly be maintained, supplemented by verifiable documentation. In general, the diary should contain at least the following information:

1. Date and type of specific wager or wagering activity.
2. Name of gambling establishment.
3. Address or location of gambling establishment.
4. Name(s) of other person(s), if any, present with the taxpayer at the gambling establishment.
5. Amount(s) won or lost.

Adds the I.R.S.: "Verifiable documentation for gambling transactions include but is not limited to Forms W-2G; Forms 5754, Statement By Person Receiving Gambling Winnings; wagering tickets, canceled checks, credit records, bank withdrawals, and statements of actual winnings or payment slips provided by the taxpayer to the gambling establishment.

"Where possible, the diary and available documentation generated with the placement and settlement of a wager should be further supported by other documentation of the taxpayer's wagering activity or visit to a gambling establishment. Such documentation includes, but is not limited to, hotel bills, airline tickets, gasoline credit cards, canceled checks, credit records, bank deposits, and bank withdrawals.

"Additional supporting evidence could also include affidavits or testimony from responsible gambling officials regarding wagering activity."[4]

If an expense arises out of the conduct of a business and is a required outlay meeting the standard definition of ordinary and necessary, it is allowed, even though the business activity is illegal under the laws of the state where it operates. The United States Supreme Court has said that "the federal income tax is a tax on net income, not a sanction against wrongdoing."[5] Where state law banned bookmaking, payments of wages and rent by the bookmaker were deductible for tax purposes because they were ordinary and necessary expenses in the accepted meaning of those terms and were not devices to avoid the consequences of violations of the law.[6]

Other expenses of an unlawful business, conceivably, could not be deemed deductions. See also **Bribes and kickbacks; Illegal business activity.**

Gasoline taxes. For taxable years beginning after December 31, 1978, gasoline taxes no longer are deductible, except when the fuel is used in business or investment activities.[7]

General sales taxes. See **Taxes.**

Gift and leaseback. See **Family transactions.**

Gifts. See **Business gifts; Contributions: Ordinary and necessary business expenses.**

Government service, company employees in. *See* **Compensation.**

Graduated payment mortgages. *See* **Interest.**

Grooming. *See* **Personal grooming.**

Group term life insurance premiums. *See* **Compensation.**

Guarantor, payments by. Where a corporate employee was advised by his supervisor that if he did not act as guarantor of a bank loan made by his company, his present position and future possibilities would be jeopardized, he guaranteed the loan. His sole purpose was to protect his employment. When the loan could not be repaid by the corporation and he was obliged to honor his guarantee, this was a fully deductible business bad-debt deduction.[8]

Guardians, expenses of. Reasonable amounts paid for the services of a guardian or committee for a ward or minor, and other expenses of guardians and committees which are ordinary and necessary in connection with the production or collection of income of the ward or minor, or in connection with the management of his property, are deductible.[9]

Guide dogs. *See* **Medical expenses.**

Gymnasium. *See* **Actors; Handball court, rental of.**

G

1. I.R.C. Section 165(d).
2. *William H. Green*, T.C. Memo. 1972-131, filed June 20, 1972.
3. *Salem et al. v. Commissioner*, T.C. Memo. 1978-142, filed April 13, 1978.
4. Revenue Procedure 77-29, 1977-2 CB 538.
5. *Commissioner v. Tellier*, 383 U.S. 687 (1966).
6. *Commissioner v. Sullivan*, 356 U.S. 27 (1958).
7. Revenue Act of 1978, Section 111.
8. Revenue Ruling 71-561, 1971-2 CB 128.
9. Regulations Section 1.212-1(j).

H

Hairpieces. *See* **Actors; Medical expenses.**

Halfway house. *See* **Medical expenses.**

Handball court, rental of. An actor who was obliged to keep himself in first-class physical condition could deduct rent for handball courts and gymnasium facilities.[1]

Handicapped persons. *See* **Blind persons, expenses of; Child care and disabled dependent care; Deaf persons, expenses of; Education; Medical expenses; Removal of impediments to the physically handicapped.**

Health and accident insurance premiums. *See* **Medical expenses.**

Health foods. *See* **Medical expenses.**

Health institute fees. *See* **Medical expenses.**

Hearing aid. A lawyer could deduct the cost of a hearing aid as a business expense.[2] *See also* **Medical expenses.**

Hearing Ear dog. *See* **Deaf persons, expenses of.**

Hedging operation. *See* **Insurance.**

Hobby, income-producing, expenses of. Expenses of an income-producing hobby are deductible.[3]

Hobby losses. Although expenses of a business are deductible whether or not profits are made, real doubt exists as to whether an activity actually is a business if profits are nonexistent. That is especially the presumption if the alleged business is something that the taxpayer enjoys doing. Rarely does a court admit, as in one case, that a "business will not be turned into a hobby merely because the owner find it pleasurable; suffering never has been made a prerequisite to deductibility."[4]

An activity may not be classified as a trade or business unless an individual can prove that he has a *bona fide* intention of making a profit therefrom. It is not necessary, however, that the expectation of profit be a reasonable one, as long as it is genuine.[5]

An individual became interested in the writings and teachings of Joanna Southcott, a religious teacher and prophetess who died in 1814. The taxpayer read Southcott's sixty-five works which were in libraries; the teacher's other works were supposed to be sealed in an ark in the custody of the British Parliament, which was to be opened in 1914 or whenever the nation's troubles demanded that it be opened. (The year 1914 seemed to qualify.) The taxpayer arranged for the publication of Southcott's works in the United States. There were some fifty thousand disciples in this country, and efforts were made to disseminate the wisdom of the prophetess. With a disciple, the taxpayer traveled widely and distributed pamphlets. Her expenses were allowable deductions. Whether the publication project would ever be financially successful was not the determining factor in whether the transaction was one entered upon for profit; more significant was whether the taxpayer thought it could be financially viable. And she was believed to have entered upon the undertaking in good faith for the purpose of making a profit. Had the ark been opened, the profit potential would have been increased greatly. She showed a willingness to invest time and capital in the future outcome of the enterprise, regardless of what actually happened. She thought it was a proper and commendable enterprise. It was not carried on primarily for recreation or pleasure; she was in deadly earnest.[6]

A diplomat who had long been interested in farming got advice on the running of his farm from a consulting firm and showed cognizance of the profit motive by eliminating unsuccessful activities and substituting others with more promise. His expenses were deductible. Perhaps he did not operate the farm in the most efficient manner, but it was not the quality of his judgment which was at stake.[7]

A government employee could deduct his expenses at the business of lapidary (the cutting, polishing, or engraving of precious or semiprecious stones). He displayed his wares at a rock showing and sold many items, he had a sales tax license, and he advertised in a national magazine. The court rejected the Internal Revenue Service claim that this was a hobby, its expenses nondeductible:

A trade or business is something more than a hobby; a trade or business, as the names imply, connotes the hope of profit. Though it also connotes something more than an act or course of activity engaged in for profit. It must refer not merely to acts engaged in for profit but to extensive activity over a substantial period of time during which the taxpayer holds himself out as selling goods or services.[8]

A businessman who collected postage stamps was allowed to take a deduction when he ultimately sold his collection for less than his cost. He was active in various enterprises and served as a director of the Philadelphia National Bank. He became impressed with the investment possibilities of stamps and was recommended to a professional philatelist. The philatelist discussed the investment features of stamps and their history of increasing value over a period of time. The businessman purchased stamps regularly, following the consultant's advice in most instances. The professional philatelist did not regard his client as a collector or a hobbyist, and for that reason no recommendations were made as to stamps that seemed to be selling over the market value (or what was generally accepted as the current market value) of the stamps. The stamps were fully insured against loss, and meticulous account books were kept. When the stamps were sold, the motive was to achieve liquidity. The court believed that the businessman's single objective was financial reward. Thus he had the "requisite greed" for a transaction entered upon for profit.[9]

An individual acquired land for the purpose of quarrying and selling rock. But because of time-consuming construction activity in the area, the roads were virtually impassable, and he had difficulty in getting his product to market. His sales efforts were not conspicuously successful. The Internal Revenue Service sought to disallow his maintenance and other expenses as hobby-related, not a transaction entered upon for profit. The court disagreed. Although hindsight revealed that there were insurmountable obstacles in the way of making the venture profitable, these were not realized during the taxable year. And this was the familiar situation of a hobby loss, where a taxpayer does not care that the undertaking never will make a cent as long as he has fun on his farm or other outlet for pleasure. The court concluded, "Try as we might, we cannot conjure up a picture of [the taxpayer] mirthfully driving his fully reconditioned 1948 GMC flatbed truck or 1948 FWD telephone pole truck along the countryside with nothing but pleasure on his mind."[10] (The year in question was 1963.)

A psychoanalyst was permitted to deduct her expenses in connection with photographic activities related to a book which she hoped to have published. The court found that she sincerely and in good faith expected to make a profit out of her activity in these years or at least an ultimate profit. It mattered not that this was a secondary occupation to her, for it was carried on in a regular, continuous manner and in a businesslike way. The court's most significant words were, "I do not think she played at this as a dilettante."[11]

A professor's wife had been engaged in artistic endeavors for twenty years. Her income from painting, etc., never equaled her expenses, but she kept steadily at work with the encouragement of some sales, various prizes, exhibits, and good critical reviews and encouragement. She satisfied the court that she had pursued her activities in the taxable years with the objective of making a profit. Perhaps her expectations of profit were not reasonable, but the court was convinced that she had a *bona fide* intention of making a profit and a belief that she could do so. She kept all the receipts of her art expenses and kept a journal recording what she had sold and to whom, which indicated that, said the court, "she carried on her activities in a businesslike manner for profit." She had a mailing list of persons to whom she sent regular notices of her exhibits and she sought to get galleries to have her work shown.[12]

To maximize the possibility of having deductions allowed as business-oriented even though the activity is one which most people pursue as a hobby, an individual should attempt to observe these court findings:

1. Operate the activity under a trade name. This is an indication that it actually is a business rather than a hobby.[13]
2. Where animals are involved, engage professional trainers.[14]
3. Be personally involved in the project. A nonfarmer who maintained a farm impressed the court with the fact that he had consulted with the county agent on agricultural problems, subscribed to Doane's *Agricultural Services*, and obtained various government and university publications on farming.[15]
4. Form a panel of experts to render advice.[16]
5. Keep good accounting records. One taxpayer had one of the eight largest accounting firms in the country audit the books.[17]
6. Constantly review operations to weed out unpromising lines.[18]
7. Where animals or produce are involved, advertise the venture. Compete in shows.[19]
8. Undertake profit-feasibility studies.[20]

If profits do not materialize, a taxpayer may be able to show that there had been a reasonable expectation of financial success, which had been thwarted by such factors as these:

1. The taxpayer had sustained a nervous breakdown which kept her from spending enough time on the venture.[21]

2. A farmer's house with all its contents had burned to the ground and his wife had left him.[22]

3. Lack of success of a racing-car venture was attributable to the fact that there had been mechanical breakdowns and several cars had crashed.[23]

4. Although the venture had been operated in a businesslike manner, a depression had prevented success.[24]

Persistent losses limit the amount of a person's deductions. A taxpayer is presumed to be engaged in an activity for profit in the current taxable year, unless established to the contrary by the Internal Revenue Service, if in two or more years of the period of five consecutive taxable years ending with the current taxable year (seven years in the case of an activity which consists in major part of the breeding, training, showing, or racing of horses), the activity was carried on at a profit, that is, if the gross income from the activity exceeds the deductions attributable to the activity which would be allowed if it were engaged in for profit. For this purpose, all deductions attributable to the activity other than that allowed for net operating loss carry-overs are taken into account.[25]

An individual may elect to suspend the application of the presumption until there are five consecutive taxable years (or seven in the case of horses) in existence from the time he first engages in the activity and then to apply it to any years in the five- or seven-year period.[26] If the activity is not deemed to be one carried on for profit, hobby losses are deductible only to the extent that there are gains from this activity.[27]

Deduction of a loss from what *could* have been a hobby requires positive proof. A physician inherited a farm. He took a great interest in activities there, maintaining sizable herds of cattle. He sold animals that proved unsatisfactory. He experimented with various strains until he found what appeared to be cattle with good profit potential. He raised horses, an operation he closed out when it proved to be unprofitable. His catfish pond activities were terminated for the same reason. He sought advice and assistance from expert farmers, cattlemen, and machinery mechanics, constantly attempting to improve his profit picture by altering his methods of operation and by abandoning those operations which proved incapable of profit. But for twelve years, the farm failed to show a profit. The Internal Revenue Service claimed that his business was medicine and the farm was primarily for recreation, so his losses were personal and nondeductible. But the court felt that he had established that his dominant motive or intention had been to derive a profit. There were no recreational facilities at the farm. He engaged in manual farm labor and machinery repair, activities that could scarcely be regarded as recreational. Although his activities evidenced a lack of good business judgment or farming knowledge, he had tried with the aid of competent advisors to operate the farm as a business for profit. Therefore the losses were deductible.[28]

Home, office at. *See* **Office at home.**

Home, sale of. *See* **Residence sold at a loss.**

Home, taxpayer's. *See* **Interest; Taxes.**

Home care. *See* **Medical expenses.**

Home for the aged. *See* **Contributions.**

Home mortgage. *See* **Interest.**

Home stereo system. *See* **Medical expenses.**

Home telephone. *See* **Employees; Executives; Telephone.**

Horses. *See* **Advertising.**

Hospitality room. *See* **Entertainment.**

Hospital services. *See* **Medical expenses.**

Host's own meals, deductibility of. *See* **Entertainment.**

Household expenses. *See* **Child care deduction.**

Household improvements for the handicapped. *See* **Medical expenses.**

Hunting, expenses of. *See* **Entertainment.**

H

1. *Charles Hutchinson*, 13 B.T.A. 1187 (1928).
2. *Paul Blanchard, Jr.*, 23 T.C. 803 (1955).
3. *Miscellaneous Deductions and Credits*, I.R.S. Publication 529, 1976 edition, page 1.
4. *Thomas W. Jackson*, 59 T.C. 312 (1972).
5. *Margit Sigray Bessenyey*, 45 T.C. 261 (1965), *aff'd*, 379 F.2d 252 (2d Cir., 1967).

6. *Doggett v. Burnet*, 65 F.2d 191 (App. D.C., 1933).
7. *Patterson et al. v. United States*, 459 F.2d 487 (Ct. Cl., 1972).
8. *Estes et al. v. United States*, D.C., S.D. Ala., 1969.
9. *George F. Tyler*, T.C. Memo., Docket No. 5508, entered March 6, 1947.
10. *Claude L. Crespeau*, T.C. Memo. 1969-236, filed November 5, 1969.
11. *Young v. United States*, D.C., Md., 1971.
12. *Churchman et al. v. Commissioner*, 68 T.C., 696 (1977).
13. *Rex B. Foster et al.*, T.C. Memo. 1973-14, filed January 23, 1973.
14. *Joan F. (Walton) Farris et al.*, T.C. Memo. 1972-165, filed August 3, 1972.
15. *Patterson et al. v. United States*, 459 F.2d 487 (Ct. Cl., 1972).
16. *Plant v. Walsh*, 280 F. 722 (D.C., Conn., 1922).
17. *Patterson et al. v. United States*, 459 F.2d 487 (Ct. Cl., 1972).
18. *Ibid.*
19. *Rex B. Foster et al.*, T.C. Memo. 1973-13, filed January 23, 1973.
20. *Irving C. Ackerman et al.*, 24 B.T.A. 512 (1931), *aff'd*, 71 F.2d 586 (9th Cir., 1935).
21. *Thelma C. Whitman*, T.C. Memo. 1960-88, filed May 6, 1960.
22. *Woodrow L. Wroblewski*, T.C. Memo. 1973-37, filed February 14, 1973.
23. *L. A. Bolt*, 50 T.C. 1007 (1968).
24. *Lucien H. Tyng et al.*, 36 B.T.A. 21 (1937), *aff'd and rev'd on other grounds*, 106 F.2d 55 (2d Cir., 1939), *rev'd*, 308 U.S. 527 (1940).
25. I.R.C. Section 183(a),(d).
26. I.R.C. Section 183(e).
27. I.R.C. Section 183(b).
28. *Gregory, Jr., et al. v. United States*, D.C., W.D. La., 1976.

I

Ice storms. *See* **Casualties.**

Illegal business activity. Expenses of an illegal business are deductible if not of a type forbidden by law, such as bribes to police officers. Accordingly, wages and rents are deductible by a gambler even though his betting establishment was forbidden by state law.[1] Although the laws of one state prohibited lotteries, the cost of producing lottery tickets was deductible as a business expense.[2] *See also* **Bribes and kickbacks; Gambling losses; Legal fees.**

Illegal operation. *See* **Abortion; Medical expenses.**

Improvement of skills. *See* **Education.**

Improvements of a capital nature. In general, all construction costs of a business must be capitalized and written off over the estimated useful life of the facility. But when the purpose of temporary partitions, heating, and the like was to allow existing buildings to operate during major construction operations, the cost was deductible.[3] Deduction was also allowed for the cost of enlarging and improving an office when the work was not in the nature of permanent improvements but was to facilitate the transaction of increasing business.[4]

Expenses related to the installation of capital equipment with a useful life of more than one year customarily must be capitalized. But labor and transportation costs in connection with moving certain of a taxpayer's capitalized assets to another location were deductible, for the relocation did not add to the value nor appreciably prolong the useful life of these assets.[5] *See* **Election to deduct or to capitalize; Expenditures for benefits lasting more than one year; Removal of impediments to the physically handicapped.**

Inclinator in home. *See* **Medical expenses.**

Income beneficiaries. *See* **Depreciation.**

Income in respect of a decedent. Sometimes a person receives income which would have been paid to the one who had earned it if he had lived. For example, a widow may receive a year-end Christmas bonus which would have been paid to her husband except that he died in early December before payment was ready to be made. Or an insurance salesman may have sold a policy to a client but died before he received his commission, so that the check eventually went to his son, the wife having died many years earlier. The *right* to receive this money must be shown as property owned by the person who died, and if his estate was large enough to be taxable, that right was part of the total property subject to Federal estate tax. The person who eventually receives income earned by the one who died must show this income on his own tax return. But he gets a deduction for *income in respect of a decedent.* He must determine what the proportion of the value of the right to receive this income in respect of a decedent is to the total property which is subject to tax. That ratio or percentage is multiplied by the estate tax paid, and the resultant figure is deducted by the person who receives the income in respect of a decedent.[6]

Incurable disease. A person may have a physical or mental condition which medicine cannot alleviate. But expenses for the purpose of offsetting the effect of this condition may be deducted as medical expenses. *Example:* parents could deduct the fees paid to a teacher who had been specially trained in reading and study skills which enabled a child with incurable brain damage to alleviate the condition.[7]

Indefinite living away-from-home expenses. *See* **Travel.**

Indemnity bond premiums. *See* **Insurance.**

Individual retirement account. For taxable years beginning after December 31, 1974, if an individual is not an active participant in a qualified or government pension plan or the special arrangement available to employees of tax-exempt organizations, he may make payments into an Individual Retirement Account, IRA (or this may be done for him by his employer or his union), the maximum deduction each year being the lower of $1,500 or 15 percent of his compensation. The assets of the IRA may be invested in a trustee or custodial account with a bank, savings and loan association, or credit union, or in a qualified retirement bond. Married couples compute the deduction separately. Each can take the deduction if each received compensation and is not a participant in another plan.[8]

For taxable years beginning after December 31, 1976, a plan may include a nonworking spouse (spousal IRA), in which event the maximum dollar contribution is $1,750.[9]

Sometimes an employer will make a contribution to an employee's IRA. Then the limitation on deductions to the account is increased to the lesser of $7,500 or 15 percent of the employee's earned income for amounts contributed by his employer to the IRA. The limits on employee contributions to the IRA are not changed. For example, if the employer contributes to an employee's account less than the usual limit on deductible contributions by the employee for a year, the employee may make up the difference. On the other hand, the employee cannot make additional deductible contributions to the account for a year in which the employer contributions exceed the usual limit. In the case of an employee who is an officer or shareholder, or in the case of an owner-employee, the deduction limit is reduced if Social Security taxes are treated as employer contributions. The employee's deduction for amounts contributed by his employer to an IRA or individual retirement annuity are allowed even though the employee is an active participant in a qualified plan, a governmental plan, or a tax-sheltered annuity. But make-up contributions are not allowed. The expanded deduction limits apply only if employer contributions to it are made under a written formula followed by the employer and if the account is maintained solely by the employee. This applies to taxable years beginning after December 31, 1978.[10]

Previously, contributions to an IRA were deductible if made up to 45 days after the close of the taxable year for which the deduction was claimed. For taxable years beginning after December 31, 1977, a deductible contribution may be made up to the prescribed date (including extensions) for filing the Federal income tax return. The IRA is considered to have been set up on the date the contribution was made.[11]

If an individual in a previous year had deducted an excessively high contribution to an IRA, he may correct this by contributing less than his maximum deduction allowable for the year he makes this correction. The maximum deduction allowed is the amount of the contribution. For example, if an individual were entitled to make a contribution of $1,000 for 1978 and 1979, an excess contribution of $400 for 1978 can be corrected by making a contribution of only $600 for 1979 ($400 less than the individual's maximum permissible contribution) and he is entitled to a $1,000 deduction for 1978 and 1979. If he erroneously took a deduction in a previous year for any part of the excess contribution and the period for assessing a deficiency for the previous year has expired, the amount allowed as a deduction is reduced correspondingly.[12]

An individual cannot deduct contributions to an IRA for any part of the year he was covered by his company's retirement program. One employee was a participant in his employer's contributory profit-sharing plan, to which no contribution had been made by the company for several years because of inadequate earnings. In the year that the company discontinued this plan, the employee established his own IRA and made payments into it. These were deductible.[13]

For taxable years beginning after December 31, 1975, a member of the Armed Forces Reserves or National Guard can qualify for an IRA deduction for a year (if otherwise qualified) despite his participation in the military retirement plan if he had eighty or fewer days of active service (other than training) during the year.[14]

Although an active participant in a governmental plan is not allowed a deduction for a contribution to an IRA, this is permitted for taxable years beginning after December 31, 1975, in the case of a person who would be eligible except for membership in a volunteer fire department or in a governmental plan for volunteer firemen. But deduction is allowed only to firefighters who have not accrued an annual benefit in excess of $1,800 (when expressed as a single-life annuity payable at age sixty-five) under a firefighters' plan.[15]

Individuals, contributions to. *See* **Contributions.**

Informant, tax, return of fees. Where a cash-basis individual receives an advance from the Internal Revenue Service for supplying information about violations of the tax law by someone else, with the understanding that he will receive more if his leads justify it, but will have to refund any portion of his receipts if they are higher than the amount of the award as finally established on the basis of tax yields, he is taxable upon the full advance. But he can deduct the amount of anything he is obliged to give back at the time of the repayment.[16]

Inheritance, expense of collecting. *See* **Contested inheritance, expenses of.**

Initiation fee. An initiation fee paid to a labor union to obtain employment is deductible.[17] *See also* **Union dues.**

Injuries to employees. *See* **Compensation; Ordinary and necessary business expenses.**

I

Insider profits. *See* **Executives.**

Institutional care. *See* **Medical expenses.**

Insurance. Deductible business insurance premiums include:
1. Fire, theft, flood, and other casualty insurance on property used in the trade or business.
2. Merchandise and inventory insurance.
3. Credit insurance on policies covering losses resulting from the nonpayment of debts owed to the business.
4. Employees' group hospitalization and medical insurance paid or incurred by the employer.
5. Public liability insurance covering liability for bodily injuries sustained by nonemployees and for damage to the property of others.
6. Workmen's compensation insurance.
7. Overhead insurance.
8. Use and occupancy insurance and business-interruption insurance.
9. Employee performance bonds. Fees are deductible in the case of fidelity, indemnity, performance, and other types of bond to ensure faithful performance by employees.
10. Bonds that must be furnished by reason of law or a contract to ensure the company's performance in a business undertaking.
11. Automobile and other vehicle insurance.[18]

Malpractive insurance premiums were deductible by a physician who could become personally liable for negligence.[19]

Insurance premiums paid or incurred by a taxpayer as the mortgagor on a mortgaged loan, which are attributable to the loan during the period of construction of business improvements covered by the loan, are deductible as business expenses.[20]

Amounts paid by policyholders as premiums on business insurance to a mutual insurance company are deductible even though there is a likelihood that a portion of the premium may be returned to them by the company.[21]

An employer may deduct indemnification insurance premiums of two types: (1) where the employer would be indemnified against damages sustained as a result of wrongful acts committed by executives in the line of their duties, and (2) where executives would be indemnified for their expenses arising from wrongful acts committed or alleged to have been committed in their capacity as executives.[22]

Standard marine insurance policies have a $100,000 deductible provision. A shipowners' protection and indemnity association set up a fund to provide insurance protection left void by that deductible clause. Amounts paid by a shipper into this fund for protection were deductible as ordinary and necessary expenses.[23]

Credit insurance premiums on policies covering losses resulting from the nonpayment of debts owed to the business are deductible.[24]

Premiums on the life of a business debtor are deductible, the payment being, in the words of one decision, "related to its business, to wit, the preservation and conservation of its funds."[25] Ordinarily, a creditor cannot deduct premiums paid on a policy on the life of a debtor assigned as collateral. But where a creditor paid premiums on life insurance on the debtor which had been given as collateral for a loan, and there was no reasonable expectancy that the debtor would reimburse the creditor for these premium payments, they could be deducted.[26]

An employer may deduct insurance premiums he pays on the life of an employee, the latter's wife being the beneficiary, where there was a clear intent that the insurance premium be a form of compensation.[27]

Where a taxpayer purchases an insurance policy which, in accordance with its terms, would reimburse him to the extent specified in the policy for certain business overhead expenses incurred by him during prolonged periods of disability due to sickness or injury, any premiums paid are deductible business expenses.[28]

The expenses of a hedging operation were deductible by a manufacturer which was interested in protecting itself against fluctuations in the price of its raw materials.[29] Deduction is not permitted where there is merely a transaction in futures contracts rather than in commodities.[30]

For group term life insurance, hospitalization, and medical insurance paid by one's employer, *see* **Compensation; Medical expenses.**

Intangible drilling and development costs. *See* **Election to deduct or to capitalize.**

Interest. Interest paid or incurred on indebtedness is tax-deductible.[31] There are few significant exceptions to this rule. One exception is that interest in connection with the purchase of single-premium life insurance is not deductible. Interest to buy or carry tax-exempt bonds generally is not deductible, although exceptions to this provision are given later in this section. And "interest" where the indebtedness is not genuine is nondeductible.

Unlike so many forms of tax deduction, interest need not be related to the taxpayer's trade or business. Thus, interest on notes given to the taxpayer's ex-wife as part of the property settlement was held to be deductible.[32]

A cash basis taxpayer can deduct items such as interest only when he actually makes the payment. And he has not actually paid out anything if he uses borrowed money (another party's funds) to satisfy his interest obligation; there merely has been a transfer of one form of debt obligation to another. But where interest was paid with borrowed money at a time when the taxpayer had ample resources to pay these obligations, the payments were deductible because they *could* have been made with the taxpayer's own money. The pay-outs thus were regarded as equivalent to cash payments that qualified for the interest deduction.[33]

Interest is deductible in the case of delinquent payments even where the payments themselves are not deductible, as for example, when a Federal income tax deficiency is imposed, the tax is not deductible but interest on the belated payments is.[34]

Unlike many other forms of expenditure, such as compensation or rent, interest need not be reasonable to be deducted.[35] If a taxpayer borrows money at a usurious rate, interest is deductible regardless of what it has been labeled to circumvent a state law on maximum percentages.[36]

Expenditures related to the acquisition of property with a remaining life of more than one year, such as a building, customarily are not deductible when made but are considered an additional cost of the property, subject to the depreciation deduction where business property is involved. But interest does not represent a cost of acquiring or developing property. It is, rather, the price paid for the use of borrowed money even where the loan is used to improve or to secure an asset with a life of more than a year. So the interest is deductible.[37]

Ordinarily, a taxpayer on the cash basis deducts expenses when paid, regardless of the period covered by his payments. However, prepaid interest in general is not deductible in this manner. A deduction for interest paid in advance on indebtedness for a period not in excess of twelve months of the taxable year immediately following the taxable year in which the payment is made will be considered on a case-by-case basis to determine whether a material distortion of income has resulted. Factors to be considered include the amount of income in the taxable year of payment, the income of previous taxable years, the amount of prepaid interest, and the existence of a varying rate of interest over the period of the loan. If a material distortion of income results from the prepayment, interest will be deductible on a prorated basis over the period covered.[38] The taxpayer has the burden of showing that prepayments of interest did not result in this material distortion.

In the case of prepayments of interest on or after January 1, 1976, the Treasury Department is authorized in certain cases to treat interest payments under a loan with variable interest rates as consisting partly of interest computed under an average level effective rate of interest and consisting partly of an interest prepayment allocable to later years of the loan.[39]

An individual borrowed money from an insurance company against a policy on his life. He was on the cash basis, that is, he reported income on his tax return when he actually received it and took deductions when payments were màde. The insurance company deducted interest on his loan in advance, when he borrowed the money in 1970. His tax deduction was in 1972, when he actually paid off the loan.[40]

Interest paid to a related party is deductible if for a *bona fide* indebtedness, as in the case where the husband agreed to pay his wife for securities he borrowed from her to provide capital for his business.[41]

Parents may legitimately deduct interest paid on money borrowed from their minor children.[42]

Loan fees withheld by a bank from the amount given to a borrower are deductible as interest.[43]

Amounts charged to customer accounts under a bank's credit card plan and designated as "finance charges" pursuant to the Truth in Lending Act are deductible as interest where no part of the charge is a carrying charge, loan fee, or similar charge.[44] Amounts levied by retail stores on customers' revolving charge accounts and designated as "finance charges" pursuant to that same act are deductible as interest, e.g., customers with approved credit may charge their purchases and then either pay for them in full or in installments. If payment is made within thirty days from the date of the statement billing date, no charge is made to his account by the store. If full payment is not made within thirty days, a charge is made to the customer's account on his unpaid balance at the beginning of the month.[45]

An individual who uses a credit card issued by an oil company can purchase gasoline, oil, special products, and services. The credit card agreement provides for the payment by the purchaser of a "finance charge" that is expressed as an annual percentage of the purchaser's billing statement. The charge is based on the customer's unpaid balance and is computed monthly. This finance charge is deductible as interest.[46]

A bank operated a credit card plan under which retail customers who were cardholders could obtain cash advances and overdraft advances. At the time an advance was made by the bank, the amount was added to the cardholder's credit card account balance, the bank charging the cardholder's account with a onetime charge of 2 percent of the amount of each cash advance and 1 percent of the amount of each overdraft advance, these charges being in addition to its regular monthly finance charges on overdue accounts. The charges for advances were held to be deductible as interest.[47]

Finance charges paid by customers under a retail installment contract and charges for the privilege of prepaying their accounts are deductible as interest.[48]

If flat fees or service charges on installment purchases are separately stated on a customer's bill, but the interest cannot be ascertained, the deduction is the lesser of (1) an amount equal to 6 percent of the average unpaid balance of the installment contract during the year, or (2) the portion of the total fee or service charge allocable to the year.

The average unpaid balance in (1) is determined by totaling the unpaid balances on the first day of each month in the year and dividing this total by twelve. The unpaid balance at the beginning of each month is determined by taking into account the payments in the amount and at the time called for in the contract, even though such payments are not made when due.

The amount in (2) is determined by dividing the fee or service charge by the total number of monthly payments to obtain a prorated monthly finance charge. This amount is then multiplied by the number of months the installment obligation was outstanding during the year.[49]

Where a contract calls for a buyer to make deferred payments in the future with no reference to any interest charge, or where the stated interest rate is less than 4 percent per year, some of the deferred payments he makes are regarded as interest. This so-called "imputed interest" may be deducted by the buyer on the ground that it is not really a purchase price of the goods he is buying. But the rule does not apply where the sales price under the contract is less than $3,000.[50]

A late-payment charge of 5 percent of the amount of the bill of customers who paid more than twenty days after the due date was deductible as interest. It was not necessary for the parties to label a payment made for the use of money as interest for it to be treated as such for tax purposes.[51]

Commitment fees incurred by a merchant under an agreement with a bank which guaranteed to have business funds available on a standby basis in case of need were deductible as charges to carry on a business. They were deductible as ordinary and necessary expenses not representing interest.[52]

Commitment fees or standby charges incurred under a mortgage agreement providing for construction funds to be available in stated amounts over a specified period are similarly deductible as current business expenses. These fees are considered to be carrying charges which the borrower may deduct currently or elect to capitalize as part of construction costs.[53]

Penalty payments made by a taxpayer to his mortgagee for the privilege of prepaying his mortgage indebtedness are deductible as interest.[54] Prepayment charges in the case of a loan are in reality an additional fee for the use of the lender's money for a shorter period of time than originally agreed upon. The fee represents the generally higher cost of a short-term loan as opposed to a long-term loan.[55]

Under the Graduated Payment Mortgages (GPM) plan of the Department of Housing and Urban Development, the mortgagor pays to the mortgagee the principal amount borrowed, plus interest at a fixed rate per annum on the unpaid mortgage balances. Various plans are available. Some plans provide for annual increases in monthly payments for a fixed period of years with level payments made thereafter. Other plans permit five years of increasing payments with annual increases, and some permit ten years of increasing payments with annual increases at 2 percent and 3 percent respectively. For the early years of the mortgage term, when the amount of monthly payment does not fully cover the interest owed, the entire amount represents interest and is deductible by the mortgagor when paid. That part of the interest owed but not paid is not allowed as a deduction to the mortgagor until paid. For subsequent years of the mortgage term, when the amount of the payments has increased to the extent that it now exceeds the current interest charge owed, the excess is to be applied against the unpaid balance of the loan. This excess will be treated as discharging first that part of the unpaid balance of the loan that represents accumulated interest carried over from prior years and is deductible by the mortgagor as interest at that time.[56]

A loan-processing fee, sometimes referred to as points, paid by a borrower as compensation to the lender solely for the use or forbearance of money is deductible in full in the year of payment.[57]

However, the term *points* is sometimes used to describe the charges paid by a mortgagor-borrower to a lender as loan origination fees, maximum loan charges, or premium charges. Expenses incident to acquiring a mortgage loan are not deductible as interest nor are they deductible in full as business expenses in the year paid. These expenses are capital expenditures, which are deductible on a *pro rata* basis over the life of the mortgage.[58] So the payor has the obligation of showing that the loan fees were an additional cost of the borrowing of money, as opposed to a charge for compensation for services rendered in obtaining the loan.[59]

A negotiated bonus or premium paid by a borrower to a lender in order to obtain a loan is characterized as interest.[60] Whether the amount of the bonus or premium is withheld by the lender rather than being paid back to the lender is immaterial.[61]

Starting on January 1, 1976, points paid by a cash-method taxpayer on indebtedness incurred in connection with the purchase or improvement of (and secured by) his principal residence may be treated as paid in the taxable year of actual payment. This exception applies only to points on a home mortgage and not to other interest costs on such a mortgage. In addition, in order to qualify for this exception, the charging of points must reflect an established business practice in the geographical area where the loan is made. The deduction allowed under this exception may not exceed the number of points generally charged in that area for a home loan.[62]

A premium charge paid by a buyer to a savings and loan association is deductible where this represented a charge of one-half of 1 percent per year for the privilege of being granted the loan.[63]

If a borrower is obligated to sign a note for more money than he receives from the lender because the interest is subtracted from the face amount of the note, the interest is deductible on this note discount when payments are made. Assume that a borrower signs a note for $1,200 on March 27, agreeing to pay it in twelve equal installments beginning on April 30. The interest ($1,200 × 6 percent = $72) is subtracted from the face value of the note, and the borrower receives $1,128. If he uses the cash method, the interest is considered to be repaid in twelve installments of $6 each. If he makes only eight payments in that year, his deduction is $48. Accrual-method taxpayers, however, prorate the interest over the period in which it accrues. So $54 (nine-twelfths of $72) is deductible in the following taxable year.[64]

If a party owes both principal and interest, any payment he makes to his creditor is credited first to his interest obligation, the balance going towards principal. If debtor and creditor agree in an arm's-length transaction that interest is to be allocated differently from what this general rule requires, the Internal Revenue Service will respect the agreement unless the Service finds that the method of accounting does not clearly reflect income. So debtor and creditor can work out an agreement which provides the debtor with the tax treatment which he prefers, usually a larger tax deduction for that year. Where the parties fail to do so, the debtor is bound by the usual rules as to the application of the payment he makes.[65]

Payments made annually or periodically on a redeemable ground rent are deductible as interest.[66] Although payments on a nonredeemable ground rent are not interest, they may be deducted as rent to the extent they are business expenses or are attributable to rental properties held for the production of income.[67]

The owner of a condominium can deduct the interest on mortgage indebtedness allocable to his property.[68]

Where two or more persons are jointly and severally liable on an obligation (that is, each person has liability for the full amount of the indebtedness), and only one of these parties makes an interest payment in a taxable year, he is entitled to the full interest deduction.[69] Where a son borrowed money under a student loan program in order to pay tuition and other expenses, his father had to co-sign a promissory note. Actually the father paid each interest installment. He could deduct the full interest as paid.[70]

Husband and wife held their personal property as tenants by the entirety. The property was encumbered with an indebtedness evidenced by a promissory note and secured by a mortgage. The note, signed by each spouse, required each and both of them to pay the mortgage interest in monthly installments. The schedule of payments given to each spouse by the mortgagee showed separately the amount of interest payable. Where the spouses filed separate Federal income tax returns, the amount of interest actually paid by the wife was deductible on her individual tax return for each year.[71]

If a husband and wife jointly own their residence as tenants by the entirety with a right of survivorship, and an agreement made a part of a divorce decree provides that from amounts the wife receives from the husband as support she is to make the principal and interest payments on the mortgage on the property (an indebtedness for which they are both liable), then the wife must include in her income, and the husband may deduct, one-half of each principal and interest payment as "alimony." He may also deduct the other half of the interest payments as "interest." If the residence is held by husband and wife as tenants in common, the wife owns one-half of the property. Therefore the husband may deduct, as "alimony," amounts he pays on the wife's half of the property for principal and interest on the mortgage.

Amounts paid by the husband on his half of the property are not deductible as alimony, nor are they taxable to the wife. But he may deduct as "interest" the portion he pays for interest on his half of the property. If the wife is sole owner of the property, and her husband agrees to make the mortgage payments on it, he may deduct these payments as "alimony," where they are taxable to her as periodic payments under a decree or agreement. If she itemizes her deductions she may deduct the portion of each payment which represents interest on the mortgage. If the husband is sole owner of the residence occupied rent-free by the wife, he may not deduct his mortgage payments as "alimony." But he may deduct as "interest" any interest he pays on the property.[72]

Interest on indebtedness incurred or continued to purchase or to carry tax-exempt obligations is not deductible.[73] But it does not follow that interest paid to lending banks or other parties must be disallowed simply because the taxpayer happens to own tax-exempt bonds. When an individual borrowed funds to operate various business ventures at a time when he was holding tax-exempt bonds, the Internal Revenue Service claimed that interest on the undeniably business indebtedness must be disallowed because to some extent at least this money *could* have been used to carry the tax-exempts. In rejecting this position, the court pointed out that this rule applies only where a taxpayer borrows and uses the borrowed funds to purchase the tax-exempts. Such was not the case here. There was no relationship between the incurring of various indebtedness by the taxpayer and his holding of tax-exempt bonds except for the general fact that incurring of indebtedness allowed him to retain his tax-exempt holdings.[74] A loan not incurred to purchase tax-exempt obligations but for the purpose of operating a taxpayer's business was not "incurred or continued to purchase or carry" tax-exempt securities, even though such securities were hypothecated (deposited as security) for the loans.[75]

Interest expense on the revolving account of a brokerage house (the account was used to purchase both taxable and tax-exempt securities for resale) was deductible. The tax-exempt securities represented only a small fraction of the bonds purchased, inasmuch as the firm had a policy against investment in tax-exempts. The statute makes no provision for proration of interest.[76]

Another broker carried on a general securities business, including tax-exempts, which amounted to less than 1 percent of the average monthly value of the firm's assets and less than one-fourth of 1 percent of the gross income. Money was borrowed to finance customers' purchases of securities in margin accounts and for general cash requirements for purchasers. It was not possible to determine how much of the loans represented dealings in tax-exempt obligations. Only that portion of the interest deduction not allocable to investments which were not tax-exempt was deductible.[77]

In the case where an individual, as the distributee of an estate's assets, paid an estate tax deficiency and interest thereon by reason of the fact that the estate no longer had assets, he could deduct the interest which had accrued on the deficiency *subsequent* to the distribution. Interest which had accrued on the deficiency prior to the distribution was not deductible.[78]

A somewhat limited deduction is allowed for interest on money borrowed for investment purposes ("investment interest"). Such interest is deductible by an individual up to the aggregate of:

1. $25,000 ($12,500 in the case of separate returns filed by married persons).

2. The amount of net investment income.

3. The excess of net long-term capital gain over net short-term capital loss for the taxable year.

4. One-half the amount by which investment interest exceeds the total of items 1, 2, and 3.

This does not refer to investment interest on indebtedness incurred before December 7, 1969, or incurred after that date pursuant to a written contract which was binding on that date.[79]

For taxable years beginning after December 31, 1975, there is a limitation on the deduction of nonbusiness interest: $10,000 plus the taxpayer's net investment income. No offset of investment income is permitted against capital gain income. An additional deduction of up to $15,000 per year is permitted for interest paid in connection with indebtedness incurred by the taxpayer to acquire the stock in a corporation, or a partnership interest, where the taxpayer, his spouse, and his children have (or acquire) at least 50 percent of the stock or capital interest in the enterprise. Interest deductions which are disallowed under these rules are subject to an unlimited carry-over and may be deducted in future years, subject to the applicable limitation. No limitation is imposed on the deductibility of personal interest.[80]

Interest on Federal income taxes owing is deductible when paid. Effective July 1, 1975, the interest rate became 9 percent instead of the previous 6 percent. In addition, a procedure was set up by which the interest rate in the future will be adjusted to the changes in the money-market rate. Interest will be adjusted, according to a formula, as the prime rate quoted by commercial banks to large businesses changes.[81] As of February 1, 1978, the rate self-adjusted to 6 percent.[82]

Interviews. An employer can deduct the costs of interviewing prospective employees.[83] *See also* **Employment, expenses in seeking.**

Inventory write-downs. If a taxpayer's business inventory is valued on the basis of the lower of cost or market value, deduction is allowed when written down to the latter figure.[84]

Any goods in an inventory which are unsalable at normal prices and are unusable in the normal way because of damage, imperfections, shop wear, change of style, odd or broken lots, or similar causes, including secondhand goods taken in exchange, are to be included in inventory as *bona fide* selling prices less the direct cost of the disposition.[85] A deduction for this write-down is allowed.

Unsalability for this purpose is not limited to damage, imperfections, etc. Unsalability was found where the only possible purchaser of the inventory, military light cargo trailers, terminated its contract.[86] Write-down was allowed when large quantities of defective merchandise were found in the inventory;[87] when there had been leaks in the inventory;[88] and where there were merchandise shortages.[89]

Investigatory expenses. *See* **Investors.**

Investors. Deduction is allowed to an individual for all ordinary and necessary expenses paid or incurred for the production or collection of income and for the management, conservation, or maintenance of property held for the production of income.[90] One of those named characterizations customarily covers what an investor does.

Office rent and similar expenses paid or incurred by an individual in connection with his investments are deductible only if they are ordinary and necessary under all the circumstances having regard to such an investment and to the relationship of the individual to such investment.[91]

If a person maintains an office at which he conducts some other activity of a personal nature, and he also carries on activities as an investor there, an allocation of rent, clerical salaries, and other expenses may be deducted.[92]

A retired octogenarian was permitted to deduct part of the cost of an office maintained for personal use and to handle his investments. Although he personally spent little time in the office, a clerk worked there regularly, collecting and recording the venerable gentleman's income. On the basis of time devoted to the production of income, 50 percent of the office expense was deemed to be deductible.[93] The cost of moving an office was also deductible in another case where the office was used for handling investments.[94]

Postage related to one's investment activities is deductible.[95] To the extent that a secretary's time is devoted to a person's investment activities, an allocation of her (or his) time is deductible.[96]

An individual may properly deduct an investment counsel's fee.[97] And the cost of statistical service is also deductible if used in the management and conservation of investments.[98] An attorney who bought and sold securities for his own account could deduct his expenses for a statistical service.[99]

An investor properly deducted fees for the collection of income.[100] But a fee paid to a broker to acquire investment property is not deductible and is added to the cost of the property. A fee paid in connection with the sale of investment property is a selling expense and may be used only to determine gain or loss from the sale.[101]

Rent for a safe deposit box is deductible if the box is used for the storage of taxable income-producing stocks, bonds, and the like. The rent is not deductible if the box is used to store personal effects or tax-exempt securities.[102] Deduction was permitted for the rent of a safe deposit box which was used to hold Series E Treasury bonds, although no income was reportable in the taxable year, election having been made to report appreciation in the year when the bonds matured.[103]

The cost of custodian services is deductible.[104]

Entertainment in connection with one's investments in taxable securities was deductible where an investor wined and dined knowledgeable persons in an effort to get investment advice from them.[105]

An individual gave purchase orders for stock, and the necessary funds, to a New York Stock Exchange member firm, calling for immediate delivery of his shares. After nine futile months of demanding his stock, he brought suit against the broker for cancellation of his orders; the stock, meanwhile, had declined drastically in value. He also sought the return of his funds. He was awarded judgment for the amount of his cash advances. But inasmuch as the broker faced bankruptcy, the customer accepted cash and stock worth considerably less than the judgment. The loss was fully deductible, for although the broker owed money to his customer, he did not owe it as a debtor and hence it was not a debt. As far as the customer was concerned, this had been a transaction entered upon for profit.[106]

A loss sustained during a taxable year with respect to expenditures incurred in search of a business or investment is deductible only where the activities are more than investigatory and the taxpayer actually has entered into a transaction for profit and the project later is abandoned. The loss is allowable only in the taxable year in which the project is abandoned.[107]

The following case is a good example of the above. After investigating a mine operation owned by another person to determine whether it might be a suitable investment for himself, an individual contributed cash and hired several men for about thirty days to rehabilitate mining equipment and to operate a mine temporarily to ascertain whether future investment was warranted. The results of the temporary operation were unsuccessful, and the project was abandoned. The individual never acquired any interest nor made any other investment in the property. A deductible loss was sustained in the taxable year in which the project was abandoned because his activities in connection with the project were more than investigatory; he had actually entered into a transaction for profit which he had later abandoned.[108]

An individual sought to operate a Holiday Inn under a franchise. He obtained a "hold" from that organization, subject to the acquisition of an appropriate site in a designated community. He found land to his liking, arranged for the financing, and was ready to go forward, when for reasons beyond his control and without his fault or neglect the land became unavailable. He was permitted to deduct his expenses for attorney, architect, and feasibility studies because they related to a transaction entered upon for profit, although this venture was not connected with his regular profession (he was a lawyer) and the motel venture never became operative.[109] A taxpayer sought, with several associates, to incorporate a savings and loan association. Funds were expended to obtain the necessary charter from the state savings and loan commissioner. The taxpayer's extensive activities in investigating the project, in holding discussions with professional advisors, and in studying the economic chances of success indicated that this was a transaction entered upon for profit. Expenses merely representing the cost of an investigation of a possible business opportunity are not deductible, but here the project could be said to have proceeded sufficiently far to establish that this was a transaction entered upon for profit, even though the deal subsequently fell apart because the charter was not issued.[110]

One case lost by a taxpayer revealed what an investor has to show in order to deduct travel expense. He studied financial data relevant to corporations in which he was interested, including annual reports, production data, and newspaper articles. As part of his investment method, he also visited corporate factories and retail outlets to see things for himself. In one year, he made fifteen trips through parts of the United States and Europe. But he could not deduct his travel expenditures as expenses for the production of income, for it appeared that he managed to visit members of his far-flung family on these trips. The value of this decision is that the court specifically stated what a traveling investor can do to get his tax deduction: "If proof had been adduced that such a trip was part of a rationally planned, systematic investigation of the business operations of such a company, if the level of costs involved had been reasonable viewed in relation to the magnitude of the investment and the value of the information reasonably expected to be derived from the trip, if the circumstances had negated a disguised personal motive for the travel, and if there had been some showing of a practical application through investment decisions of the kind of information gained from such trips, we might have been favorably disposed to [the investor's] contentions. We need not, and do not, hold that as a matter of law the legitimate costs of travel by an investor to places of business of firms in which he holds a substantial stake may never be deducted. We hold merely that under the circumstances of this case [the investor] has not persuaded us that the costs he incurred here were ordinary and necessary."[111]

If an individual's attempts to acquire a business are unsuccessful, deduction is not allowed for expenses incurred in the course of a general search for, or preliminary investigation of, a business or investment. This includes expenses related to decisions *whether* to enter a transaction and *which* transaction to enter. Typical are expenses for advertisements, travel to search for a new business, and the cost of audits that were designed to help the investor to decide to attempt an acquisition. But once efforts are made to acquire a specific business or investment, expenses for attorneys to draft purchase agreements and any other costs incurred in an attempt to complete the purchase of the business are deductible.[112]

Expenses incurred in the search for suitable business income are not deductible; they are not business expenses before the taxpayer is engaged in that business. But if a transaction has reached the point where he is justified in thinking he has found such a business, the expenses are deductible on the ground that they are related to a transaction entered upon for profit. An individual sought to make a substantial investment in some business. Through a broker, he made contact with a distributing corporation. After consultations with bankers, accountants, and lawyers as to the status and prospects of the corporation, plus considerable personal investigation, terms were worked out and a draft acquisition agreement was prepared. But before the papers were signed, he discovered that there had been some misrepresentations to him and that the company's financial position was not so rosy as he had believed. He called the deal off. His expenses for legal and accounting fees, and for travel and living expenses in investigating the proposition, were deductible. These expenses had not been incurred by him in preparing to consummate the purchase. So they were not nondeductible prebusiness expenses before he could be said to have entered upon a transaction for profit.[113]

An individual was a corporate employee and never was in the business of buying and selling oil leases or other mining property. But he did purchase interests in leases and royalties solely for the purpose of utilizing his personal funds. It was held that expenses incident to travel to investigate investment possibilities were deductible when the investigations did not result in the acquisition of leases or royalties as investments.[114]

A United States investor could deduct his expenses in looking after his investments in Canada. The properties were held for the production of income, and legal matters in connection with these properties called for the investor's attention.[115]

A taxpayer was an employee of a bookshop. She also managed her own investments, noted the court, "in a businesslike manner." She subscribed to the Wall Street Journal and several investment services; she also collected a variety of information about investments such as corporate financial reports, news releases, and brokers' recommendations. She was permitted to deduct the costs of weekly trips to the manager of her custodial account and monthly trips to meet with her broker.[116]

Investors in securities or investors in real estate may deduct stock transfer and real estate transfer taxes, respectively, to the extent that they are expenses incurred in carrying on a trade or business or are an activity for the production of income.[117]

Taxes incurred in the production of rental income, such as real property taxes and personal property taxes, are deductible as rental expenses.[118]

If a dealer in securities makes a short sale of stock and is required to pay the lender for dividends distributed while he maintained his short position, he may deduct this amount as a business expense. These payments made by individuals who are investors may be claimed only when deductions are itemized on Schedule A ("Itemized Deductions"), which certainly means a substantial proportion of all investors.[119]

If the payment is in lieu of a liquidating or stock dividend or if the borrower buys additional shares of stock equal to a stock dividend issued during his short position, that amount must be added to the cost of the stock sold short, whether the payment is made by the dealer or an investor.[120]

Loan premiums equal to cash dividends paid by an investor on stock borrowed to cover short sales are similarly deductible.[121]

Where a stockholder surrenders a part of his stock to improve the financial condition of the corporation, he sustains a deductible loss, measured by the cost or other basis of the stock surrendered, less the resulting improvement in the value of the stock retained.[122] Where a stockholder surrenders some of his shares disproportionately with respect to other shareholders to the issuing corporation for no consideration other than whatever enhancement in the book value results from this surrender, he realizes an ordinary as opposed to a capital loss.[123]

Generally, a payment by a stockholder to his corporation to protect his existing investment and to prevent a loss is regarded as a capital contribution and must be added to the cost or other basis of his stock. But when a stockholder surrenders a part of his stock to improve the financial condition of the corporation, he has a deductible loss, measured by his basis in the shares surrendered. Such was the case where the two principal stockholder-officers of a corporation with more than 800 shareholders transferred some of their stock back to the corporation. All they received in return was a belief that the corporation would not be plunged into insolvency, a circumstance which might have caused the company's principal creditor to sue these officer-shareholders for mismanagement that had triggered bankruptcy and creditor losses.[124]

Several individuals owned the controlling stock interest in a corporation. In order to prevent a takeover of their interest by another group, they engaged counsel. Legal fees were deductible as an expenditure for the conservation of property held for the production of income. The stock could be regarded as held for the production of income if the individuals' continued gainful employment would be lost as the result of the takeover, or if continuance of dividends on their stock was likely to be jeopardized.[125]

A minority stockholder in a Delaware corporation was dissatisfied with the terms of a merger that the corporation entered into with a larger company. As authorized by Delaware law, inasmuch as she had dissented to the merger, she was entitled to be paid a price based upon an appraisal of the value of her stock. She could deduct her legal fees in forcing the appraisal and the correlative payment to her. She incurred the legal expenses solely in an attempt to increase the amount of income the sale of the stock would produce over the amount she previously had been offered. Although the fees related to a capital asset, they were not necessary to the disposition of a capital asset and hence were not capital expenditures. Her purpose in engaging counsel was to determine the amount of income due her from the sale of her stock.[126]

Pro rata expenses of members of a stockholders' committee were deductible where far-reaching changes in the management of the corporation were sought. These objectives were sought by attempting to elect a new board of directors. The payments by the stockholders were made in anticipation that profit would result, as shown in a document published by the committee entitled Let's Rebuild Montgomery Ward. It may have been a long chance that a stockholder was taking, but it was an attempt (actually successful) to increase corporate profits and stockholder dividends.[127]

Payments by an investor to a bondholders' protective committee as a proportionate share of expenses were deductible as money paid for the conservation of property held for the production of income.[128]

Costs incurred by a stockholder in a proxy fight opposing management are deductible, at least to the extent that they are closely related to his income-producing activities.[129] Deduction similarly is allowed where the existing management is being supported in a proxy fight.[130]

A director and stockholder of a major railroad corporation joined with other individuals in soliciting proxies from the stockholders in an attempt to unseat the incumbent management. The group's efforts were unsuccessful, and the corporation saw fit to reimburse their expenses. Several other stockholders brought suit against this group for improperly claiming this reimbursement, and each of the group members bore his proportionate share of the compromise settlement worked out with those bringing the suit. The amounts paid out in the compromise were deductible. The expenses arose because of an effort by major stockholders to affect the policies of the railroad corporation and were moneys spent to conserve and to maintain income-producing property (stock) which they held.[131]

That situation differs markedly from the following: A person holding a small stock interest in a large corporation takes it upon himself to crusade for a particular point of view on a particular issue. However worthy his motives, he cannot reasonably expect to affect his dividend income in relation to his corporate investments to such an extent as would justify defining his activity as an ordinary and necessary expense.[132]

If holders of stock decide to sell their shares by means of a public offering of their holdings, the cost is not deductible, being deemed to be capital. But if they change their minds and abandon the project, they can deduct the costs which they had incurred.[133]

There are two types of fees paid by subscribers to sponsored investment plans:

1. The creation fee is deducted by the custodian from subscriber deposits and is paid to the sponsor for its services in developing, selling, and administering the plan. It is a fee paid for the privilege of acquiring stock through the plan and is not deductible. This fee is a capital expenditure and must be added to the cost of the shares acquired through the investment plan.[134]

2. The custody fee is paid for services performed by the custodian in holding the shares acquired through the plan, maintaining individual records, and providing detailed statements of account to subscribers. This is deductible.[135]

A bank established a plan known as the automatic dividend reinvestment service. Under the plan, cash dividends paid by the corporation were reinvested by the bank as agent for participating shareholders in full or fractional shares of the corporation. The bank was authorized by each member to receive all the cash dividends from the payor corporation that were otherwise payable to the shareholders. The bank's service charge and brokerage commissions were apportioned among subscribers to the plan. The service charge was deductible.[136]

If an individual purchases a fully taxable bond at a premium (above par), he may elect to amortize the premium over the life of the bond. The amortizable bond premium is then subtracted from his basis or adjusted basis for the bond. This treatment is mandatory in the case of tax-exempt bonds.[137]

Premiums paid to purchase a bond of indemnity so that a

new stock certificate will be issued to replace a missing one are deductible.[138] So are incidental expenses to secure replacement if securities are mislaid, stolen, or destroyed.[139]

A theft-loss deduction depends upon whether the event meets the definition of "theft" under the law of the state where it takes place. When investments were made with a certain party under fraudulent misrepresentations by him, and under state law the taking of money under false representations or false pretenses is theft, there is a theft-loss deduction for tax purposes.[140] An individual loaned money to a corporation in exchange for an unsecured interest-bearing note of the corporation. His decision to loan the corporation funds was based upon information contained in financial reports issued by the corporation. Subsequently, it was established that the financial statements were fraudulent in that they did not reflect large liabilities which made the corporation insolvent. Inasmuch as the misrepresentation as to the corporation's financial condition had been deliberate, the lender was entitled to a theft-loss deduction.[141]

Loss from failure to exercise a stock option is deductible if the option is not a capital asset in the holder's hands.[142] (Whether or not the option is a capital asset is a technical question, which the taxpayer may have to ask an accountant, lawyer, or I.R.S. employee.)

An expense incurred for the acquisition of capital assets is not deductible and must be added to the cost of the property. But deduction for lawyers' expenses in getting back investment property is deductible, as where a minority stockholder had lent shares to the corporation because it needed collateral for a bank loan but which subsequently became reluctant to give back the stock. Her status as a lender was independent of her position as a shareholder.[143]

If an individual holds income-producing securities, expenses in connection with incompetency proceedings which involve the securities' holder are deductible as expenses for the management and conservation of property. Without the appointment of a committee to handle her affairs, the income-producing property could not be conserved.[144]

If an individual incurs expenses to produce both taxable and tax-exempt income, but he cannot identify specifically the expenses which produce each type of income, then he must prorate them in order to determine the amount deductible.[145] Typical items subject to such proration are investment counsel fees, accounting services, interest on borrowed money. Where an investor borrowed money to make real estate investments at the time when he also was holding tax-exempt bonds, the interest was deductible. A reasonable person is not expected to sacrifice liquidity and security by selling tax-exempt bonds in lieu of incurring mortgage indebtedness for business purposes.[146]

Fees paid to a fiduciary for the management, conservation, or maintenance of a trust were deductible to the extent that taxable income was involved. When both taxable and tax-free securities were in the same trust fund, deduction was determined upon the ratio of taxable to nontaxable income.[147]

Other interest paid by an investor is determined in the same manner that applies to individuals in general. Interest on margin accounts is deductible for the taxable year when it is paid.[148]

For taxable years beginning after 1975, the amount of any loss (otherwise allowable for the year) in connection with one of certain activities cannot exceed the aggregate amount with respect to which the taxpayer is at risk in the activity at the close of the taxable year. This "at risk" limitation applies to the following activities: (1) farming (except farming operations involving trees other than fruit or nut trees), (2) exploring for, or exploiting, oil and gas resources, (3) holding, producing, or distributing motion picture films or video tapes, and (4) equipment leasing. A taxpayer is generally considered "at risk" with respect to an activity to the extent of his cash and the adjusted basis of other property contributed to the activity, any amounts borrowed for use in the activity with respect to which he has personal liability for payment from his personal assets, and his net fair market value of personal assets which secure non-recourse borrowings. This provision does not apply to net leases under binding contracts for equipment-leasing activities finalized on or before December 31, 1975.[149] For taxable years beginning after 1978, the specific "at risk" rule applies to all activities other than real estate.[150] See also **Capital losses; Mineral leases, cost of acquisition.**

Involuntary conversions. See **Property used in the trade or business and involuntary conversions.**

IRA. See **Individual retirement account.**

I

1. *Commissioner v. Sullivan et al.,* 356 U.S. 27 (1958).
2. *Louis Cohen,* T.C. Memo., Docket No. 63366, entered April 8, 1958.
3. *Robert Buedingen,* 6 B.T.A. 335 (1927).
4. *Connecticut Mutual Life Insurance Company v. Eaton,* 218 F. 206 (D.C., Conn., 1914).
5. Revenue Ruling 70-392, 1970-2 CB 33.
6. I.R.C. Section 691(c).

7. Revenue Ruling 69-607, 1969-2 CB 40.

8. Pension Reform Act of 1974, Section 2002.

9. Revenue Act of 1978, Section 157(e).

10. Revenue Act of 1978, Section 702(c).

11. Revenue Act of 1978, Section 157(a).

12. Revenue Act of 1978, Section 157(b).

13. I.R.S. Letter Ruling 7740008, June 28, 1977.

14. Tax Reform Act of 1976, Section 1503.

15. Tax Reform Act of 1976, Section 2715.

16. Revenue Ruling 76-374, 1976-2 CB 19.

17. I.T. 3634, 1944 CB 90.

18. *Tax Guide for Small Business*, 1975 edition, page 112.

19. Revenue Ruling 60-365, 1960-2 CB 49.

20. Revenue Ruling 56-26, 1956-1 CB 153.

21. Revenue Ruling 60-275, 1960-2 CB 43.

22. Revenue Ruling 69-491, 1969-2 CB 22.

23. Revenue Ruling 55-189, 1955-1 CB 265.

24. *Tax Guide for Small Business*, 1976 edition, page 112.

25. *General Smelting Company*, 4 T.C. 313 (1944).

26. *The First National Bank and Trust Company of Tulsa v. Jones*, 143 F.2d 652 (10th Cir., 1944).

27. *N. Loring Danforth*, 18 B.T.A. 1221 (1930).

28. Revenue Ruling 55-264, 1955-1 CB 11.

29. *Corn Products Refining Company v. Commissioner*, 350 U.S. 46 (1955).

30. *Farroll v. Jarecki*, 231 F.2d 281 (7th Cir., 1956).

31. I.R.C. Section 163.

32. *Thomas v. Dierks*, 132 F.2d 224 (5th Cir., 1942).

33. *In the Matter of Battelstein*, D.C., S.D. Texas, 1977.

34. Revenue Ruling 70-284, 1970-1 CB 34.

35. *Goldstein et al. v. Commissioner*, 364 F.2d 734 (2d Cir., 1966).

36. *Arthur R. Jones Syndicate v. Commissioner*, 23 F.2d 833 (7th Cir., 1927).

37. *Margaret E. Johnson Malmstedt et al.*, T.C. Memo. 1976-46, filed February 24, 1976.

38. Revenue Ruling 68-643, 1968-2 CB 76.

39. Tax Reform Act of 1976, Section 208.

40. Revenue Ruling 73-482, 1973-2 CB 44.

41. *M. A. Long*, 8 B.T.A. 737 (1927).

42. *Cook et ux. v. United States*, D.C., W.D. La., 1977.

43. *Dustin et al. v. Commissioner*, T.C. Memo. 1977-409, filed November 29, 1977.

44. Revenue Ruling 71-98, 1971-1 CB 57.

45. Revenue Ruling 72-315, 1972-1 CB 60.

46. Revenue Ruling 73-136, 1973-1 CB 68.

47. Revenue Ruling 77-417, 1977-2 CB 60.

48. Revenue Ruling 73-137, 1973-1 CB 68.

49. Regulations Section 1.163-2.

50. I.R.C. Section 483.

51. Revenue Ruling 74-187, 1974-1 CB 48.

52. Revenue Ruling 54-43, 1954-1 CB 119.

53. *Tax Information on Business Expenses*, I.R.S. Publication 535, 1976 edition, page 3.

54. Revenue Ruling 57-198, 1957-1 CB 94.

55. *General American Life Insurance Company*, 25 T.C. 1265 (1956).

56. Internal Revenue News Release IR-1795, April 15, 1977.

57. Revenue Ruling 69-582, 1969-2 CB 29.

58. *Tax Information on Business Expenses*, I.R.S. Publication 535, 1976 edition, page 14.
59. *Herbert Enoch et al.*, 57 T.C. 781 (1972).
60. Revenue Ruling 74-395, 1974-2 CB 45.
61. *L–R Heat Treating Company*, 28 T.C. 894 (1957).
62. Tax Reform Act of 1976, Section 208.
63. Revenue Ruling 69-290, 1969-1 CB 55.
64. *Your Federal Income Tax*, 1976 edition, page 98.
65. *Mason et al. v. United States*, 453 F. Supp. 845 (D.C., N.D. Cal., 1978).
66. I.R.C. Section 163(c).
67. *Your Federal Income Tax*, 1976 edition, page 96.
68. Revenue Ruling 64-31, 1964-1 CB (Part 1) 300.
69. *Kate Baker Sherman*, 18 T.C. 746 (1952).
70. Revenue Ruling 71-179, 1971-1 CB 58.
71. Revenue Ruling 71-268, 1971-1 CB 58.
72. *Income Tax Deductions for Alimony Payments*, I.R.S. Publication 504, 1976 edition, page 3.
73. I.R.C. Section 265(2).
74. *Edmund F. Ball et al.*, 54 T.C. 1200 (1970).
75. *R. B. Machinery Co.*, 26 B.T.A. 594 (1932).
76. *Wynn, Jr., et al. v. United States*, 288 F. Supp. 797 (D.C., E.D. Pa., 1968).
77. *Leslie et al. v. Commissioner*, 413 F.2d 636 (2d Cir., 1969).
78. Revenue Ruling 72-544, 1972-2 CB 96.
79. I.R.C. Section 163(d).
80. Tax Reform Act of 1976, Section 209.
81. I.R.C. Section 6621.
82. Internal Revenue News Release IR-1897, October 14, 1977.
83. *Charles O. Gunther, Jr., et al.*, T.C. Memo. 1954-181, filed October 21, 1954.
84. *E. W. Bliss Company et al. v. United States*, 351 F.2d 449 (6th Cir., 1965).
87. Regulations Section 1.471-2(c).
86. *Space Controls, Inc., v. Commissioner*, 322 F.2d 144 (5th Cir., 1963).
87. *Celluloid Company*, 9 B.T.A. 989 (1927).
88. *Otto Huber Brewery Company*, 2 B.T.A. 1193 (1925).
89. *Long Broom Co.*, 9 B.T.A. 39 (1927).
90. I.R.C. Section 212.
91. Regulations Section 1.212–1(g).
92. *Charles Oster*, T.C. Memo. 1964-335, filed December 20, 1964.
93. *Kenneth A. Scott*, T.C. Memo. 1972-109, filed May 10, 1972.
94. *Samuel Abrams et al.*, T.C. Memo. 1964-256, filed September 29, 1964.
95. *E. N. Fry*, 5 T.C. 1058 (1945).
96. *Frederick B. Rentschler*, 1 T.C. 814 (1943).
97. *Raymond Fitzgerald*, T.C. Memo., Docket No. 52539, entered December 27, 1956.
98. *Edward E. Bishop*, 4 T.C. 862 (1945).
99. *L. T. Alverson*, 35 B.T.A. 482 (1937).
100. *Edward Mallinckrodt, Jr.*, 2 T.C. 1128 (1943), *aff'd*, 146 F.2d 1 (8th Cir., 1945).
101. *Tax Information on Investment Income and Expenses*, I.R.S. Publication 550, 1976 edition, page 22.
102. *Ibid.*
103. *Daniel S. W. Kelly*, 23 T.C. 682 (1955), *aff'd on another issue*, 228 F.2d 512 (7th Cir., 1956).
104. *M. A. P. Coolidge et al.*, T.C. Memo., Docket Nos. 103648–103653, entered December 31, 1942.

<table>
<tr><td>105.</td><td>Samuel Abrams et al., T.C. Memo. 1964-256, filed September 29, 1964.</td></tr>
</table>

105. *Samuel Abrams et al.*, T.C. Memo. 1964-256, filed September 29, 1964.
106. *Fred G. Meyer et al.*, T.C. Memo. 1975-349, filed December 8, 1975.
107. Revenue Ruling 57-418, 1957-2 CB 143.
108. *Charles T. Parker*, 1 T.C. 509 (1943).
109. *Finch et al. v. United States*, D.C., Minn., 1966.
110. *Harris W. Seed et al.*, 52 T.C. 880 (1969).
111. *William R. Kinney*, 66 T.C. 122 (1976).
112. Revenue Ruling 77-254, 1977-2 CB 63.
113. *Johan Domenie et al.*, T.C. Memo. 1975-94, filed April 7, 1975.
114. *Colman et al. v. United States*, D.C., Utah, 1961.
115. *E. M. Godson et al.*, T.C. Memo., Docket Nos. 4913-4, entered July 24, 1946.
116. *Martha E. Henderson*, T.C. Memo. 1968-22, filed January 13, 1968.
117. Regulations Section 1.164(a).
118. *Income Tax Deduction for Taxes*, I.R.S. Publication 546, 1976 edition, page 5.
119. *Tax Information on Business Expenses*, I.R.S. Publication 535, 1976 edition, page 4.
120. *Ibid.*
121. Revenue Ruling 72-521, 1972-2 CB 178.
122. *Commissioner v. Burdick*, 59 F.2d 395 (3d Cir., 1932).
123. *Estate of William H. Foster*, 9 T.C. 930 (1947).
124. *David N. Smith et al.*, 66 T.C. 622 (1976).
125. *Powell, Jr., v. United States*, 294 F. Supp. 977 (D.C., S.D. S.D., 1969).
126. *Stemfel v. United States*, D.C., M.D. Tenn., 1969.
127. *Surasky v. United States*, 325 F.2d 191 (5th Cir., 1963).
128. *Truman H. Newberry et al.*, T.C. Memo., Docket Nos. 4122-3, entered June 6, 1945.
129. *Graham v. Commissioner*, 326 F.2d 878 (4th Cir., 1964).
130. *Locke Manufacturing Companies v. United States*, 237 F. Supp. 80 (D.C., Conn., 1964).
131. *Graham et al. v. Commissioner*, 326 F.2d 878 (4th Cir., 1964).
132. *J. Raymond Dyer*, 36 T.C. 456 (1961).
133. Revenue Ruling 79-2, I.R.B. 1979-1, 10.
134. *Tax Information on Investment Income and Expenses*, I.R.S. Publication 550, 1976 edition, page 23.
135. Revenue Ruling 55-23, 1955-1 CB 275.
136. Revenue Ruling 70-627, 1970-2 CB 159.
137. I.R.C. Section 171.
138. Revenue Ruling 62-21, 1962-1 CB 37.
139. *Tax Information on Investment Income and Expenses*, I.R.S. Publication 550, 1976 edition, page 23.
140. *Michele Monteleone et al.*, 34 T.C. 688 (1960).
141. Revenue Ruling 71-381, 1971-2 CB 126.
142. Regulations Section 1.1234-1(b)
143. *Cruttenden et al. v. Commissioner*, 70 T.C. 191 (1978).
144. *Elsie Weil Estate*, T.C. Memo. 1954-96, filed July 12, 1954.
145. *Tax Information on Investment Income and Expenses*, I.R.S. Publication 550, 1976 edition, page 23.
146. *Edmund F. Ball et al.*, 54 T.C. 1200 (1970).
147. *Whittemore, Jr., et al. v. United States*, 383 F.2d 824 (8th Cir., 1967).
148. *Miscellaneous Deductions and Credits*, I.R.S. Publication 529, 1976 edition, page 3.
149. Tax Reform Act of 1976, Section 204.
150. Revenue Act of 1978, Section 201.

J

Job evaluation. *See* **Career counseling.**

Job hunting. *See* **Employment, expenses in seeking; Employment agency fees.**

Jockeys. A professional jockey who is required to supply his own uniforms, without possibility of reimbursement, is entitled to deduct the cost.[1]

Joint Federal income tax returns. *See* **Carry-overs; Child care deduction; Contributions; Medical expenses; Taxes; Tax-option corporations.**

Joint ownership of property. *See* **Interest; Taxes.**

J

---

1. Revenue Ruling 70-475 1970-2 CB 35.

K

Keogh plans. *See* Self-employment plans.

Kickbacks. *See* Bribes and kickbacks.

Kidnapper, payments to. *See* Casualties.

L

Laboratory services. *See* **Medical expenses.**

Labor problems, expenses due to. *See* **Ordinary and necessary business expenses.**

Labor union. *See* **Union dues.**

Laetrile. The cost of laetrile is deductible as medical expense if prescribed by a doctor, provided the product was purchased and used where legally permitted.[1]

Land clearing. *See* **Farmers.**

Late payment charge. *See* **Interest.**

Laundry expenses. Deductible travel expenses while away from home include cleaning and laundry costs.[2]

Law school, study at. *See* **Education.**

Learning disabilities, expenses to cope with. *See* **Education; Medical expenses.**

Leasehold improvements as rent. *See* **Rent.**

Leases, expenses for obtaining. *See* **Expenditures for benefits lasting more than one year.**

Legal fees. Legal expenses which are a necessary factor in producing taxable income normally are deductible. Deduction is allowed where legal assistance is related directly to keeping one's employment, whether in performing duties or in litigating to keep one's job.[3] Legal fees incurred in an effort to get a person rehired by a corporation after his dismissal were deductible.[4]

An individual took an examination for assistant building

inspector of the New Jersey Civil Service Commission, and he was certified number one on the list. There was then a vacancy, and his appointment to the post was mandatory. But at the request of the municipality where the vacancy existed, his name was removed. He sued and won reinstatement. His attorneys' fees were deductible. Although he had no "job" in the usual sense, there was a position of status to be protected. It related to the production of future income. He was endeavoring to protect an already existing employment advantage.[5]

Attorneys' fees incurred to protect one's employment are deductible, despite the apparently indirect nature of the expenditures in some circumstances. In order to keep stockholders from voting her out of office, the president of a corporation needed all of the votes she could muster. Previously she had transferred stock amounting to about 5 percent of the shares outstanding to trusts for the benefit of her children. As the trustees might vote this stock against her retention of her salaried position, she engaged counsel to arrange for the replacement of the trustees with other persons who would vote on her side. The fees were deductible.[6]

Expenses of resisting his attempted discharge were deductible by a corporate officer.[7] Attorneys' fees paid by the president of a corporation were similarly deductible, as action had been brought against the corporation to remove him from control and management.[8] An officer and director of a corporation which was involved in various litigation properly deducted the fees of a lawyer he had engaged to advise him as to his liabilities, if any, as an officer and director.[9]

An individual was president and a stockholder of a family corporation in which his father was the dominant person. The father was strongly opposed to his son's expressed intention of marrying a certain woman. The father threatened that if the marriage were consummated (presumably in the legal sense) against his wishes, he would starve his son into submission by cutting his income from all sources. When the son got married anyway, the father discharged him. Then, as the son now was "retired," the father sought to have the corporation reacquire the son's shares under a buy-sell agreement which had been adopted. The purchase price offered was totally inadequate.

The son's mother was loyal to her husband and sought to have the son declared mentally incompetent. The son engaged counsel, and there were thirty instances of litigation in the next four years, including derivative suits by minority shareholders. Typically, the son filed suit against the corporation to require it to pay dividends because he continued to hold some stock. After the father died, an accommodation was reached, and the son regained his presidency, with substantial salary increases. His legal fees were deductible, for, said the court, without the assistance he received from his lawyers, he would not have regained his executive position, which provided the compensation on which he paid substantial income tax. And his stockholdings would have been swept away by an inadequate purchase price. Dividends would have been much smaller if not nonexistent. The fees were to protect his position and his income.[10]

The United States government brought suit against the directors of a corporation which went into bankruptcy, seeking to recover $250,000 from the directors collectively. The matter was settled. A director could deduct legal fees related to her participation in the matter, for they were in line with the performance of her duties.[11] An individual could deduct legal fees to defend himself against charges of breach of fiduciary duties owed to a corporation as a director and officer.[12] A retired businessman properly deducted his attorneys' fees in defending himself in a lawsuit directed against his activities while still a corporate director and officer. The suit had resulted from his business as a director and officer, when he was still engaged in the business.[13]

An individual was secretary-treasurer of a corporation with the responsibility of filing the corporation's Federal income tax returns. He diverted substantial corporate funds to his personal use and did not report these amounts as income on either the corporate or his personal income tax return. As a consequence he was indicted for causing the corporation to file a fraudulent tax return and for filing a false individual return. He employed counsel and incurred legal fees. Inasmuch as his duties included the filing of the corporate tax returns, the legal expenses incurred in his defense for evading the corporation's taxes by filing a false return arose in connection with acts committed by him in his trade or business as an employee of the corporation and were deductible as ordinary and necessary expenses on his own return. He could, moreover, deduct attorneys' fees in connection with his own defense of tax evasion.[14]

In general, attorneys' fees are deductible only if related to the taxpayer's trade or business or to the production of income. Such was the case where an individual paid a lawyer for claims resulting from a business in which he was no longer engaged.[15]

Legal expenses in defense of professional acts arising from one's trade or business are deductible.[16] An individual may deduct fees in defense of his own activities in connection with an antitrust suit involving his corporation as long as they are incurred in defending activities related to the business of the corporation and not to personal policies.[17] A broker was put to the cost of defending a lawsuit wherein he was charged with "churning" the portfolio of a trust under his supervision simply for the purpose of increasing his commissions. His expenses incurred in resisting the claim were held to be deductible.[18] An attorney could deduct legal fees related to his successful defense against disbarment.[19] Legal expenses incurred by a physician in defending a suit for malpractice were deductible.[20]

But the person paying the fees must establish that they were related to his trade or business. That could not be done by a physician who had to pay substantial costs arising from a stockholder's suit for mismanagement against a board of directors of which he was a member. This director served solely at the request of the chief stockholder and was not paid for so doing.[21]

An author could deduct legal fees in connection with the negotiation of contracts and the resisting of a libel suit.[22] Legal expenses were allowed in a matter involving alleged violation of the Fair Labor Standards Act.[23] A physician could deduct fees paid to an attorney to settle any possible civil action which might arise out of an altercation with a third party to prevent the doctor from removing a patient from a hotel.[24]

Deductibility of counsel fees is not limited to instances where the defense was successful, however, because deduction was allowed for the defense of a damage suit based on malpractice or fraud or breach of fiduciary duty without regard to the success of the defense.[25]

Legal fees are deductible in the case of an unsuccessful defense of a criminal action arising from the carrying on of a trade or business. In the words of one decision which the United States Supreme Court affirmed:

So long as the expense arises out of the conduct of the business and is a required outlay it ought to be considered ordinary and necessary. . . . There had been no "governmental declaration" of any "sharply defined" national or state policy of discouraging the hiring of counsel and the incurring of other legal expense in defense of a criminal charge. In fact, it is highly doubtful whether such a public policy could exist in the face of the Sixth Amendment's guaranty of the right to counsel.[26]

Attorneys' fees and related legal expenses paid or incurred in the unsuccessful defense of a prosecution for violation of the Sherman Anti-Trust Act or of claims by the government under the Clayton Act or the Federal False Claims Act, if otherwise deductible as ordinary and necessary expenses, no longer will be denied deduction on the ground that allowance of these deductions would frustrate sharply defined public policy.[27] Attorneys' fees in connection with defense before the National Labor Relations Board are also deductible.[28]

Attorneys' fees resulting from resistance to foreclosure suits for alleged nonpayment of bills were deductible.[29]

Attorneys' fees in an action to recover the amount of a bill which a customer or client refused to pay are deductible.[30]

And an executor could deduct the legal expenses involved in collecting his fee.[31]

Deduction was allowed for the fees of attorneys hired to collect a business insurance claim. The expenditure was to collect a sum of money, and the dispute did not concern title to a capital asset nor an additional expenditure undertaken to improve or to increase the value of any capital asset then owned by the taxpayer.[32]

Legal expenses in an attempt to recover damages for illegal patent infringement were allowed.[33]

Legal fees paid to collect income are deductible, even though the income collected happens to be capital gain.[34]

Legal fees incurred in conection with a suit to recover interest on a loan are deductible, but that portion of the legal expenses attributed to the collection of the principal of the loan is not.[35]

Although consulting fees pertaining to the acquisition of additional business properties with a life of more than one year are not deductible, deduction is allowed for that part of the fees which relates to problems of administration of property already held.[36]

Lawyers' fees in connection with the leasing of land are not currently deductible, for they must be spread over the life of the lease. Deduction is proper, however, where the efforts to acquire leases were unsuccessful.[37] Legal fees in the compromising of litigation with a onetime business associate were deductible, even though the suit had been brought against other persons in addition to the taxpayer.[38]

An individual could deduct attorney's fees paid in an effort to salvage something from the dissolution of a corporation in which he was interested.[39]

Costs of legal work in applying for a Federal income tax ruling were held to be deductible.[40] Fees paid for consultation and advice in tax matters arising from a divorce settlement are deductible.[41] (See the discussion on legal expenses related to divorce proceedings later under this heading.)

Legal fees incurred in defending the legality of a divorce are not deductible. Expenses for getting tax advice, however, are deductible. Where a lawyer handling divorce litigation shows a breakdown on his bill of how much of it represented the tax problems involved, that portion could be deducted, whereas nothing is deductible in the absence of such an analysis of his charges.[42]

Legal fees paid in connection with a compromise of taxes are deductible.[43]

Fees paid to a law firm to prepare an estate plan for an individual and his wife are deductible to the extent that the services involve Federal income, estate, and gift tax advice. A proration which includes an itemized list of the services performed and the time spent on each element of the estate planning must therefore be made available, preferably on the lawyer's bill. Without such a proration into the deductible and nondeductible portions of the estate-planning work, the entire deduction may be lost; otherwise, an allowable percentage of the bill is deductible.[44]

Deduction was permitted for attorneys' fees in a case where the fees were to pay for a study of the merits and legal aspects of a plan to rearrange and to reinvest an entire estate. The plan had been submitted by a firm of estate planners.[45]

Professional fees in connection with obtaining a ruling from the Internal Revenue Service on the tax consequences of corporate reorganization were deductible in part. That part of the fee which was allocated to ascertain the basis of a shareholder's stock under the proposed reorganization was not deductible.[46]

Deductible attorneys' fees are not restricted to litigation or even to essentially legal work. A business could deduct fees paid to lawyers to work on credit problems.[47] The expenses incurred in hiring an attorney to determine the advisability of a change in organization are deductible.[48]

Fees paid to a lawyer to facilitate the shipment of undelivered purchases could be deducted.[49] Payments to an attorney for collecting a business debt were properly deducted.[50] A creditor was able to take a deduction for his payment to a lawyer for locating a debtor's property.[51]

Legal expenses arising from the defense of a suit for an accounting are deductible.[52] Where a former partner sued a copartner for an accounting of the receipts of the dissolved partnership, the copartner could deduct legal expenses arising from his defense of the suit.[53] Also, a legal expenditure made in defending a suit for an accounting and damages resulting from an alleged patent infringement was deductible as a business expense.[54]

Ordinarily, attorneys' fees incident to a condemnation action, which is an involuntary conversion, are capital expenditures. But in a case in which the owner of a building held as rental property brought suit for negligence against a salvage company (the negligence had resulted in the destruction of her building) she could deduct the legal fees. They were spent in an attempt to require a negligent party to pay for the loss of an income-producing property, that is, they were expenses in connection with the conservation of property held for the production of income.[55]

A retired noncommissioned officer in the United States Army could deduct legal fees related to successful efforts in increasing his retirement pay.[56] And the cost of court-martial counsel was deductible by a member of the Army Reserve.[57] See **Armed Forces.**

Expenses incurred in "defending or perfecting title to property" are nondeductible. The Internal Revenue Service sought to use this principle to disallow legal expenses of an individual who had inherited corporate stock from her father. A shareholder in the corporation in which her father had been an officer instituted a shareholder's derivative suit claiming that her father and other officers had obtained the stock in breach of their fiduciary duty to the corporation and that the corporation should have been the owner of the shares. This suit was unsuccessful. The daughter could deduct her legal expenses in connection with the conservation of the shares, for she was protecting her income, that is, dividends on these shares. The issue of title was not the main and primary purpose of her expenditures.[58]

When the broker to whom an individual had given funds to buy stock became financially unable to do so, the individual went to an attorney to cancel the agreement and to get back his money. A settlement was reached, under which the customer got back most of his advances in the form of cash and stock. Legal fees are not deductible if incurred in connection with the acquisition of a capital asset, as the stock was. The total dollar value of what the broker paid over was split percentagewise into stock and cash ratios. The legal fee was multiplied by the ratio representing the stock, and the result was nondeductible as a capital expenditure. The legal fee then was multiplied by the ratio representing the cash proportion of the total proceeds, and this was a deductible legal expense.[59]

Even though defense of title (for example, title of stock) ordinarily is a nondeductible capital expenditure, an individual was permitted to deduct legal fees in defending her title to stock in a suit which was completely without merit and was utterly unjustified.[60]

When the holders of a substantial minority interest in a corporation became dissatisfied with the manner in which it was operated, they sought the advice of counsel on what to do. He ascertained that enough stock could be purchased to acquire control. Legal fees for his services were deductible, being for the rendition of advice as to a method by which the shareholders could protect their existing interests in the corporation.[61]

Individuals were permitted to deduct legal fees incurred in an effort to prevent a takeover of their controlling interest in a corporation. Inasmuch as the litigation represented an attempt to conserve property held for the production of income, this was not a capital expenditure.[62]

In another stock case, a minority shareholder of a corporation, who had dissented to a merger, could deduct her legal fees in demanding an appraisal of her stock; under state law she was permitted to be paid for her shares on the basis of an appraisal and she was merely enforcing this right.[63]

The successor to a defunct business could deduct attorneys' fees in resisting taxes imposed against the defunct company, whose liabilities the successor had assumed.[64]

Legal fees relating to the payment of alimony are deductible to the extent that they were concerned with the tax deductibility of such payments.[65]

A contractor could deduct legal fees in connection with damage claims against him for inadequate construction work.[66] The sole stockholder of a corporation was able to deduct legal expenses in resisting claims that charged him and other officers of conspiracy against the corporation after it had been liquidated, for he could look to no one else for reimbursement.[67]

In general, attorneys' fees in connection with a divorce, separation, or decree for support are not deductible by either the husband or the wife. But the expense of legal advice to determine the tax consequences incident to divorce is deductible in each of these situations:

1. Where at the time of his divorce a taxpayer engaged a law firm specializing in taxation to advise him as to a proposed settlement agreement in which he transferred his interest in certain properties to his wife in exchange for the transfer to him of her interest in other properties and the release by her of marital rights in certain other properties owned by him.

2. Where at the time of his divorce the taxpayer engaged tax counsel to advise him of the Federal income, estate, and gift tax consequences to him of establishing a trust to make periodic payments to his wife during her life in discharge of his obligations under state law to support her, with a remainder interest in the property to pass to their children at her death.

3. Where for an agreed fee the taxpayer engaged a practitioner to represent him in connection with his divorce, the services including tax counsel concerning the right of the taxpayer to claim the children as dependents for Federal income tax purposes in years subsequent to the divorce. The practitioner's statement allocated his fee between the deductible tax advice and other nondeductible nontax matters.[68]

Any part of an attorney's fee paid in connection with a divorce, legal separation, written separation agreement, or a decree of divorce which is properly attributable to the production or collection of money includible in one spouse's gross income is deductible by that spouse.[69]

Where tax advice is given in a divorce settlement and one spouse pays the fees to attorneys of both parties, the payor can deduct both fees.[70]

Attorneys' fees for collecting alimony which is owing are deductible.[71]

A large investor incurred legal expenses in objecting to Securities and Exchange Commission proceedings for the dissolution of a corporation. These costs were deductible. Inasmuch as the S.E.C. objective was dissolution of the corporation, which could have resulted in the loss of an attractive investment, the expenditures were a necessary expense of carrying on the investor's business of conservation of existing investments. The attorneys' fees were not for the primary purpose of realization of a capital gain. That a gain did in fact result from the contest was a consequence of the investor's unsuccessful effort to hold on to an investment and of being forced to sell; that did not change the nature of the expenditures.[72]

Legal fees paid by shareholders in defending an action instituted by the S.E.C. for the purpose of imposing trusts on the shareholders' stock were deductible as ordinary and necessary expenses for the collection of income. None of the issues in this litigation was of a nature which would require disallowance of the deduction to prevent the frustration of public policy.[73]

An individual was allowed to deduct legal expenses incurred in reestablishing her right to act as coexecutor of an estate after her disqualification by a state court.[74]

A life tenant properly deducted legal expenses arising from a contested will involving the amount of income payable to her.[75]

Attorneys' fees in acquiring a life estate for an individual, while not deductible in the year of payment, may be spread over the acquirer's life expectancy for tax purposes.[76]

An individual who had acquired property by gift contested

the Internal Revenue Service valuation of the property. He was required to pay the Federal gift tax because the donor, who should have done so, had not made this payment. Accordingly, the recipient of the gift was permitted to deduct his cost in keeping the valuation, and his tax upon it, low.[77]

An individual whose professional livelihood was dependent upon the goodwill of the public before whom he appeared as an entertainer could deduct legal fees in undertaking suit against a person who allegedly had libeled him publicly. The primary purpose of the litigation was to vindicate the personal reputation and character of the taxpayer in order to protect his business.[78]

Attorney's fees incurred in resisting condemnation of business property by a state agency were deductible. The court pointed out that an individual undoubtedly could deduct payments to a watchman to remain on this very property to prevent unlawful entry or misuse by trespassers. And if court action was necessary to oust the trespasser from this property, the fee of a lawyer engaged to eject him would be a business expense. Here the state agency proved to be the trespasser, and legal fees were deductible just as the watchman's wages would have been.[79]

Expenditures made in order to produce a benefit lasting more than one year generally must be capitalized, deduction each year being the amount spread ratably over the period of benefit. But legal fees could be deducted in full when incurred to have declared invalid a municipal ordinance which would have prohibited the operation of the taxpayer's business. Here it was deemed to be immaterial that the benefits gained would last indefinitely.[80]

A professional writer was permitted to deduct legal fees for obtaining advice on his rights when he appeared before a Congressional investigation.[81]

Where property which had been contributed to a tax-exempt organization was in danger of having a public highway constructed through it, the original donor of the land could deduct the legal fees spent in resisting condemnation as a charitable deduction.[82]

When an attorney's fee covers both business and personal matters, an allocation into the deductible and nondeductible portion is allowed. However, the burden of establishing the percentage to which he is entitled rests on the taxpayer. A yacht was used only to the extent of 5 percent for business purposes. In a case in which a lawyer was engaged to handle an action brought against the taxpayer for false imprisonment by a member of the crew, 5 percent of the fee was the allowable deduction.[83] *See also* **Contested inheritance, expenses of.**

Legal separation. *See* **Alimony.**

Lettercarriers. *See* **Uniforms.**

Liability insurance. *See* **Executives; Insurance.**

Libel award, payment of. *See* **Business-related losses.**

Library, depreciation on. A depreciation deduction is allowable for a library which is used in the taxpayer's trade or business. *See also* **Depreciation.**[84]

License and franchise costs. *See* **Expenditures for benefits lasting more than one year.**

Life care. *See* **Retirement homes.**

Life insurance. *See* **Alimony; Compensation; Insurance.**

Life tenant. *See* **Depreciation; Legal fees.**

Limited partner. *See* **Carry-overs.**

Lip reading. *See* **Deaf persons, expenses of.**

Liquor. *See* **Medical expenses; Ordinary and necessary business expenses.**

Living expenses. *See* **Employees.**

Loan commitment fees. *See* **Interest.**

Loan origination fee (points). *See* **Interest.**

Loan premiums. *See* **Investors.**

Loan processing fee. A loan processing fee (points) paid by a mortgagor-borrower as compensation to a lender solely for the use or forebearance of money is deductible as interest.[85] In such a situation, the borrower must establish that the fee was not paid for any specific services that the lender had performed, or had agreed to perform, in connection with the loan.[86]

Loan repayment. *See* **Penalty fee for loan repayment.**

Loans and advances. A bank director and several of his associates personally advanced funds to the bank's creditors in an effort to relieve the institution, which had been paying them compensation, of certain obligations when its financial situation became precarious. When this advance became uncollectible, he could deduct it as related to his trade or business of being a director.[87] *See also* **Bad debts.**

Lobbying. Expenditures in an effort to influence legislation are not deductible, but deduction is permitted for certain types of activity dealing with legislative matters:
1. Appearances before, or communications with, committees or individual members of Federal, state, or local legislative bodies.
2. Communication of information on legislative matters to business or trade organizations.
3. The portion of membership dues in such organizations which are attributable to the activities mentioned in items 1 and 2.[88]
An individual was permitted to deduct as a business expense his costs in lobbying for employment benefits for all the state employees of a department in which he worked.[89]

Local benefit taxes. *See* **Taxes.**

Local taxes. *See* **Taxes.**

Long service award. An employer may deduct the cost, but not in excess of $100, of tangible personal property awarded to an employee by reason of length of service.[90] *See also* **Employee awards.**

Looting, losses from. *See* **Casualties.**

Losses. *See* **Abandonment loss; Bad debts; Business-related losses; Capital losses; Casualties; Demolition; Family transactions; Gambling losses; Hobby losses; Illegal business activity; Inventory write-downs; Purchase of stock to get assets; Small business corporation stock; Small business investment company; Tax-option corporations; Transactions entered into for profit.**

Low-income rental housing. *See* **Depreciation.**

1. Revenue Ruling 78-425, I.R.B. 1978-36, 24.
2. *Travel, Entertainment and Gift Expenses*, I.R.S. Publication No. 463, 1976 edition, page 2.
3. *Miscellaneous Deductions and Credits*, I.R.S. Publication 529, 1965 edition, page 3.
4. *Stanley V. Waldheim et al.*, 25 T.C. 839 (1956), *aff'd on another issue*, 244 F.2d 1 (7th Cir., 1957).
5. *Caruso et al. v. United States*, 236 F. Supp. 88 (D.C., N.J. 1964).
6. *Nidetch v. Commissioner*, T.C. Memo. 1978-313, filed August 11, 1978.
7. *Stanley V. Waldheim et al.*, 25 T.C. 839 (1956), *aff'd on other issues*, 244 F.2d 1 (7th Cir., 1957).
8. *E. L. Potter*, 20 B.T.A. 252 (1930).
9. *Durden v. Patterson*, D.C., N.D. Ala., 1956, *rev'd and rem'd'd on another issue*, 5th Cir., 1957.
10. *Ingalls, Jr., et al. v. Patterson*, 158 F. Supp. 627 (D.C., N.D. Ala., 1958).
11. *Mrs. A. B. Hurt, Jr., et al.*, 30 B.T.A. 653 (1934).
12. *Hochschild v. Commissioner*, 161 F.2d 817 (2d Cir., 1947).
13. *The First National Bank of Atlanta et al. v. United States*, 202 F. Supp. 702 (D.C., N.D. Ga., 1962).
14. Revenue Ruling 68-662, 1968-2 CB 69.
15 *Sylvester G. Miller*, T.C. Memo., Docket No. 111238, entered July 21, 1943.
16. S.M. 4078, V-1 CB 226.
17. *Central Coat, Apron & Linen Service, Inc., v. United States*, 298 F. Supp. 1201 (D.C., S.D. N. Y., 1969).
18. *Ditmars v. Commissioner*, 302 F.2d 481 (2d Cir., 1962).
19. *Morgan S. Kaufman*, 12 T.C. 1114 (1949).
20. S.M. 4078, V-1 CB 226.
21. *DePinto et al. v. United States*, ... F.2d ... (9th Cir., 1978).
22. *Cornelius Vanderbilt, Jr.*, T.C. Memo. 1957-235, filed December 23, 1957.
23. I.T. 3762, 1945 CB 95.
24. *Henry M. Rodney et al.*, 53 T.C. 287 (1969).
25. *Commissioner v. Heininger*, 320 U.S. 467 (1943).
26. *Tellier et al. v. Commissioner*, 342 F.2d 690 (2d Cir., 1965), *aff'd*, 383 U.S. 687 (1966).
27. Revenue Ruling 66-330, 1966-2 CB 44.
28. Revenue Ruling 69-547, 1969-2 CB 24.
29. *Lena G. Hill*, 8 B.T.A. 1159 (1927).
30. *Kornhauser v. United States*, 276 U.S. 145 (1928).
31. *Buder et al. v. United States*, 235 F. Supp. 479 (D.C., E.D. Mo., 1964), *aff'd on another issue*, 354 F.2d 941 (8th Cir., 1966).
32. *Ticket Office Equipment Co., Inc.*, 20 T.C. 272 (1953), *aff'd on another issue*, 213 F.2d 318 (2d Cir., 1954).
33. *Urquhart v. Commissioner*, 215 F.2d 17 (3d Cir., 1954).
34. *Commissioner v. Doering, Jr., et al.*, 335 F.2d 738 (2d Cir., 1964).
35. *John Kurkjian et al.*, 65 T.C. 862 (1976).
36. *Harry Bourg et al.*, T.C. Memo. 1961-95, filed March 31, 1961.
37. *Watson P. Davidson*, 27 B.T.A. 158 (1932).
38. *H. M. Howard*, 22 B.T.A. 375 (1931).
39. *Jay A. Mount*, T.C. Memo., Docket No. 8401, entered November 29, 1946.
40. Revenue Ruling 67-401, 1967-2 CB 123.
41. *Davis et al. v United States*, 287 F.2d 168 (Ct. Cl., 1961).

L

198

42. *Hall et al. v. United States,* ... F.2d ... (Ct. Cl., 1977).
43. *B. E. Levinstein,* 19 B.T.A. 99 (1930).
44. *Sidney Merians et al.,* 60 T.C. 187 (1973).
45. *Nancy Reynolds Bagley,* 8 T.C. 130 (1947).
46. *Kaufman et al. v. United States,* 227 F. Supp. 807 (D.C., W.D. Mo., 1963).
47. *Meldrum & Fewsmith, Inc.,* 20 T.C. 790 (1953).
48. *Francis A. Parker,* 6 T.C. 974 (1946).
49. *B. F. Crabbe et al.,* T.C. Memo. 1956-52, filed March 5, 1956.
50. *Richard Croker, Jr.,* 12 B.T.A. 408 (1928).
51. *H. R. MacMillan,* 14 B.T.A. 1367 (1929).
52. *Kornhauser v. United States,* 276 U.S. 145 (1928).
53. Revenue Ruling 72-169, 1972-1 CB 178.
54. *F. Meyer & Brother Co.,* 4 B.T.A. 481 (1926).
55. *United States v. Pate et al.,* 254 F.2d 480 (10th Cir., 1958).
56. I.T. 3325, 1939-2 CB 151.
57. Revenue Ruling 64-277, 1964-2 CB 55.
58. *Sergievsky v. McNamara et al.,* 135 F. Supp. 233 (D.C., S.D. N.Y., 1955).
59. *Fred G. Meyer et al.,* T.C. Memo. 1975-349, filed December 8, 1975.
60. *Samuel Galewitz et al.,* 50 T.C. 104 (1968).
61. *Straub et al. v. Granger,* 143 F. Supp. 250 (D.C., W.D. Pa., 1956).
62. *Powell, Jr., v. United States,* 294 F. Supp. 977 (D.C., S.D. S.D., 1969).
63. *Stemfel v. United States,* D.C., M.D. Tenn., 1969.
64. *W. D. Haden Company v. United States,* 165 F.2d 588 (5th Cir., 1948).
65. *Carpenter et al. v. United States,* 338 F.2d 366 (Ct. Cl., 1964).
66. *Connecticut Valley Realty Co.,* B.T.A. Memo., Docket No. 62678, entered April 8, 1933.
67. *Russell et al. v. Riddell,* D.C., S.D. Cal., 1966.
68. Revenue Ruling 72-545, 1972-2 CB 179.
69. Regulations Section 1.262-1(b)(7).
70. *United States v. Davis et al.,* 370 U.S. 65 (1962).
71. *Ruth K. Wild,* 42 T.C. 706 (1964).
72. *Allied Chemical Corporation v. United States,* 305 F.2d 433 (Ct. Cl., 1962).
73. *Guttmann et al. v. United States,* 181 F. Supp. 290 (D.C., W.D. Pa., 1960).
74. *Annie Laurie Crawford,* 5 T.C. 91 (1945).
75. *Stella Elkins Tyler,* 6 T.C. 135 (1946).
76. *Marianne Crocker Elrick,* 56 T.C. 903 (1971).
77. *United States v. Bonnyman et al.,* 261 F.2d 885 (6th Cir., 1958).
78. *Paul Draper et al.,* 26 T.C. 201 (1956).
79. *L. B. Reakirt,* 29 B.T.A. 1296 (1934).
80. Revenue Ruling 78-389, I.R.B. 1978-44, 7.
81. *Waldo Salt,* 18 T.C. 182 (1952).
82. *Archbold v. United States,* 449 F.2d 1120 (Ct., Cl., 1971).
83. *Larrabee et al. v. United States,* D.C., C.D. Cal., 1968.
84. *Beaudry v. Commissioner,* 150 F.2d 20 (2d Cir., 1945).
85. Revenue Ruling 74-187, 1974-1 CB 48.
86. Revenue Ruling 69-188, 1969-1 CB 54.
87. *Stephenson v. Commissioner,* 43 F.2d 348 (8th Cir., 1930).
88. I.R.C. Section 162(e).
89. *James M. Jordan,* 60 T.C. 770 (1973).
90. Regulations Section 1.274-3(b)(2)(iii).

M

Magazines. *See* **Subscriptions to periodicals.**

Mailpersons. *See* **Uniforms.**

Maintenance. The operator of a drive-in food stand could deduct the cost of cleaning a canopy and coating it with a plastic finish. Although there was a five-year guarantee for the plastic finish, the work was not done to prolong the life of the building but to maintain it in an efficient operating condition.[1] *See also* **Repairs.**

Maintenance of employment, expenses for. *See* **Employees; Executives; Legal fees.**

Malpractice insurance. Premiums on malpractice insurance are deductible by a doctor who could become personally liable for negligence.[2]

Malpractice judgments. A physician was permitted to deduct malpractice judgments and attendant costs.[3]

Malpractice suits. *See* **Legal fees.**

Management survey. *See* **Expenditures for benefits lasting more than one year.**

Managerial skills, improvement of. *See* **Education; Executives.**

Materials used to build a new home. *See* **Taxes.**

Meals. *See* **Employees; Entertainment.**

Meals and lodging as medical expense. *See* **Medical expenses.**

Medical bill of employee injured on job. *See* **Ordinary and necessary business expenses.**

Medical expenses. An individual may deduct expenditures which qualify as "medical expenses" for himself, his spouse, and his dependents as defined in the tax law. The allowable deduction is that amount which exceeds 3 percent of his adjusted gross income.[4] (For an explanation of "adjusted gross income," see the box below.)

One of the tests for a dependency exemption in computing Federal income tax is that the dependent not have gross income in excess of $1,000 for taxable years beginning after 1978. But medical expense of a dependent otherwise qualifying for this treatment may be taken even though the dependent's income is in excess of this figure.[5]

Adjusted gross income is the total of all your income less the following deductions:

Expenses that are ordinary and necessary to a trade or business, other than as an employee.

Ordinary and necessary expenses and certain other deductions in connection with property held for producing rents and royalties.

Expenses incurred by an employee in connection with the performance of services as an employee. These may include travel, meals, and lodging away from home, local transportation expenses, moving expenses, and other reimbursed expenses if they otherwise qualify.

Certain losses on sales or exchanges of property.

50 percent of the excess of net long-term capital gain over net short-term capital loss.

Payments by self-employed persons to their own retirement plans.

Allowable depreciation and depletion if you are a life tenant or an income beneficiary of property held in trust or are an heir, legatee, or devisee of an estate if the depreciation or depletion is not deductible by the estate or trust.

Multiple-support arrangement. In some cases, no one person contributes more than half the support of a dependent. Instead, two or more persons—any one of whom could claim the individual as a dependent if it were not for the support test—together contribute more than half of the dependent's support.

In such a case, any one of those who individually contribute more than 10 percent of the mutual dependent's support, but *only one* of them, may claim the exemption for the dependent. Each of the others must file a written statement that he will not claim the exemption for that year.

The statements must be filed with the income tax returns of the person who claims the exemption. Form 2120 may be obtained for this purpose from your Internal Revenue Service office.

The deduction allowed for medical expenses includes expenditures on behalf of a person whom the taxpayer can claim as a dependent under a multiple-support arrangement, except to the extent that the taxpayer is reimbursed by other relatives or friends.

For example, Fred Johnson and his brothers Harry and Jack each contribute equally to the support of their aged mother. Fred, however, claims his mother as a dependent under a multiple-support arrangement. (See the box above for an explanation of "multiple-support arrangement.") Because Fred claims his mother as a dependent, he also pays her medical bills. He may deduct the expenditure even though he does not contribute more than half of her support. If Harry or Jack reimburse Fred for any part of the medical bills, Fred must reduce his medical deduction by the amount of the reimbursement. And neither Harry nor Jack can deduct their share of the medical bills. Therefore, a deduction is lost for this amount.[6]

Medical care, the basis for the deduction, means amounts paid for the diagnosis, cure, mitigation, treatment, or prevention of disease or for the purpose of affecting any structure or function of the body.[7]

It is irrelevant that the medical expense is incurred in connection with a self-inflicted condition.[8]

Mental defects or illnesses are covered as well as the physical ones.[9]

A mental disorder is a "disease" for this purpose.[10] Expenses to provide care for the mentally ill in order to keep them from harming themselves or others constitute deductible medical care.[11]

Deductible medical expenses include payments primarily for medical care made for the following:

1. Hospital services.

2. Nursing services (including nurses' board when it is paid by the taxpayer).

3. Medical, laboratory, surgical, dental, and other diagnostic and healing services.

4. X rays.

5. Medicine and drugs to the extent that they exceed 1 percent of the taxpayer's adjusted gross income.

6. Artificial teeth and limbs.

7. Ambulance hire.[12]

Also covered are expenditures for the following:

1. Chiropodists (podiatrists).

2. Chiropractors.

3. Christian Science practitioners.

4. Crutches.

5. Dental care; dentists.

6. Doctors.

7. Guide dogs and their maintenance.

8. Hearing aids and their component parts.

9. Meals and lodging furnished by a hospital or similar institution incident to medical care.

10. Optometrists; eyeglasses.

11. Psychiatrists.

12. Special equipment, such as wheelchairs.

13. Therapy.[13]

14. Vaccines.[14]

Elastic stockings qualified as medical expenses in the case of an elderly woman.[15]

The cost of a sacroiliac belt prescribed by a doctor was deductible.[16]

The cost of high blood pressure medication and a blood sugar test was deductible.[17]

Payments for vitamins, iron supplements, and the like may qualify for medical expenses if prescribed or recommended by a physician.[18]

On the advice of a dentist, an individual paid for a device for adding fluoride into a home water supply and also paid monthly rentals for the equipment. The fluoridating device was installed for the purpose of adding fluoride at a controlled rate into the home water supply. It was represented that fluoride is a chemical which strengthens the dental enamel as the teeth grow, making them more resistant to decay. The primary and only purpose of the installation and use of the device was to prevent tooth decay. The costs were deductible.[19]

Amounts paid for "medical care" may be deductible even if they were for purposes which do not have the sanction of the medical profession or if the payments are made to persons without medical qualifications. Thus, payments to qualified psychologists are deductible medical expenses even though such persons may be devoid of any medical training.[20]

Payments for acupuncture treatments qualify as medical expenses, even if the medical association in the state where the treatment was performed did not sanction this procedure.[21] Whether laetrile is an effective drug or a food is a controversial question in the medical profession. But its cost was deductible as medical expense where a taxpayer's physician has prescribed the use of laetrile for treatment of illness and the prescribed quantity was purchased and used in a locality where sale and use of the product were legal.[22]

Amounts which are paid to practitioners such as psychotherapists for services rendered are categorized as medical care for tax purposes even though those who perform the services are not required to be, or are not (even though required by law), licensed, certified, or otherwise qualified to perform such services. In other words, payments to unlicensed practitioners are deductible if the type and quality of their services are not illegal.[23]

An individual paid amounts to a nonprofessional person who helped conduct "patterning" exercises for his mentally retarded child. One system of therapy consists mainly of coordinated physical manipulation of the child's limbs to stimulate crawling and other normal movements. The manipulation exercises, known as "patterning," are conducted in an attempt to trace the pattern of normal physical movements on undamaged portions of the child's brain thereby causing the undamaged portions to assume the function of controlling the child's basic movements. After his evaluation at a medical institute, physical therapists designed a therapy program for the child and instructed the parent in the techniques of patterning so the therapy could be continued at home. The physical therapists at the institute periodically reevaluated the program and the child's responses to the therapy. The costs were deductible as medical expense, because the program was given for the purpose of alleviating physical and mental defects.[24]

A taxpayer's son had a congenital defect which resulted in severe malocclusion (an improper meeting of the upper and lower teeth). An orthodontist recommended that the child take lessons in playing the clarinet because he considered the continued practice with the clarinet would serve as therapeutic treatment and alleviate the severe malocclusion of the boy's teeth. The cost of the clarinet and the lessons necessary for the child to play the instrument to the degree required to obtain the benefits of the prescribed treatment were deductible.[25]

The purchase of birth control pills by a woman for her personal use was a deductible medical expense since she obtained the pills under a prescription provided by her physician.[26]

A husband and wife underwent treatment for sexual inadequacy and incompatibility at a hospital which utilized procedures developed by foundation researchers. The couple followed its own doctors' recommendations in taking this treatment. In the opinion of the psychiatrists conducting the program, the probability of successful treatment was greater if their patients resided at a hotel in the vicinity of the hospital during the two-week duration of the treatment. Fees paid to the psychiatrists were deductible as medical expenses, although deduction was not allowed for payments for hotel accommodations, these not being a part of the institutional medical care.[27] Possibly the couple would have won a complete victory if their doctors had testified that hotel occupancy was an indispensable part of the therapy, the home environment being hostile to their treatment because of the presence of certain other parties.

Also, the cost of an operation legally performed on a taxpayer at her own request to render her incapable of having children qualifies as a medical expense.[28]

A vasectomy performed in a doctor's office under local anesthetic for the purpose of preventing conception is a deductible medical expense, even if the operation is performed at the man's own request.[29]

Payments made in lieu of what would have been a deductible medical expense are allowable as a legal medical expense. For example, a businessman was obliged to be in his office during normal working hours. His wife, a semi-invalid after a series of strokes, was unable to take care of herself, nor was she able to get about without the benefit of a walker. In addition, she had to take certain pills for her ailment three times a day. Rather than put his wife in a nursing home, he engaged a woman to attend to his wife's needs while he was away at work. The hired woman's only duties were to give the wife her medication at prescribed times, to wash and dress her, and to cook her meals. She also prepared evening dinner for the couple and did some light housework and laundry. The hired woman had absolutely no training in nursing nor was she qualified to provide medical care. But the businessman's deduction of her salary, which was labeled "nursing care," was allowed by the court to the extent of 75 percent of what the businessman claimed. The unallowable portion presumably was what had been spent (estimated) for purposes other than caring for the semi-invalid. Because the cost of a nursing home would have been included in medical-care expense, the cost of the hired woman was merely an acceptable substitution.[30]

An individual had the problem of having someone take care of his seventy-eight-year-old wife, who had a bad case of arthritis and was unable to take care of herself. Her physician advised the husband to engage a person to take care of her, and so the man had his wife brought to the home of their daughter, who took care of the physical and other needs of her mother. The father paid his daughter $72 a month to take over this care, which he deducted as medical expense. The court allowed one-half of that amount on the ground that some of the assistance was personal and did not relate to physical or mental matters. That the payee was a close relative without medical or nursing training was deemed to be irrelevant.[31]

When hospital stays failed to alleviate his wife's mental disorders, an individual obtained her release by agreeing to have a woman reside in his home to look after her. Failing to find anyone available in the vicinity of his farm, he prevailed upon his niece to move in with her seven children, the oldest of whom was fourteen, in return for their board and lodging. He was permitted to deduct the value of such board and lodging as medical expense. The cost of maintaining his wife in a hospital would have been deductible. So was this alternative arrangement. "It is the nature of the services and the purpose for which they are rendered," said the court, "rather than the place where they are performed or the title of the person performing them that determine whether they constitute [deductible] medical care. . . ."[32]

When his mentally retarded dependent son was released from a mental hospital, the father was advised by a psychiatrist to have the youth spend a transition period in a private home with these specifications: (1) that it be near the hospital, (2) that there be in the home both a husband and a wife who were emotionally stable, (3) that they accept the doctor's recommendations regarding the manner in which they related to the patient, and (4) that there be no other patients ("rivals") in the house. The costs qualified as medical care, although this care was provided by persons with no medical training at a place without hospital facilities.[33]

A Milwaukee businessman, while on a trip to New York, had an attack of appendicitis and underwent immediate surgery. Seventeen days later he was still too weak to return to Milwaukee. His wound was still draining, but the hospital needed his room. On the recommendation of his doctor, the Milwaukee businessman stayed in a New York hotel until he was recovered enough to return home. His wife changed his bandages, assisted him in walking and bathing, and provided him with such nursing services as he required. The hotel room was a substitute for a hospital room, and the cost was similarly deductible.[34]

A ninety-year-old woman had a brain hemorrhage. She wished to stay at the home of her daughter rather than in a hospital. The daughter agreed to take care of her mother if her brother paid the salary of a clerk to take her (the daughter's) place in her husband's store during her absence. The brother could deduct the store clerk's salary as medical expense, for it avoided a larger, more direct expenditure for the required nursing care.[35]

One taxpayer had a seven-year-old child who was blind. Because of this condition the child was unable to attend school unless someone accompanied him throughout the day and guided him about. An individual, not a dependent, was engaged by the taxpayer solely for the purpose of guiding the child's steps throughout the school day. Inasmuch as the expenditure was to alleviate the child's physical condition of blindness, the expenses constituted medical care.[36]

Medical expense includes amounts paid for oxygen equipment and for oxygen used to alleviate difficulty in breathing due to a heart condition.[37]

The cost of a reclining chair purchased on his doctor's advice by a person with a cardiac condition qualified as medical-care deduction but only under the condition that such "equipment" was not used generally as an article of furniture.[38]

A special mattress and a certain thickness of plywood boards had been prescribed for an individual who had arthritis of the spine. The cost of the mattress and the plywood boards was deductible.[39]

A medical-expense deduction was allowed when a sick or disabled person acquired an "autoette," or wheelchair that was manually operated or self-propelled. This equipment was primarily used for the alleviation of his sickness or disability and was not merely to provide transportation between his residence and his place of employment.[40]

An individual paid fees in connection with plastic surgery that improved the taxpayer's personal appearance. The operation, commonly referred to as facelifting, involved the elimination or removal of chin and neck sag, jowls, bags under the eyes, and excess tissues under the eyelids. Although the operation was not the result of a recommendation by a physician, the cost was deductible as medical care, the purpose being to affect a structure of the human body.[41]

The cost of a whirlpool for baths for medical purposes was deductible.[42]

The cost of a wig was deductible when purchased on a physician's orders as necessary to avoid mental upset by a patient who had lost her hair.[43]

Capital expenditures generally are not deductible for Federal income tax purposes. That means those expenditures, for example, which add to the value or prolong the life of some property and whose benefits are expected to extend beyond one taxable year. But in the case of medical expenses, an expenditure which otherwise qualifies as medical expense will not be disqualified merely because it is a capital expenditure. If the primary purpose of the expenditure is for the medical care of the taxpayer, his spouse, or his dependent, it may qualify as medical expense. However, the "capital nature" of the asset will be a consideration in determining the amount of medical-expense deduction. If such expenditures are for permanent improvements which increase the value of any property, they will be allowed as medical expense only to the extent they exceed the increase in the value of the property.

Let's take a couple of examples. In the first case, an individual with a heart ailment, on his doctor's advice, installs an elevator in his home so that he will not need to climb stairs. The elevator costs $1,000. A competent appraiser says the elevator increases the value of the home by $700. The $300 difference is medical expense. If the elevator had not increased the value of the home, the entire installation cost would have been medical expense.[44]

In the second case, that is what happened. The physician had advised the installation of an elevator to alleviate an acute coronary insufficiency of a taxpayer's wife. The elevator was regarded as a permanent installation, but in the court's judgment it did not have the effect of increasing the value of the property. The full cost was deductible.[45]

Deduction was approved for the cost of an inclinator which was detachable from one's residence and had been purchased only for the use of a sick person.[46]

A taxpayer who was physically unable to walk and was confined to a wheelchair purchased an automobile that was specially designed for transporting people confined to wheelchairs. The vehicle had ramps for entry and exit, rear doors that opened 180 degrees, floor locks to hold wheelchairs in place, and a raised roof giving the required headroom to accommodate wheelchair patients. The individual paid $6,000 for this specially designed automobile, whereas the cost of a comparable car of standard design was $4,500. Inasmuch as the car was designed for transporting persons confined to wheelchairs, the cost to the purchaser of the special model was a capital expenditure which was related only to the sick person. So the amount paid which was attributable to the special design, $1,500, was deductible as medical expense.[47]

A taxpayer's wife had multiple sclerosis. Special features in a residence built for her were allowed to the extent they did not add to the value of the house. This included a stereo system.[48]

A man was handicapped with arthritis and a severe heart condition. As a result, he could not climb stairs or get into or out of a bathtub. On the advice of his physician he had bathroom plumbing fixtures installed on the first floor of a two-story house he rented. The lessor (an unrelated party) did not assume any of the costs of acquiring or installing the special plumbing fixtures nor did he reduce the rent; the entire costs were paid by the tenant. As the primary purpose of the acquisition and installation of the plumbing fixtures was for medical care, the tenant could deduct them as medical expenses.[49]

Improvements to a person's grounds to enable him to move more freely to get from one part of a split-level home to another were deductible by a handicapped person. "There is nothing in the statute, regulations, or the cases," said the court, "which limits deductions to those which are necessary for eating, sleeping, and using the bathroom."[50]

The expense of a pool may or may not be a medical deduction even though it was installed in the first place because of a physician's recommendation. If the person who installed the pool on his property cannot prove that the installation of the pool alleviated in any way his physical condition, then a deduction is not allowed.[51]

On the other hand, if it can be proved that the pool was installed on the advice of a physician and was used for a specific medical purpose—for example, to provide hydrotherapeutic purpose—and did therefore serve a medical purpose, the deduction is allowed.[52]

After being advised by a physician to provide pure, humid air for his child, who was restricted to her home by cystic fibrosis, an individual installed central air-conditioning in his home. The alternative, air-conditioning the child's room and confining her to this area, was thought by the taxpayer to be psychologically dangerous. The cost of the installation was $1,300; the value of the house was increased $800 according to the authoritative estimates. The $500 difference could be deducted as medical expense.[53] (See also **Air-conditioning equipment.**)

To the extent that medical expenses for a year exceed three

percent of adjusted gross income, there may be question as to *how much* a person may deduct. In most areas of taxation, there *is* a limit: an individual may deduct an expense, such as business salaries or entertainment, only to the extent that they are reasonable. One person, on doctor's orders, installed a swimming pool on his estate in an effort to prevent his wife's spinal disorder from resulting in lifelong paralysis. "Permanent" improvements to a home to alleviate one's physical condition are deductible as medical expenses to the extent that they do not increase the value of the property. Addition of this pool increased the value of the estate, but certainly not by the amount which had been lavished on the pool, housed as it was in a building that matched the palatial residence, with similar hand-cut stone, cedar woodwork, and a cathedral ceiling built without thought of cost. Taxpayers are not limited to choosing the cheapest form of medical treatment available to them, held the court which originally heard the case, and a taxpayer of means can deduct the cost of an extremely expensive private room at a hospital instead of entering a ward. True, an appeals court subsequently ruled, but at the hospital the costs incurred were directly related to medical care. That was not the situation here. The use of ceramic tile and fantastically luxurious appointments for this oversized pool were not necessary for medical care. The first court was directed to find out how much of the cost of the pool could be said to provide a functionally adequate facility for therapeutic purposes. But, admitted the higher court, in the market of potential buyers of luxury residences, a facility of mere functional adequacy might add nothing to the property value of the taxpayer's swank estate, in which event the entire cost of the pool would be deductible medical expense.[54]

percent of adjusted gross income, there may be question as to *how much* a person may deduct. In most areas of taxation, there *is* a limit: an individual may deduct an expense, such as business salaries or entertainment, only to the extent that they are reasonable. One person, on doctor's orders, installed a swimming pool on his estate in an effort to prevent his wife's spinal disorder from resulting in lifelong paralysis. "Permanent" improvements to a home to alleviate one's physical condition are deductible as medical expenses to the extent that they do not increase the value of the property. Addition of this pool increased the value of the estate, but certainly not by the amount which had been lavished on the pool, housed as it was in a building that matched the palatial residence, with similar hand-cut stone, cedar woodwork, and a cathedral ceiling built without thought of cost. Taxpayers are not limited to choosing the cheapest form of medical treatment available to them, held the court which originally heard the case, and a taxpayer of means can deduct the cost of an extremely expensive private room at a hospital instead of entering a ward. True, an appeals court subsequently ruled, but at the hospital the costs incurred were directly related to medical care. That was not the situation here. The use of ceramic tile and fantastically luxurious appointments for this oversized pool were not necessary for medical care. The first court was directed to find out how much of the cost of the pool could be said to provide a functionally adequate facility for therapeutic purposes. But, admitted the higher court, in the market of potential buyers of luxury residences, a facility of mere functional adequacy might add nothing to the property value of the taxpayer's swank estate, in which event the entire cost of the pool would be deductible medical expense.[54]

If the capital expenditure relates to the permanent improvement or betterment of property (such as a swimming pool or an elevator in a home), the cost is not deducted but becomes part of the total cost of the property. Otherwise, it is deductible as medical expense, such as in the case of oxygen equipment used to alleviate difficulty in one's breathing due to a heart condition. Medical expenses are deductible only to the extent that in total they exceed three percent of the taxpayer's adjusted gross income for the year. So part of the cost of the oxygen equipment may not have been deducted as medical expense up to the time this equipment subsequently is sold. In that case, for the purpose of determining any gain on the sale of the equipment, its cost is deemed to be increased by amounts not deductible as medical expense because of the 3 percent limitation.[55]

Generally, the cost of special food or beverages does not

qualify as medical expenses. But in special cases, depending upon the circumstances, such costs are deductible medical expenses. If the prescribed food or beverage is taken solely for the alleviation or treatment of an illness, is in no way a part of the nutritional needs of the patient, and a statement as to the particular facts and as to the food or beverage prescribed is submitted by a physician, the cost may be deductible. But if the special food or beverage is taken as a substitute for food or beverage normally consumed by a person and satisfies his nutritional needs, there is no deduction allowed. If the special food or beverage is prescribed by a physician for medicinal purposes and is in addition to the normal diet of the patient, then the deduction is allowed.[56]

An individual had hypoglycemia, a condition caused by abnormally low blood sugar in the body. A specialist prescribed frequent feedings of a high protein diet as the major treatment. The high protein supplements were not in addition to her normal nutritional needs and, not being replacements for any of her normal consumption of food, qualified as medical expense. By comparing her food bills with those of her friends without this condition, she estimated that 30 percent of her bills represented the cost of the extra protein needed to treat her disease. This additional cost was deductible.[57]

In a case where a physician had prescribed that a person take two ounces of whiskey twice a day for relief of angina pain resulting from a coronary disease, the cost of the prescribed amount of whiskey was a deductible medical expense.[58]

An individual had been placed on a salt-free diet regimen by his physician. The additional charge made by restaurants for preparing such meals was deductible as medical expense. And for good measure, the court allowed as additional medical expense the cost of getting to and from such accommodating restaurants.[59]

Artificially ripened, stored, sweetened, colored, and preserved foods, or those which have been canned in phenollined tins, cause allergic reactions in some persons which bring about headaches, nausea, or other severe distress in some bodies. Such was the situation of both a husband and wife, whose physicians testified that the only treatment was to restrict their patients' diets to uncontaminated organic foods. Specially grown, transported, packaged, and marketed foods were used exclusively by the spouses at a cost of approximately double that of ordinary foods. So 50 percent of the cost of the specially processed foods was deductible as medical expense. The organic foods were not a substitute for ordinary nondeductible food but represented an additional cost for the relief of medical infirmities.[60] This decision is not likely to give comfort to people who buy "health foods" for philosophical or other personal reasons.

Expenses paid for transportation primarily for, and essential to, the rendition of medical care are allowed as medical-care expenses. This does not include, however, the cost of any meals or lodging while away from home receiving medical treatment.[61]

Transportation to and from a physician's office, such as taxi fare, is deductible.[62]

Food and lodging expense while traveling to the place of medication and incurred prior to receiving medical treatment are deductible.[63]

Amounts paid for bus, train, or plane fares or ambulance hire are similarly deductible.[64]

An individual's son, while on a vacation cruise at sea, manifested signs of mental disorder and threatened to blow up the ship. He was put ashore by the captain at the nearest port. The father, after having been notified by the ship's doctor that the youth could not travel by himself, flew to where his son had been disembarked. The father could deduct as medical expenses his round-trip costs in flying to Europe to fetch his son, as well as the excess cost of the son's return trip by air over the cost of sea travel.[65]

When a patient uses his own automobile for transportation to and from a physician's office or for other medical-care purposes, a flat figure of 7 cents per mile may be claimed in lieu of itemizing expenditures. Parking fees and tolls attributable to such transportation may be deducted as separate items. If the patient prefers, he may deduct his actual substantiated expenditures.[66]

If on the basis of competent medical advice it is deemed necessary for the parents of a child at a specially equipped psychiatric therapy center to visit their child, the cost of the transportation for these visits qualifies as the cost of transportation primarily for, and essential to, medical care and is therefore deductible.[67]

The deductions for medical expenses also include the money paid for the transportation of a parent who must accompany a child to get medical care as well as for the transportation expenses of a nurse familiar with injections, medications, and other treatment required by a patient who is traveling to get medical care and is unable to travel alone.[68]

If a wife has been trained to handle emergency situations which ordinarily a nurse would take care of, then the deduction would also apply to the taxpayer's wife.[69]

A deduction was allowed for the transportation costs of both a taxpayer and his nurse when in accordance with his physician's advice he went to a predetermined location where the temperature was suitable to his condition (the taxpayer had arteriosclerotic heart disease) and where he would receive proper medical care. Any further travel or sightseeing was precluded by his physician's orders. The nurse was necessary to give him the medication and injections which he required continually.[70]

Expenses which were incurred annually by an individual who traveled from Los Angeles to New York and back to consult a physician in whom he had confidence were regarded as medical-care expenses. It was determined that such consultation was the primary purpose for the travel and otherwise the patient would not have made the trip.[71]

An individual who went to Europe on a freighter for a vacation was afflicted with a severe kidney ailment. He could deduct as medical expense the higher fare for an airline trip back to San Francisco for treatment by a urologist there.[72]

A taxpayer could deduct the cost of transporting his wheelchair-confined daughter, the victim of an incurable disease, to a public high school. Although the child could have received competent instruction at home, the taxpayer's primary purpose in sending her to a public high school was for psychotherapeutic reasons, as explained by her physician, to keep her in school with children of her own age.[73]

The cost of operating an automobile as a means of transportation that is not primarily for, and essential to, medical care is not an allowable medical expense. In other words, Mrs. Martha Hennings, who is confined to a wheelchair but who uses her specially equipped automobile to drive around for shopping and pleasure purposes, cannot claim the operating expense of her automobile as a medical-care deduction when the automobile is used for those purposes.[74]

But driving a car was part of a doctor's prescribed treatment for one patient, and therefore the cost of operating the car was deductible as medical expense. The doctor had advised the taxpayer, who had suffered severe facial mutilations after an accident, to mix with other people. Driving a car was part of the doctor's treatment for her mental state.[75]

A war-wounded veteran could deduct that portion of his automobile expenses in going from home to work at a veterans' hospital which the mileage involved bore to the total miles he drove that year. His physician had recommended employment as therapy for his physical condition, and the use of a car also had been advised for improving the patient's physical health.

He testified that after he started to work, he felt much better.[76]

An individual who was almost wholly disabled was advised by her physician to seek remunerative employment as occupational therapy. It was understood that in so doing, she would be obliged to spend sums in excess of what a normal person would have to pay for transportation. She had to travel by taxi, with special demands upon the drivers for assistance. Her expenses were deductible in the course of occupational therapy as, and for, medical expenses.[77]

To distinguish when it is allowable to deduct the cost of operating an automobile as medical expense, let us give you two examples. In the first case, an individual could deduct the cost of driving to work because his physician had recommended that he undertake employment and that he use a car for the improvement of his health. His driving was part of a physician's prescribed treatment and therefore deductible.

In the second case, where the cost of operating an automobile was not deductible, the individual had an artificial limb, and she used her car to get to work as she could not use public transportation. But there was no determination that driving a car was in any way an alleviation of her physical or mental condition, and there was no evidence to support her allegation that she had to work "for physical and occupational therapy," because her physician had not prescribed it.[78]

Special equipment such as hand controls and other devices which are especially adapted to permit the operation of an automobile by a physically handicapped individual and a mechanical device to lift and to place such a handicapped person in an automobile are medical expenses.[79]

How to get a medical expense deduction for the cost of installation of a telephone in one's car is suggested by how one person lost such a deduction. He was paralyzed from the waist down. Subsequently he suffered a heart attack. When he was able to drive again, he had his automobile equipped with a mobile telephone service, the cost of which he sought to deduct as medical expense. This, he claimed, was so that he could contact a doctor immediately in the case of another heart attack while on the road. But if that was primarily the reason for installing a car telephone, why did he have this phone number listed in the public directory? That careless act cost him a tax deduction, for the directory listing indicated that social or other nondeductible personal purposes might have been the reason for this printed announcement of where he could be contacted by callers.[80]

When an individual is in an institution because his physical condition is such that the availability of medical care in the institution is the principal reason for his presence there, the entire cost of medical care, including meals and lodging at the institution, is deductible as medical expense. For example, medical care includes the entire cost of institutional care for a person who is mentally ill and unsafe when left alone.[81]

While ordinary education is not medical care, when the individual is attending a special school for a mentally or physically handicapped individual, his medical care includes the cost of attending such a school. However, the following requirement has to be met: His condition has to be such that the resources of the institution for alleviating such mental or physical handicap are a principal reason for his presence there.[82]

Deduction of the entire cost of a special school for mentally retarded children is allowed. The cost of ordinary education provided by a special school is deductible only if it is incidental to medical care. For an example of this, see the following.[83]

A taxpayer's daughter, a girl of average to above-average intelligence, suffered from an emotional disturbance which caused her to withdraw from reality and to be incapable of functioning normally at school. Upon the recommendation of a psychiatrist, the taxpayer enrolled her in a private school which specialized in treating children with problems of this nature and in remedying their learning disabilities. The institution was regarded as a "special school," and the tuition paid by the taxpayer as medical care.[84]

Tuition of an individual's deaf son was deductible at a school where individual attention and opportunity for lip reading was available. The special resources of the school were the primary and principal reason for enrollment, and the enrollment was also at the recommendation of an otologist, a physician who specializes in treatment of diseases of the ear.[85]

A university provided medical and hospital care for its students, contracting such care at a stipulated rate per student and paying actual hospital bills for those students hospitalized during the academic year. The amount of the fee for the health plan, which was included in the tuition charge, was not billed separately. It was ruled that if a student pays a lump-sum fee which includes his education, board, medical care, etc., and no breakdown is made of this fee as to the amount apportioned to medical care, no specific part of the tuition fee is deductible medical care. But if this breakdown is provided or is readily obtainable from the university, that portion of the fee which is allocated to medical care will constitute a proper deduction.[86]

In some cases an allocation is made between deductible medical-care cost and nondeductible personal expenses. One individual sent his son, who had hearing and vision difficulties, to a school for boys of normal intelligence who had failed to achieve success at other schools because of mental or emotional problems. This was not a "special school" for a mentally or physically handicapped person. Nevertheless, an allocation of the school's $10,682.81 fee was allowed between deductible medical-care and nondeductible education expense. That portion of the fee which was in excess of what other private schools in the state were charging was characterized as medical expense.[87]

In another case where an allocation was made, an emotionally disturbed child, who was not retarded or physically handicapped, was sent to a school primarily to receive an education. The desire to obtain psychological and psychiatric help was merely one of the reasons for selecting this particular school. The court allowed $3,000 of the $6,270 fee as medical-care expense.[88]

Following the recommendation of his psychiatrist, an individual paid the cost of maintaining his mentally retarded dependent son in a specially selected home to aid his adjustment to life in the community after life in a mental hospital; the expenses were deductible.[89]

Parents could deduct the fees paid to a teacher who was specially trained and qualified to teach remedial reading to mitigate the dyslexic condition of their child. The dyslexia was caused by congenital damage to the brain; the only treatment is training and study skills which permit the student to overcome the results of his handicap.[90]

Fees paid to a special school were deductible, where there was a program designed to educate children with severe learning disabilities so that they could return to a regular school within a few years. Here the taxpayer's minor child had congenital impairment in the areas of visual memory and visual matching. Competent medical authorities who examined the child determined that the learning disabilities were caused by a neurological disorder, and the child's physician recommended special schooling.[91]

Similarly, deduction was allowed for expenses of maintaining a dependent at a "halfway" house which aided individuals in adjusting from life in a mental hospital to life in the community after such people had outgrown the protective environment afforded by psychiatric institutions and for whom further hospitalization was not indicated.[92]

Amounts paid by a taxpayer to maintain a dependent in a therapeutic center for drug addicts, including the cost of the dependent's meals and lodging at the center which were furnished as a necessary incident to his treatment, were expenses for medical care.[93]

Ordinarily, fees paid to a health institute where a taxpayer takes exercise, rubdowns, etc., are nondeductible personal expenses. But fees paid to health institutes may be deductible as medical expenses when such treatments are prescribed by physicians and are substantiated by a doctor's statement that the treatments are necessary for the alleviation of a physical or mental defect or illness of the individual receiving the treatment.[94]

The amount of bills paid to a nursing home, including the costs of meals and lodging, were deductible if the principal reason for a person's presence in the home was the availability of medical care for him.[95]

Social Security taxes on wages of private nurses providing medical care are deductible as medical expense.[96]

An individual entered a hospital as a patient for a kidney transplant. The donor traveled from a distant city and was entered at the same hospital for the purpose of donating a kidney to the patient. The patient paid all surgical, hospital, and transportation costs of the donor and was entitled to deduct such payments as medical expenses.[97] Ordinarily, only medical expenses for the benefit of the taxpayer, his spouse, or a dependent are deductible by him. But surgical, laboratory, and transportation expenses paid by a donor and a prospective donor in connection with a kidney transplant operation were deductible medical expenses.[98]

Attorneys' fees to collect for the cost of medical care following an accident can be deducted under certain circumstances as medical expenses. To be deductible, they must exceed the amount of insurance recovered or other reimbursement for the expenses.[99]

Legal expenses incident to the establishing and conducting of an individual's guardianship were deductible as medical-care payments in the special case that follows. The taxpayer's physicians had advised that the girl for whom he was a potential guardian should be treated for mental and emotional problems and that the treatment would be successful only if she were institutionalized. The girl refused voluntary institutionalization; therefore, the taxpayer became her legal guardian in order to give the girl the necessary medical treatment which she needed. His expenses incident to the establishment and conduct of the guardianship were therefore deductible.[100]

Legal fees paid by a father in connection with the commitment of his son to a state mental institution are deductible as medical care.[101]

Psychoanalysis is usually deductible as medical expense. However, if an individual undertakes psychoanalysis for the purpose of qualifying for admission to a psychiatric or psychological institution or to equip himself for specialization as an analyst, the costs are nondeductible. The reasons, of course, for the nondeduction in the above case is that the psychoanalysis was undertaken not for the purpose of affecting the health of the taxpayer but for qualification of that taxpayer for a job or profession.

But where the psychoanalysis is obtained for the purpose of diagnosis, cure, mitigation, treatment, or prevention of disease or for the purpose of affecting any function of the body, the amount spent for the psychoanalysis is therefore medical care, even though a further and additional benefit is obtained as qualification for admission to a school of psychoanalytic training. Here the individual's purposes were dual and of equal weight. That is, to help alleviate his own problems and to qualify for admission to the training curriculum of an institute.[102]

Payment of an ex-wife's medical and dental expenses under a divorce decree or agreement qualifies as deductible alimony if the amounts meet the test of periodic payments and if separate tax returns are filed. (Periodic payments are payments of a fixed amount [for example, $100 per month] for either a fixed or indefinite period. The payments need not be made at regular intervals.) The wife includes the payments in her gross income. But she may claim them as medical expenses if she itemizes her deductions.[103]

In a *community property state*, such as California, married couples are treated as though each spouse earned one-half of the income and owned one-half of the property of the other spouse. Where a husband and wife reside in a community property state and file separate income tax returns on a community property basis, amounts paid for the medical care of one spouse out of funds they both own are considered as paid one-half by each spouse. Where expenses are paid out of the separate funds of one spouse, only the spouse paying the medical expense is entitled to the deduction.[104]

A deduction is allowed without regard to the previously mentioned 3-percent limitation for one-half of the premiums for medical insurance. The deduction, however, may not exceed $150. The balance is added to the taxpayer's other medical expenses and is subject to the 3-percent limitation.[105]

This provision also covers premiums paid for an insurance

policy which provides only for reimbursement of the cost of prescription drugs, but not in excess of $150 as a total paid for *all* premiums for medical-care insurance, without regard to the 3-percent limitation.[106]

Medical care includes amounts paid for insurance covering medical care.[107] Amounts paid for hospitalization insurance for membership in an association furnishing cooperative or so-called free choice medical service, or for group hospitalization and clinical care, are expenses for medical care.[108] Premiums are deductible for policies covering accidental loss of life, limb, sight, and time.[109]

An otherwise allowable medical expense is deductible even if paid to a party other than the one who or which provided the services. An individual's medical bills were paid by his parents, who brought along a standard form of promissory note for him to sign on their condolence call. The individual paid off the note to his parents a year later. Medical expense deduction was allowed in the year his parents paid the physician.[110]

If an individual is fitted with contact lenses by an optometrist, the individual may make an agreement with the optometrist, for a nonrefundable fixed amount, to replace the lenses if they become lost or damaged within one year. Or the individual may take out insurance on the lenses, covering replacement if they are lost or damaged within that time. In either event, the payments are deductible as medical expenses.[111]

Amounts paid as premiums under Part B of Medicare (Supplementary Medical Insurance for the Aged) are deductible as medical expenses.[112]

A middle-aged couple had an eighteen-year-old daughter who was physically and mentally handicapped to the extent she was confined to a wheelchair and required continued and extensive care. To ensure that the daughter receive appropriate care after their death or at such time as they would otherwise be unable to care for her, they entered into a contract with a private institution specializing in the care and custody of such individuals to provide for her care, supervision, and training in the institution during her lifetime. In order for the girl to be accepted in the institution and receive lifetime care, the institution required payments from the couple of a specified amount, 20 percent payable when the contract was signed, 10 percent within twelve months, an additional 10 percent within twenty-four months, and the final 60 percent when the daughter entered the institution. No portion of the payments was refundable. The fee was not medical insurance, being calculated without regard to contracts for care involving other patients. Under the contract, the obligation to pay was incurred at the time the payments were made, and the payments were made to secure medical services for a dependent, even though these services were not to be performed until a future time, if at all. The payments were deductible as expenses for medical care in the year paid.[113]

A couple living together as common-law man and wife in a state recognizing such marriages can file a joint return on which medical-care expenses can be claimed for a woman's dependent parents.[114]

Preadoption medical expenses are deductible if the child adopted qualifies as a dependent *when* these expenses were paid or incurred. If, for example, the taxpayer reimburses an adoption agency or other persons for medical expenses they paid out under an agreement with the taxpayer, the taxpayer is considered to have paid these expenses, and they are deductible if the adoption has been completed at the time of reimbursement.

On the other hand, if the reimbursement of such expenses are incurred and paid *before* the adoption negotiations, then the taxpayer is not allowed the medical expenses as a deduction.[115]

The above two paragraphs refer both to doctor and to hospital bills.[116] It is immaterial that the taxpayer's adopted child was not born at the time the medical services were rendered.[117]

One can deduct the cost of a periodic physical examination if it is required by an employer.[118] But any additional expenses for medical or physical correction would be deductible only if they met the requirements for a medical expense deduction.[119]

Physicians, psychologists, and others frequently notice that the payments they receive for personal services are in the form of company checks. But when a revenue agent seeking substantiation for such a medical-expense deduction sees these checks, he is likely to disallow the deduction with some witticism such as, "If the company is sick, the company gets the medical deduction." One individual subjected to that treatment won his case by showing that the company checks had been left over from the days when he still was in business for himself and that the bank actually charged the medical-expense payments to his personal account.[120]

Payments were made on a subscription basis to a plan that provided for the storage and locating of personal medical information by a computer data bank. The services thus provided by the computer equipment consisted of storing medical information that was furnished by the personal physician of each subscriber regarding his illnesses, diseases, allergies, medication prescribed on a long-term basis, vital-sign statistics, blood type, and family medical history. This information could be located and furnished rapidly to any physician who was attending the subscriber, subscribers being furnished with a special identification card to facilitate speedy supplying of data. The subscription cost of this service was deductible as medical expense.[121]

One of the major requirements of allowable medical-care deduction is concrete *proof*. But in at least one case the court was willing to estimate what the allowable medical expenses were. The case was that of an elderly taxpayer who had no such proof, but there was credible testimony that the woman was consulting a physician. Evidently the court believed that a person of her advanced years could be presumed to have physical infirmities, and without concrete proof it allowed an estimate of medical expenses to be deducted.[122]

Poorly documented medical expenses were allowed where the husband was seventy-nine and his wife was seventy-eight, the court deeming the total claimed as not too unreasonable in the light of their advanced ages.[123] In *any* situation where an individual can show that he had some medical expenses but has little specific proof of the amount he actually spent, the court, if it chooses, may arrive at its own figure for the medical-expense deduction, treating the taxpayer rather severely becuase the insufficient records resulted from his own doing.[124] So it was where an individual supplying services which alleviated a physical condition required food and lodging at substantial cost, although actual figures were not available.[125]

Expenses for the medical care of an individual who died are treated for tax purposes as *his* medical expenses if they are paid out of his estate by his executor during the one-year period beginning with the day following his death. But this can be done only if the executor agrees not to deduct the same amount on the Federal estate-tax return as a debt of the deceased taxpayer.[126]

Medical expenses are deductible only to the extent that, in aggregate, they exceed 3 percent of an individual's adjusted gross income for the taxable year. Business expenses are fully deductible. When a businessperson has medical expenses in order that he can transact business, the question is whether such expenses are characterized as *medical* or *business*. Here is how the Internal Revenue Service draws the line: (1) A businessperson was paralyzed from the waist down. When he had to go to business meetings out of town, his wife, a friend, or an associate went along to help him negotiate the stairs and narrow doors and to handle baggage. He needed no such assistance in his hometown. (2) Another individual, an amputee, required medication several times a day. When he went out of town on business, his wife, a friend, or an associate helped him to get about, as in (1). But his helper also took care of the replacement and removal of his prosthesis (artificial limb) and the daily administration of his medicine, and was prepared to render assistance should an allergic reaction to his medication occur. In both (1) and (2), the taxpayer did not pay for this aid, but he assumed all travel, meal, and lodging expenses. The expenses of the helper in (1) were deductible as *business expenses,* inasmuch as they were intrinsically a part of the expenses for travel paid by an individual in connection with business services. But the outlays in (2) were *medical expenses,* being more in the nature of payments for nursing services, the services being required *regularly* in the conduct of the individual's personal activities as well as incidentally in his business activities.[127] *See also* **Alcoholics Anonymous; Alcoholism, treatment for; Blind persons, expenses of; Credit card, charges to; Deaf persons, expenses of; Incurable disease; Retirement homes; Wigs.**

If a medical expenditure is deducted on the decedent's final Federal income tax return, it is subject to the regular limitation that medical expenses are deductible only to the extent that in aggregate they exceed 3 percent of adjusted gross income. There is no limitation to the amount that the decedent's estate can deduct. Where part of the medical expenditure is taken on the decedent's income tax return and the remaining portion is shown as a claim against the estate on the Federal estate tax return, the 3 percent portion of the medical expenses not allowable on the income tax return is also not deductible from the gross estate on the estate tax return.[128]

Allowance of the medical expense deduction can depend upon willingness to identify names. An individual considered it to be damaging to the patient to write down the name of a dependent who was getting psychiatric treatment. He was also concerned lest identification of the doctors lead to tax investigation of them. (The record did not indicate *whose* idea that was. Result: loss of the medical expense deduction for lack of substantiation.)[129]

Medical malpractice insurance. Certain physicians formed a trust for the creation of a statewide medical malpractice insurance risk pool to provide coverage to participants for any medical malpractice claim in excess of a specified amount. Each physician was obliged to arrange for coverage up to that specified amount. Compliance was effected with the state insurance department's rules as to reserves, deficit assessments, and the like. Premiums paid by the physicians could not be recovered by them. Premiums paid for medical malpractice insurance paid by the participating doctors were deductible as ordinary and necessary business expenses.[130]

Medicare, premiums under Part B. *See* **Medical expenses.**

Merchandise shortages. *See* **Inventory write-downs.**

Mileage allowance. In the case of expenses for business travel away from home (other than costs of transportation to and from the destination), the requirements of substantiation are deemed to be met where an employer reimburses his employees for subsistence in an amount not exceeding $44 per day or in lieu of subsistence provides his employees with a *per diem* allowance not to exceed $44 a day. But the employer must reasonably limit payment of such travel expenses to those which are ordinary and necessary in the conduct of his trade or business, and the elements of time, place, and business purpose of the travel must be substantiated. For this purpose the employer must maintain adequate internal audit controls, such as verification by a responsible person other than the employee himself. The term "subsistence" includes, but is not limited to, cleaning and pressing of clothes, and fees and tips for services. Alternatively, in the case of travel away from home, a fixed mileage may be used.[131] This standard mileage rate is 17 cents on the first 15,000 miles and 10 cents on each additional mile.[132] Such an arrangement is not acceptable where an employer and an employee are related parties unless the related parties are other than an individual and his spouse, brothers and sisters, ancestors, and lineal descendants. If the employer is a corporation, the employee may not own, directly or indirectly, more than 10 percent of the stock.[133]

If an employer's mileage allowance exceeds 17 cents per mile, the presence of unusual circumstances which account for his excess may constitute grounds for considering the higher allowance as equivalent to substantiation and adequate accounting to the employer. But the Internal Revenue Service refused to allow 20 cents per mile to be used even where local gasoline prices were running above the national average or other normal operating costs had been increasing.[134]

Where a car used for business purposes is fully depreciated for tax purposes, that is, the amount of its cost already has been deducted over a period of years, the standard mileage deduction is 10 cents per mile for all miles of business use. This applies to taxable years beginning after December 31, 1974.[135]

The maximum automatic allowable rate can be greater than $44 if the maximum *per diem* rate paid by the government is higher in the locality in which the travel is performed, as may be the case where travel is outside the United States.[136]

Where a person uses a car for the rendering of gratuitous services to a charitable organization, for transportation for medical care, or for allowable moving expenses, 7 cents per mile may be claimed as a deduction in lieu of itemizing costs individually.[137]

See also **Medical expenses; Moving expenses.**

Military officers. *See* **Armed Forces.**

Mine cave-in damage to one's property. The amount of such damage qualifies as a deductible casualty loss.[138]

Mineral leases, cost of acquiring. An individual may pay fees to a person who solicits applicants to participate in the bidding on non-competitive government oil and gas leases on Federal lands which are held monthly by the United States Interior Department's Bureau of Land Management. The fees may cover such services as: expert geological advice on government lands available for noncompetitive leasing, timely and accurate filing of offers to lease approved lands on behalf of the applicant, and payment of the standard filing fee to the Bureau on behalf of the applicant. If no lease is obtained, the fee is fully deductible.[139] If a lease is obtained, the cost is a capital expenditure recoverable through annual depletion deductions.[140]

Mink coat. *See* **Uniforms.**

Minor children, interest paid to. Parents legitimately may deduct interest on loans from minor children.[141] *See* **Family transactions.**

Minority stockholders, expenses of. *See* **Investors; Legal expenses.**

Minors, expenses for. *See* **Guardians.**

Misappropriation, restitution for. *See* **Restitution payments.**

Mismanagement suits, cost of. *See* **Executives.**

Misrepresentation. *See* **Reliance upon misrepresentation.**

Mortgage, payments on. *See* **Interest.**

Mortgage insurance premiums. *See* **Insurance.**

Mortgage loan fees and commissions. Ordinarily, fees and commissions paid in connection with a mortgage loan are not deductible, for the benefit of the expenditures is expected to last over the period of the loan. The deduction of fees must be spread over the life of the loan. But the unamortized portion of the fees and commissions is deductible in the year the mortgaged property is sold.[142] (If the loan is called ahead of time by reason of a default, any unamortized portion of the fee is deductible in the year the property is disposed of.[143] *See also* **Expenditures for periods lasting more than one year.**

Mortgage payments as alimony. *See* **Alimony.**

Motor fuel tax. Except in the case of vehicles used for business and investment purposes, gasoline, diesel fuel, and other motor fuel taxes are not deductible in taxable years beginning after December 31, 1978.[144]

Moving expenses. The rules as to moving expenses apply both to employees and to self-employed persons. Moving expenses are deductible if an individual can meet these guidelines:
1. The distance between his new place of work and his old principal residence is at least thirty-five miles farther than the distance from his old residence to his old place of work. The distance between the two points is measured by the shortest of the more commonly traveled routes between the two places. A part-time residence or a seasonal one, such as a summer beach cottage, does not qualify for this purpose.
2. The individual must work at least thirty-nine weeks during the twelve-month period immediately after his arrival in the general location of his new principal place of work. It is not necessary that he work for a single employer for that thirty-nine weeks, nor must the weeks be consecutive. It is required only that he be employed on a full-time basis within the same general commuting area. Whether a person is deemed to be employed full-time depends upon the customary practice for a particular occupation. For example, a schoolteacher whose employment contract covers a twelve-month period and who teaches on a full-time basis for more than six months is considered a full-time employee during the entire twelve-month period. A person is considered as working during any week he is, through no fault of his own, temporarily absent from work

because of illness, strikes, shutouts, layoffs, natural disasters, and the like. Self-employed persons must perform services on a full-time basis for at least seventy-eight weeks during the twenty-four-month period immediately after their arrival.

The thirty-nine- or seventy-eight-week test is waived only if an individual is unable to satisfy it because of death, disability, involuntary separation from work (other than for willful misconduct), or transfer for the benefit of the employer after obtaining full-time work in which he reasonably could have been expected to satisfy the test. In the case of married persons filing a joint Federal income tax return, if both spouses are employees either one may satisfy the full-time work requirement. But the weeks worked by the two spouses may not be added to satisfy the requirement.[145]

The move must be reasonably close in time and in place to a person's commencement of work at his new principal place of work. In general, moving expenses incurred within one year of the date of commencement of work are considered to be reasonably close in time. Moving expenses incurred after the one-year period may be considered reasonably close if it can be shown that circumstances prevented the taxpayer from incurring the moving expenses within the one-year period allowed. An individual was transferred by his employer from Los Angeles to Chicago in December 1974. He and his wife decided that she would remain in Los Angeles until the youngest child was graduated from junior high school in June 1977. He thereupon rented a furnished one-room apartment in Chicago and lived there until the family home in Los Angeles was sold, at which time his wife and children moved to join him in their newly purchased home in Chicago. The cost of the 1977 move to Chicago was deductible although he already had been working there for two and a half years.[146]

No deduction is allowed for an individual's moving expenses unless his new principal place of residence is at least thirty-five miles farther from his former residence than was his former principal place of residence. If he had no former principal place of residence, the new principal one must be at least thirty-five miles from the former residence. This latter category includes persons who are seeking full-time employment for the first time or those who are reentering the labor force after a substantial period of unemployment or part-time employment. An out-of-work individual found work elsewhere and moved to a new residence. The distance between his former residence and his former principal place of work was twenty-five miles. The distance between his former residence and his new principal place of work was fifty-five miles, thus exceeding by thirty miles the distance from his former residence to his former principal place of work. He could not deduct the moving expenses. Although his new principal place of work was fifty-five miles from his former residence, it was only thirty miles farther than his former residence was from his former principal place of work and thus did not meet the "at least thirty-five miles farther" minimum distance condition. He was not seeking full-time employment for the first time, nor was he reentering the labor market after a substantial period of unemployment in view of the fact that he had been unemployed for only two months.[147]

The time periods referred to previously are measured from the date of an employee's arrival in the general location of his new principal place of work. Generally, date of arrival is the date of the termination of the last trip preceding the person's commencement of work on a regular basis and is not the date his family or household goods and effects arrive.

Where a person has more than one place of employment (for example, he works for more than one employer), his principal place of work is determined by his principal employment. The more important factors are: (1) the total time ordinarily spent at each place, (2) the person's activity at each place, and (3) the relative significance of the financial return from each place.

The term *moving expenses* includes only those expenses which are reasonable under the circumstances of the particular move. They cover the following categories:

1.   Travel expenses, including meals and lodging, for the taxpayer and his family while en route from his old principal residence to his new one. Family, for this purpose, includes any member of one's household other than a tenant or employee, unless he happens to be a genuine dependent whose principal place of abode is the taxpayer's residence. It does not include a servant, chauffeur, nurse, or other attendant who is not a member of the household. The deduction for traveling expenses from the taxpayer's former principal residence to his new residence is allowable for only one trip. But it is not necessary that the taxpayer and all members of his household travel together or at one time. If a person used his own automobile for this transportation, he can compute the transportation expense in either of two ways: (1) by actual out-of-pocket expenses, or (2) at a rate of 7 cents a mile.

2.   The cost of moving household goods, personal effects, and automobiles of the taxpayer and of the members of his household as outlined in item 1 above. This covers the cost of transportation from the old principal residence to the new one, the cost of packing and crating, in-transit storage, and insurance.

Storage can include charges for a thirty-day period after the day of the move. If the property was not at the taxpayer's old residence at the time of the move, expenses are deductible only if he owned it at the time, and the cost of transportation does not exceed what the tariff would have been from his old residence.

3. The cost of house-hunting trips prior to the move from the old principal residence to the new principal place of work, including return after obtaining work. The deduction is not available, however, unless the taxpayer (1) has obtained employment at a new principal place of work before the trip begins, and (2) travels from his former residence to the general area of his principal place of work and returns.

4. The cost of temporary quarters (meals and lodgings are covered) at the new location of work during any period of thirty consecutive days after obtaining work.

5. The cost of selling an old, or acquiring a new, residence are deductible. When a person sells his old home he may deduct real estate commissions, attorneys' fees, title fees, escrow fees, points or loan-placement charges he is obligated to pay, and state-transfer taxes and similar expenses in connection with the sale or exchange of his former residence. When he buys a new residence, he may deduct attorneys' fees, escrow fees, appraisal fees, title costs, points or loan-placement charges not representing payment or prepayment of interest, and similar charges in connection with the purchase of a new residence.

6. The expenses incurred in obtaining a settlement on the lease to a person's former residence and the expenses incident to the acquisition of a lease for a new residence.

The total deduction for items 3, 4, 5, and 6 for taxable years beginning after December 31, 1976, is limited to $3,000 (previously it had been $2,500), of which no more than $1,500 (previously it had been $1,000), can be for items 3 and 4.[148]

If a husband and wife both commence work at a new principal place of employment within the same general location, the same $2,500 limit applies as if there were only one commencement of work. Where a married couple file separate returns, the overall limitation for these additional living expenses is $1,250 for each, and the house-hunting and temporary living expenses are limited to $500 of the $1,250. In those cases where the moving expenses relate to an individual other than the taxpayer, a deduction is allowed only if the individual lives in both the former and the new residence and is a member of the taxpayer's household.

Transportation expenses of the move cover any pets owned

by the taxpayer.[149] It is not necessary to consider whether a pet is regarded as a member of the household or a personal effect.

Certain expenses are not deductible if the purpose is to obtain tax-exempt income, such as interest on money borrowed to purchase or to carry state or municipal bonds. (This has been discussed under **Interest**.) Similarly, moving expenses to change jobs from one producing taxable income to one producing tax-exempt income are not deductible. A person moved from the United States to a foreign country, where his income was exempt from United States tax because his principal residence and his place of work were abroad. No deduction was allowed for moving expenses.[150] See also **Armed Forces; Expenditures for benefits lasting more than one year.**

In the case of moves to foreign work locations, the period during which the cost of temporary living arrangements is allowed as deductible moving expenses is ninety days rather than thirty, and the ceiling on those temporary living costs is $4,500 rather than $1,500. Moving expenses include the cost of storing goods while abroad. The moving expenses deduction has been expanded to permit *bona fide* retirees returning to the United States after working abroad and survivors of Americans who die overseas to deduct the cost of moving back to the United States, subject to the regular limitations.[151]

When to take the moving expense deduction can be perplexing because it is not known until a year after the move if one really qualifies. Deduction cannot be taken in the later year when one's entitlement to the deduction becomes known. Deduction thus should be claimed in the year of the move, subject to later verification, although at filing time it is not known whether the deduction is proper. Or an amended return may be filed subsequently for that year.[152]

Multiple-support arrangement. See **Medical expenses.**

Municipality, contributions to. See **Contributions.**

Musicians. See **Commuting; Education; Uniforms.**

Music lessons as medical expense. See **Medical expenses.**

M

1. *Giles Frozen Custard, Inc.,* T.C. Memo 1970-73, filed March 26, 1970.
2. Revenue Ruling 60-365, 1960-2 CB 49.

3. I.R.S. Letter Ruling 7816021, January 17, 1978.
4. I.R.C. Section 213(a)(1).
5. Regulations Section 1.213-1(a)(3)(i).
6. *Litchfield v. Commissioner*, 330 F.2d 509 (1st Cir., 1964).
7. I.R.C. Section 213(e)(1).
8. Revenue Ruling 72-226, 1972-1 CB 96.
9. Regulations Section 1.213-1(e)(ii).
10. *Walter D. Bye et al.*, T.C. Memo. 1972-57, filed February 29, 1972.
11. Regulations Section 1.213-1(e)(1)(v)(a).
12. *Ibid.*
13. *Your Federal Income Tax*, 1976 edition, page 86.
14. *Protecting Older Americans Against Overpayment of Income Taxes*, Special Committee on Aging, United States Senate, 1976, page 2.
15. *Bessie Cohen*, T.C. Memo., Docket No. 22263, entered January 12, 1951.
16. *Protecting Older Americans Against Overpayment of Income Taxes*, Special Committee on Aging, United States Senate, 1976, page 2.
17. *Owens et al. v. Commissioner*, T.C. Memo, 1977-319, filed September 19, 1977.
18. *Tax Benefits for Older Americans*, I.R.S. Publication 554, 1976 edition, page 25.
19. Revenue Ruling 64-267, 1964-2 CB 69.
20. Letter from Assistant Commissioner of Internal Revenue to the author, March 19, 1953, on behalf of the Joint Council of New York State Psychologists on Legislation.
21. Revenue Ruling 72-593, 1972-2 CB 180.
22. Revenue Ruling 78-325, I.R.B. 1978-36, 24.
23. Revenue Ruling 63-91, 1963-1 CB 54.
24. Revenue Ruling 70-170, 1970-1 CB 51.
25. Revenue Ruling 62-210, 1962-2 CB 89.
26. Revenue Ruling 73-200, 1973-1 CB 140.
27. Revenue Ruling 75-187, 1975-1 CB 92.
28. Revenue Ruling 73-603, 1973-2 CB 76.
29. Revenue Ruling 73-201, 1973-1 CB 140.
30. *John Frier et al.*, T.C. Memo. 1971-84, filed April 26, 1971.
31. *Myrtle P. Dodge Estate*, T.C. Memo. 1961-346, filed December 27, 1961.
32. *Walter D. Bye et al.*, T.C. Memo, 1972-57, filed February 29, 1972.
33. Revenue Ruling 69-499, 1969-2 CB 39.
34. *Kelly v. Commissioner*, 440 F.2d 307 (7th Cir., 1971).
35. *Sidney J. Ungar et al.*, T.C. Memo. 1963-159, filed June 10, 1963.
36. Revenue Ruling 64-173, 1964-1 CB (Part 1) 121.
37. Revenue Ruling 55-261, 1955-1 CB 307.
38. Revenue Ruling 58-155, 1958-1 CB 156.
39. Revenue Ruling 55-261, 1955-1 CB 307.
40. Revenue Ruling 58-8, 1958-1 CB 154.
41. Revenue Ruling 76-332, 1976-2 CB 81.
42. *Protecting Older Americans Against Overpayment of Income Taxes*, Special Committee on Aging, United States Senate, 1976, page 2.
43. Revenue Ruling 62-189, 1962-2 CB 88.
44. Regulations Section 1.213-1(c)(iii).
45. *Berry et al. v. Wiseman*, 174 F. Supp. 748 (D.C., Okla., 1958).
46. Revenue Ruling 66-80, 1966-1 CB 57.
47. Revenue Ruling 70-605, 1970-2 CB 209.
48. *Oliver et al. v. Commissioner*, 364 F.2d 575 (8th Cir., 1966).
49. Revenue Ruling 70-395, 1970 2 CB 34.

M

230

50. *Riach et al. v. Frank*, 302 F.2d 374 (9th Cir., 1962).
51. Revenue Ruling 54-57, 1954-1 CB 67.
52. *Mason et al. v. United States*, D.C., Hawaii, 1957.
53. *Raymond Gerard et al.*, 37 T.C. 826 (1962).
54. *Ferris et al. v. Commissioner*, ... F.2d ... (7th Cir., 1978).
55. Revenue Ruling 78-221, I.R.B. 1978-24, 9.
56. Revenue Ruling 55-261, 1955-1 CB 307.
57. *Von Kalb v. Commissioner*, T.C. Memo. 1978-366, filed September 13, 1978.
58. *Tax Benefits for Older Americans*, I.R.S. Publication 554, 1976 edition, page 25.
59. *Leo R. Cohn et al.*, 38 T.C. 387 (1962).
60. *Thereon G. Randolph et al.*, 67 T.C. 481 (1976).
61. Regulations Section 1.213-1(e)(iv).
62. Revenue Ruling 55-261, 1955-1 CB 307.
63. *Montgomery et al. v. Commissioner*, 428 F.2d 243 (6th Cir., 1970).
64. *Your Federal Income Tax*, 1976 edition, page 86.
65. I.R.S. Letter Ruling 7813004, December 20, 1977.
66. Revenue Procedure 70-24, 1970-2 CB 505.
67. Revenue Ruling 58-533, 1958-2 CB 108.
68. *Your Federal Income Tax*, 1976 edition, page 86.
69. *Allenberg Cotton Company, Inc., et al. v. United States*, D.C., W.D. Tenn., 1960.
70. Revenue Ruling 58-110, 1958-1 CB 155.
71. *Stanley D. Winderman*, 32 T.C. 1147 (1959).
72. *William B. Meister et al.*, T.C. Memo. 1959-202, filed October 26, 1959.
73. Revenue Ruling 65-255, 1965-2 CB 76.
74. Revenue Ruling 55-261, 1955-1 CB 307.
75. *Michael R. Bordas et al.*, T.C. Memo. 1970-97, filed April 27, 1970.
76. *Sanford H. Weinzimer et al.*, T.C. Memo. 1958-137, filed July 16, 1958.
77. *Misfeldt v. Kelm*, D.C., Minn., 1957.
78. *Ann Coopersmith*, T.C. Memo. 1971-280, filed November 2, 1971.
79. Revenue Ruling 66-80, 1966-1 CB 57.
80. *George M. Womack*. T.C. Memo. 1975-232, filed July 15, 1975.
81. Revenue Ruling 58-481, 1958-2 CB 107.
82. Regulations Section 1.212-1(e)(1)(v)(a).
83. Revenue Ruling 70-285, 1970-1 CB 52.
84. *Lawrence D. Greisdorf et al.*, 54 T.C. 1684 (1970).
85. *Donovan et al. v. Campbell, Jr.*, D.C., N.D. Texas, 1961.
86. Revenue Ruling 54-457, 1954-1 CB 100.
87. *C. Fink Fischer et al.*, 50 T.C. 164 (1968).
88. *Hobart J. Hendrick et al.*, 35 T.C. 1223 (1961).
89. Revenue Ruling 69-499, 1969-2 CB 39.
90. Revenue Ruling 69-407, 1969-2 CB 40.
91. Revenue Ruling 78-340, I.R.B. 1978-38, 7.
92. I.R.S. Letter Ruling 7714016, January 10, 1977.
93. Revenue Ruling 72-226, 1972-1 CB 96.
94. Revenue Ruling 55-261, 1955-1 CB 307.
95. *W. B. Counts et al.*, 42 T.C. 755 (1964).
96. Revenue Ruling 57-489, 1957-2 CB 207.
97. Revenue Ruling 68-452, 1968-2 CB 111.
98. Revenue Ruling 73-189, 1973-1 CB 139.
99. *Edward J. Cullen*, T.C. Memo. 1973-158, filed July 23, 1973.

100. *Gerstacker et al. v. Commissioner*, 414 F.2d 548 (6th Cir., 1969).
101. Revenue Ruling 71-281, 1971-2 CB 165.
102. *David E. Starrett et al.*, 41 T.C. 877 (1964).
103. *Income Tax Deductions for Alimony Payments*, I.R.S. Publication 504, 1976 edition, page 1.
104. Revenue Ruling 55-479, 1955-2 CB 18.
105. I.R.C. Section 213(a)(2).
106. Revenue Ruling 68-433, 1968-2 CB 110.
107. I.R.C. Section 213(e)(1).
108. Regulations Section 1.213-1(e)(4).
109. *Richard H. Marriott et al.*, T.C. Memo. 1966-86, filed April 22, 1966.
110. Revenue Ruling 78-173, 1978-19, 9.
111. Revenue Ruling 74-429, 1974-2 CB 83.
112. *Donovan et al. v. Campbell, Jr.*, D.C., N.D. Texas, 1961.
113. Revenue Ruling 75-303, 1975-2 CB 87.
114. *James M. Ross*, T.C. Memo. 1972-122, filed May 25, 1972.
115. *Your Federal Income Tax*, 1976 edition, page 89.
116. Revenue Ruling 60-255, 1960-2 CB 105.
117. *Kilpatrick et al. v. Commissioner*, 68 T.C. 469 (1970).
118. *Protecting Older Americans Against Overpayment of Income Taxes*, Special Committee on Aging, United States Senate, 1976, page 5.
119. Revenue Ruling 58-382, 1958-2 CB 59.
120. *John B. Dougherty et al.*, T.C. Memo. 1976-135, filed April 20, 1976.
121. Revenue Ruling 71-282, 1971-1 CB 166.
122. *Bessie Cohen*, T.C. Memo., Docket No. 22263, entered January 12, 1951.
123. *Myrtle P. Dodge Estate*, T.C. Memo. 1961-346, filed December 27, 1961.
124. *Teichner et al. v. Commissioner*, 453 F.2d 944 (2d Cir., 1972).
125. *Walter D. Bye et al.*, T.C. Memo. 1972-57, filed February 29, 1972.
126. I.R.C. Section 213(d).
127. Revenue Ruling 75-317, 1975-2 CB 57.
128. Revenue Ruling 77-357, 1977-2 CB 328.
129. *Dodov et al. v. Commissioner*, T.C. Memo. 1977-362, filed October 11, 1977.
130. I.R.S. Letter Ruling 7751021, September 21, 1977.
131. Revenue Ruling 71-412, 1971-1 CB 170.
132. Revenue Ruling 75-433, 1974-2 CB 92, as amended by I.R.S. News Release IR-1893, October 7, 1977.
133. Revenue Ruling 71-412, 1971-1 CB 170.
134. I.R.S. Letter Ruling 7736018, June 9, 1977.
135. Revenue Procedure 75-3, 1975-1 CB 643.
136. Revenue Procedure 72-508, 1972-2 CB 200.
137. Revenue Procedure 74-24, 1974-2 CB 477.
138. *Tax Guide for Small Businesses*, 1978 edition, I.R.S. Publication 334, page 111.
139. Revenue Ruling 71-191, 1971-1 CB 77.
140. Revenue Ruling 67-141, 1967-1 CB 153.
141. *Cook et ux. v. United States*, ... F. Supp. ... (D.C., W.D. La., 1977).
142. *Herbert Enoch et al.*, 57 T.C. 781 (1972).
143. *Malmstedt et al. v. Commissioner*, 578 F.2d 520 (4th Cir., 1978).
144. Revenue Act of 1978, Section 111.
145. This entire division is based upon I.R.C. Section 217 and the correlative Treasury Regulations.
146. Revenue Ruling 78-200, I.R.B. 1978-22, 9.
147. Revenue Ruling 78-174, I.R.B. 1978-19, 10.

148. Tax Reform Act of 1976, Section 506.
149. Revenue Ruling 66-305, 1966-2 CB 102.
150. *Hartung et al. v. Commissioner*, 484 F.2d 953 (9th Cir., 1973).
151. Foreign Earned Income Act of 1978, Section 204.
152. *Della M. Meadows*, 66 T.C. 51 (1976).

M

232

N

Narcotics addiction, treatment for. Amounts spent at a therapeutic center for drug abusers is deductible as medical expense.[1]

Nationalization by foreign government. *See* **Foreign expropriation losses.**

Naval officers. *See* **Armed Forces.**

Negligence. *See* **Casualties; Repairs.**

Net operating loss. *See* **Carry-overs; Family transactions; Foreign expropriation losses; Tax-option corporations; Unused carry-over of fiduciary.**

Newsletter fund, contributions to. *See* **Contributions.**

Nonbusiness casualties. *See* **Casualties.**

Nonbusiness interest. *See* **Interest.**

Noncompetition agreements. *See* **Expenditures for benefits lasting more than one year.**

Nonprofit organizations, contributions to. *See* **Contributions.**

Normal obsolescence. *See* **Depreciation.**

Notetaker for deaf student. *See* **Deaf persons, expenses of.**

Nurses. *See* **Uniforms.**

Nursing home, contributions to. *See* **Contributions.**

Nursing home, services at. *See* **Medical expenses; Retirement homes.**

1. Revenue Ruling 72–226, 1972–1 CB 96.

O

Obsolescence. The depreciation allowance includes "a reasonable allowance for obsolescence."[1] This refers to *normal* obsolescence, the general awareness that sooner or later most depreciable property will be supplanted by something better.

Abnormal obsolescence, which is the subject of this section, is another matter entirely. Here there is not merely a leisurely period of something becoming out of date; there is a dramatic occurrence, not necessarily all at once, which requires that an asset be replaced before it wears out physically. If this abnormal obsolescence and the steps to replace the asset take place in a single year, there is a deduction at that time.[2] Generally, recognition of the problem and doing something about it take more than one year.[3] Then the unrecovered cost of the asset is amortized over that period.

Obsolescence in this sense may arise from changes in the art, shifting of business centers, loss of trade, inadequacy, supersession, prohibitory laws, and other things which, apart from physical deterioration, operate to cause business assets to suffer diminution in value.[4] Where an asset is permanently retired from use in the trade or business or in the production of income but is not disposed of by the taxpayer or physically abandoned, loss is recognized upon an abnormal retirement. This is measured by the excess of the adjusted basis of the asset at the time of retirement over the estimated salvage value or the fair market value at that time if it is higher. A retirement may be abnormal if the asset is withdrawn at an earlier time or under different circumstances than had been contemplated as, for example, where the property has lost its usefulness suddenly as the result of extraordinary obsolescence.[5]

A manufacturer lost a contract to manufacture shells for the government at the war's end. The full value of specialized machinery for such production (less estimated salvage) was deductible as obsolescence upon the termination date of the contract.[6] Additional buildings that had been constructed for a manufacturer under like circumstances were subject to a write-off.[7]

Changes in the character of a neighborhood and in the activities engaged in it by the taxpayer were bound to make the structures economically valueless because the changes had recast the neighborhood from residential to business. An obsolescence deduction was allowed where the conditions were known to exist at the end of the taxable year, although the buildings were not abandoned until the following year.[8]

Usually an asset cannot be written off at one time, even though its obsolescent state is recognized, because it takes time to procure a replacement. So the unrecovered cost of the asset is amortized over the length of time that will be required for that.[9] For example, a retail merchant undertook plans to replace his obsolete store with a modern, up-to-date building; he could amortize his unrecovered cost over a period of time until the new facilities would be available.[10]

Occupational taxes. Taxes imposed at a flat rate by a locality, for the privilege of working there, are deductible.[11]

Office at home. For taxable years beginning after December 31, 1975, an individual is not permitted to deduct any expenses attributable to the use of his home for business purposes except to the extent attributable to the portion of his home that is used exclusively on a regular basis: (1) as his principal place of business, (2) as a place of business which is used by patients, clients, or customers in meeting or dealing with the taxpayer in the normal course of his trade or business, or (3) in the case of a separate structure which is not attached to his dwelling unit (such as an artist's studio in a structure adjacent to but unattached to the residence), in connection with his trade or business. In the case of an employee, the business use of the home must be for the convenience of the employer. The use of a portion of a dwelling unit (such as a den) for both personal purposes and for the purposes of carrying on a trade or business does not meet the exclusive-use test. An exception to the exclusive-use test is provided where the dwelling unit is the sole fixed location of a trade or business which consists of selling products at retail or wholesale and the taxpayer regularly uses a separately identifiable portion of the residence for inventory storage. An overall limitation limits the amount of the deduction to the gross income generated by the business activity of the taxpayer in his home.[12]

Photographs may be a useful mechanism to show what

proportion of an apartment or home is used for business purposes.[13]

Olympic games, contributions to sponsoring organization. Deduction is allowed for contributions made after October 4, 1976, to tax-exempt organizations which sponsor athletic competitions.[14]

Optometrist, payments to. *See* **Medical expenses.**

Ordinary and necessary business expenses. Deduction is allowed for all ordinary and necessary expenses paid or incurred during the taxable year in carrying on any trade or business.[15]

It is difficult to argue that expenditures are *ordinary* if other parties customarily do not make such payments. Disbursements by a brokerage firm to an ordained minister for spiritual help were not deductible in the absence of proof that such help was sought by other concerns in solving business problems.[16] Deduction was allowed for a small part of the payment as compensation because the minister did run some business errands, which the court apparently regarded as an ordinary function for him.

In the case of an individual, deduction is allowed for all ordinary and necessary expenses paid or incurred for all the production or collection of income or for the management, conservation or maintenance of property held for the production of income.[17]

An executive who is required, such as in the corporate bylaws, to reimburse his employer for any of his entertainment expenses which the Internal Revenue Service refuses to permit the corporation to deduct may himself take a tax deduction for the amount of the reimbursement he makes.[18]

Compensation paid by a business as an inducement to a regular employee who is in the Armed Forces to return upon his discharge is deductible as a business expense.[19]

Expenses prior to the time one is engaged in a business are not deductible; prebusiness expenses are not "paid or incurred in carrying on the business," for the business is not a fact as yet. But expenses during a transitional period between businesses are deductible. Thus, gifts and entertainment for buyers of jewelry were deductible by a salesman in that line during a transitional period until he found a new connection.[20]

Where a corporation incurs travel and entertainment and other legitimate expenses in territory where it has not yet received state approval to do business, these expenses are not tax-deductible, for they are not related to the corporation's business if it is not authorized to do any there. An individual may get a better deal. A salesman for a prominent national manufacturer had a specific geographical territory, Greater Oklahoma City, where he received commissions on products he sold. He was highly ambitious, so he solicited orders from firms outside his territory. The Internal Revenue Service sought to disallow his expenses in connection with soliciting these outside orders because they did not relate to *his* business, which was restricted by his employer to Oklahoma City. But the court allowed him to take the deduction. Those business trips to cities outside his own territory were made only after approval had been obtained from his sales manager, which legitimized his invasion of districts not his own.[21]

Expenses of trying out a business venture are deductible if the venture is abandoned, provided the activities were more than a matter of investigating or looking into a proposition. The taxpayer must actually have been engaged in a transaction carried on for profit.[22]

Amounts paid to a client by an individual because of his failure to protect the client's interest are deductible.[23]

If a salesman is allowed to draw commissions before they are earned, and he draws against sales not yet paid for by his customers, he may be called upon to repay those commissions he drew out against customer bills that never did get paid. If he paid Federal income tax on commissions when he received them, he then is entitled to a business-expense deduction in the year he returns the unearned commissions to his employer.[24]

A manufacturer entered into an agreement with an established day care center to provide child care for the preschool children of employees. The stated purpose of the taxpayer in providing for the availability of the day care center was (1) to provide employees with a place to send their children during working hours, knowing that the children would receive proper care, (2) to reduce absenteeism and to increase productivity, and (3) to reduce employee turnover. The amounts paid by the manufacturer to the day care center were directly related to its business and hence were deductible business expenses.[25]

An employer could deduct fees paid to a tax-exempt organization for advice as to housing for employees of a minority group.[26]

An employer, as a matter of policy, may encourage employees to enroll in outside educational courses which will help them more quickly absorb the employer's business background and discharge the duties of their jobs. On behalf of employees who take the courses and maintain satisfactory grades, the employer either pays the tuition costs directly to the educational institution or reimburses the employees for the costs of the courses taken. Assuming that the courses are of a type which will be beneficial to a career in the employer's business and that they have the prior approval of the employer, the employer's costs are deductible as business expenses, because the degree to which an employee effectively and successfully performs his duties directly affects the degree to which the employer achieves business objectives. So the employer's costs are deducted as business expenses of a noncompensatory character and are not subject to wage withholding.[27]

Consultation fees for management and financial advice during contract negotiations were held to be deductible. (Such might not have been the case where the transaction involved the sale of capital assets, the cost then appearing to be a capital expenditure.)[28] Professional or technical journals and books, etc., are deductible if they have short useful lives, such as less than one year; otherwise, the costs would have to be written off as depreciation over the useful lives of the assets.[29] Gifts to subordinates by a sales supervisor were deductible, because greater cooperation from these persons was likely to increase his own performance.[30]

A businessperson could deduct the cost of liquor purchased in reasonable amounts for people who regularly supplied merchandise.[31] A business-expense deduction was allowed for payments to a physician for treating someone injured on the premises.[32] Research expenses incurred by a professor for the purpose of teaching, lecturing, and writing in his own field were deductible as a means of carrying out the duties expected of him as a professor without expectation of profit apart from his salary.[33]

Testimonial dinner costs in the case of important customers were deductible business expenses.[34]

Fines and penalties are not deductible for Federal income tax purposes. But some of the by-products of fines and penalties are deductible, such as legal fees and related expenses paid or incurred in the defense of a prosecution or civil action arising from the violation of the law imposing the fine or civil penalty. Court costs assessed against the taxpayer, as well as stenographic and printing charges, are not regarded as part of the fine or penalty, nor are compensatory damages (including damages under Section 4A of the Clayton Anti-Trust Act) paid to a government.[35]

A partner in a brokerage firm could deduct his contributions to an undertaking which was formed to get evidence against a bucket shop. His payment was to protect his own business interest.[36] Amounts paid by various employers to a protective service association that was to protect them from unjust labor demands were deductible.[37]

Some physicians organized a private hospital to serve their own patients exclusively. To keep the hospital solvent, the doctors paid the operating deficits that resulted at first. Each doctor was permitted to deduct such payments, as the purpose was to continue to earn fees from patients who were hospitalized there. The payments were made to preserve income from loss or reduction.[38]

Payments to a nonprofit organization for protection against labor demands were deductible.[39] A printing concern with labor problems was allowed to deduct the cost of recruiting personnel to break a strike.[40] Expenses incurred while investigating employees in order to avoid embezzlement losses was a legitimate deduction.[41]

Costs of resisting efforts to put the taxpayer out of business were deductible, as where an entertainer incurred legal fees in a libel action against a person who had called him a Communist and who had published calls to the public "to hit these boys in their box-office."[42]

A commercial firm could deduct payments to the Union of Soviet Socialist Republics that were based upon a percentage of the value of its imports and exports, in order to obtain a license to do business.[43] Deduction was allowed for the cost of Christmas cards, including the postage thereon, which were sent to customers.[44]

When an individual engaged in a trade or business makes a payment to an exempt organization with a reasonable expectation of financial return to himself, which is in line with the amount of his gift, it is not subject to the percentage limitations of charitable contributions but is fully deductible as ordinary and necessary business expense. Such was the ruling when money was given to a pollution-control fund established by a municipality, where the donor's business had been hurt in the past because of polluted atmosphere.[45]

A manufacturer can deduct as research and experimental expenditures the cost of developing and designing, at the manufacturer's risk, a specially built automated manufacturing system for a single customer's specific order.[46]

An employer's contribution to an unemployment-benefit fund to pay a "layoff moving allowance," when an employee who is laid off at one plant accepts employment at another plant, is deductible as an ordinary and necessary business expense.[47]

Where income is earned outside the United States by a person under certain conditions, it is not taxed in the U.S. Expenses in connection with that income similarly are not deductible. But expenses not related to income earned outside the country are deductible. Examples of such items include personal and family medical expenses, real estate taxes on a personal residence, interest on a mortgage on a personal residence, and charitable contributions.[48]

An industry association and a union made an agreement, which provided that companies belonging to the association would make monthly contributions of $x per employee into a trust fund for the benefit of covered employees. The trust was to maintain a health facility for the benefit of the union members and to maintain accident, health, and hospitalization insurance for the employees and their families. If the plan were terminated, any remaining moneys were to be used as the trustees saw fit, which meant that the companies would not get back their contributions under any circumstances. The amounts thus contributed under the plan were deductible as ordinary and necessary business expenses.[49]

Dental bills paid for an employee because of an accident sustained at work are deductible.[50]

A taxpayer could deduct the cost of repairs and replacements in the form of a complete cleaning, overhauling, and replacing of axles, transmissions, and brakes of motor equipment used for business purposes. Although the repairs were extensive and the new materials had some advantages over those replaced, they did not materially increase the value or the life of the equipment but only kept it in usable condition.[51]

The cost of repairs was deductible where the business equipment was of no greater efficiency or utility after the repair, even if the work done was not a reasonable facsimile of the original item, as in the case of an elevator.[52]

After a fire had partially destroyed a plant, expenditures for temporary electrical installations and other emergency activities to place the plant in running order were deductible.[53] *See also* **Repairs.**

The cost of tickets for benefit performances, purchased to maintain goodwill in the community, was deductible as a form of advertising.[54] A tavern owner was permitted to deduct as advertising the cost of a Christmas party given for the children of the neighborhood to promote goodwill with their parents.[55] A restaurant could deduct the cost of an automobile given to the patron who drew a winning ticket.[56] *See also* **Advertising.**

To promote sales and net profits, a business agreed to pay to an approved charitable organization a certain amount for each label from one of its products that the organization mailed to the business enterprise. In return, the charitable organization agreed to permit the use of its name in the business's advertising and to obtain testimonial letters for use in a sales campaign. The amounts turned over to the charity by the business were deductible as ordinary and necessary expenses, without the percentage limitations imposed upon charitable contributions.[57]

An attorney bought stock in a finance company. When the company became insolvent, his loss on the stock was not a capital loss but a fully deductible ordinary loss. He had purchased the stock, not as an investment, but for the purpose of getting profitable law work for himself. His investment was large enough to enable him to be elected president, and as such, he thought he could turn over some of the finance company's legal work to himself in his capacity as a lawyer. He expected through this connection to be engaged for title searches on property offered as security by borrowers, to obtain collection fees of up to 25 percent when the company had to get some lawyer to go after delinquent parties, and to obtain document recording and notarial fees. The loss was fully deductible, being in connection with a business transaction entered upon for profit.[58] See also **Actors; Armed Forces; Contributions; Employees; Executives; Teachers.**

Organic foods. See **Medical expenses.**

Outside salesmen, expenses of. See **Employees.**

Overhead insurance. See **Insurance.**

Over sixty-month period. See **Expenditures for benefits lasting more than one year.**

O

1. I.R.C. Section 167(a).
2. *Keller Street Development Company v. Commissioner*, 323 F.2d 166 (9th Cir., 1963).
3. *Zwetchkenbaum et al. v. Commissioner*, 326 F.2d 477 (1st Cir., 1964).
4. *United States Cartridge Company v. United States*, 284 U.S. 511 (1932).
5. Regulations Section 1.167(a)–8.
6. *United States v. Wagner Electric Mfg. Co.*, 61 F.2d 204 (8th Cir., 1932).
7. *United States Cartridge Company v. United States*, 284 U.S. 511 (1932).
8. *Cosmopolitan Corporation et al.*, T.C. Memo. 1959–112, filed June 12, 1959.
9. *Corsicana Gas & Electric Company*, 6 B.T.A. 565 (1927).
10. *Townsend-Ueberrhein Clothing Company v. Crooks*, 41 F.2d 66 (D.C., W.D. Mo., 1930).

11. *Your Federal Income Tax*, 1978 edition, page 90.
12. Tax Reform Act of 1976, Section 601.
13. *Frank A. Thomas et al.*, T.C. Memo. 1969–108, filed May 26, 1969.
14. I.R.C. Section 170(c)(2)(B).
15. I.R.C. Section 162.
16. *Trebilcock et al. v. Commissioner*, 557 F.2d 1226 (6th Cir., 1977).
17. I.R.C. Section 212.
18. I.R.S. Letter Ruling 7811004, November 29, 1977.
19. *Berkshire Oil Co.*, 9 T.C. 903 (1947).
20. *Harold Haft et al.*, 40 T.C. 2 (1963).
21. *Raymond Warren Jackson et al.*, T.C. Memo 1975–301, filed September 30, 1975.
22. *Charles I. Parker*, 1 T.C. 709 (1943).
23. *Henry F. Cochrane*, 23 B.T.A. 202 (1931).
24. Revenue Ruling 72–28, 1972–1 CB 45.
25. Revenue Ruling 73–348, 1973–2 CB 31.
26. Revenue Ruling 68–2, 1968–1 CB 61.
27. Revenue Ruling 76–71, 1976–1 CB 308.
28. *United States Freight Company et al. v. United States*, 422 F.2d 887 (Ct. Cl., 1970).
29. *Beaudry v. Commissioner*, 150 F.2d 20 (2d Cir., 1945).
30. *Harold A. Christensen*, 17 T.C. 1456 (1952).
31. *Rodgers Dairy Co.*, 14 T.C. 66 (1950).
32. *Fred W. Staudt*, T.C. Memo., Docket No. 32244, entered December 17, 1953.
33. Revenue Ruling 63–275, 1963–2 CB 85.
34. *First National Bank of Omaha v. United States*, 276 F. Supp. (D.C., Neb., 1967).
35. T.D. 7366, 1975–2 CB 64.
36. *Edward A. Pierce*, 18 B.T.A. 447 (1921).
37. *Mrs. H. A. Allan*, 7 B.T.A. 1256 (1927).
38. *Charles J. Dinardo*, 22 T.C. 430 (1954).
39. *Fritz B. Campen*, 16 B.T.A. 543 (1929).
40. *Queen City Printing Company*, 6 B.T.A. 521 (1927).
41. *Desmonds, Inc.*, 15 B.T.A. 738 (1929).
42. *Paul Draper et al.*, 26 T.C. 201 (1956).
43. *Allied American Corporation*, 25 B.T.A. 1276 (1932).
44. *Arthur S. McKenzie et al.*, T.C. Memo., Docket No. 30042, entered May 2, 1952.
45. Revenue Ruling 73–113, 1973–1 CB 65.
46. Revenue Ruling 73–275, 1973–1 CB 134.
47. Revenue Ruling 73–245, 1973–1 CB 64.
48. Regulations Section 1.911–1(a)(3).
49. Revenue Ruling 77–406, 1977–2 CB 56.
50. *Bearl Sprott et al.*, T.C. Memo., Docket Nos. 32340–1, entered February 17, 1953.
51. *Mark C. Nottingham*, T.C. Memo., Docket No. 31415, entered May 8, 1953.
52. *Mellie Esperson*, B.T.A. Memo., Docket No. 98737, entered February 5, 1941.
53. *Ticket Office Equipment Co., Inc.*, 20 T.C. 272 (1953) aff'd, 213 F.2d 318 (2d Cir., 1954).
54. *Victor J. McQuade*, 4 B.T.A. 837 (1926).
55. *A. D. Miller*, T.C. Memo., Docket No. 23754, entered January 18, 1951.
56. I.T. 1667, II-1 CB 83.
57. Revenue Ruling 63–73, 1963–1 CB 35.
58. *Irwin v. United States*, D.C., E.D. La., 1975

P

Parking fees. Where an automobile is used for business purposes, parking charges are one of the legitimate expenses deductible in producing taxable income. Such fees may be deductible even if not used in producing income. Such was the case where an individual was a member of his state's Advisory Committee to the Small Business Administration. He was not compensated for his services in this connection. But he could deduct his parking fees as "out-of-pocket transportation expenses necessarily incurred in performing donated services."[1] See also **Contributions.**

Parking fees incurred in connection with business are separately deductible even where a person uses the zero bracket amount in lieu of itemizing deductions.[2] See also **Employees; Medical expenses; Mileage allowance.**

Partial bad debts. See **Bad debts.**

Partners, lunches for. See **Entertainment.**

Partnerships. For deduction of a partner's share of partnership losses, see **Carry-overs.**

A partner can deduct unreimbursed travel and entertainment expenses he incurred for the partnership, where under the partnership agreement he was obliged to assume such expenses.[3]

A sum paid to one's partner to bring about an early dissolution of the partnership is deductible.[4] See also **Legal fees.**

Passport. The fee paid for a passport is not deductible as a tax. But if it is procured in connection with a trip for business purposes, it is deductible as a business expense.[5]

Past-due premium on fidelity bond. A belated premium on a fiduciary bond required under a previous employment was held to be deductible.[6]

Patent infringement, losses from. *See* **Compensable injuries.**

Payment of debt of another person. Generally, voluntary payments of the debt of another party are not a deductible business expense. But deduction is allowed where payments are made to protect and to preserve an existing business reputation.[7] *See also* **Reputation, maintenance of.**

Payola. *See* **Bribes and kickbacks.**

Penalty fee for loan repayment. A borrower may wish to prepay loan installments to speed up the termination of his loan. Ordinarily, a cash-basis taxpayer is not entitled in a single year to the deduction of interest related to a period of more than twelve months because that would result in a material distortion of his income for that year. One loan agreement allowed the borrower to make prepayments on any future installments. But if prepayments in a 12-month period equaled or exceeded 20 percent of the principal of the loan, the borrower would be liable to a prepayment penalty equal to 180 days' interest on the original principal of the loan. Prepaid interest in the year of payment was deductible to the extent of the penalty for the prepayment of installments.[8]

Penalty payments, as interest. *See* **Interest.**

Pension contributions not completely regained. If an individual contributes his required amount to a plan which is approved by the Internal Revenue Service, he may be entitled to receive from the pension fund when he retires a lump-sum payment of the amount due him. But because of the fund's investment losses, the amount which he receives when he retires may be less than he had put into the fund. The difference between what he had put into the fund and what he gets out is deductible as an ordinary loss in the year he gets the money.[9]

Pensions. *See* **Individual retirement account; Self-employment plans.**

Percentage depletion. *See* **Depletion.**

Percentage rental. If business is good, a company can afford to pay higher rent for its premises, and of course the tax deduction goes up. If business is poor, a rent reduction is desirable. Both objectives are facilitated by a percentage lease. The landlord is protected against inflation by the automatic escalation factor, while if the tenant's business deteriorates, the automatically lowered rent is at least better than having the tenant become unable to afford the original rent. Customarily, the percentage lease is geared to receipts or profits, with a minimum rent to provide a reasonable return on the landlord's investment. Even if a tenant's rent is unusually large in a particular year under a percentage lease, no part of the rent will be disallowed as unreasonable. But if tenant and landlord are related parties, the Internal Revenue Service may question the legitimacy of the arrangement. In one case, the Service questioned the tax deduction when a corporation rented its premises from the chief stockholder under a percentage lease, which yielded a rental that exceeded the flat rental rate previously used. But the court permitted the full rent deduction even though the percentage rental had been recommended by the accountant who also handled the company's taxes because (1) percentage rentals are fair to both landlord and tenant in principle by reason of the factors of inflation and business fluctuations, and (2) the arithmetic of this percentage lease was in line with other percentage leases in the area involving unrelated parties.[10] See also **Rent.**

Per diem allowance. See **Mileage allowance.**

Performance bonds. See **Contracts, expenses; Insurance.**

Periodicals. See **Subscriptions to periodicals.**

Periodic payments. See **Alimony.**

Personal grooming. Although the cost of personal grooming (such as haircuts) is not deductible as a business expense, an American Airlines pilot could deduct the cost of shoeshines, which the court regarded as part of the upkeep of his uniform. The company had suspended other persons who had failed to present a well-groomed appearance to the public.[11] An employee was permitted to deduct the cost of the daily cleaning of his work clothes, which, having become saturated with oil, could be worn only one day and then had to be cleaned. Dirty clothing was dangerous in his business, because his garments became saggy and could catch in revolving machinery.[12] A police officer could deduct the cost of having his uniform cleaned, possibly because he had little choice in the selection of persons with whom he came in contact.[13]

Personal liability insurance. See **Executives.**

Personal property taxes. *See* **Taxes.**

Pets, transportation of. *See* **Moving expenses.**

Physical examination. *See* **Employees; Medical expenses.**

Physicians, expenses of. *See* **Depreciation; Education; Expenditures for benefits lasting more than one year; Legal fees; Malpractice insurance; Office at home; Ordinary and necessary business expenses; Subscriptions to periodicals; Travel.**

Physicians' fees. *See* **Medical expenses.**

Podiatrists. *See* **Medical expenses.**

Points. *See* **Interest.**

Policemen. *See* **Personal grooming; Uniforms.**

Political bad debts. *See* **Bad debts.**

Political contributions. *See* **Contributions.**

Political lobbying. *See* **Lobbying.**

Pollution-control facilities. The cost of certified pollution-control facilities in connection with a plant or other property in operation before January 1, 1969, may, at the taxpayer's election, be amortized over a sixty-month period.[14]

Pool. *See* **Medical expenses.**

Postage stamps, loss on sale. *See* **Hobby losses.**

Postcards. Deduction was allowed for the cost of mailing postcards to his patients back in the United States by a physician, for the addressees were persons whose patronage reasonably was expected and who were being reminded of the continuing availability of the sender.[15]

Postmen. *See* **Uniforms.**

Practical nurses. *See* **Medical expenses.**

Preadoption medical expenses. *See* **Medical expenses.**

Prebusiness expenses. Where a manufacturer's retail outlets in city stores suffered falling sales, advertising and promotional activities were undertaken in individual suburban stores, in an effort to stimulate products' sales. Such expenses were deductible as an expense of the manufacturer's existing business, not costs related to the development of a new business.[16] See **Feasibility studies; Investors; Ordinary and necessary business expenses.**

Premature withdrawal of interest. Some financial institutions offer a higher than standard rate of interest to depositors who agree to leave a designated principal amount on deposit for a period of time which may range from sixty days to ten years. If the depositor withdraws the principal prior to the expiration of the term of the account, he must forfeit an amount equivalent to the interest for a stipulated period. A deduction from principal is made in the event the depositor has made a premature withdrawal and if the interest has already been paid to or withdrawn by him. The financial institution must report to the Internal Revenue Service any interest payments aggregating $10 or more during a taxable year, and the amount thus reported cannot be reduced by any forfeiture incurred. The depositor must report the full interest. But he may deduct the amount of the forfeiture as a loss incurred in a transaction entered upon for profit. Where the deposit arrangement is entered into as part of the depositor's trade or business, the forfeiture is a loss incurred in a trade or business, and in arriving at adjusted gross income, it is deductible in the year of the forfeiture.[17]

Premium charges. See **Interest.**

Premiums, insurance. See **Executives; Insurance.**

Premiums on medical insurance. See **Medical expenses.**

Prepaid interest. See **Interest.**

Preparation of tax returns, cost of. Deduction is permitted for all ordinary and necessary expenses in connection with the determination, collection, or refund of any tax.[18] Expenses of obtaining guidance on tax matters are deductible.[19] So it is worth preserving the bill or invoice of this book.

Prepayment charges. See **Interest.**

Preservation of reputation. *See* **Earning power, payments to protect; Reputation, maintenance of.**

Preventative maintenance. *See* **Repairs.**

Prevention of casualties, cost of. *See* **Casualties.**

Probation, expenses to obtain. *See* **Restitution payments.**

Professional seminars. *See* **Conventions.**

Promotion, expenses in obtaining. An employee, dissatisfied with his compensation and prospects at his employer's business, paid a fee to an executive search agency for help in finding him something better. The search agency did locate a better position for him elsewhere, but his old employer matched this with a promotion and higher pay. The fee paid to the agency was disallowed by the Internal Revenue Service on the ground that it was not a payment to obtain another job. The court, however, allowed the deduction.[20] Eight years later, the I.R.S. has announced that it will apply this decision in similar situations.[21]

Promotion expenses. *See* **Advertising.**

Property used in the trade or business and involuntary conversions. In the case of so-called "Section 1231 assets," long-term capital gain is reported if the assets are sold or otherwise disposed of at a gain after having been held for more than one year. But losses are fully deductible. Section 1231 assets are property used in the taxpayer's trade or business which is either real property or depreciable property. This does not include inventory, copyright, artistic composition, or certain livestock.[22] This treatment also applies under specified circumstances to timber, coal, or domestic iron ore, and to livestock and unharvested crops.[23] This preferential tax treatment applies to the *netted* gain or loss for all transactions in Section 1231 assets within the taxable year.

Capital assets subject to Section 1231 treatment are limited to assets involuntarily converted, as by fire or governmental seizure.[24] *See also* **Farmers.**

Protection. *See* **Bodyguard.**

Protective clothing. *See* **Work clothes.**

Proxy fight. Expenses of an investor in seeking to cause the removal of an incompetent management of a corporation in which he owns stock are deductible.[25] See *also* **Investors.**

Psychiatrists. See **Medical expenses.**

Psychoanalysis. See **Medical expenses.**

Psychologists. See **Medical expenses.**

Psychotherapists. See **Medical expenses.**

Purchase of stock to get assets. In the standard situation, sale of stock at a loss produces capital loss. But the loss is fully deductible as a business expense where the purpose of the stock's acquisition was not investment but a business objective.

A wholesale liquor dealer purchased shares of stock in a distillery during a whiskey shortage in order to exercise rights offered by the distiller to acquire liquor; loss on the sale of the shares after the rights had been exercised was fully deductible.[26] A business enterprise could deduct as a business expense its cost of purchasing stock in a manufacturing company that went bankrupt. The only purpose of the acquisition was to ensure a steady supply of equipment.[27]

Loss similarly was deductible where stock in a retailing organization had been purchased by a manufacturer in order to have a continuing outlet for its products.[28] Deduction of a loss on the disposition of shares was allowed where the purpose of the acquisition had been to get the technical expertise of the employees of the company taken over.[29]

A manufacturer entered into a contract with the representative of a foreign country for the sale of machinery. The foreign government required that United States government bonds be deposited with a New York financial institution as security for the performance of the contract. Such bonds were purchased and were sold at a loss when the contract was completed. The loss was deductible in full, having been incurred in the regular course of the taxpayer's business.[30]

A business paid a certain dollar amount for the stock of a corporation which was dissolved immediately. Inasmuch as the only purpose for acquiring the stock was to be relieved of a burdensome contract, and as there was no intention to buy or to hold the stock as an investment, the payment was deductible as an ordinary and necessary expense of doing business or as a business loss.[31] See *also* **Ordinary and necessary business expenses.**

1. *Oliver et al. v. Commissioner*, 553 F.2d 560 (8th Cir., 1977).
2. Revenue Procedure 74–23, 1974–2 CB 476.
3. *Frederick A. Klein*, 25 T.C. 1045 (1956).
4. *A. King Aitkin et al.*, 12 B.T.A. 692 (1928).
5. Revenue Ruling 72–608, 1972–2 CB 100.
6. *Raymond Warren Jackson et al.*, T.C. Memo. 1975–301, filed September 30, 1975.
7. *Allen et al. v. Commissioner*, 283 F.2d 785 (7th Cir., 1960).
8. *Jackson P. Howard et al.*, T.C. Memo, 1976–5, filed January 7, 1976.
9. Revenue Ruling 73–305, 1973–2 CB 43.
10. *A. H. Phillips Co., Inc., v. Commissioner*, T.C. Memo, 1977–150, filed May 18, 1977.
11. *Robert C. Fryer et al.*, T.C. Memo. 1974–26, filed January 30, 1974.
12. *Elwood J. Clark et al.*, T.C. Memo., Docket Nos. 9059, 9135, and 9167, entered April 1, 1946.
13. *Commissioner v. Benson*, 146 F.2d 191 (9th Cir., 1944).
14. I.R.C. Section 169.
15. *Ralph E. Duncan*, 30 T.C. 386 (1958).
16. *Briarcliff Candy Corporation v. Commissioner*, 475 F.2d 775 (2d Cir., 1973).
17. Revenue Ruling 73–511, 1973–2 CB 402.
18. I.R.C. Section 212(3).
19. *Higgins v. Commissioner*, 143 F.2d 654 (1st Cir., 1944).
20. *Kenneth R. Kenfield*, 54 T.C. 1197 (1970).
21. I.R.B. 1978–37.
22. I.R.C. Section 1231(a),(b)(1).
23. I.R.C. Section 1231(b)(2),(3),(4).
24. Regulations Section 1.1231–1(a).
25. *Central Foundry Company*, 49 T.C. 234 (1967).
26. *Western Wine & Liquor Co.*, 18 T.C. 1090 (1952).
27. *Arlington Bowling Corporation*, T.C. Memo. 1959–201, filed October 26, 1959.
28. *Weather-Seal, Inc.*, T.C. Memo. 1963–102, filed April 8, 1963.
29. *Schlumberger Technology Corporation v. United States*, 443 F.2d 1115 (1971).
30. *Commissioner v. Bagley Sewell Company*, 221 F.2d 944 (2d Cir., 1955).
31. *Pressed Steel Car Company, Inc.*, 20 T.C. 198 (1953).

R

Racial discrimination suit. *See* **Violation of rights, payments to settle.**

Railroad rolling stock. The cost of certain railroad rolling stock may be amortized for Federal income tax purposes over a sixty-month period.[1]

Ransom, payment of. *See* **Casualties.**

Razing of property. *See* **Demolition.**

Real estate. *See* **Interest; Taxes.**

Real estate transfer taxes. *See* **Taxes.**

Real property. *See* **Election to deduct or to capitalize.**

Rebates. Under various circumstances a business is not permitted to sell below stipulated prices. Example: in a regulated industry such as liquor or milk, state law may ban sales below posted prices. In California, state law forbade wholesale liquor dealers from selling below prices on file at a state agency. One dealer billed favored customers at the official prices required by state law but allowed credits which brought down the actual costs to these customers. Then the pet customers asked for wet goods they desired, and these were furnished without cost up to the amount of the credits, cost of sales being charged for the figures represented in the credit memoranda. Gross income of the wholesale liquor dealer for income tax purposes was based upon actual net prices paid by customers and not upon the legal minimum prices which should have been paid. This amounted to a deduction of the amount of the rebates or credits, which served to reduce gross income. The court distinguished between (1) rebates to which customers became entitled at the time of sale, as here, and (2) costs incurred in the form of bribes and kickbacks that were not made pursuant to an agreement that was part of the original sales. Item (2) is not deductible, but (1) is.[2] See *also* **Bribes and kickbacks.**

Recapitalization of corporation, contributions opportunity. See **Contributions.**

Reclining chair, as medical expense. *See* **Medical expenses.**

Redeemable ground rent. *See* **Interest.**

Referral fees. Payments to persons who are in position to refer business to the payor are deductible.[3] *But see* **Bribes and kickbacks.**

Refinancing fee. The refinancing fee for a loan customarily is not deductible in the year paid. It provides a benefit intended to last for more than one year and thus has to be deducted ratably over the remaining period of the loan. But if the loan is called prematurely because of a default, any remaining unamortized portion of the fee is deductible in the year the property is sold.[4] *See* **Expenditures for benefits lasting more than one year.**

Refresher course. *See* **Education.**

Reimbursement of client or customer. See **Ordinary and necessary business expenses.**

Related parties. *See* **Family transactions.**

Reliance upon misrepresentation. A theft-loss deduction depends upon whether the event meets the definition of "theft" under the law of the state where it takes place. An individual subscribed $25,000 for stock in a corporation, and the persons who solicited the funds kept them. The individual was parted from his money by deceit and trickery amounting to a criminal taking of his property with felonious intent, that is, theft.[5] A woman received a substantial sum in a divorce settlement, which was publicized in the newspapers. Shortly after this, an individual interested her in a project to acquire a nightclub, and she advanced money for the purpose. She was led to believe that the money would be set aside in a special fund until the club could be purchased. She never saw the money again. Her loss was treated as a deductible theft loss even though the fast talker actually had not been convicted as a criminal.[6] A theft-loss deduction was allowed where money was given to a person to bet on fixed races, and the trusted recipient disappeared with the funds. The individual who provided the funds had not participated in the fixing of the races.[7]

A bad debt deduction may be fully allowable as a theft loss, if it can be shown that a loan had been made on the basis of a financial statement which was fraudulent by reason of the deliberate omission of large liabilities that made the borrower insolvent.[8]

An individual taxpayer engaged a contractor to build a home. The contractor requested and obtained advance money to buy materials. But he actually ordered the materials on credit and disappeared with the money, as a result of which the taxpayer had to pay the charges to free his property from the lien which suppliers had placed upon it. When the contractor filed a voluntary petition in bankruptcy, the taxpayer objected to releasing the contractor from debts on the ground that the contractor had taken money by fraud. But a state court was not convinced that the contractor had the guilty intent required by law, and he was discharged of his debts. The Internal Revenue Service resisted the theft loss deduction because the contractor had not been found guilty of fraud. The court allowed deduction, however, because the weight of the evidence was that fraud indeed had been committed although no conviction had been obtained.[9]

An engineer consulted a business broker about the possibility of buying into a business where his engineering talents would be useful. The broker suggested that his business was a good one in which to invest, as there were acquisitions and merger deals that required the expertise of an engineer. So the engineer, relying upon assurances of important clients, paid $10,000 for a 20 percent interest in the business. The broker and the money disappeared. As the engineer had been parted from his money through trick or deceit after relying upon knowingly false misrepresentations, he had a deductible theft loss.[10]

See also **Casualties; Investors.**

Remainder interest, contribution in form of. See **Contributions.**

Remedial reading. A child suffered from a mental handicap known as dyslexia, or cross dominance, which makes it very difficult to learn to read. Only education, rather than medical procedures, can be used to overcome the results of this condition. Fees paid to a teacher trained to administer such instruction are deductible as medical expenses.[11]

Removal of impediments to the physically handicapped. For taxable years beginning after December 31, 1976, and ending before January 1, 1980, a taxpayer may elect to deduct rather than to capitalize the cost of removing certain impedimenta to physically impaired persons. This refers to the removal of architectural and transportation barriers to the handicapped (including the deaf and blind) and the elderly (age sixty-five or over) in any facility or public-transportation vehicle owned or leased for use in a trade or business. The maximum deduction for a taxpayer for any taxable year is $25,000. In order to qualify for the deduction, the expenses must meet certain government standards.[12] See also **Election to deduct or to capitalize.**

Rent. Rent of business premises is deductible.[13] The value of leasehold improvements installed by a tenant on the landlord's property is deductible if the parties had intended this to be equivalent to a nonmonetary form of payment for the use of the leased premises.[14] Where an apartment is used both for business and for personal purposes, an allocation of the rent between these two uses is to be made, and that part of the rent thus allocated to business purposes is deductible.[15] See also **Apartment use for business purposes; Family transactions; Office at home.**

Rent, forgiveness of. A taxpayer reported income on the accrual basis. When a tenant who was in arrears on his rent requested that he be relieved of his back rent although he was not insolvent, the taxpayer forgave the delinquent rent which he had already included in his income. A deduction was allowed for the forgiven rent. The premises benefited from the fine appearance of the tenant's enterprise and attracted a superior type of clientele which the taxpayer felt would improve his own business.[16]

Rental payments by a business tenant to an unrelated landlord are deductible; they may also be deductible when paid to a related party under appropriate circumstances. This simple rule is complicated by a lease with option to purchase. Are the annual payments deductible rent or installments on the purchase price? The test is whether the tenant's annual payments are in excess of the going rental rate, so that actually he is acquiring an equity in the property. If, at the end of the lease, the tenant can buy the property for much less than its worth, usually he is regarded as having in fact paid for the property over the years. But when one tenant at the end of the lease acquired property under the option for $30,000 and immediately sold it for $48,000, his payments in prior years still were deductible. They were just about at the going rate for flat rentals. The low option price, in the court's judgment, had been the result of a fortunate business bargain he had made and had not been an attempt to cast a sales transaction in the form of a lease.[17]

Repairing of damaged property. See **Casualties.**

Repairs. The nature of a deductible repair was analyzed by a court decision which has been quoted with approval in hundreds of later decisions:

> In determining whether an expenditure is a capital one or is chargeable against operating income, it is necessary to bear in mind the purpose for which the expenditure is made. To repair is to restore to a sound state or to mend, while a replacement connotes a substitution. A repair is an expenditure for the purpose of keeping the property in an ordinary efficient operating condition. It does not add to the value of the property, nor does it appreciably prolong its life. It merely keeps the property in an operating condition over its probably useful life for the uses for which it was acquired. Expenditures for the purpose are distinguishable from those for replacements, alterations, improvements, or additions which prolong the life of the property, increase its value, or make it acceptable to a different use. The one is a maintenance charge, while the others are additions to capital investment which should not be applied against current earnings.[18]

Deductible repairs are confined to business properties, as is indicated by the allowance in the Treasury Regulations under the heading of business deductions.[19]

The general rule is that the cost of a business repair is deductible only if the property is not improved as to length of life or of usefulness. If the property ends up in some more valuable form, the cost must be deducted over the years of expected useful life. An individual purchased a farm on which there was an earthen dam. Water subsequently began to seep through the dam. A contractor was hired to drain the reservoir and to excavate soil from one area for replacement with clay. Upon completion of this work, the general appearance of the dam seemed unchanged but the water seepage had stopped. The full cost was deductible. The sole purpose of the expenditure was to prevent leaks and to keep the dam in an ordinary operating condition over its probable useful life for the use for which it was acquired. The work did not create a replacement for the dam but merely restored its original capacity of retaining water. Explained the court: "To some extent, of course, every repair or restoration, no matter how minor or how soon after acquisition it is done, will add some value to the thing repaired or restored." Fixing leaks is hardly extraordinary, and the differences in the condition of the property before and after the work was done were insufficient to require the expense to be treated as a capital expenditure to be spread over the life of the work performed.[20]

A repair is deductible if the purpose of the expenditure is merely a restoration of the *status quo*. Thus, the replacement of pipes containing potential defects was allowed, even though repairs could have been performed on a leak-by-leak basis as they occurred, for the expenditures did not enhance the property's value nor adapt the property to a different use. The primary purpose for making these repairs was not to achieve improvements.[21]

A taxpayer could deduct the cost of repairs and replacements in the form of a complete cleaning, overhauling, and replacing of axles, transmissions, and brakes of motor equipment used for business purposes. Although the repairs were extensive and the new materials had some advantages over those replaced, they did not materially increase the value or the life of the equipment but only kept it in usable condition.[22]

Modifications to a mine hoist made solely for safety reasons, when the anticipated life of the equipment was not extended materially, were deductible repairs even though the asset after this work was not precisely the same as originally it had been.[23]

Where the work is to improve the life, utility, or performance of the asset, the expenditure is not deductible, being considered an investment in a capital asset, recoverable only through annual depreciation deductions. A business experienced many leaks in its underground piping. Rather than replace the pipes, the business installed clamps to cover deteriorated places. Whenever pipes were uncovered in connection with new construction or other activities, clamps would be installed at places which seemed to be weakened. The costs, primarily for excavating to get at the pipes, were deductible as repairs. The clamping of a pipe did not adapt it to a new or different use, nor was the original estimated useful life extended by this work.[24]

Repairs are deductible even though they were occasioned by the taxpayer's negligence.[25]

Frequently it is stated that a repair, to be deductible, must be made with the same materials as those being replaced, for otherwise the work would be more than a restoration of the *status quo*. That is not necessarily the case. Costs were deductible where a roof was repaired with a different material from the original one, because the new materials did not add to the value nor prolong the life of the roof.[26]

The cost of repairs was deductible where the business

equipment was of no greater efficiency or utility after the repair, even if the work done was not a reasonable facsimile of the original item, as in the case of an elevator.[27]

After a fire had partially destroyed a plant, expenditures for temporary electrical installations and other emergency activities to place the plant in running order were deductible.[28]

Repair expense was allowed in the case of drilling and grouting (filling with a kind of cement) and some replacements to prevent further cave-ins of a plant.[29]

A business owned and operated docks and piers on a river location. Silt accumulated regularly to such an extent that dredging had to be performed at times to maintain the necessary water depth for passage of shipping. The expenses did not improve the taxpayer's property but merely permitted continued operation of its facilities. Deduction was allowed.[30]

If a taxpayer elects to use the Asset Depreciation Range system, deduction is permitted in the form of a repair allowance percentage.[31] For example, office partitions have been given an asset guideline period of ten years (plus or minus 20 percent), and the annual guideline repair allowance is 7½ percent of "repair allowance property" as defined for this purpose.[32] See *also* **Ordinary and necessary business expenses; Watch repairs.**

Repairs as measure of casualty loss. See **Casualties.**

Repayment of excessive compensation. Where an executive was required by a corporate by-law to reimburse the company for any amount of his compensation disallowed as excessive pay when the Internal Revenue Service audited the corporate tax return, he can deduct the amount he repays to the company.[33]

If he repays an amount disallowed as excessive to his employer, he can deduct only the amounts attributable to the periods after an agreement is signed.[34]

Reputation, maintenance of. The regular rule is that a taxpayer cannot deduct the expenses of another party. But deduction is allowed if the expenditures are for the payor's benefit. Such was the case where an individual's name was used by a personal service (public relations) company which he headed. When the company was financially unable to pay its bills, the president paid them. He was allowed the deduction because of his belief, which the court found reasonable, that if he had permitted the corporation which bore his name to go into bankruptcy, his reputation and standing in the public relations community where his livelihood was to be gained would have been injured. So his payments to trade creditors of the corporation were deductible as ordinary and necessary expenditures of his business of being an executive.[35]

Payment by an investment banker to a corporation of which he was a director, to avoid possible liability under the Securities and Exchange Act and to protect his reputation as a banker, was deductible.[36]

A lawyer was engaged in performing legal services primarily for insurance companies. He purchased stock in one such company, which he later sold at a profit. A state attorney-general maintained that under the technical provisions of his state's law, the profit belonged to the corporation. The lawyer doubted this and the matter went to court; but fearful that controversy would damage his status and reputation with the insurance companies, and that his professional career would be endangered, he paid the amount of the profits over to the corporation. He could deduct this amount as an ordinary and necessary expense in connection with his trade or business.[37]

See also **Earning power, payments to protect; Executives; Legal fees.**

Research. Research expenses incurred by a professor for the purpose of teaching, lecturing, and writing in his own field were deductible as a means of carrying out the duties expected of him as a professor without expectation of profit apart from his salary.[38]

A professional writer was permitted to deduct travel and away-from-home lodgings while conducting research for a book he had reasonable expectations of marketing.[39]

Research and experimental expenses. A manufacturer can deduct as research and experimental expenditures the cost of developing and designing, at the manufacturer's risk, a specially built automated manufacturing system for a single customer's specific order.[40]

Expenditures which are expected to produce benefits lasting more than one year must be capitalized and not deducted currently. But the cost of economic analysis of projects which never were undertaken could be written off when the project was abandoned.[41] See also **Election to deduct or to capitalize.**

Reserve for bad debts, additions to. See **Bad debts.**

Residence sold at a loss. If an individual sells his residence at a loss, deduction depends upon whether this had been a transaction entered into for profit or was the sale of his personal home. An individual purchased land and commissioned a builder to construct a home for his family there. But the purchaser and his wife had such violent arguments about the details of their dream house that their marital relationship was threatened. At that point they decided to abandon plans to build a home. The builder was instructed to eliminate all the personalized custom features of the structure and to substitute cheap materials wherever possible so that persons interested primarily in buying a cheap residence would be attracted. But the finished building was sold at a loss. This was deductible because, by abandoning his intention to construct a personal home in which to live, the taxpayer had converted the house's construction and other costs into a transaction entered upon for profit. Actually, he had never lived there.[42]

Restitution payments. Fines and penalties generally are not deductible. Restitution payments are something else. An officer of a contracting company was convicted of misappropriation of funds paid by a client for the construction of a house. As a condition of his probation, the executive was directed by a court to pay $5,000 to the client. This was deductible, not being a fine or similar payment imposed by a state legislature or the local law. It merely represented the payment of an amount due and owing in connection with a business transaction.[43]

Restitution to customers. See **Business-related losses.**

Restoration of damaged property. See **Casualties.**

Restrictive easement, contribution in form of. See **Contributions.**

Resumé. See **Employment, expenses in seeking.**

Retarded persons. See **Education; Medical expenses.**

Retirement homes. If a husband and wife pay a monthly life-care fee to a retirement home and are able to prove that a specific portion of the fee covers the cost of providing medical care for them, that portion of the fee is deductible by the couple as an expense for medical care in the year paid.[44]

Ordinarily, personal living expenses, even in a retirement home, are not deductible. And advance payments for medical services to be rendered in subsequent years are not allowed. But where proper records have been kept, a medical-expense deduction is allowed at the time of payment. An individual paid a lump-sum fee to a retirement home under an agreement entitling him to live in the home and to receive lifetime care. The fee was calculated (whether by negotiation or on a what-the-traffic-will-bear basis) without regard to any similar contracts with other patients at the home, and hence no part of it could be called medical insurance. The retirement home demonstrated that a stipulated percentage of the life-care fee covered the home's obligation to provide medical care, medicines, and hospitalization and gave him a separate statement to that effect. It was agreed that on the basis of past experience, the medical-expense allocation of this lump-sum fee conformed to actuality. Because the individual's obligation to pay the lump-sum amount (including the percentage allocable to medical care) was incurred at the time the payment was made in return for the retirement home's promise to provide lifetime care, that part of the charge to secure medical protection was deductible when paid despite the fact that the medical services were not to be performed until a future time—if at all. Accordingly, the portion of the charge allocated to this medical care was deductible as medical expense.[45]

An individual entered into a written agreement with a tax-exempt organization, which provided that he would live at its facility and would receive lifetime care, including his main meal in the dining room and medical attention. The entrance fees charged by this home were determined by a projection of costs of providing services for the average period of residency of each resident. That portion of the entrance fees and monthly service charges were deductible to the extent that they could properly be allocated to medical care.[46]

An individual entered into an agreement with a retirement home, under which agreement he became entitled to live there and to receive lifetime care that included specified residential accommodations, meals, and medical care. In consideration for this provision of lifetime care, he paid a "founder's fee" upon commencing residence there plus a specified monthly fee. The fees were negotiated individually with each retiree and were not regarded as medical insurance. Because the home demonstrated that 15 percent of the monthly fee and 10 percent of the founder's fee would be used to discharge its obligations to provide medical care for its residents, a written statement being provided to the individual to this effect, these percentages of the monthly fees and founder's fee were treated as medical expenses. But an allocation of his payments to the construction of health facilities was not deductible.[47]

A seventy-six-year-old woman with developing cataracts and the prospects of surgery sold the family house and movod with her aging, infirm husband into a retirement center. The center had been built with funds supplied by the corporation which owned it, a charitable foundation, and fees charged to residents did not provide enough money to pay off these construction costs. So "sponsorship gifts" to repay building costs were solicited by the center in its brochures. Two weeks after the couple had been admitted to the center, the woman made a sponsorship gift. She was permitted to deduct this as a charitable contribution, for although 80 percent of the center's population had made such gifts, there was no compulsion to do so, no special benefit was anticipated for making a gift, the center had not prepared the check for her signature, and the couple had been accepted before she made the gift. She had not even known, when she applied for admission and when she was accepted, that a gift was expected.[48]

Retirement of property. See **Obsolescence.**

Retirement pay, expenses to establish. See **Armed Forces.**

Return of embezzled funds. When an individual returns to his victim any money or property which had been embezzled from the latter, a deduction is allowed in the year of this repayment.[49]

Revolving charge account fees. See **Interest.**

Reward for return of stolen property. A taxpayer engaged in a trade or business can deduct the amount of a reward given to a person who found and returned stolen property.[50]

Risk, limitation on investment at. See **Investors.**

Robbery losses. See **Casualties.**

Rulings on tax matters, expense of obtaining. The cost of legal and accounting work in obtaining a Federal income tax ruling from the Internal Revenue Service is deductible.[51]

R

1. I.R.C. Section 184.
2. *Max Sobel Wholesale Liquors v. Commissioner,* 69 T.C. 477 (1977).
3. *Robert Wright et al.,* T.C. Memo. 1967–86, filed April 21, 1967.
4. *Malmstedt et al. v. Commissioner,* 578 F.2d 520 (4th Cir., 1978).

5. *Paul C. F. Vietske*, 37 T.C. 504 (1961).
6. *Michele Monteleone et al.*, 34 T.C. 688 (1960).
7. *Edwards v. Bromberg et al.*, 232 F.2d 107 (5th Cir., 1956).
8. Revenue Ruling 71–381, 1971–2 CB 126.
9. *Hartley et al. v. Commissioner*, T.C. Memo. 1977–317, filed September 19, 1977.
10. *McComb v. Commissioner*, T.C. Memo. 1977–176, filed June 9, 1977.
11. Revenue Ruling 69–607, 1969–2 CB 40.
12. Revenue Act of 1976, Section 2122.
13. I.R.C. Section 162(a)(3).
14. *Blatt v. United States*, 305 U.S. 267 (1938).
15. *Ray Harroun*, T.C. Memo., Docket No. 5869, entered July 20, 1945.
16. *Lab Estates, Inc.*, 13 T.C. 811 (1949).
17. *Daniel et al. v. Commissioner*, T.C. Memo. 1978–277, filed July 24, 1978.
18. *Illinois Merchants Trust Co.*, 4 B.T.A. 103 (1926).
19. Regulations Section 1.162–4.
20. *Evans et al. v. Commissioner*, 557 F.2d 1095 (5th Cir., 1977).
21. *Mountain Fuel Supply Company v. United States*, D.C., Utah, 1970.
22. *Mark C. Nottingham*, T.C. Memo., Docket No. 31415, entered May 8, 1953.
23. *Ranchers Exploration and Development Corporation v. United States*, . . . F. Supp. . . . (D.C., N.M., 1978).
24. *Niagara Mohawk Power Corporation v. United States*, 558 F.2d 1379 (Ct. Cl., 1977).
25. *Brier Hill Collieries*, 12 B.T.A. 500 (1928).
26. *Munroe Land Company*, T.C. Memo. 1966–2, filed January 4, 1966.
27. *Mellie Esperson*, B.T.A. Memo., Docket No. 98737, entered February 5, 1941.
28. *Ticket Office Equipment Co., Inc.*, 20 T.C. 272 (1953), *aff'd*, 213 F.2d 318 (2d Cir., 1954).
29. *American Bemberg Corporation*, 10 T.C. 361 (1948), *aff'd*, 177 F.2d 200 (6th Cir., 1949).
30. *Kingston River Terminal, Inc., v. United States*, D.C., S.D. Ill., 1977.
31. These repair allowance percentages have been published in Revenue Procedure 71–25, 1971–2 CB 553.
32. Regulations Section 1.167(a)–11(d)(2).
33. *Vincent E. Oswald*, 49 T.C. 645 (1968).
34. I.R.S. Letter Ruling 7811004, November 29, 1977.
35. *Conley et al. v. Commissioner*, T. C. Memo. 1977–406, filed November 23, 1977.
36. *Laurence M. Marks*, 27 T.C. 464 (1956).
37. *Joseph P. Pike et al.*, 44 T.C. 787 (1965).
38. Revenue Ruling 63–275, 1963–2 CB 85.
39. *Stern et al. v. United States*, D.C., C.D. Cal., 1971.
40. Revenue Ruling 73–275, 1973–1 CB 134.
41. *Ranchers Exploration and Development Corporation v. United States*, . . . F. Supp. . . . (D.C., N.M., 1978).
42. *Albert W. Bassett et al.*, T.C. Memo, 1976–14, filed January 20, 1976.
43. *Spitz et al. v. United States*, 432 F. Supp. 148 (D.C., E.D. Wis., 1977).
44. Revenue Ruling 67–185, 1967–1 CB 70.
45. Revenue Ruling 75–301, 1975–2 CB 66.
46. I.R.S. Letter Ruling 7807093, November 21, 1977.
47. Revenue Ruling 76–481, 1976–2 CB 82.
48. *Dowell v. United States*, 553 F.2d 1233 (10th Cir., 1977).
49. *James v. United States*, 366 U.S. 213 (1961).
50. Revenue Ruling 67–98, 1967–1 CB 29.
51. Revenue Ruling 67–401, 1967–2 CB 123.

S

Safe deposit box, rental on. *See* **Investors.**

Safety award. An employer may deduct the cost, but not in excess of $100, of tangible personal property given to an employee for safety achievement.[1]

Safety equipment. See **Work clothes.**

Safety measures, expenses to achieve. Expenditures to make machinery or other assets safer, or to conform to safety standards, frequently involve costs which provide benefits that will last for more than one year. Such costs, being capital, are not deductible. But modifications to an asset solely for safety reasons, where the life of the asset is not prolonged appreciably nor is the asset improved as to performance, are deductible.[2]

Sale and lease-back. The owner of property may sell it to another party (sometimes called, for the purpose of convenience, the "investor") and then immediately lease it back. Depending upon the relationship of the sale price to the adjusted value at the time, the rent to obtain the use of the property again may be higher than the normal price (if the sale price was more than the property was worth) or lower than the normal rent (if the sale price was less than the property was worth). But even if a higher than normal rent was paid, this is fully deductible.[3] When the parties to such a transaction are related, a rental in excess of normal rates may not be recognized for tax purposes on the ground that the transaction lacks reality.[4]

Sales and exchanges between related parties. See **Family transactions.**

Sales promotion expense. Deductible advertising includes sales promotion expenses.[5] *See also* **Advertising.**

Sales tax. *See* **Taxes.**

Samples. In some states, distribution of samples by businesses is
against the law. That means the cost of the samples is not
deductible for Federal income tax purposes because it represents an expense for an illegal purpose. But where the taxpayer
can show that the state was not enforcing its own law and in
fact had issued an order to enforcement officers to ignore it, the
deduction was allowed.[6]

S

265

Satisfaction of claims, payments in. *See* **Business-related losses.**

Schools, specialized, as medical expense. *See* **Medical expenses.**

Season tickets. A business dependent upon the general public for
patronage was allowed to deduct its entire expenditure
for home-game season tickets for baseball and hockey encounter sessions in Boston. The Internal Revenue Service had allowed deduction of one half of the cost, but the court considered that the business benefits derived from supporting the
local teams and the occasional use of these tickets to entertain
customers was justification for full deductibility.[7]

"Section 1231" property deductions. *See* **Property used in the
trade or business and involuntary conversions.**

Security deposit. Often a landlord requires a tenant to make a security deposit, for example, of the last month's rent under a lease.
State law customarily requires the landlord to segregate such
deposits and to pay or to credit interest thereon. Often the state
law permits the landlord to take as administration expense an
amount equivalent to 1 percent per annum of the deposit.
When such is the case, a tenant can deduct this 1-percent
charge as an expense paid or incurred during the taxable year
for the production or collection of income or for the management, conservation, or maintenance of property held for the
production of income.[8] Although this deduction would seem
to apply to businesses only, it may be taken for residences too.

Seeing Eye dog. *See* **Blind persons, expenses of.**

Self-employment plans. Self-employed persons may be covered by
qualified (that is, Treasury-approved) pension, profit-sharing,
annuity, and bond-purchase plans, with some of the favorable
tax benefits available to corporate stockholder-employees.
These often are referred to as Keogh plans. The owner-

employee of a trade or business with earned income from personal services rendered to that trade or business may set up a self-employment plan. A person is an owner-employee if he is a self-employed individual who is a sole proprietor or a partner who owns more than a 10-percent interest in either the capital or profits of the partnership.

If a sole proprietor sets up such a plan for himself, he must cover all full-time employees who have worked for him for three or more years. If he has not been in business for at least three years, he must cover full-time employees who have had as much service as he has had. A full-time employee for this purpose is one who normally works more than twenty hours a week for more than five months a year. A longer waiting period for employees than for the proprietor is not permitted.[9] For taxable years beginning after December 31, 1973, a sole proprietor's deduction for a self-employed person's pension is the lesser of 15 percent of the earned income from the trade or business or $7,500.[10] In applying the 15-percent limitation, not more than $100,000 of earned income is taken into account.[11] For years beginning after December 31, 1975, a self-employed individual may set aside up to $750 of self-employment income without regard to the percentage limitation if his adjusted gross income does not exceed $15,000.[12]

Where an individual is covered under a corporate pension or profit-sharing plan and he also derives income from a business he operates during the evening hours, he can set up a plan and make deductible contributions to it out of the self-employment income from his moonlighting operations.[13]

Self-inflicted wounds. See **Medical expenses.** Maintenance at a center for drug abusers is deductible as medical expense.[14]

Senior citizens. See **Blind persons, expenses of; Contributions; Deaf persons, expenses of; Medical expenses; Removal of impediments to the physically handicapped; Retirement homes.**

Separation agreements. See **Alimony.**

Services, as contributions. See **Contributions.**

Settlement payments. Damages paid for breach of contract entered into in the ordinary course of a taxpayer's business and directly related to it are normally considered to be a business expense, deductible if not a fine or penalty.[15]

In general, fines and penalties are not deductible. But a carefully worded settlement offer may be used to describe the payment as something which is deductible. The government brought action against a businessperson for violation of the Federal False Claims Act on the ground that shipments to a governmental agency had not lived up to the materials specifications. The business carefully worded a settlement offer, stating that a stipulated amount was being offered for ordinary breach of contract. The government accepted this offer as written, and the payment thus was characterized for tax purposes as a proper business deduction.[16]

Government claims against a taxpayer for fraud, deceit, malpractice, and the like which involve wrongs of some moral turpitude may be settled by compromise. The amounts paid out in settlement are then deductible as allowable business expenses if there has been no admission of guilt.[17]

A taxpayer purchased the business of a competitor with which it had been engaged in lawsuits involving restraint of trade. The price paid included a negotiated sum to settle lawsuits which had been brought by this competitor. Ordinarily, when a lump sum is paid to acquire the assets of a going business, the amount paid in excess of the value of the operating assets is attributed to intangible capital assets (e.g., goodwill) and thus is not currently deductible. But to the extent that the excess amount was attributable to disposition of the lawsuits pending against the buyer, the payment was deductible as ordinary and necessary business expense. Strong support was given to the buyer's claim that no part of the payment was for nondeductible capital assets by reason of the fact that they were not needed or used by the buyer.[18]

A corporate director could deduct settlement costs resulting from lawsuits against him by the stockholders. He was a member of the board of directors of a corporation which had gone through several reorganizations, the results of which the stockholders had felt were not to their best interests. The amount he paid to the stockholders to settle the affair was deductible.[19]

See also **Violation of rights, payments to settle.**

Severance pay. Payments to terminate the employment of a business employee are deductible.[20] See also **Compensation.**

Sex discrimination suit, payments under. See **Violation of rights, payments to settle.**

Sexual inadequacy, efforts to overcome. See **Medical expenses.**

Shoeshines, cost of. See **Personal grooming.**

Shooting preserve, expenses of. *See* **Entertainment.**

Shop fees. Where a union obtains a contract which requires an employer to check off dues from members, and also an equivalent amount from nonmembers, for transmittal to the union, nonmembers can deduct these shop fees on their income tax returns.[21]

Shortages, repayment of. *See* **Armed Forces; Business-related losses; Cash shortages; Executives; Inventory write-downs.**

Short sales expenses. *See* **Investors.**

Skills, improvement of. *See* **Education.**

Ski lodge. *See* **Entertainment.**

Small Business Corporation Stock. An individual may deduct as an ordinary loss, rather than as a capital loss, his loss on the sale, exchange, or worthlessness of certain stock he owns in a Small Business Corporation. (Gain on this stock, however, is capital gain if the stock is a capital asset in his hands. If in doubt as to the status, he should consult an accountant, attorney, or I.R.S. office.) Small Business Stock for this purpose is voting or nonvoting common stock of a domestic corporation, provided:
1. The stock is not convertible into other securities of the corporation.
2. The stock has been offered under a written plan adopted by the corporation after June 30, 1958. The plan must specify the maximum amount in dollars to be received by the corporation in consideration for the stock to be issued under the plan and the period during which it can be offered. That period must end not later than two years after the date the plan was adopted.
3. At the time the plan in item 2 above was adopted (but not necessarily at the time the stock was issued or the loss occurred), the corporation qualified as a Small Business Corporation and no portion of any other stock offering was outstanding.
4. The stock was issued under the plan in item 2 above for money or property other than stock or securities.[22]
   A corporation qualifies as a Small Business Corporation if at the time the written plan is adopted the following requirements are met:
1. The amount of the offering, plus money or other property

received by the corporation after June 30, 1958, for its stock as a contribution to capital and as paid-in surplus, does not exceed $500,000.

2. The amount offered under the plan plus the equity capital of the corporation (as of the date the plan is adopted) does not exceed $1,000,000.

The amount deductible as ordinary loss on this stock is limited to $50,000 on a separate return and $100,000 on a joint return in the case of stock issued after November 6, 1978.[23] Previously it had been one half of these amounts.

The loss on Small Business Stock which is treated as ordinary loss is a business loss when determining a net operating loss.[24]

For computing the ordinary loss on Small Business Stock, the basis of the stock is reduced by the difference between the adjusted basis of the property and its fair market value. The reduction is made for this purpose only and does not affect the basis of the stock for any other purpose.[25]

Small Business Investment Company. Investors in a Small Business Investment Company are allowed as ordinary loss rather than as capital loss any losses arising from the sale or exchange or worthlessness of stock. Losses of this nature are allowed in determining the net operating loss.[26]

Small Business Investment Companies, as authorized by the Small Business Investment Act of 1958, are private corporations with paid-in capital and surplus of at least $150,000 which are empowered to provide equity capital and long-term loans as well as management assistance to small business concerns.

Smog damage. *See* **Accident, as casualty loss.**

Snow removal. The owner of business property was permitted to deduct the cost of snow removal from the parking areas of his enterprise.[27]

Social club dues. *See* **Entertainment.**

Soil conservation expenditures. *See* **Farmers.**

Sole proprietor. *See* **Self-employment plans.**

Sonic-boom damage. *See* **Accident, as casualty loss.**

Special assessments, deductibility as taxes. *See* **Taxes.**

Special food. *See* **Medical expenses.**

Special schools. *See* **Medical expenses.**

Sponsored investment plans. *See* **Investors.**

Sponsorship gift. *See* **Retirement homes.**

Spouses. *See* **Alimony; Carry-overs; Child care and disabled dependent care; Contributions; Entertainment; Family transactions; Interest; Medical expenses; Taxes; Tax-option corporations; Travel.**

Stamp collection, loss on. *See* **Hobby losses.**

Standard mileage deduction. *See* **Mileage allowance.**

Standby charges. *See* **Interest.**

Standby expense. A corporation, which operated a shopping center, rented an airplane and pilot. This enabled prospective tenants to visit the center and to return home in a minimum amount of time and to survey the population density of the surrounding areas. In addition, company personnel could make business trips more rapidly. The Internal Revenue Service claimed that the rent deduction of the plane should be limited to the going time rate for leasing, the actual payment made having been much larger because the craft had been rented on a twenty-four-hour-per-day basis so as to have it available at all times on a "standby basis." The court allowed the full deduction. Having the plane available on a standby basis had resulted in some considerable savings to the business. On one of the three occasions when the plane was needed on instant notice, a savings of many times the full rent charge had resulted because an executive was able to obtain a great discount on interest payable on a loan by taking immediate action where a fast decision was necessary.[28]

State disability insurance. Some states have disability insurance laws. One in California, for example, required employers to withhold 1 percent of the first $9,000 of wages for deposit with the California State Disability Fund, which applied unless the employer established a suitable private disability plan meeting all state standards. Employees subjected to this withholding could take a Federal tax deduction of the amount as a state income tax.[29]

State taxes, deductibility of. *See* **Taxes.**

Statistical services. *See* **Investors.**

Stereo system, as medical expense. *See* **Medical expenses.**

Sterilization. *See* **Medical expenses.**

Stock acquired to get assets. *See* **Purchase of stock to get assets.**

Stockholders' committee, expenses of. *See* **Investors.**

Stock transfer taxes. *See* **Investors; Taxes.**

Stop watch. *See* **Employees.**

Strikebreakers. *See* **Ordinary and necessary business expenses; Travel.**

Student's maintenance, as charitable deduction. *See* **Contributions.**

Subchapter S corporations. *See* **Tax-option corporations.**

Subscriptions to periodicals. Subscriptions to professional magazines are a deductible expense of being an employee.[30] Likewise, subscriptions to periodicals appropriate to their income-producing activities are deductible by investors,[31] by members of the Armed Forces,[32] by farmers,[33] by teachers,[34] and by physicians.[35]

A Federal law enforcement agency issued an official work manual, which was revised frequently. An agency employee, who traveled extensively on business, purchased a year's subscription to the manual at his own expense so that he could have it readily available at all times. This was a deductible business expense.[36]

A salesperson could deduct subscription and single-purchase costs of trade publications which described new products that were competitive to the line she sold, in order to learn what she was up against.[37]

Subsistence expenses. *See* **Conventions; Mileage allowance.**

Substitute, payments to. *See* **Executives.**

Subterranean disturbances. *See* **Casualties.**

Suggestion awards. Payments to employees for the submission of suggestions to increase the efficiency of a business are considered to be a form of wages.[38] Consequently they are deductible in line with the ground rules for other types of compensation.

Supplementary medical insurance for the aged (Medicare B). *See* **Medical expenses.**

Support payments. *See* **Alimony.**

Surrender of stock to issuing corporation. *See* **Executives; Investors.**

Swimming pool, deductibility of. *See* **Entertainment; Medical expenses.**

Swindling loss. *See* **Casualties.**

Sword. *See* **Armed Forces.**

S

1. Regulations Section 1.274–3(b)(2)(iii).
2. *Ranchers Exploration and Development Corporation v. United States,* . . . F. Supp. . . . (D.C., N.M., 1978).
3. *Barran v. Commissioner,* 334 F.2d 58 (5th Cir., 1964).
4. *Shaffer Terminal, Inc., v. Commissioner,* 194 F.2d 539 (9th Cir., 1952).
5. Revenue Ruling 56–181, 1956–1 CB 96.
6. *Sterling Distributors, Inc., v. Patterson,* 236 F. Supp. 479 (D.C., N.D. Ala., 1964).
7. *Cambridge Hotels, Inc.,* T.C. Memo. 1968–263, filed November 19, 1968.
8. Revenue Ruling 75–363, 1975–2 CB 463.
9. Regulations Section 1.404(e)–1.
10. Pension Reform Act of 1974, Section 2001(a).
11. Pension Reform Act of 1974, Section 2001(c).
12. Tax Reform Act of 1976, Section 1502.
13. Regulations Section 1.401–10(b)(3)(ii).
14. Revenue Ruling 72–226, 1972–1 CB 96.
15. *Great Island Holding Corporation,* 5 T.C. 150 (1945).
16. *Grossman & Sons, Inc., et al.,* 48 T.C. 15 (1967).
17. *Milner Enterprises, Inc., v. United States,* D.C., S.D. Miss., 1965.
18. *Entwicklung und Finanzierungs A.G. v. Commissioner,* 68 T.C., 749 (1977).
19. I.R.S. Letter Ruling 7728004.
20. *Driskill Hotel Company,* T.C. Memo., Docket No. 31562, entered May 22, 1953.
21. I.R.S. Letter Ruling 7828050, April 13, 1978.

22. I.R.C. Section 1244.
23. Revenue Act of 1978, Section 345.
24. *Tax Information on Investment Income and Expenses,* I.R.S. Publication 550, 1976 edition, page 23.
25. *Ibid.,* p. 19.
26. I.R.C. Section 1243.
27. *Ward v. Commissioner,* T.C. Memo., 1978–216, filed June 8, 1978.
28. *Palo Alto Town & Country Village, Inc., et al. v. Commissioner,* 565 F.2d 1388 (9th Cir., 1977).
29. *Anthony Trujillo et al. v. Commissioner,* 68 T.C. 670 (1977).
30. *Your Federal Income Tax,* 1976 edition, page 105.
31. *Martha E. Henderson,* T.C. Memo., 1968–22, filed January 31, 1968.
32. *Armed Forces Federal Income Tax,* 1976 edition, page 41.
33. Schedule F listing for Form 1040.
34. *Beaudry v. Commissioner,* 150 F.2d 20 (2d Cir., 1945).
35. *Wolfson et al. v. Commissioner,* T.C. Memo. 1978–445, filed November 7, 1978.
36. Revenue Ruling 78–265, I.R.B. 1978–28, 7.
37. *Marilyn Finley,* T.C. Memo. 1977–9, filed January 17, 1977.
38. Revenue Ruling 70–471, 1970–2 CB 199.

T

Takeover, expenses to prevent. *See* **Executives; Investors; Legal fees.**

Taxes. The following taxes, paid or accrued, are deductible for Federal income tax purposes:
1.   State, local, and foreign real property taxes.
2.   State and local personal property taxes.
3.   State, local, and foreign income, war profits, and excess profits taxes.
4.   State and local general sales taxes.
5.   State and local taxes on the sale of gasoline, diesel fuel, and other motor fuels, but only if the vehicle is used for business or investment purposes.[1]

In addition, taxes not described above which are paid or accrued within a taxable year in the process of carrying on a trade or business or an activity relating to expenses for the production of income are allowed as a deduction.[2]

Ordinarily, taxes cannot be deducted by a party other than the one upon whom that tax is imposed. But if the amount of any general sales tax is stated separately, then to the extent that the consumer pays the tax separately, it will be treated as a tax imposed upon, and paid by, the consumer.[3]

A *compensating use* tax is treated for deduction purposes as if it were a general sales tax. A compensating use tax means a tax (1) which is imposed on the use, storage, or consumption of such items as would normally have been subjected to a general sales tax under ordinary circumstances, and (2) which is complementary to a general sales tax.[4]

As an example of such a tax, consider the following: A municipality has a sales tax upon the purchase of tangible personal property within the jurisdiction of that municipality. To protect local merchants from loss of business in cases where residents go outside the city to make purchases, such as automobiles, a compensating use tax may be imposed upon all residents who have brought in cars without payment of the sales tax. This is deductible.[5]

When a joint state income tax is filed and there is joint (and several) liability to pay the tax (that is, each spouse can be held liable not only for his portion of the tax but for all of it), if one spouse pays the entire amount, that is what he may deduct in computing his Federal income tax. It is assumed, of course, that separate Federal income tax forms are filed for the two individuals.

Let's say that George and Mary Travil filed a joint state income tax return in 1976. Although each owed an equal share of the total amount, George paid the entire amount when the form was filed in 1977. George can now deduct the entire amount when computing his Federal income tax, and Mary, who files separately, can deduct none of it.[6]

If husband and wife are each liable for the full amount of the state income tax actually paid, and each paid an equal amount, each may deduct on separately filed Federal income tax returns the amount of state tax actually paid by him or her.[7]

If separate state income tax returns are filed by married taxpayers who at the same time file a joint Federal income tax return, the sum of the state income taxes imposed on and paid by both spouses during the taxable year may be deducted on the joint Federal income tax return.[8] The state income taxes imposed upon a married taxpayer and paid during the taxable year are deductible on a joint Federal income tax return regardless of which spouse actually paid the taxes.[9]

Foreign income taxes paid to a foreign country or to a United States possession may either be taken as a deduction or claimed as a credit against the individual's Federal income tax. Usually such a decision whether a deduction or a credit should be taken on such taxes should be made after figuring out the amounts owed (or to be returned) under each method.[10]

A taxpayer, who was a citizen of the United States residing permanently in the Republic of Ireland, was permitted to deduct the Irish wealth tax, which was levied annually on the net market value each year of every assessable person at 1 percent.[11]

Deduction was allowed for the Zurich, Switzerland, personal fortune tax based upon stocks and bonds owned by a taxpayer and held for the production of income.[12]

Property taxes are deductible even if paid with borrowed money, provided that the taxpayer at that time had sufficient resources of his own to make these payments.[13]

Frequently, when a person borrows money from a bank on a mortgage, the bank requires him to put one-twelfth of the estimated real property taxes into an escrow fund each month so that, by the time the tax payment date to the government authority comes around, the bank will have all of the necessary funds in hand, any shortage then to be made up by the borrower on demand. These taxes are deductible by the borrower, not when he pays the bank, but when the bank pays the local taxing authority. And that payment, or a large portion of it, could be in the year after the borrower "paid" his tax installments.[14]

An individual who owed property taxes on his realty could deduct payments made to the governmental authority. The satisfaction of his tax obligation took place regardless of whether the payment had the character of a loan or gift to him or represented some form of income to him.[15]

Real property (or real estate) taxes are any state, local, or foreign taxes on real property which are levied for the general public welfare. They are deductible.

Local benefit taxes are not deductible in most instances. These taxes are so called because they are for local benefits, such as assessments for local streets, sidewalks, and other like improvements which are imposed because of, and measured by, some benefits applying directly to the property against which the assessment is levied. A "tax" is considered to be assessed against local benefits when the property subject to the tax is limited to the property benefited.

But if these assessments are made for the purpose of maintenance or repair of such local benefits or for the purpose of meeting interest charges with respect to such benefits, then they are deductible. For example, if your city assesses you a city property tax for the purpose of installing new street lamps on your street, these taxes are not deductible. But if in the future further taxes are assessed for the maintenance of such street lamps, then these future taxes will be deductible.[16]

Thus, when a special assessment was imposed against the owners of property on Main Street and Broadway in Oklahoma City to finance the resurfacing of the pavement when a street railway system was abandoned, this special assessment did not tend to increase the value of the property assessed, for existing curbs, gutters, and surfacing were repaired. None of the streets in the district was widened or lengthened or other "new" work done.[17]

Similarly, a sprinkling tax imposed upon the residents of Duluth, Minnesota, for the use of water to sprinkle their lawns, etc., was a deductible tax, for it did not constitute a benefit to the property against which the tax was imposed.[18]

If in the case of a local benefit tax assessment the property owner believes at least part of the assessment is going to maintenance, repair, or interest, he may deduct that part of the assessment which he is able to establish is going to such maintenance, repair, or interest.[19]

Water bills, sewerage, and other service charges (e.g., "water taxes") assessed against property used for business purposes are deductible, not as taxes but as business expenses.[20]

Generally, real estate taxes are an equal responsibility of all the owners of a property, no matter how many there are. Therefore, if one owner, who owns only one-sixth of the property, pays the entire real estate tax, she may deduct the entire amount.

This is true if the taxpayer in question is a *tenant in common* (defined as having the right to occupy the whole property in common with her cotenants). In order to preserve her individual rights and interest, which she could have lost had she not paid the entire tax (due to a possible foreclosure for nonpayment of taxes), she was entitled to the full deduction.[21]

In the case where the joint owners of property are individually and collectively liable for expenses such as real estate taxes on the property, whichever owner actually pays the taxes is entitled to the deduction on his or her Federal income tax return.[22]

An individual conveyed his house and lot to the ownership of his church, reserving possession for five years and promising to pay real estate taxes assessed on the property. He could deduct these taxes because the liability to pay them was his.[23]

A person may deduct taxes on property to which someone else has legal title if the person paying the taxes has a beneficial interest to protect.[24]

If real estate is sold, the deduction for real estate taxes must be apportioned between the buyer and the seller according to the number of days in the "real property year" that each held the property (a real property year is the period of time which a real estate tax covers). The taxes are apportioned to the seller up to, but not including, the date of sale, and to the buyer beginning with the date of sale, regardless of the accrual or lien dates under local laws.

If the seller uses the cash method and cannot deduct the property taxes until they are paid, and the buyer is personally liable for the tax, the seller is considered to have paid the portion of the tax imposed at the time of the sale. This permits him to deduct the portion of the tax to the date of the sale even though he does not actually pay it.[25]

Tenant-shareholders in a cooperative housing or apartment corporation who utilize their alloted space as their principal residence may take as their own deductions the amounts they pay to the corporation as their proportionate shares of the real estate taxes the corporation pays or incurs on the property. But shareholders may not deduct any portion of the real estate taxes where the corporation does not own the property, even though the corporation pays these taxes under its rental agreement with the actual owner.[26]

The owner of an apartment in a condominium apartment project which he uses as his principal residence may deduct taxes which he pays with respect to the apartment *if* he is liable to the local tax authority for the tax assessment according to his interest in the condominium.[27]

In lieu of itemizing sales taxes, an individual has the choice of using tables prepared by the government for this purpose. These tables are printed in such places as the instruction forms which accompany personal income tax packets. They also are reproduced in various Internal Revenue Service publications such as *Your Federal Income Tax* and *Income Tax Deductions for Taxes*. If he thinks it would give him a higher deduction and if he thinks he can meet the requirements as to substantiation, an individual may elect not to use these optional tables. The tables are geared to an individual's adjusted gross income plus any nontaxable receipts such as Social Security, veterans' and railroad retirement benefits, and workmen's compensation payments.[28]

Should a person use the sales tax tables to determine his tax deduction, he may *add* to the amount shown on the tables the sales tax which he pays on the following five classes of items:
1. Automobiles.
2. Airplanes.
3. Boats.
4. Mobile homes.
5. Material used to build a new home when the individual taxpayer is his own contractor.[29]

If an individual engages a contractor to construct a personal home, the contract could provide for separate listings for supervision, labor, materials, and sales tax on these materials. Sales tax is deductible by the person upon whom it is imposed. In some states the law provides that sales tax on materials which are incorporated into realty are imposed on the purchaser of the realty rather than on the contractor: for example, if the contract identifies the final consumer of the materials as the customer and not the contractor. Where such is the case, the homeowner can deduct sales taxes on materials going into the house.[30]

When an individual engages a private nurse under circumstances which qualify as medical expenses, the Social Security taxes which he pays on the nurse's wages are also deductible as medical expenses.[31]

An employer who absorbs the employee portion of his business employees' Social Security taxes may claim them as a deduction under the heading of compensation, assuming that these absorbed taxes plus regular salary do not constitute unreasonable compensation.[32]

The Federal Insurance Contributions Act (FICA) tax on wages, which are deductible as amounts paid for household and dependent-care expenses, is an essential part of these services and is deductible as employment-related expenses, but only if the expenses are incurred to enable a taxpayer to be gainfully employed.[33]

Dealers or investors in securities can deduct state stock transfer taxes to the extent that they are expenses incurred in carrying on a trade or business or an activity for the production of income. Dealers or investors in real estate may deduct the real estate transfer taxes in the same manner for the same reasons.[34]

When the separate taxable existence of a trust was denied the grantor by the Internal Revenue Service on the ground that he had not sufficiently "let go" of control of the trust moneys, the income was taxed to the grantor rather than to the trust.

But by the same token he was allowed to deduct state income taxes originally claimed by the trust.[35]

Taxes paid on real estate which has the complication of being a factor in a divorce case are deductible according to the facts in each particular case. For instance, when a residence is held jointly by the erstwhile husband and wife as tenants by the entirety with a right to survivorship, the husband may deduct any real estate taxes he pays on the property as "taxes." This refers to real property owned by both spouses, to belong to the survivor after one spouse dies. Neither can sell without the approval of the other.

When the residence is held by the onetime husband and wife as tenants in common, each party owns one-half of the property. So the former husband may deduct, as "alimony," amounts he pays for taxes on the ex-wife's half of the property. The half he pays on his 50 percent of the property he deducts as "taxes."

In the case where the ex-wife is the sole owner of the residence and the former husband agrees to pay the real estate taxes, he may deduct the payments as "alimony" if they are taxable to her as periodic payments under a divorce decree or agreement. The wife then may deduct the portion of each payment which represents taxes.

If the husband is the sole owner of the residence occupied rent-free by his ex-wife, he may deduct any real estate taxes he pays on the property.[36]

See *also* **State disability insurance.**

Taxes, election to deduct or to capitalize. *See* **Election to deduct or to capitalize.**

Tax evasion, expenses relating to. An individual was permitted to deduct attorneys' fees in connection with his defense of the charge of tax evasion.[37]

Tax-exempt bonds. If an individual purchases a fully taxable bond as opposed to a tax-free municipal bond at a premium (above par), he may elect to amortize the premium over the life of the bond. The amortizable bond premium then is subtracted from his basis or adjusted basis for the bond. This treatment is mandatory in the case of a tax-exempt bond.[38] *See also* **Interest.**

Tax-free reorganization, use in obtaining contributions deduction. *See* **Contributions.**

Tax informant. *See* **Informant, tax, return of fees.**

Tax-option corporations. Under stipulated circumstances, corporate shareholders may elect to have the Federal income tax applied only at the shareholder level. Then there is a pass-through of corporate income and losses (the excess of deductions over income) to the shareholders on a *pro rata* basis. To qualify for the election, the corporation must be a domestic one and not a member of an affiliated group, except that it may own stock in an inactive subsidiary. There can be only one class of stock, which may be held by not more than ten shareholders, who can only be individuals or estates (not corporations, trusts, or partnerships).[39] For taxable years beginning after December 31, 1976, the number of permissible stockholders has been increased from ten to fifteen, after tax-option status has been elected for five consecutive years. In addition, a corporation may have up to fifteen shareholders during the five-year period if additional shareholders acquire their interests through inheritance. In addition, certain trusts are now deemed to be eligible shareholders, including any type of trust which receives stock under a will, but only for a period of sixty days.[40] The shareholders cannot be nonresident aliens. Every co-owner is considered a shareholder for determining whether the corporation has more than ten shareholders, and each must file a consent on Form 2553 within specified times.[41] But for taxable years beginning after December 31, 1976, the election will not be terminated merely because a new shareholder fails to consent to the election. The election will terminate only if he "affirmatively refuses" to consent to an election within sixty days.[42]

An individual who is a shareholder of an electing tax-option corporation during the taxable year in which it has a net operating loss is allowed as a deduction from gross income for his taxable year in which or with which the taxable year of the corporation ends, an amount equal to his portion of the corporation's net operating loss. But his share of the corporation's net operating loss for the year cannot exceed the sum of (1) the adjusted basis for his stock and (2) the adjusted basis of any indebtedness of the corporation to him. Both (1) and (2) are determined as of the close of the corporation's taxable year.[43]

Tax preparation, fees related to. Deduction is allowed for expenses in the determination, collection, or refund of any tax.[44] This includes estate taxes[45] and gift taxes,[46] as well as property taxes. Thus, expenses incurred by an individual for tax counsel or expenses in connection with the preparation of his tax returns or in connection with any proceedings involved in determining the extent of his tax liability or in contesting it are deductible. Fees paid to a consultant to advise on the tax consequences of a transaction,[47] and fees paid to an appraiser to determine the amount of a casualty loss for tax purposes,[48] are deductible. Deduction was allowed for the costs of resisting a tax assessment[49] and for the defense against a tax-evasion charge.[50] The propriety of a deduction is not affected by the fact that the taxpayer is unsuccessful.[51]

After a corporation was liquidated, tax was assessed against it; and as the corporation no longer existed, a stockholder was called upon to pay this tax up to the value of the property he had received from the corporation when it was dissolved. In order to avoid this personal tax liability, he contested the imposition of the tax against the corporation and was successful in having the assessment canceled. He could deduct his legal fees, regardless of the fact that the tax had been imposed against the corporation and not against him, for as transferee of corporate properties he would have had to pay the tax himself if he had not successfully resisted the claim against the corporation. His expenses had been to establish his own tax liability.[52]

Tax rulings, expenses in obtaining. The costs of legal and accounting work in applying for a Federal tax ruling are deductible.[53]

Teachers, expenses of. Professional or technical journals and books, etc., are deductible if they have short useful lives, such as less than one year; otherwise, the costs have to be written off over the useful lives of the assets.[54]

A teacher of trainable mentally retarded children could deduct the cost of educational materials he purchased for use in his classes or as a student in courses for the handicapped in which he was enrolled.[55] *See also* **Advanced degree, study for; Education; Educational materials; Employees; Library, depreciation of; Office at home; Research; Transportation; Travel.**

Telephone. The cost of a telephone is deductible to the extent that the calls are for business as opposed to personal purposes.[56] A businessperson could deduct the expenses of his telephone at a time when he was confined to his home by reason of illness.[57] Telephone expenses are deductible as part of travel expense by a person who is away from home overnight on business.[58] *See also* **Deaf persons, expenses of; Executives.**

Telephone answering service. *See* **Answering service.**

Telephone in car. *See* **Medical expenses.**

Temporary employment, expenses of. *See* **Employees.**

Temporary living-away-from-home expenses. *See* **Travel.**

Temporary partitions, cost of. *See* **Repairs.**

Tenants in common, expenses of. *See* **Alimony; Interest; Taxes.**

Tenant-stockholders. *See* **Cooperative housing, deductions of tenant-shareholder in.**

Tennis courts. *See* **Entertainment.**

Tenure, expenses of obtaining. *See* **Advanced degree, study for; Education.**

Termination of trust or estate. If an estate or a trust has deductions in excess of gross income and other than personal exemptions and charitable contributions for its last taxable year upon termination of the trust or estate, the excess is allowed as a deduction to the beneficiaries succeeding to the property of the trust or estate. The deduction is allowed only in the taxable year of a beneficiary in which or with which the estate or trust terminates.[59]

Termites, damage caused by. Ordinarily, loss brought about by termite damage is not deductible as a casualty loss because there is not the *sudden* destruction necessary for a casualty deduction, the termites presumably having been at work on a foundation, etc., for a long, long time. But deduction was allowed where it could be shown that the building had been free of termites when examined by an expert less than a year before the loss occurred.[60]

Testimonial dinners. *See* **Ordinary and necessary business expenses.**

Theft losses. *See* **Casualties; Family transactions.**

Therapy. *See* **Medical expenses.**

Tickets for theater, etc. *See* **Advertising; Benefit performances, tickets for; Business expenses; Contributions.**

Timber. *See* **Forest management expenses.**

Time savings account or deposit, premature withdrawal. *See* **Premature withdrawal of interest.**

Tips. Tips for business purposes are deductible. But usually the deduction is lost through lack of proof that the payments were appropriate and necessary or that a specific business purpose had been sought to be gained. In the words of one court decision, "Indeed, a reasonable case can be made that such tips are ordinary and necessary and proximately related to a salesman's duty of entertaining his customers." But here, as usually is the case where there is no contemporary record of who the recipient was and the business purpose, the amount claimed was disallowed for tax purposes.[61] *See also* **Bribes and kickbacks.**

Title insurance company, payments to. Deduction was allowed for payments made to a title insurance company to ascertain whether local tax assessments made against a person's property were in order.[62]

Tolls. When a car is used for business purposes, highway, bridge, or similar tolls are separately deductible even where the zero bracket amount option is selected.[63]

Tools. Although the cost of business assets with an estimated useful life of more than one year ordinarily must be capitalized and written off only in the form of annual depreciation, the cost of small tools is deductible.[64]

A sales representative, who had to service equipment bought by his customers, could deduct the cost of tools for which he was not entitled to reimbursement by his employer.[65]

Although expenditures for business assets with an estimated life of more than one year ordinarily must be capitalized and not expensed, the cost of small tools was held to be deductible.[66]

Tools, transportation of. See **Commuting.**

Trade or business. Deduction is allowed for all ordinary and necessary expenses paid or incurred during the taxable year in carrying on any trade or business.[67] Where premises are used to carry on a trade or business, depreciation is a proper expense even in the case of assets which ordinarily would be regarded as personal, such as a radio, a cocktail table, a grandfather clock, and a painting in a lawyer's library.[68] See also **Ordinary and necessary business expenses.**

Transaction entered into for profit. Deduction is allowed for losses resulting from "any transaction entered into for profit, though not connected with a trade or business."[69] An individual who collected postage stamps was allowed a loss upon ultimate disposition for less than his cost. Evidence disclosed that although he enjoyed his collection, he had been guided in his purchases by the advice of professionals as to which stamps had the greatest potential for enhancement in value because he was interested in making money.[70] An attorney bought stock in a finance company. When the company became insolvent, his loss on the stock was not a capital loss but a fully deductible ordinary loss. He had purchased the stock, not as an investment, but for the purpose of getting profitable law work for himself. His investment was large enough to enable him to be elected president, and as such, he thought he could turn over some of the finance company's legal work to himself in his capacity as a lawyer. He expected through this connection to be engaged for title searches on property offered as security by borrowers, to obtain collection fees of up to 25 percent when the company had to get *some* lawyer to go after delinquent parties, and to obtain document recording and notarial fees. The loss was fully deductible, being in connection with a business transaction entered upon for profit.[71]

A real estate developer's deduction of operating expenses was disallowed by the Internal Revenue Service on the ground that his business was exclusively in residential properties. Thus, it was claimed, expenses in connection with the development of commercial properties were unrelated to his trade or business. But the court considered the I.R.S.'s differentiation to be mere hair-splitting. Enlarging the scope of the developer's activities was only a reasonable and natural expansion of an existing business activity. It was but the cultivation of a business within the normal scope of real estate development generally.[72]

Expenses of trying out a business venture are deductible if the venture is abandoned, provided the activities were more than a matter of investigating or looking into a proposition. The taxpayer must actually have been engaged in a transaction carried on for profit.[73] See *also* **Hobby losses.**

Transactions between related parties. See **Family transactions.**

Transferee liability, payments representing. See **Legal fees.**

Transplant of organs, expenses related to. See **Medical expenses.**

Transportation. See **Conventions; Travel.**

Travel. According to the United States Supreme Court, three conditions must be satisfied before a traveling-expense deduction will be allowed:
1. The expense must be a reasonable and necessary traveling expense, as that term is generally understood. This includes such items as transportation fares and food and lodging expenses incurred while traveling.
2. The expense must be incurred "while away from home."
3. The expense must be incurred in pursuit of business. This means that there must be a direct connection between the expenditure and the carrying on of the trade or business of the taxpayer or of his employer. Such an expenditure, moreover,

must be necessary or appropriate to the development and pursuit of the trade or business.[74]

An individual may deduct living expenses while away from home. This rule applies when a person who maintains a residence at one location accepts employment away from the vicinity of this residence, the duration of which is *temporary* as distinguished from *indefinite*. A professional news and speech writer was out of employment. He took a job as a construction site carpenter. The work could have lasted indefinitely, but he intended it to be only temporary because (1) he wanted to get back to his chosen form of work as soon as a position could be found, and (2) he was physically unable to perform carpentry for a long period of time because of a muscle condition caused by childhood polio. Thus he chose not to move to the area of the construction site, and his expenses there were deductible as "away-from-home."[75]

Where an individual is engaged in more than one trade or business, and such businesses require a division of his time between two distant cities, he may deduct his travel expenses incurred in discharging his duties at that city which is removed from his principal post of duty. In other words, where a person has more than one place of business or employment, his principal place of business or employment constitutes his "home" to serve as a point of origin for determining his deduction for traveling expenses.[76]

"Away from home" means overnight if one's duties require him to be away from the general area of his tax home for a period substantially longer than an ordinary day's work; and during released time while he is away ("released time" being, naturally, time when he is not actively pursuing business or employment), it is reasonable for him to need and to get sleep or rest to meet the requirements of his employment or business. A person need not be away from his tax home for an entire twenty-four-hour day or from dusk to dawn so long as his relief from duty during his absence is a sufficient period of time in which to get necessary sleep and rest.[77]

The fact that the home from which he was away was the residence of his father did not make it any less the son's home for this purpose, as he paid rent there in the form of contributions to the support of the father's home, had his furnishings there, and made regular trips there while employed on temporary jobs elsewhere.[78]

The travel must be business-oriented. A free-lance lecturer and writer could deduct his travel and related expenses in making movies to show at lectures. Although he had a substantial income from a trust fund, his activity was regarded as a trade or business. For many years he had been a journalist, and this activity at one time had supported him and his family. The potential for profit still was good despite some lean years.[79]

An accomplished scientist with a Ph.D. degree and one hundred published papers to her credit went to Europe to do further research in her field. Her objective was to maintain her professional standing in order to be eligible for prospective research appointments and financial gain. Since the death of her husband she needed a source of income; the profit motive was supplied by the good prospects for remuneration by salaries from foundations. Her travel expenses were held to be deductible. The activity engaged in was part of a profit-making scheme. Her activity was not merely a stepping-stone into another type of work; her existing activity was the potentially profitable one.[80]

An established professional writer could deduct travel and away-from-home lodging expenses while researching, writing, and arranging material for a book. The manuscript material on which he worked was in a museum 3,000 miles from his home, and he spent most of a year working at the museum. Although he received no compensation for his work on the book that year, it was a transaction into which he had entered with a good faith expectation of making a profit.[81]

A University of Alabama professor went to Egypt one summer for personal pleasure. While there, he accepted invitations from two universities to lecture upon his field of expertise. As these lectures helped to maintain his professional reputation, although he was not paid for his appearances, he could deduct that proportion of the cost of his trip which represented the number of days devoted to the lectures.[82]

An assistant principal of a racially and culturally integrated high school could deduct travel expenses to various countries while on sabbatical leave. Her major responsibilities were the handling of racial and riot problems and attempting to better race relations in a school characterized by racial, cultural, and social diversity. She achieved her objectives by repeatedly visiting foreign schools and talking to teachers, administrators, and students. Upon returning to her school, she instituted a new curriculum concentrating on techniques often used abroad for classrooms of diverse cultural backgrounds.[83]

An individual was permitted to deduct his travel expenses to and from Ireland to collect his earnings from the Irish Sweepstakes. There were hazards of loss if the funds were transmitted to him from Europe. He established that no time was spent on unrelated travel or sightseeing.[84]

Deduction is limited to what actually was paid, not to what

might have been paid, despite the circumstances. An individual had *bona fide* business to conduct in a foreign country for fourteen days. The charter fare for a twenty-five-day stopover was considerably less, and that was the ticket he purchased. As travel expense, he claimed the right to deduct either (1) the cost of a regular flight, as charter rates did not apply to an eleven-day visit, or (2) expenses for eleven nonbusiness days that the charter flight terms required him to stay abroad. He struck out on both arguments. Deductions are allowed only for actual expenses and not for theoretical calculations based upon expenses which might have been but were not actually incurred on business.[85]

A teacher could deduct his expenses in taking mentally retarded educable students to places where they could be exposed to different aspects of community life.[86]

An individual held real estate for investment. He received word in a distant city where he lived from county officials where the property was located that under local law he was required to keep unimproved property free from brush, dead trees, and trash or be subjected to a penalty. Inasmuch as he had been unsuccessful in getting anyone else to take care of the property, he was obliged to travel to his land and to perform the work himself. Said the court: "The need to comply with such ordinances makes his travel expenditures . . . both ordinary and necessary."[87]

A businessman could deduct the expenses of his journey to recruit strikebreakers for his business.[88]

Deduction of the travel expenses of a businessperson's spouse usually is not successful because of the strong presumption that the spouse's presence was pleasure- rather than business-oriented. But where an individual is on a valid business trip, the travel expenses of the spouse are deductible if "it can be adequately shown that the wife's presence on the trip had a *bona fide* business purpose."[89] Such was the case where an employee went abroad with the assignment of reporting back on the operation of the foreign branch offices. Specifically, he was to accumulate information on physical facilities, staffing, housing, office space, recreational facilities, school facilities, and other problem areas. His wife, by contacting the families of the foreign employees, was able to relay to her husband information which otherwise he might not have been able to gather himself.[90]

An individual was a vice-president and director of a New York Stock Exchange-listed tobacco company. European sales were negotiated primarily by senior executives of the company, who dealt directly with major officials of potential customers. Officers were encouraged and required to have very close friendly relations with foreign customers, and the president told his executives how much his wife had contributed to cementing the type of relationship deemed of greatest value to the company. So the vice-president took his own wife with him on his annual European visits to major customers. She was not a trained salesperson, but a susceptible judge pointed out that she "presents a very personable and attractive appearance."

She entertained customers and their wives in her hotel and made it possible and congenial for her husband to be entertained in customers' homes. She was invited to come to Europe by customers. She did no sightseeing on these trips, and the itinerary was constructed solely in accordance with business requirements. The trips were not regarded as for her pleasure or vacation. The only reason she went, concluded the court, was because of her husband's business. Her trip was directly attributable to his business. "It assisted him in his business and assisted in the production of income."[91]

Roy Disney was president and board chairman of Walt Disney Productions, a publicly held corporation engaged in the production of family-type entertainment. He and other executives frequently traveled in connection with business meetings, conferences, meetings with the press, and business-related social engagements. Usually he took his wife with him. On these trips she did nothing of a business nature, such as acting as her husband's secretary, but she attended various events at which women were present. The court found that the trips were part of *his* job. The primary question was whether the dominant purpose of her presence on the trips was to serve her husband's business purpose. And the answer was yes. The company specialized in providing "wholesome entertainment" based largely upon the ideals of Americanism and the home. Inasmuch as executives identified with the company were frequently in the public eye, management believed that the company's special image would be enhanced if its representatives traveled with their wives. True, the chief executive would scarcely be likely to lose his job if he left his wife at home. But he was warranted in believing that even the president should conform to the company's policy.[92]

Expenses of the wife of a businessman who accompanied him to Europe on a *bona fide* commercial trip were deductible. He was a diabetic and could not have made the journey without the constant presence of someone who had been trained to minister to his emergency needs, as his wife had been.[93]

How to get a deduction for travel expenses of a businessman's wife is emphasized by what the Internal Revenue Service says should be avoided: "Although the taxpayer was continually contacting actual or potential customers on these trips, he and his wife generally managed to include stops at resort cities or visits with relatives in their itineraries."[94] In one case where a wife accompanied her husband on a business trip, the court pointed out that during her husband's commercial journey to Hawaii, the wife neither went swimming nor shopping.[95] One must wonder how that was proved.

In a case where a businessman goes on a valid trip and is accompanied by his wife, whose expenses do not qualify for deduction, the couple's cost of transportation and lodging may exceed the cost for single fare and accommodations but is less than twice the single tariff. The amount deductible is the cost at the single rate for similar accommodations.[96]

Substantiation is a critical phase of the deduction for travel expense. An interstate truck driver, under Interstate Commerce Commission regulations, carried a driver's log book. He had to show the date of each trip, times of departure and arrival, destinations, and number and place of each stop of any length en route. Entries had to be made within a very short period after completion of each shift. These data were not kept for tax purposes, but they were exactly what the Internal Revenue Service may demand.[97]

The operation and maintenance charges for a private airplane are regarded as away-from-home travel expenses and are deductible if related to the taxpayer's business.[98] *See also* **Apartment used for business purposes; Education; Investors; Medical expenses; Moving expenses; Ordinary and necessary business expenses.**

Trickery, loss because of. *See* **Casualties.**

Trustee. *See* **Fiduciaries.**

Trusts. *See* **Capital losses; Carry-overs; Depreciation.**

Turnover, reduction of. A business is permitted to deduct the cost of current expenses which are incurred for the purpose of reducing turnover of employees. Amounts paid to provide child care for the preschool children of employees was permitted where persons on the payroll resigned frequently because of problems connected with not having facilities available to take care of their children during working hours.[99]

Tutoring, cost of. *See* **Education.**

1. Revenue Act of 1978, Section 111.
2. I.R.C. Section 164(a).
3. I.R.C. Section 164(b)(S).
4. I.R.C. Section 164(b)(1)(D).
5. *Income Tax Deduction for Taxes*, I.R.S. Publication 546, 1976 edition, page 3.
6. G.C.M. 17570, 1937–1 CB 193.
7. Revenue Ruling 72–79, 1972–1 CB 51.
8. Revenue Ruling 74–486, 1974–2 CB 86.
9. Revenue Ruling 75–47, 1975–1 CB 62.
10. I.R.C. Section 901.
11. Revenue Ruling 78–81, I.R.B. 1978–10, 6.
12. Revenue Ruling 70–464, 1970–2 CB 152.
13. *In the Matter of Battelstein*, D.C., S.D. Texas, 1977.
14. Revenue Ruling 78–103, I.R.B. 1978–12, 10.
15. *Ronald G. Peters et al.*, T.C. Memo. 1977–314, filed November 16, 1970.
16. Regulations Section 1.164–4(b)(1).
17. *Walker v. United States*, D.C., W.D. Okla., 1959.
18. *Oscar Mitchell*, 27 B.T.A. 101 (1932).
19. *Tax Information on Business Expenses*, I.R.S. Publication 535, 1976 edition, page 3.
20. *Ibid.*, page 16.
21. *Lulu Lung Powell*, T.C. Memo, 1967–32, filed February 20, 1967.
22. *Gilbert J. Kraus*, T.C. Memo., Docket No. 22594, entered October 31, 1951.
23. Revenue Ruling 67–21, 1967–1 CB 45.
24. *Mary Rumsey Mavius Estate*, 22 T.C. 391 (1954).
25. Regulations Section 1.164–6.
26. I.R.C. Section 216(a)(1).
27. Revenue Ruling 64–31, 1964–1 CB (Part 1) 300.
28. *Income Tax Deduction for Taxes*, I.R.S. Publication 546, 1976 edition, page 6.
29. *Ibid.*
30. I.R.S. Letter Ruling 7733068, May 20, 1977.
31. Revenue Ruling 57–489, 1957–2 CB 207.
32. *R. J. Nicholl Co.*, 59 T.C. 37 (1972).
33. Revenue Ruling 75–176, 1974–1 CB 68.
34. Regulations Section 1.164–1(a).
35. *United States v. Green, Jr., et al.*, 170 F. Supp. 359 (D.C., S.D. N.Y., 1959).
36. *Income Tax Deductions for Alimony Payments*, I.R.S. Publication 504, 1976 edition, page 3.
37. Revenue Ruling 68–662, 1968–2 CB 69.
38. I.R.C. Section 171.
39. I.R.C. Section 1370 *et seq.*
40. Tax Reform Act of 1976, Section 902.
41. I.R.C. Section 1371.
42. Tax Reform Act of 1976, Section 902.
43. I.R.C. Section 1374(b)(2).
44. Regulations Section 1.212–1(1).
45. *Sidney Merians et al.*, 60 T.C. 187 (1973).
46. *United States v. Bonnyman et al.*, 261 F.2d 835 (6th Cir., 1958).
47. *Michael J. Ippolito et al.*, T.C. Memo. 1965–167, filed June 24, 1965.
48. *Ben R. Stein et al.*, T.C. Memo. 1972–140, filed June 29, 1972.

49. *Carlos Marcello et al.,* T.C. Memo. 1964–299, filed November 18, 1964.
50. Revenue Ruling 68–662, 1968–2 CB 69.
51. *W. Brown Morton et al.,* T.C. Memo. 1957–101, filed June 25, 1957.
52. *Sharples et al. v. United States,* 533 F.2d 550 (Ct. Cl., 1976).
53. Revenue Ruling 67–401, 1967–2 CB 123.
54. *Beaudry v. Commissioner,* 150 F.2d 20 (2d Cir., 1945).
55. *Gudmundsson et al. v. Commissioner,* T.C. Memo. 1978–299, filed August 1, 1978.
56. *Biggs et al. v. Commissioner,* 440 F.2d 1 (6th Cir., 1971).
57. *Dan R. Hanna, Jr., et al.,* T.C. Memo., Docket Nos. 25706–7, entered June 6, 1951.
58. Regulations Section 1.162–2(a).
59. I.R.C. Section 642(h).
60. *Rosenberg v. Commissioner,* 198 F.2d 46 (8th Cir., 1952).
61. *George H. Newi et al.,* T.C. Memo. 1969–131, filed June 26, 1969, *aff'd on another issue,* 432 F.2d 998 (2d Cir., 1970).
62. *Byron H. Farwell et al.,* 35 T.C. 454 (1960).
63. Revenue Procedure 74–23, 1974–2 CB 476.
64. *Arnold Roy Bushey,* T.C. Memo. 1971–149, filed June 21, 1971.
65. *McCollum et al. v. Commissioner,* T.C. Memo. 1978–435, filed November 1, 1978.
66. *Henry G. Lewis et al.,* T.C. Memo. 1972–168, filed August 7, 1972.
67. I.R.C. Section 162(a).
68. *Beaudry v. Commissioner,* 150 F.2d 20 (2d Cir., 1945).
69. I.R.C. Section 165(c)(2).
70. *George F. Tyler,* T.C. Memo., Docket No. 5508, entered March 6, 1947.
71. *Irwin v. United States,* D.C., E.D. La., 1975.
72. *Malmstedt et al. v. Commissioner,* 578 F.2d 520 (14th Cir., 1978).
73. *Charles T. Parker,* 1 T.C. 709 (1943).
74. *Commissioner v. Flowers,* 326 U.S. 465 (1946).
75. *Waldrop v. Commissioner,* T.C. Memo. 1977–190, filed June 21, 1977.
76. Revenue Ruling 54–147, 1954–1 CB 51.
77. *Your Federal Income Tax,* 1976 edition, page 70.
78. *Jim Lee Wilson,* T.C. Memo, 1976–235, filed July 27, 1976.
79. *Cornelius Vanderbilt, Jr.,* T.C. Memo. 1957–235, filed December 23, 1957.
80. *Brooks v. Commissioner,* 274 F.2d 96 (9th Cir., 1959).
81. *Stern et al. v. United States,* D.C., C.D. Cal., 1971.
82. *Ahmed F. Habeeb et al.,* T.C. Memo. 1976–259, filed August 19, 1976.
83. *Haynie v. Commissioner,* T.C. Memo. 1977–330, filed September 26, 1977.
84. *Harry Kanelos et al.,* T.C. Memo., Docket Nos. 112053 and 112090, entered September 21, 1943.
85. *Habeeb et al. v. Commissioner,* 559 F.2d 435 (5th Cir., 1977).
86. *Gudmundsson et al. v. Commissioner,* T.C. Memo. 1978–299, filed August 1, 1978.
87. *Harris v. Commissioner,* T.C. Memo. 1978–332, filed August 23, 1978.
88. *Queen City Printing Co.,* 6 B.T.A. 521 (1927).
89. Regulations Section 1.162–2(c).
90. *Wilkins et al. v. United States,* 348 F. Supp. 1282 (D.C., Neb., 1972).
91. *Warwick et al. v. United States,* 236 F. Supp. 761 (D.C., E.D. Va., 1964).
92. *United States v. Disney et al.,* 413 F.2d 783 (9th Cir., 1969).
93. *Allenberg Cotton Company, Inc., et al. v. United States,* D.C., W.D. Tenn., 1960.
94. Revenue Ruling 55–57, 1955–1 CB 315.

95. *Allen J. McDonnell et al.*, T.C. Memo. 1967–18, filed January 31, 1967.
96. Revenue Ruling 56–168, 1956–1 CB 93.
97. *B.J. Culwell et al.*, D.C., New Mexico, 1967.
98. *Gibson Products Company, Inc.*, 8 T.C. 654 (1947).
99. Revenue Ruling 73–348, 1973–2 CB 31.

T

293

U

Uncollectible accounts. *See* **Bad debts.**

Undivided interest in property, contribution in form of. *See* **Contributions.**

Unearned commissions, repayment of. If a salesman is allowed to draw commissions before they are earned, and he draws against sales not yet paid for by his customers, he may be called upon to repay those commissions he drew out against customer bills that never did get paid. If he paid Federal income tax on commissions when he received them, he then is entitled to a business-expense deduction in the year he returns the unearned commissions to his employer.[1]

Unemployment-benefit fund, contributions to. An employer's contribution to an unemployment-benefit fund to pay a "layoff moving allowance" when an employee who is laid off at one plant accepts employment at another plant is deductible as an ordinary and necessary business expense.[2]

Uniforms. The cost of acquisition and maintenance of uniforms is deductible as an ordinary and necessary expense if the uniforms (1) are specially required as a condition of employment and (2) are not of a type adaptable to general or continued usage to the extent that they take the place of regular clothing. The fact that a uniform might be required as a condition of employment is not, of itself, sufficient to allow a deduction, as in the case of military apparel, which replaces regular clothing. Likewise, the deduction is not allowed if the uniform is suitable for ordinary wear.[3]

The fact that the employer's name could be removed from an employee's jacket did not mean that the garment was adaptable to street use. As long as he still was on the payroll and wore the clothing in connection with his business duties, the cost of the attire was deductible.[4]

A woman employee of an airplane company during World War II was required to wear slacks at work. She was allowed to deduct the cost, for the court believed she would not have worn such apparel other than at work.[5]

An art teacher could deduct the cost of protective-clothing smocks as an ordinary and necessary expense of her business.[6]

The cost of uniforms used by air, rail, and bus employees is deducted if the uniforms are used solely in the course of their employment. But the cost is not deductible if uniforms are equipped with snap buttons that can be removed to convert the uniform to general use.[7]

Deduction is allowed for the cost of uniforms for firemen[8] and for policemen.[9] A California highway patrolman could deduct the cost of his uniform, which he was required to purchase and to wear while on duty. He was not permitted to wear it while employed for compensation outside his official duties. He did not wear the uniform while not working because civilian attire was more comfortable and less expensive.[10] But an examiner in the same state's department of motor vehicles could not deduct the cost of purchasing the prescribed regulation dress for use while on duty in the driver-licensing function. It was a slate-gray suit indistinguishable from regular civilian attire and could have been worn off duty. Perhaps he made a mistake in wearing his uniform to court, for the judge admitted that the most convincing evidence against the taxpayer's argument that the required attire was a uniform was that, in His Honor's words, he "looked too normal and too well in the suit he wore to court."[11] Next time, perhaps, he could do something about *that*.

A commercial airline navigator was allowed to deduct the cost of his uniforms.[12]

The cost of a nurse's costume is deductible.[13] A private-duty nurse properly deducted the cost of her uniform, for it served as a mark of her profession and was necessary in the care of her patient from an aseptic standpoint.[14]

The cost of acquisition and maintenance of uniforms of lettercarriers is deductible if the persons are required to wear distinctive types of uniform while at work and the garb is not suitable for ordinary wear.[15]

A hospital attendant could deduct the cost of clothing which he wore when exposed to contagious diseases.[16]

The office manager of a dental clinic was allowed to deduct the cost of upkeep of the uniform she wore.[17]

A waitress could deduct the cost of yellow uniforms and aprons, plus appropriate shoes that she wore at work.[18]

Where an employer required his service employees to wear a shirt, jacket, and cap bearing the company name, one of these employees was able to deduct not only the cost of these items but also the cost of trousers made of identical material which were not adaptable to general use.[19]

A fashion coordinator was able to deduct the cost of very advanced styles she wore for special meetings.[20] But an advertising executive could not deduct the cost of a mink coat which his wife wore to places where clients were apt to be because he could not show that a mink coat was an essential uniform for the wife of a successful executive.[21]

A professional musician could deduct the cost of dress clothes which were used exclusively for his business of playing the piano and the Solovox.[22]

A professional baseball player who was required to furnish his own uniform was permitted to deduct its cost even though conceivably this attire could have been worn socially.[23]

A jockey was allowed to deduct the cost of uniforms which he wore professionally, where no reimbursement from anyone was possible.[24]

A plant employee properly deducted as work clothes a plain white coat marked with large letters "Foreman."[25] Presumably his wife would not have let him wear this at home.

The cost and upkeep of uniforms used in charitable activities (for example, as a scoutmaster) are deductible as a charitable contribution.[26]

An amateur ski enthusiast devoted much of his spare time to serving as a member of the safety patrol of a tax-exempt organization which performed rescues and administered first aid to injured skiers. He was allowed to deduct the cost of a certain type of parka and dark ski trousers which the patrol members were required to wear while on duty.[27]

A civilian employee of an aircraft company could deduct the cost (less salvage value) of an army officer's uniform without insignia which he was required to wear in combat areas so that if he were captured, he would be treated as a prisoner of war.[28]
See also **Armed Forces; Work clothes.**

Union dues. Monthly dues and assessments paid by members of a labor union are deductible business expenses except for any portion of the assessments used to provide death benefits.[29] An initiation fee is deductible when it is paid to the union in order to obtain employment.[30]

Sometimes a union contract provides that employers must

deduct the equivalent of check-off dues from employees who do not belong to the union, which nevertheless receives these amounts. Such employees may deduct the "shop fees."[31]

Fines assessed against a member by his union are deductible, where nonpayment would have meant being dropped from the union.[32] See *also* **Employees.**

United States, expenses related to income earned outside. Where income is earned outside the United States by a person under certain conditions, it is not taxed in the U.S. Expenses in connection with that income similarly are not deductible. But expenses not related to income earned outside the country are deductible. Examples of such items include personal and family medical expenses, real estate taxes on a personal residence, interest on a mortgage on a personal residence, and charitable contributions.[33]

Unlawful business, expenses of. See **Gambling losses.**

Unlimited deduction for contribution to charitable organization. When an individual engaged in a trade or business makes a payment to an exempt organization with a reasonable expectation of financial return to himself, which is in line with the amount of his gift, it is not subject to the percentage limitations of charitable contributions but is fully deductible as ordinary and necessary business expense. Such was the ruling when money was given to a pollution-control fund established by a municipality where the donor's business had been hurt in the past because of polluted atmosphere.[34]

Unrecovered loss for damages. Damages received under a judgment or settlement of a civil action for United States patent infringement, breach of contract or fiduciary duty, and recoveries (except for punitive damages) under the Clayton Act for anti-trust violation, are deductible. The deduction is the smaller of (1) the amounts paid in the taxable year concerning the award, or (2) the unrecovered loss. The unrecovered loss is the sum of net operating losses attributable to the damages, arising during the period the damages were sustained, to the extent they were not absorbed in carry-overs or carry-backs and also less any deductions for prior recoveries allowed in any prior year.[35]

Unreimbursed expenses. See **Employees; Executives; Partnerships.**

Unsalable inventory. See **Inventory write-downs.**

Unsuccessful acquisition costs. *See* **Mineral leases, cost of acquiring.**

U

Unused capital loss carry-overs. *See* **Capital losses.**

Unused carry-over of fiduciary. If an estate or trust, when it is terminated, has a net operating-loss carry-over or a capital-loss carry-over, this is allowed as a deduction to the beneficiaries succeeding to the property.[36]

Use tax. *See* **Taxes.**

Usurious interest. *See* **Interest.**

U

1. Revenue Ruling 72–28, 1972–1 CB 45.
2. Revenue Ruling 73–245, 1973–1 CB 64.
3. Revenue Ruling 70–474, 1970–2 CB 34.
4. *Bennie Blatt*, T.C. Memo., Docket No. 10064, entered February 10, 1947.
5. *Morgan et al. v. United States*, 80 F. Supp. 537 (D.C., N.D. Texas, 1948).
6. *Kellner v. Commissioner*, 2d Cir., 1977.
7. *Miscellaneous Deductions and Credits*, I.R.S. Publication 529, 1976 edition, page 3.
8. *Jess H. Taylor et al.*, T.C. Memo., Docket No. 28821, entered June 24, 1952.
9. Revenue Ruling 70–474, 1970–2 CB 34.
10. *Commissioner v. Benson et al.*, 146 F.2d 191 (9th Cir., 1944).
11. *Harry J. Sanner*, T.C. Memo, 1969–84, filed April 30, 1969.
12. *Dean L. Philips*, T.C. Memo., Docket Nos. 18410–12, entered June 9, 1950.
13. Revenue Ruling 70–474, 1970–2 CB 34.
14. *Helen Krusko Harsaghy*, 2 T.C. 484 (1943).
15. Revenue Ruling 70–474, 1970–2 CB 34.
16. *Oliver W. Bryant et al.*, T.C. Memo., Docket No. 27114, entered May 2, 1952.
17. *Floyd Gilbert Bickel II et al.*, T.C. Memo. 1966–202, filed September 19, 1966.
18. *Owens et al. v. Commissioner*, T.C. Memo. 1977–319, filed September 19, 1977.
19. *Jerome Mortrud et al.*, 44 T.C. 208 (1965).
20. *Betsy L. Yeomans*, 30 T.C. 757 (1958).
21. *Paul E. Jackson et al.*, T.C. Memo. 1954–235, filed December 27, 1954.
22. *Wilson J. Fisher*, 23 T.C. 218 (1954), *aff'd on another issue*, 230 F.2d 230 (7th Cir., 1956).
23. Revenue Ruling 70–474, 1970–2 CB 34.
24. Revenue Ruling 70–475, 1970–2 CB 35.
25. *Morgan et al. v. United States*, 80 F. Supp. 537 (D.C., N.D. Texas, 1948).
26. *Protecting Older Americans Against Overpayment of Income Taxes*, Special Committee on Aging, United States Senate, 1976, page 3.

27. *McCollum et al. v. Commissioner*, T.C. Memo. 1978–435, filed November 1, 1978.
28. *Henry Ralph Leacock*, T.C. Memo., Docket No. 7730, entered December 19, 1947.
29. Revenue Ruling 72–463, 1972–2 CB 93.
30. I.T. 3634, 1944 CB 90.
31. I.R.S. Letter Ruling 7828050, April 13, 1978.
32. Revenue Ruling 69–214, 1969–1 CB 52.
33. Regulations Section 1.911–1(a)(3).
34. Revenue Ruling 73–113, 1973–1 CB 65.
35. I.R.C. Section 186.
36. I.R.C. Section 642(h).

V

Vaccine. *See* **Medical expenses.**

Vandalism. Deduction was allowed in the case of deliberate destruction of works of art.[1] *See also* **Casualties.**

Vasectomy. *See* **Birth control measures.**

Veterans' organizations, contributions to. *See* **Contributions.**

Veterinarians. *See* **Depreciation; Farmers.**

Veterinary expenses. A commercial farmer is entitled to deduct costs of this nature.[2]

Violation of rights, payments to settle. Several women brought action against an employer for violations of the Civil Rights Act of 1964. They claimed that they had not been given work because of sex or color or that they had lost their jobs because of pregnancy. To settle the matter, but without admitting violation of the Civil Rights Act, the employer agreed to make settlements to the claimants in lieu of salaries or promotion increases. These were deductible as ordinary and necessary business expenses.[3]

Vitamins. *See* **Medical expenses.**

Volunteer fire companies, contributions to. *See* **Contributions.**

Volunteer firemen. *See* **Individual retirement account.**

1. *Lattimore v. United States,* D.C., N.D. Cal., 1967.
2. Per Form 1040, Schedule F.
3. I.R.S. Letter Ruling 7720011, February 7, 1977.

W

Wagering losses. *See* **Gambling losses.**

Ward, expenses of. *See* **Guardians, expenses of.**

War profits taxes. *See* **Taxes.**

Watch repairs. Deduction is permitted for the cost of repairs to a personal watch which is required by the nature of the job as, for example, the case of a railroad employee.[1] Deduction is not permitted in the absence of evidence that the employer required the employee to carry a watch or that employment was of a character that necessitated such use of a watch.[2] *See also* **Employees.**

Water conservation expenditures. *See* **Farmers.**

Water taxes. *See* **Taxes.**

Weevils. Payments by a cotton broker to a fund for the stamping out of boll weevils were deductible.[3]

Well, abandonment of. *See* **Abandonment loss.**

Wheelchair. *See* **Medical expenses.**

Whirlpool bath. *See* **Medical expenses.**

Whiskey. *See* **Medical expenses.**

Wigs. Where a doctor prescribed the wearing of a wig by a patient who had lost her hair in order to alleviate mental distress, the cost was characterized as deductible medical expense.[4] Where a businessperson finds it necessary to wear a hairpiece in order to achieve the appearance of youth called for by the job, this is treated as a business expense.[5] *See also* **Actors; Medical expenses.**

Will contest, expenses of. *See* **Legal fees.**

Withdrawal of interest, premature. *See* **Premature withdrawal of interest.**

Work clothes. A maintenance electrician and electronic technician could deduct the cost of prescription safety glasses and special work clothes that would tear readily in the event that his clothing should be caught in any of the machinery around which he worked daily.[6]

An airline stewardess was allowed to deduct the cost of an in-flight smock.[7]

Work shoes that were not suitable or acceptable for general usage were a business expense.[8]

A worker at a chemical plant could deduct the cost of work clothes, safety shoes, and gloves in order to protect himself from the acid fumes of the plant.[9]

A construction worker was allowed to deduct the cost of safety lenses, shoes, and equipment.[10]

A carpenter was allowed to deduct what he paid for overalls and special work shoes.[11]

A truck driver could deduct the cost of safety gloves and special shoes he wore when driving loads of blacktop because of the high temperature to which he was exposed.[12]

A worker at a fish processing plant was able to deduct the cost of rubber gloves and boots. The court was willing to assume that these particular items could not have been used socially after work.[13] Commercial fishermen were allowed to deduct the cost of oil clothes.[14]

Workmen's compensation insurance. *See* **Insurance.**

Worthless debts. *See* **Bad debts.**

Write-downs, inventory. *See* **Inventory write-downs.**

Writer. *See* **Research; Travel**

1. *O. G. Russell,* T.C. Memo., Docket No. 26963, entered April 2, 1952.
2. *Charles H. Boston et al.,* T.C. Memo., Docket No. 25564, entered June 17, 1952.
3. *Alexander Sprunt & Sons, Inc.,* 24 B.T.A. 599 (1931).
4. Revenue Ruling 62–189, 1962–2 CB 88.
5. *Reginald Denny,* 33 B.T.A. 738 (1935).
6. *Arnold Roy Bushey,* T.C. Memo. 1971–149, filed June 21, 1971.
7. *Stiner et al. v. United States,* 524 F.2d 640 (10th Cir., 1975).
8. *Cavic et al. v. Commissioner,* T.C. Memo. 1977–192, filed June 21, 1977.
9. *Joseph Swiderski et al.,* T.C. Memo., Docket No. 33281, entered August 27, 1952.
10. *Armes et al. v. Commissioner,* T.C. Memo. 1978–258, filed July 12, 1978.
11. *Busking et al. v. Commissioner,* T.C. Memo. 1978–415, filed October 16, 1978.
12. *Robert S. Henke,* T.C. Memo. 1973–186, filed August 21, 1973.
13. *Clark v. Commissioner,* T.C. Memo. 1978–276, filed July 24, 1978.
14. Revenue Ruling 55–235, 1955–1 CB 274.

Y

Yacht. *See* **Entertainment.**

You can deduct the expenses of obtaining guidance on tax matters.[1] That includes the cost of this book.

Y

1. *Higgins v. Commissioner,* 143 F.2d 654 (1st Cir., 1944).